The Polish Deportees of World War II

Also by Tadeusz Piotrowski
and from McFarland

The Indian Heritage of New Hampshire and Northern New England (2002)

Genocide and Rescue in Wołyń: Recollections of the Ukrainian Nationalist Ethnic Cleansing Campaign Against the Poles During World War II (2000)

Poland's Holocaust: Ethnic Strife, Collaboration with Occupying Forces and Genocide in the Second Republic, 1918–1947 (1998; paperback 2006)

Vengeance of the Swallows: Memoir of a Polish Family's Ordeal Under Soviet Aggression, Ukrainian Ethnic Cleansing and Nazi Enslavement, and Their Emigration to America (1995)

The Polish Deportees of World War II

Recollections of Removal to the Soviet Union and Dispersal Throughout the World

Edited by
TADEUSZ PIOTROWSKI

McFarland & Company, Inc., Publishers
Jefferson, North Carolina, and London

To the victims of Soviet
crimes against humanity

The present work is a reprint of the illustrated case bound edition of The Polish Deportees of World War II: Recollections of Removal to the Soviet Union and Dispersal Throughout the World, *first published in 2004 by McFarland.*

LIBRARY OF CONGRESS CATALOGUING-IN-PUBLICATION DATA

The Polish deportees of World War II : recollections of removal
to the Soviet Union and dispersal throughout the world /
edited by Tadeusz Piotrowski.
p. cm.
Includes bibliographical references and index.

ISBN-13: 978-0-7864-3258-5
softcover : 50# alkaline paper ♾

1. World War, 1939–1945 — Deportations from Poland.
2. Forced migration — Poland — History — 20th century.
3. World War, 1939–1945 — Personal narratives, Polish.
4. Poland — Biography.
5. Poles — Soviet Union — History — 20th century.
I. Piotrowski, Tadeusz, 1940–
D810.D5P64 2008 940.53'161'09239185 — dc22 2004005130

British Library cataloguing data are available

On the cover: Polish exiles on the U.S.S.R.–Iran border
(courtesy Józef Piłsudski Institute of America)

Manufactured in the United States of America

McFarland & Company, Inc., Publishers
Box 611, Jefferson, North Carolina 28640
www.mcfarlandpub.com

Table of Contents

Preface

Among the great tragedies that befell Poland during World War II was the forced deportation of its citizens by the Soviet Union during the first Soviet occupation of that country from 1939 to 1941. This is the story of that brutal Soviet ethnic cleansing campaign told in the words of a few of the survivors. It is an unforgettable human drama of excruciating martyrdom in the Gulag and, after the "amnesty," miraculous rebirth in the non–European countries that extended a helping hand to the exiles in their hour of need. Sad to say, America was not one of those countries.

Who would not be moved by a straightforward observation such as this in one of the accounts? "A young woman who had given birth on the train threw herself and her newborn under the wheels of an approaching train. She left behind her two older children." Or these despairing words of one mother who wrote in the diary she shared with her daughter: "Our situation now is hopeless… The children are very sick… My psychological state is terrible. Will I be able to carry on?…. Can anyone know what I feel in my heart?… I think I am going mad; I am breaking down… I think God is abandoning us."

Who would not be moved by this same mother's heartfelt gratitude upon receiving two packages from Poland? "We are overwhelmed by the tremendous goodness of people, which saved our lives. God is good." It was but a temporary reprieve, for later she wrote "Thoughts of suicide tempt us. Our suffering is beyond description."

And when these deportees were finally free and far away from the horrors of their Soviet nightmare, the lessons they had learned in that "inhuman land" were not soon forgotten. One refugee, who wound up in the African bush, writes: "[T]he obligatory regimen of the settlement clearly forbade a display of friendship toward the natives, but having gone through the Siberian Gehenna we did not always understand the reason for this prohibition and explained our behavior by our felt need to treat everyone equally no mater what the color of their skin. Moved by pity for the poor black mothers, we gave them our clothing, blankets and some home furnishings as well. We even began to purchase chickens, eggs and fruits from them — an activity that was forbidden."

The accounts of deportation herein come from diaries and memoirs, some of which have never been published previously and many of which were written in Polish and never translated. Except when noted otherwise, all translations are my own.

The first three chapters deal with deportation, life in the Soviet Union, and the "amnesty." Subsequent chapters are organized by the countries that opened their doors to the refugees and, specifically, the various refugee camps in these countries. It was my intention through this organizational framework and through the personal narratives of the survivors to give the reader an understanding of the general conditions at that time in Eastern Poland, the Soviet Union, and the Polish refugee settlements in the Near and Middle East, India, Africa, New Zealand and Mexico.

At the back of the book there are three documents from the Soviet Union and one from Great Britain, a detailed and revealing 1943 confidential report from London. I thank my Australian correspondent, Joseph Poprzeczny, for bringing it to my attention.

I am grateful to the University of New Hampshire for the Carpenter Professorship Award and the sabbatical during which I was able to complete much of this work.

My heartfelt thanks go to the following individuals and publishers for allowing me to quote from unpublished and published diaries and memoirs: Dunmore Press (New Zealand) for Maria van der Linden, *An Unforgettable Journey*; *Dziennik Związkowy* (Chicago) for Elżbieta Wróbel and Janusz Wróbel, "Spotkanie w Santa Rosa"; Maria Gabiniewicz for her *W stronę domu ojczystego przez Syberię, Kazachstan, Uzbekistan, Turkmenię, Persję, Indie, Afrykę,* and especially for facilitating the permission I obtained from the Rada Fundacji "Archiwum Fotograficzne Tułaczy" in Warsaw to use the accounts in the Polish publication *Tułacze dzieci, Exiled Children*; Stanisław Milewski for the Milewski family memoir, which includes his mother's and sister's diary; the recently deceased Michael Mineyko for the work of his late mother, Anna Mineyko, "Through the Mists of Time"; Anita Paschwa-Kozicka for her *My Flight to Freedom: An Autobiography* and her article "My Road to Freedom" in *Poles of Santa Rosa: Our 50th Anniversary, 1946–1996;* Tadeusz Pieczko for his memoir; Marysia Pienta, for her article "Only a Chapter in the Road to Freedom," in the previously-mentioned *Poles of Santa Rosa*; Janusz Smenda for facilitating the permission I obtained from the Committee of the Siberian Group of Western Australia for Nina and Janusz Smenda (eds.), *Unforgettable Memories: Memoirs of Polish Exiles in the Soviet Union, 1940-1942;* Ursula Sowińska and the University Archives, University of Illinois at Chicago, for her article, under the pseudonym Eva, "Trial by Torture: Out of the Depths" in *Pier Illini*; Krystyna Tomaszyk (née Skwarko) for the work of her late mother, Krystyna Skwarko, *The Invited: The Story of 733 Polish Children Who Grew Up in New Zealand;* Alicia A. Zarzycki and Stefania Buczak-Zarzycka for their *Kwaheri Africa: A Polish Experience 1939–1950, from Deportation to Freedom*; Jane [Janina] Żebrowski-Bulmahn and her publisher, iUniverse.com, for her *Long Journey Home*; and *Związkowiec* (Toronto) for Henryka Utnik-Łappo, "Afrykańczycy — Wspominając tamte dni." Finally, I would also like to thank the Jósef Piłsudski Institute of America for permission to use the cover photograph and Radio Free Europe/Radio Liberty for permission to use the translation of the Katyn document from Louisa Vinton, "The Katyn Documents: Politics and History."

My love, as always, to my wife Terri and to Renia, Ala, and Andrzej, my children.

Tadeusz Piotrowski
Manchester, New Hampshire
May 2004

Introduction

The Great Patriotic War, as the Russians like to call it, which claimed the lives of millions of Soviet soldiers and civilians and landed millions of other Soviet citizens in the slave-labor camps of Germany, was greatly facilitated by the August 23, 1939, Soviet-German Pact of Non-Aggression that allied Communist Soviet Union with the Nazi Third Reich. In that pact a secret protocol was also drawn up for the reorganization of Central Europe.

That September, in violation of their own treaties with Poland, both of these allies invaded and partitioned the Second Polish Republic. Thus began World War II.

According to Stalin, the joint aim of the Soviet Union and Germany was "to restore peace and order in Poland, which had been destroyed by the disintegration of the Polish State, and to help the Polish people establish new conditions for its political life."[1] Needless to say, that "disintegration of the Polish State" had been brought about by the very powers which now promised to restore "peace and order." On September 28, 1939, the German-Soviet Boundary and Friendship Treaty announced the new borders of the "respective national interests" of Germany and the Soviet Union in "the former Polish State" and promised to "assure the people living there a peaceful life in keeping with their national character."[2]

In keeping with the terms of the German-Soviet Boundary and Friendship Treaty, the Soviet government also pledged to actively support and *did* actively support the German war effort against Poland and the West. This support took many forms: the breaking of the British blockade of Germany; the permission to establish German navy bases in the USSR; the allowance for the passage over Soviet territory of raw materials bound for Germany from other nations; and the supplying of goods such as food, cattle, cotton, phosphates, chromium and iron ore, platinum, zinc, rubber, flax, lumber, and oil directly to Germany. Each month, for the duration of the Soviet-German alliance, 200–300 Soviet trains carried these goods into the heart of the Third Reich.[3]

Meanwhile, instead of assuring "peace and order" in the "former Polish State," both allies subjected the populace of Poland to a reign of terror the likes of which had seldom been seen before in the annals of human history. Their mutual aim was to completely suppress the political and sociocultural life of the Polish people forever. Their official policies included outright murder, "extermination through work," "resettlement," deportation, enslavement, assimilation, and — in the case of more scientific Germany — the kidnaping and Germanization of Polish children and the involuntary sterilization of Polish women of childbearing age.[4]

One of these monstrous measures carried out by the Soviet government was the massive deportation of Polish citizens from the Soviet zone, or the so-called Soviet sphere of influence, to the "inhuman land" where, as we know from Aleksandr Solzhenitsyn's masterful epic *The Gulag Archipelago,* millions of Soviet citizens were dumped after the Bolshevik Revolution. There, they all became the slaves of the Soviet Union.

Similar deportations and enslavement of Polish citizens occurred under the tsars in 1832, 1864, and 1906. Another earlier and less known two-volume work on the topic is George Kennan's *Siberia and the Exile System*, penned in 1891. Although this pioneering work does not deal specifically with Polish exiles, the author states that "First and last, about 100,000 Poles have been banished."[5] Official Russian records indicate that between 1863 and 1866 alone, 18,623 Poles were deported to Siberia.[6]

Between 1930 and 1933, during Stalin's war against the kulaks, 10,000 Poles were deported from Soviet Ukraine to the interior of the Soviet Union. In 1935, in the interest of securing the Soviet western borders, another 40,000 Poles were deported eastward. In 1936 there were additional massive deportations from this area for a grand total of 120,000 Poles in this seven-year period. The Poles in Soviet Belorussia fared no better: before 1936, about 20,000 ethnic Poles suffered some form of Soviet repression; in 1937–38, some 20,000 Poles were deported to the east.[7]

Just before the outbreak of World War II, in 1937 and 1938, 143,810 (all these "precise" figures are NKVD's) Poles living in the Soviet Union were officially charged with one thing or another as a part of Stalin's war on national minorities — they were the first to be targeted on purely ethnic grounds. Of these, 139,835 were sentenced administratively, i.e., without following the usual legal procedures. All told, 111,091 of them were executed. Poles accounted for about ten percent of the total number of victims of the 1936–38 Great Purge, and for about 40 percent of the victims of the Stalinist purges aimed at national minorities.[8] Such abysmal numbers are absolutely staggering to the normal, healthy mind. And every one of these "numbers" had a first and last name and a life, such as it was, before his or her dislocation or "liquidation." But a greater tragedy was yet to follow during the 1939–41 Soviet occupation of Poland and in the postwar years.

It is a well-documented fact that after the Soviet "liberation" of Poland, that is, after the second Soviet occupation of Poland beginning in January 1944, 42,000 Poles were interned (over 40 percent of them were members of the anti-Nazi Polish underground) and that an additional 50,000 Poles were arrested and deported to northern Russia.[9] This same tragic fate befell all the other captive nations in the Soviet bloc. A much greater number of Soviet citizens, including a vast number of returning Soviet POWs and repatriated non-combatants, shared that same fate after that victorious Great Patriotic War which Stalin himself had helped set in motion.

In the nineteenth and twentieth centuries, therefore, the threat of deportation was all too real to the Poles. Jan Plater-Gajewski's family history was shared by many of them: His great-grandfather spent seven years, his grandfather eleven, his father five, and he himself seventeen years in that barren wasteland of Siberia.[10]

Sources

The sources dealing with the four major waves of deportations from Eastern Poland in 1940–41 include the NKVD (Order No. 0054) instructions relating to "anti-Soviet elements" (see Document A at the back of the book). This document identifies the various categories of people deemed subversive to the Soviet Union and its interests. These categories include "all citizens of foreign countries," "repatriates," "Polish refugees," land and shop owners, and the clergy — to name but a few. But there are many more categories and they are all-embracing.

We also have Ivan Serov's "Basic Instructions on Deportations, Order No. 001223" (see Document B). These instructions detail the procedures for carrying out the deportation of the "anti-Soviet elements."

We also have the March 5, 1940, document signed by Stalin and his Politburo members, a document that orders the summary execution (or in the words of the document itself, "the supreme penalty: shooting") of some 25,700 Polish citizens, both military and civilian (see Document C).

And now, thanks to the diligent work of the Polish Military Archives Commission and the cooperation of the Russian authorities, we have several thousand pages of NKVD records which document the Soviet atrocities against Poles,[11] records that are now being analyzed and recorded in the *Index of the Repressed*, compiled by the Karta Centre.[12]

In addition, the Polish Government Collection, the Władysław Anders Collection, and the Poland, Ambasada (USSR) Collection at the Hoover Institution on War, Revolution and Peace at Stanford, California, contain over 20,000 accounts and transcripts of interviews conducted with Polish citizens deported to the Soviet Union between 1939 and 1941. All this information was gathered shortly after the "amnesty" — while it was still fresh in the minds of the victims. Among the most moving of these accounts are the ones written by children in the Polish settlements of the British-controlled Middle East where they were sent. One hundred twenty of these essays have been published in the English language by Irena Grudzińska-Gross and Jan Tomasz Gross in a 1981 book entitled *War Through Children's Eyes.*

The General Sikorski Historical Institute Archives in London and the Karta Centre in Warsaw are two other sources of invaluable information.

An important document, one that heretofore has escaped the scholarly attention it deserves, is a confidential report from London dated December 1943: "Soviet Deportation of the Inhabitants of Eastern Poland in 1939–1941." It is located in the U.S. State Department, National Archives and Research Administration, Washington, D.C. (see Document D).

Finally, a number of worthwhile publications — many of them memoirs — that deal with the deportations have come out in both Polish and English. Three of these works deserve a special mention: *Sprawiedliwość sowiecka [Soviet Justice],* the first popular book in the Polish language, self-published in Italy in 1945 by Sylwester Mora [Kazimierz Zamorski] and Piotr Zwierniak [Stanisław Starzewski] and reissued in Warsaw in 1994; *The Dark Side of the Moon*, a work published anonymously in London in 1946 by Zoe Zajdlerowa, with a preface by T. S. Eliot, and reissued in 1989; and *The Black Book of Communism*, which came out in English in 1999.

Statistics

The four previously-mentioned major deportations of Polish citizens from the Soviet zone took place on February 10, April 13, and June 29 in 1940, and from mid-June 1941 until the invasion of the Soviet Union by Germany. (Daniel Boćkowski, however, contends that in addition there was a fairly large deportation in October 1939 as well.[13]) How many people were deported? No one really knows and chances are that no one will ever know the full scale of that Soviet ethnic cleansing campaign.

The most conservative Polish count based on Soviet documents is as follows: 140,000 (mostly Poles) during the first, 60,000 (again, mostly Poles) during the second, 80,000 (mostly Jewish refugees) during the third, and 40,000 Polish citizens mainly from the Wilno area during the fourth deportation for a grand total of 320,000 persons. These figures were published in 1997 by the Main Commission in Warsaw,[14] repeated in the Warsaw daily, *Rzeczpospolita* (April 18, 2000), and presented in text and table format in a 2000, and subsequently revised 2002, Karta Centre publication.[15] The information in these sources came from the *Index of the Repressed*. According to that *Index* (as of 2002), during the war and after 1944, 570,387 Polish citizens had been subjected to some form of Soviet repression. Józef Lewandowski summarized the findings of Russian historians as follows:

> [During the February, April, and June 1940 mass deportations] over 270,000 [sic, 280,000] persons were expelled, of whom 60 percent were residents of the occupied territories (82–83 percent of these, in turn, were Poles), and 40 percent were refugees [from western and central Poland]. Jews constituted 82–84 percent of the latter category. Then there was an additional deportation just before the outbreak of the German-Soviet war ... involving between 34,000 and 44,000 Polish citizens. Altogether 314,000–324,000 persons were deported.... As of August 1, 1941, there were 381,000 Polish prisoners and deportees in the Soviet Union. Of these, 335,000 were deportees and their families.[16]

These Soviet figures, even if accurate (and some scholars question their veracity), do not give us a complete picture of that horrendous Soviet ethnic cleansing campaign aimed against Polish citizens. If to them we add the various other deportations, smaller in scale, resulting in the displacement of civilians, prisoners of war, and people arrested for political reasons and detained in the prisons of Eastern Poland, about half of whom were eventually deported to Soviet forced-labor camps, we will arrive at 400,000 to 500,000 as the grand total of those deported using the Soviet documents as our point of departure. By including voluntary workers, those who fled in June and July 1941, Red Army draftees, and other such categories we arrive at approximately 750,000 to 780,000 as the total number of Polish citizens who found themselves in the Soviet Union during the Soviet occupation of Eastern Poland.[17]

A contemporary source, the previously-mentioned 1943 report from London, informs us that "Independently of the four mass deportations small batches of a dozen or even several score persons were continually being banished to the interior of the USSR. The deportation plan was not carried out in full on account of the outbreak of the Russo-German war. The four mass deportations included only a part of those figuring in the registers, and this part amounted to about 1.000.000 men, women and children." (See Document D.)

One promising approach to this question of numbers is provided by Polish railway employees who, after all, had firsthand knowledge of the preparations being made for the deportations and who operated the trains bound for the interior of the Soviet Union. According to their reckoning, the occupation authorities utilized from 120 to 150 trains for each of the deportations, each train carrying an average of 2,000 persons. Using this information and relying on additional information provided by the deportees, Bohdan Podoski — himself a victim of NKVD arrest and exile — estimates that 110 trains were used in the first deportation, 160 in the second, 120 in the third, and 120 in the deportation of June of 1941. Moreover, he estimates that about ten percent of the deportees and prisoners were marched or transported by trucks into the Soviet Union just before the German invasion. Thus, according to Podoski, 220,000 persons were deported in February, 320,000 in April, 240,000 in June 1940, and 265,000 in June of the following year. That last deportation consisted of 170,000 exiles and 95,000 prisoners. In addition, there were approximately 647,000 POWs, Red Army recruits, and concentration camp victims in the Soviet Union as of June 1941. Podoski's grand total, therefore, of all Polish citizens deported to the Soviet Union in 1939–41 stands at 1,692,000.[18]

CATEGORIES

Ethnic Poles, an overall minority in Eastern Poland, constituted the majority of those deported, but no social category or Polish minority group was spared.

The social categories included workers, artisans, peasants, foresters, soldiers, judges, the clergy, professors, scientists, attorneys, engineers, and teachers. But anyone listed in the index of "anti-Soviet elements" could have been deported and many were.

The minority groups included Jews, Ukrainians, Belorussians, Lithuanians, and other Polish citizens. As can be seen, among these masses were the "oppressed minorities" that Stalin came to rescue from "Polish oppression" — his official excuse for the invasion of Poland. The Soviet line, that at least they were spared the horrors of war, that they were "saved," means little considering the existence of places like Katyn, the sprawling network of various Soviet detention camps, and life in the Gulag where Poles and others suffered untold misery and where so many of them perished in circumstances defying description.

About 20 percent of those deported to the Soviet Union from Eastern Poland were Jews. The largest group was not the indigenous Jews but the refugees from the Nazi zone. After arriving in Eastern Poland, rather than opting for Soviet citizenship many registered for repatriation in accordance with the terms of the September 28, 1939, German-Soviet Boundary and Friendship Treaty. Their motives for so doing were their wish to rejoin their families, their disillusionment with the Soviet system, and their fear of losing their homes and properties in Poland. Since Germany and the Soviet Union were allies at the time, and since the "Final Solution" was not implemented until after the German invasion of the Soviet Union, how were they to know that their request for repatriation to the Nazi zone would make them suspect in the eyes of the Soviets and thus make them eligible for deportation? But that's exactly what happened: the Nazis didn't want them back and the Soviets no longer trusted them. Other Jews were deported for engaging in illicit trade, for illegal border crossing, for political activity, and, in the case of the well-to-do, for being "class enemies."

By the time this Soviet reign of terror was over, Jewish communal life in Eastern Poland was in shambles and approximately 70,000 of them (of the total number deported by Soviet count: 320,000) wound up in Siberia together with the rest. Of the 70,000, from 1,500 to 2,000 may have perished. In all, some form of repression was carried out against 120,000 Jews and between 2,300 and 2,900 were murdered by the Soviets, including 500–600 in Katyn, Kharkov, and Kalinin (now Tver).[19] It should not surprise us, therefore, that so many Jews willingly joined Gen. Anders' Free Polish Army after the "amnesty" (despite official Soviet efforts to prevent them from doing so) and that so many of them willingly chose to be repatriated to Soviet-occupied Poland after the war rather than to remain under direct Soviet rule. For many this exodus ended not in Poland but in Palestine or the West.

The number of Ukrainian and Belorussian deportees (of the 320,000) is estimated at 25,000 and 20,000, respectively. The rest, with few exceptions, were ethnic Poles.

Other, less conservative but not necessarily inaccurate, estimates would greatly inflate all these figures.

Political prisoners kept in Eastern Poland constituted yet another category of deportees. Thousands of such prisoners perished in the course of the Soviet occupation and, according to Soviet documents, at least 10,000 were slaughtered in local jails on the eve of the German invasion of the Soviet Union. Those who were not killed, and they numbered into the thousands as well, were evacuated with the retreating Red Army; many of them were executed later.[20]

Procedures

In spite of the Soviet directives for a well-orchestrated mass exodus, the deportation process left much to be desired. Lists of those to be deported were drawn up on the basis of information provided by collaborators from among the ethnic minorities, including the Jews and Ukrainians. (In the German zone, it was the Volksdeutschen, or German nationals, who generally prepared such lists of Poles.) Long trains stood waiting at the railway stations. In towns and villages, columns of trucks along with wagons — and in winter, sleighs — requisitioned from the peasants stood ready. Soviet army units as well as the NKVD and the local militia — very often composed of Jews and Ukrainians[21] — awaited orders. And when they came, regardless of weather conditions or time of day or rather night, the village or colony would be surrounded and forcible entries would be made into people's homes. At gunpoint, the family would be given from ten minutes to two hours in which to pack their belongings and then be driven or made to walk to the nearest railway station. Janina Karpa from the province of Lwów provides us with one description of the way in which it was done:

> On the 10th of February, a Saturday, at five-thirty in the morning, came seven Soviets armed with rifles, two men from the Ukrainian police and five Jews, who were also

> armed. There were six of us in the family, and they were fifteen armed men. One of the seven Soviets read an official order, which was like a death sentence. We were given fifteen minutes to get ourselves and our children ready. We didn't have enough time to get ready and were fearful of what would happen to us, so we were only half dressed. We were not allowed to take anything at all. It was only about a mile to our train station, but they took us to the station in Winniki, fourteen kilometers away. We stood all day in freight wagons like in a shed because they were not heated. At night they transported us to Lwów where we stayed for another whole day. When our family found out that we were taken from our home under guard without being allowed to take anything with us, they brought us some food. The Soviets and Jews did not want to allow our parents to come close to the wagons, so we started screaming and crying and jumped out of the wagons not paying attention to the guards because it didn't matter to us any more. We only wanted to get some food for our children. The next night they left Lwów with us. There were 58 people in this wagon.[22]

A child from Stanisławów Province gives us another glimpse at what was going on at that time:

> It was a cold night, the snow fell and the wind blew. It was on February 10 at three in the morning, when everyone slept soundly. Suddenly there was a loud knocking. I jumped up from my bed it frightened me very much and also my mommy. Daddy got up put on the light and opened the door, four Russians rush into the apartment and two Ukrainians with rifles drawn, at this sight I became even more frightened and rushed out from bed got dressed and sat down. After a moment they gathered the whole family into one room daddy, mommy, my brother, sister, and me. They asked daddy where we wanted to go, to Russia or to Germany, daddy said to America. Then they became very angry.... A few minutes later we put our things on the sleigh and we went to the station on foot.... When we got to the station it was already getting light, we waited at the station for 3 hours and then we were ordered to get into the freight cars. It was very cold in them.... We stood at that station for two days, there was nothing hot to eat because there was no coal or wood.[23]

The winter of 1939–40 was extremely severe. I was born in the province of Wołyń from which tens of thousands of us were deported. February 10, 1940, was my birthday. The thermometer registered 30 degrees below zero on the Celsius scale that night, and both children and adults froze to death by the thousands on their way to the stations and in the boxcars in Poland and all along their long journeys to their final destinations. During the summer deportations it was just the opposite, and people perished from the stifling heat. The rations of food and water were meager; there were no sanitary facilities, no time for burials, and no time to mourn.

In the Soviet Union

The destination of the exiled Polish citizens was the northern, central, and eastern regions of the Soviet Union — the area between the Arctic Circle in the north and the Mongolian border in the south: Arkhangelsk, Komi and Kolyma regions, Siberia, Kazakhstan and Uzbekistan. Some ended up in prisons or in penal, POW, "special," concentration, or forced-labor camps; others were dumped into remote settlements; and still others wound up in kolkhozes (Soviet collective farms). They lived, or rather suffered, in 2,800 locations in 56 Russian oblasts (districts). Their fate was the same wherever they were sent: slave labor in exchange for the barest necessities of life. And they died by the thousands — by tens of thousands — of cold, hunger and disease. Here is one vivid description of what life was like out there on the frozen tundra:

> So they sent me then to Siberia with my wife and children, and of the many and great privations on the way, had I the time there would be much to tell....
>
> There began to be nothing to eat, the folk began to die of hunger and from ceaseless working in the water; shallow was the river, heavy were the rafts, merciless were the taskmasters, stout were the sticks, gnarled were the cudgels, cutting were the knouts, cruel were the sufferings —fire and rack.... Ah me! What a time!.... and we dragged on for another year living on the Nercha River, and keeping ourselves alive with roots and herbs that grew on the banks. One after another the folk died of hunger.... And in the winter we would live on fir cones.... A mare foaled, and in secret, the starving folk devoured the foal together with the caul.... And another mare died, and desperation seized them all, inasmuch as they had pulled the foal out of her, stealing a march on nature. When nought but the head had as yet emerged from the womb, they tore it out, yea, and they began to eat the blood that came away with it. Ah, me! What a time! And two of my little sons died from these sore straits, and roaming the hills and the sharp rocks with my children that survived, naked and barefoot, living on grass and roots, what did I not endure? And I, sinful man, partook willy-nilly of mare's flesh and foul carrion and the flesh of birds. Woe for my sinful soul! Who will pour water on my head and unseal for me the fountain of tears?[24]

That description comes from a Russian classic, *The Life of Archpriest Avvakum by Himself.* He was deported to Siberia three times for a total of over 25 years and then, with three of his comrades, burned at the stake. He was born in 1621 and died in 1682. But were the conditions of life in the early 1940s any different out there than in the 17th century? The following personal account comes from Maria Skałka, one of the World War II deportees:

> The conditions in which we lived were simply impossible. Our damp places of residence, full of different kinds of bugs, had a negative impact on our health. These conditions exacted a toll on our family as well. In May my mother became grievously ill. Not having any medical care or even the slightest assistance from any quarter ... she bade farewell to this vale of tears on October 30, 1940. In December of that year my youngest brother, Władysław, died. He was hardly 15 months old. The following year, in February, my six-year-old brother, Ludwik, slipped into eternity. A terrible emptiness surrounded us. The loss of these three beloved persons affected us greatly.[25]

And "who will pour water on [Maria's] head and unseal for [her and the hundreds of thousands like her] the fountain of tears?"[26]

"Amnesty"

Such was the lot of the deportees until the invasion of the Soviet Union by Germany on June 22, 1941. A protocol of the Polish-Soviet (Sikorski-Maisky) agreement of July 30, 1941, provided for the release of all Poles in Soviet exile as well as for the formation of a Polish army on Soviet soil. The document, signed in the presence of Winston Churchill and Anthony Eden, used the unfortunate term "amnesty" (the word should have been "manumission" or "emancipation") to characterize the release of the exiles; they were Stalin's bargaining chip in the contest for the *status quo ante* borders of Poland. According to a January 15, 1943, note from Beria to Stalin, 389,041 Polish citizens were freed as a result of that "amnesty." These included 200,828 ethnic Poles, 90,662 Jews, 31,392 Ukrainians, 27,418 Belorussians, 3,421 Russians, and 2,291 persons of other nationalities.[27] There was no need to inform Stalin of the fact that the Soviet authorities often impeded the release of the deportees from their various places of confinement and absolved themselves from assisting them in any way whatsoever upon their release. This utter lack of concern brought about a crisis of unimaginable proportions.

Nevertheless, elated by this turn of events the far-flung Polish exiles began to make their way as best they could southward, to where Gen. Anders' army was forming, in the hope of liberation. These journeys, often several weeks long, brought new suffering and tens of thousands died from hunger, cold, heat, disease, and exhaustion on that trip to freedom. For many, the help provided by the United States and Great Britain was too little and too late. Czesława Żukowska, a Wołynian, recalls:

> We, together with the others, left Siberia and made our way towards central Russia whose wonders were being praised everywhere. Unfortunately, although we only spent a few months in that new place, we lost our father and mother who, unable to tolerate the murderous climate, died there.[28]

Stanisława Sawko's mother, not wishing to abandon her ailing husband, sent their children on that trip by themselves. Stella Synowiec-Tobis lost her mother at a railway station; her mother went to look for some provisions and the train suddenly departed, leaving her behind. Józefa Stroczyńska's father died on a train. Another woman lost not only her husband but her four children as well.[29] Such tragic stories are a legion. In the Samarkand district alone, over a two-and-a-half-month period in 1942, out of 27,000, 1,632 Polish citizens perished from typhus and malnutrition.[30] The Polish embassy estimated that between December 1941 and June 1942, 10 percent of the 200,000 Polish citizens that gathered in the central Soviet republics died of typhus alone.[31]

Meanwhile, by June 1942 the Polish authorities had gathered over 77,000 lost children and orphans and with the help offered by Great Britain, Canada, and the American Red Cross, planned to evacuate about 50,000 of them. But Moscow would not agree to such a massive evacuation of children citing transportation problems as the reason and denying that the Polish children were in any danger.[32] The words of reassurance offered by Deputy Commissar Andrei Vyshinsky to Polish Ambassador Stanisław Kot must surely rank among the most cynical ever uttered by a Soviet official. "The welfare of the children," he said, "is assured by the Soviet authorities."[33] In reality, the Russians were afraid that the evacuation of these children and the disclosure of their condition — at times indistinguishable from that of Nazi concentration-camp victims — would have earned them the scorn of the civilized world.

As the negotiations, or rather pleas, for the children's release continued, on January 16, 1943 — when there were still hundreds of thousands of Poles in the USSR — the Polish embassy was informed that since the number of Poles in the Soviet Union had become negligible, there was no longer a need for the Polish social welfare agencies on Soviet soil, and 400 of them, including numerous orphanages and hospitals, were immediately closed or taken over, along with all their internationally-donated supplies, by Soviet authorities. That March, the remaining Poles were forced to accept Soviet citizenship.[34] So much for "amnesty," the Soviet version. On April 13, 1943, the Germans announced to the world their discovery of the mass graves at Katyn. On April 25 of that same year Stalin broke off diplomatic relations with the Polish government-in-exile using the Polish protests over the executions at Katyn as a pretext.

Nevertheless, during the two great evacuations (the first, between March 24 and the beginning of April 1942; the second, between August 10 and September 1, 1942), from Krasnovodsk across the Caspian Sea to Pahlavi, and the smaller overland evacuations from Ashkhabad to Mashhad (in March and September 1942), about 115,000 people (including some 37,000 civilians, of whom about 18,300 were children) left the Soviet Union. The soldiers of Gen. Anders' army went on to fight in many battles, including the one at Monte Cassino; the civilians, because they could not be repatriated, were forced to remain in foreign lands for the remainder of the war.

In addition to the refugees who left with Gen. Anders' Polish army, a number of Poles returned to Poland later with Zygmunt Berling's communist armed forces.

After Leaving the Soviet Union

The first stop of the refugees evacuated with Gen. Anders' army was Iran, where they found temporary quarters in large temporary camps initially located in Pahlavi and Mashhad, and later in Tehran and Ahvaz. While Gen. Anders' troops were subsequently transferred to Palestine and from there to Iraq, the civilians remained in Iran. To accommodate the refugees, a sprawling stationary camp was established in Isfahan (Eṣfahān). Because it housed several camps for the thousands of orphaned Polish children, it came to be known as the "City of Polish Children." The relief assistance afforded by Polish, British, American, and Iranian authorities soon improved their living conditions and brought the devastating contagious diseases under control, diseases acquired in the Soviet Union which continued to rob the refugees of their lives even after liberation. (Over 2,000 refugees died in Iran alone.) In time, various Polish institutions, including 24 schools serving some 3,000 students, were established in Iran and several Polish periodicals and newspapers appeared.

Their stay in Iran, however, was cut short because of the hostility of the Soviet army units occupying northern Iran and because of the threat of the German armies which had already reached the Caucasus. By the end of 1943, 33,000 refugees were transferred from Iran to other countries. By the end of 1945, another 4,300 were evacuated to Lebanon; by 1946, that number rose to 6,000. From a temporary camp near Beirut they were sent to more permanent quarters such as those located in Ghazir, Zauk Michael, Ajaltoun, and Boladoun. Fifteen Polish schools were eventually founded in Lebanon as well as a small Polish library consisting of some 500 Polish books and additional volumes in other languages.

In Palestine, the camps for the over 5,000 refugees transferred there were located in Jerusalem, Nazareth, Rehovot, Ain-Karem, and Barbara. Several Scout groups, yunak (young men's labor brigade) schools, training centers, a women's auxiliary service, and an officers' legion were established. A Polish press, located in Palestine and Iran, printed the much-needed educational materials used in refugee schools throughout the Middle East.

Some exiles also found asylum in India in temporary camps set up in Quetta, Mount Abu, Panchgani, Bandra, and in and near Karachi (such as the Country Club Camp, Haji Pilgrims Camp, and the Malir Camp). But more stable settlements also emerged such as those in Balachadi, near the city of Jamnagar, and in Valivade, near Kolhapur. Balachadi became a refuge for some 1,000 Polish children. Valivade housed 5,000 Polish refugees; there, they had their own self-government and succeeded in establishing three kindergartens, four elementary schools, a secondary school, and a trade school. In all, 16 Polish schools were attended by some 2,500 Polish children in India. Moreover, several Polish periodicals were published, Polish amateur theaters were founded, and Polish business enterprises flourished.

Africa provided another safe harbor for the Poles. In mid-1944, East Africa hosted over 13,000 Polish citizens. They settled in temporary and stationary camps in the British colonies of Uganda, Kenya, and Tanganyika. In Uganda, the camps were located in Masindi and Koya on Lake Victoria. In Kenya, they were located in Rongai, Manira, Makindu, Nairobi, and Nyali near Mombasa. In Tanganyika, the largest settlement was Tengeru (4,000 refugees) and smaller camps were located in Kigoma, Kidugala, Ifunda, Kondoa, and Morogoro.

South Africa, North Rhodesia, and South Rhodesia also became the home of Poles. The largest of these settlements were: in the Union of South Africa — Oudtshoorn; in North Rhodesia — Abercorn, Bwana M'Kubwa, Fort Jameson, Livingstone, and Lusaka; in South Rhodesia — Digglefold, Marandellas, Rusape, and Gatooma.

In Africa, Polish schools, churches, hospitals, civic centers, and manufacturing and service cooperatives were founded and Polish culture prospered. African radio stations ran programs in the Polish language and there was even a Polish press. In South Africa alone there were 18 Polish schools with about 1,800 students in attendance.

A large Polish settlement was also founded in Mexico. Although provisions were made to resettle several thousand Poles in that country, only two transports arrived in the summer and fall of 1943 with a total of 1,432 refugees. Their home became a deserted hacienda in Santa Rosa, near León. The settlement was financed by the Polish government-in-exile in London and by American institutions, including the National Catholic Welfare Conference and the Polish-American Council.

Finally, 733 Polish children with their 105 caretakers arrived in New Zealand on November 1, 1944. They were housed in the Polish Children's Camp located in Pahiatua. As elsewhere, kindergartens and grammar schools provided for the educational needs of the youngsters. Unlike elsewhere, upon graduation the teens were placed either in schools operated by religious orders or in technical schools. Two hostels were also established: one in Island Bay for girls, the other in Lyall Bay for boys.

Wherever they went the Polish refugees encountered effusive goodwill not only on the part of the respective governments that invited them but also on the part of the native populations. Welcoming signs with Polish flags, white eagles, and words of encouragement often greeted them upon their arrival, high government officials paid them visits, and commemorative monuments were erected in their honor. Unlike the Soviet Union, these were, after all, ancient civilized cultures.

Why didn't America open its doors, and open them wide, to the Polish refugees? That the Western Allies knew all about the deportations is clear from their relief efforts both in the Soviet Union and in the Middle East as well as from the December 1943 report reprinted herein as Document D. It is also clear from that document that they opted for the suppression of this information. (The report, stamped "Confidential," was reserved for the eyes of "a few persons, especially selected for this purpose" who were to be "confidentially informed of the fate of Polish citizens under Soviet rule.") Moreover, even while in Iran, although debriefed, the refugees were not encouraged to speak about their experiences in the Soviet Union with outsiders. In America, the date of the arrival of the first transport aboard the USS *Hermitage* (on June 25, 1943, consisting of 706 refugees, including 166 children) was a State secret, no doubt also marked "Confidential" on Washington inter-departmental missives. After disembarking at the San Pedro navel dock near Los Angeles, the women and children under 14 years of age were placed in the Griffith Park *Internment* Camp in Burbank and the men in the *Alien* Camp in Tuna Canyon (emphases added).

When the Polish community found out about the arrival of the transport they rallied around the exiles and demanded to know why the refugees were placed in camps. Father Wacław Zajączkowski even recruited families willing to take in a hundred orphans. But that was not in the plans, and two days later all of the refugees were shipped off to Mexico. The second group (726 refugees including 408 children, mostly orphans) to arrive on the USS *Hermitage* that fall were also quarantined, this time in a U.S. army camp near Los Angeles called Santa Anita. After a short stay, they too were dispatched across the border to Colonia Santa Rosa. The delicate balance between the Soviet Union and the Western Allies had to be maintained, it seems, at any cost.

Among the victims on this altar of silence were the 14,500 prisoners of war interned in Kozelsk, Starobelsk, and Ostashkov and executed in cold blood in Katyn, Kharkov, and Kalinin in April and May 1940. The Allies never officially contradicted the Soviet line that the Germans, who dug up the graves in the Katyn forest, were responsible for the murders.

No doubt "Uncle Joe"—*homo sovieticus barbarosus* incarnate—must have been grateful to the Western Allies for their conspiracy of silence, for preserving the "good name" of his evil empire. He was even more grateful at Yalta, when the Western Allies granted him the right to enslave all of eastern and half of central Europe.

But was there ever a real need for this cover-up, this concern for maintaining the "delicate balance," this appeasement of Stalin after the revocation of the "amnesty" and the April 25, 1943, rupture of diplomatic relations with the Polish government-in-exile? He was committed to fighting the Germans whether he wanted to or not, he needed the help of the West, and it was abundantly clear that he would not allow any more evacuations out of the Soviet Union. Moreover, a full, timely, and well-orchestrated disclosure of the Soviet atrocities in Eastern Poland, the deportations, and Katyn—in effect the moral equivalent of a Soviet Nuremberg Trial—may have had a significant impact on the events at Yalta which, in turn, would have had a profound effect on the immediate postwar forced repatriation to the Soviet block of Soviet citizens (who were often executed upon their return to the Soviet Union because they were considered to be "tainted") as well as the displaced persons of other nations — and there were hundreds of thousands in both categories. More important, it may have given the Allies that much-needed edge to withstand Stalin's postwar territorial demands and thereby would have also prevented the additional Soviet postwar atrocities in those countries which, as the result of Yalta, became captive nations behind the Iron Curtain. Appeasement, as we know, only emboldens the aggressor. The revelations of the Soviet war crimes, crimes against peace, and crimes against humanity, when they finally came out in the Western media during the cold-war period, were like crying over spilled milk. As for the victims, insults were sometimes added to injuries. When Hank Birecki, one of the orphans of Colonia Santa Rosa brought to Chicago in 1946, was put on stage with the other children and asked to tell about his life in the Soviet Union

> Hank told them how he and his family were taken from home, about the Red Army soldiers pounding at the door, about having to pack within a half-hour's time, and about their transport in freight cars after waiting on a railroad siding for three days without food or water. He spoke about the young woman passing her infant through the bars, the shouts and the shot, and how every day during their transport the Soviet soldiers removed the dead bodies from the cars and just dumped them by the side of the tracks; about their stay in Siberia, how they existed in the run-down horse barn, and their daily struggle to survive. Near tears he mentioned the death of his mother, and that he was never able to see her grave, that his grandmother had to go and bury her, and her words afterwards: "I had to split her nightgown in order to bury her in it. She was all in pieces, the arms the legs, the head."[35]

After Hank finished his tragic tale and walked off the stage he overheard comments like: "Those things could not have happened" and "The boy does not know what he is talking about." And this from a Polish-American audience! And this in 1946! Hank responded by withdrawing, and for years afterwards he would not speak to anyone at all about his exile. "What happened to Hank as a young boy," comments the German author of this biography to whom Hank finally did speak after 50 years, "was, in early 1946, still beyond the imagination of many people this side of the Atlantic. Revelations such as Hank's often came as too much of a shock."[36]

After Yalta

The camps and settlements established in the Near and Middle East, India, Africa and Mexico (New Zealand from the beginning offered resident status to the orphaned children) were meant to be temporary quarters for the Polish refugees until the end of the war and the expected liberation of their country. However, after Yalta and the substantive changes in Poland's borders this became an impossible dream, although a few did return to join their families in Poland.

What became of the rest? Many of those who wound up in New Zealand and the Union of South Africa remained where they were brought. The Polish refugees housed in the various camps in Iran, Lebanon, Palestine, India, and Africa moved to Great Britain and its dominions, Canada and Australia, from where some of them later emigrated to the United States; some also settled in Argentina and other countries in South America. And in 1996, in Chicago, the Poles of Santa Rosa celebrated the 50th anniversary of their arrival in the United States.

Thus ended the saga of the deportees from Eastern Poland who managed to get out of the Soviet Union under the provisions of that tenuous "amnesty" of 1941. But what happened to the rest of the hundreds of thousands of deportees who did not leave with Gen. Anders' army? For many the Soviet Union became their final resting place before the war's end. (According to the 1943 report, Document D, "about 200.000 Polish citizen children and adults died during the period of deportation.") Another quarter of a million — including, no doubt, some deportees — were repatriated to the "recovered territories" of western Poland during the massive population exchanges following World War II. As for what happened to those who never got out, God only knows. Some, no doubt, are still there.

1. Deportation

Milewski family memoir

(Stanisław) I was born on June 16, 1930, on the Bagrowo estate, near Środa, in the county of Poznań. My father Alfred and my mother Sabina moved there from the Kijewo estate, where my father was an administrator and where my brother Andrzej (August 11, 1924) and sister Teresa (February 1, 1926) were born. In 1933 we moved to Polesie to a farm in Staniewicze, near the town of Iwacewicze.

On February 10, 1940, at four o'clock in the morning, in total darkness, our neighbor knocked on our window and warned us that Russian soldiers were coming. The soldiers and three members of the local communist committee entered the house and stood us up against the wall. We thought they were going to shoot us. The Russian officer told us that we had an hour to pack. He would not tell us where they were taking us but was nice enough to tell us to take warm clothing, blankets, jewelry and money. That saved our lives later on.

Mother, Andrzej and I were put on a sled and taken to the railroad station in Iwacewicze. The station was filled with civilians and soldiers. They put us all — men, women, the young and the old — into freight railroad cars. There was a large sliding door on each side of the wagon which could be bolted from the outside. Inside were two-tier wooden benches on which we slept. In the middle there was an iron stove and a few scraps of wood for the fire. A hole in the floor served as a toilet. There were four small windows secured with iron bars. Once a day they gave us bread and soup. It was very cold, particularly at night when the fire died out. We did not know where we were going but we suspected that they were deporting us to Siberia, just as they had deported so many other generations of Poles in the past. There was one near tragedy: our sister Teresa was left behind because she was not on the list.

(The dated entries below come from the diary kept by my mother Sabina and sister Teresa during our exile.)

> February 10, 1940 (Teresa) Terrible day. They took Mother and the boys away. Rumor has it that they are deporting them to Vladivostok. I was left at home with Aunt Janina Milewska and Halina Szulc-Rembowska; they forgot about me. I begged them to take me with my family.

February 11, 1940 People from the local communist committee came for me. We reached Iwacewicze in the evening and spent the night in freezing cold at the station while snowdrifts covered the platforms.

February 12, 1940 This morning a soldier took me along a very long line of freight cars loaded with people and we searched for the Milewski family.

February 13, 1940 (Sabina) We are happy to have Teresa with us. For three days we stayed at the station in the freight cars. Today the train started moving in the direction of Baranowicze.

February 14, 1940 The train arrived at the station in Baranowicze. There are 27 people in the freight car: our family and the families of Szalantrów, Lubelski and Górecki. There are twelve grown ups, two babies about three months old, and the rest are children. There's terrible disorder and mess inside and it's impossible to do anything about it because the train jerks and moves rapidly. We have to do everything inside the train (go to the toilet, cook, etc.) since they let us out only for water and wood. We have food supplies only for one week which we share with other people. It's extremely cold; the fire burns only during the day because we have very little firewood.

February 15, 1940 We arrived at Pogorzelce, 20 km from Baranowicze, where we had to wait 24 hours because the locomotive could not pull the train over the frozen railroad tracks. The same thing happened to the train next to ours. It was filled with Polish people from Święta Wola, Kolońsk, etc. We found out that our friends, the Brzeskis, were there.[1]

Account of Vala Lewicki (née Miron)

On a severely cold morning on Saturday, 10th of February 1940, Nadya, Uncle's eldest daughter, and I went to school as usual. We were both 12 years old and we shared a boarding room in Jeziory. We found the school was closed. Little we knew that that day would change our lives dramatically and permanently. Why was the school closed? What made us walk home, six kilometres away, instead of going back to the boarding room?...

Nadya and I did not make it home. We walked only two kilometres to the crossroads from where four heavily snow-covered roads branched out in four different directions. Two of them, scarcely visible in the forest, led to two different train stations: Jeziory (2 km away) and Żydomla, 9 km in the opposite direction.

Right there, under the cross, we met a cavalcade of sledges with my father and my brother Jan (19 years old) walking in front of them, followed by three NKVD men holding their guns in readiness. Our families, with bundles of their belongings on the sledges, were, as enemies of communism, being taken to Żydomla station for deportation. Had the two of us reached the crossroads a few minutes later we would have missed our families and remained parentless and homeless in Russian-occupied Poland, as our property automatically fell under Soviet ownership. But the cross is a powerful thing. So, too, is the love and the blessing of parents.

Seeing us both, Nadya's mother, my mother and our 70-year-old grandmother who was perpetually praying, stopped murmuring and began to cry—probably overcome by sorrow and happiness at the same time. My youngest sister Veronica (8 years old) and my cousins, Nina, Victor, Mary and Michael were sobbing too. I suppose that they did not understand what the commotion was all about. Nadya and I did not cry at all. But our older sister Ola (15 years old) wept all the way down to Grodno. She had left her first boyfriend behind. As for my grandmother, when I think of her now, I feel a very great affection for her, but in prewar Poland I was afraid of her. My grandmother was a big, autocratic-looking lady in spite of a slight stoop. Normally she would never surrender to anybody. But at that time the tragedy of war had crushed her completely. Her world had collapsed....

A young married couple had been hoisted into our wagon a couple of nights previously. The lady was expecting their first baby. When the all-important time came the whole carriage was in turmoil. The father-to-be paced nervously around the pot-belly stove. This was covered in pots of melting snow. (The snow had been pulled up in containers through the tin louvres which had been forced open by our men.) Time was running out. There was no bell with which to call the officials or conductors of the two locomotives in order to stop the train. In fact there was no comfort of any kind. My grandmother, who seemed to be unaffected by the panic of the husband and others, solemnly announced that she would deliver their baby safely. Both parents were astounded — and probably horrified — on hearing this. But when reassured by the nine positive confirmations of us children, they calmed down. Silence fell among the passengers. Waiting for a new life to begin was a most peculiar sensation. There was a holy quality about it, as if one were in the church. The silence was broken, occasionally, by the lady herself.

And then — wonder of wonders! — we heard the baby's first cry. Its parents were moved beyond words. A gasp of amazement came from the passengers. Ecstatic parents' faces displayed a mixture of gratitude and exhilaration for grandmother's courage and skill. A broad grin of pure pleasure crossed her face.[2]

Account of Stefania Buczak-Zarzycka

We lived on a farm near the Zbrucz River which formed the natural border between Poland and the USSR. Our family was composed of our parents and four children: Marysia, Alexandra, Stefania (myself) and Antek....

Winter deepened its hold on the countryside; the wind howled, throwing great snowdrifts over natural and man-made constructions. The 10th February 1940, began ominously. Dogs that could not settle yelped throughout the night and our sleep was broken by the continuous sound of sleigh bells. Only those with very urgent business would venture out on such nights!

Who could these travellers be?

The answer to our question began with a thud of fists on our door and a voice shouting: "*Otkroyte dvyere*" (Open the door).

We woke to find our mother opening the door, through which three uniformed NKVD men crowded into the room. Grabbing my father they pushed him into a chair and placed a bayonet into his mouth demanding that we hand over our weapons.

The other soldiers began to ransack our home. We could see that our father was about to pass out so we began to scream at the tops of our lungs: "Father's dying, our father's dying!"

So loud were our screams that they were heard by my uncle, living next door, who rushed over to investigate the reason for our screams. However, the Russians threatened and forced him to return to his home.

Of course the NKVD found no weapons, whereupon we were told that we had ten minutes to dress and to collect any possessions we could carry with us. It was about four in the morning and we could see that outside there were two sleighs waiting for us. We were the first family from this settlement to be detained in this manner....

Muszka, our Pomeranian, trotted out to Antek, who picked her up and tucked her into his coat. On board the sleigh the excited dog growled at the strangers, whereupon a guard grabbed the dog by a clump of fur and tossed her over the side of the sleigh. Again we all began to cry out because we could see that the little dog was unable to dig herself out of the fresh, deep snowfall. And so crying, we hardly noticed the journey to the railway station and we did not realise that this would be the last time we ever would see our home.

For the first time in our short lives we began to witness the misery of human tragedy. Amongst the huge crowds we could see from the clothes that no classes had been spared. We could see the aged, the pregnant, the infirm, even those on stretchers, and crying babies all being forcibly herded into carriages for animal transportation. In the confusion, families were divided and we could see people begging the Russians to allow them to remain as family units. I could almost physically see and touch terror, panic, despair and I thought that I could only be witnessing the end of the world.

Once inside these animal trucks, we could see that there were no windows (therefore no light), bedding or toilet facilities. We were so overcrowded that we could not sit down, and so the adults stood and slept in turn. We were kept in the carriage for about twelve hours before our journey began. Once the train began moving, the men moved quickly to break the boards for ventilation slits and floorboards for a toilet. Provided with no water, the men collected snow from the roof... At midnight we were awakened and told that the direction post "Podwoloczyska-Woloczyska" had been sighted, signifying that we had just crossed the border into USSR. Everyone in the carriage sobbed with the realisation of our destination. Our journey took three weeks and during that time we were given very little food. On the days we were given a very salty soup made from dried fish we were given no water. We received two pieces of bread four times during our relocation.[3]

Account of Tadeusz Pieczko

We were awakened in the middle of one cold winter night by a loud voice and banging on the front door. The dog barked frantically as a stranger called for us to open the door. When the door was opened, we saw a group of armed men in uniforms with rifles in hand and fixed bayonets: they were Russian soldiers. We were frightened as they ordered us to pack in a hurry and get ready to be moved out. We loaded a few belongings on the sled. All this time the dog kept barking and the cattle became restless in the barn. Dad asked them if he could take the barrel of salted pork that he had in the cellar. They gave him permission to take it. The long string of sleds proceeded to the nearest railroad station. We noticed that the neighbor's family was also loaded up and that they started heading for the road. The children were crying because they wanted to take their dog with them. A Russian soldier took aim and shot the dog. I was horrified because I knew that dog. Farther down the road our sled slowed down to pick up an old woman, whom my parents knew, who was walking alone. She was so old that she frightened me. She kept looking at me and smiling. She had hardly any teeth in her mouth. This was February 10, 1940, a day on which my life changed completely.

When we arrived at the railroad station we saw some of our neighbors there and people from other villages. Awaiting us were rows of freight cars attached to coal-burning locomotives spewing black smoke and steam. Many people were crying and the Russian soldiers tried to quiet them down. An old man who was made to wait at the railroad yard almost the whole night froze to death. His despairing family was ordered to get into the boxcar and leave him behind. The soldiers promised that they or someone from the village would bury him. When the family refused to get on the train, they were beaten by the soldiers. The soldiers then dragged the man's body, in sitting position, away from the people. The day had just begun and it was very cold. I couldn't see very well because snow was falling, so I don't know what happened to the body after that.

We were loaded onto cold, wooden freight cars wherein we huddled together to keep warm. Everyone was sad, depressed and crying. The children were confused and scared. (I remember experiencing this same kind of fright one time when I attended a wake, which was held — according to the custom of those days — in the home of the deceased.) On the train, I stayed close to my parents and tried to hold on to them. This frightful experience lasted for days and days, all the way to Siberia. The Russians were able to put quite a few people inside the boxcar because it was divided into two tiers. In the center was a coal-burning stove which we used later whenever we could get some coal. The boxcar had no toilet. A hole was cut out in the floor to serve as a toilet. When not in use, it was covered with boards to keep out the cold. With some help, my dad loaded the barrel of pork onto the boxcar. (The pork turned out to be a lifesaver later on). After a few hours of heading east, we realized that we were leaving Poland for good and entering the vast territory of Russia. The doors on the boxcars were always kept locked from the outside so that no one could escape. The windows were small and had iron bars. Since we had no water on the train, we had to stick our hands through the iron bars and scrape snow from the roof for water. It tasted of soot.

The trip took over three weeks. Cold, hunger and dirt were our constant companions. Our dad tried to keep everyone alive in our boxcar by carefully rationing the salted pork, but it eventually ran out. By the time we reached the labor camps of Siberia about ten percent of the people had already died. These were almost all old people who were ill when they were put on the train. In addition, some infants also died. I don't think, however, that anyone in our boxcar died. My youngest brother, who had not yet turned two, had a couple of close calls mainly because he was ill and because of the poor diet. Since the train seldom stopped (generally, it was only to take on water and coal for the locomotive and provisions for the crew and guards), the dead were sometimes kept in the boxcars for the entire day. When the train did make a stop, the bodies were collected and placed onto a flat car. Thus they continued their journey until we came to a larger town or city where they were dumped for burial. Sometimes, looking out of the small window, I could see the snow-covered bodies lying on the flat car when the train passed a curve in the tracks. That, together with the dumping, was a horrible sight to see. I knew some of those people personally.[4]

Account of Sabina Kukla (née Lukasiewicz)

On the 10th of February 1940 at 3:00 A.M. NKVD men with fixed bayonets broke into our home and arrested my father. He was not allowed to move an inch. One of them stood by him with bayonet at the ready while others searched for weapons through all rooms. We were overcome by fear. My mother began to cry and lost her head completely. My two younger sisters and small brother, wakened from sleep, cried also. Although I was older than they I could not understand why we were subjected to such an armed raid in the night. Throughout the district dogs howled terribly, perhaps instinctively anticipating tragedy. All settlers met with a similar fate at the same time.

After some time, following the search for weapons and interrogation of my father, they ordered us to pack, saying that they were moving us to another region "for our own safety." Mama had a foreboding that they would transport us to Siberia. A similar misfortune struck my grandfather and the whole family during World War I, when she was a young girl. They lost all their property at that time. Also lost was one of grandfather's daughters, the eldest, who was never found. Only those who remained alive returned to Poland.

We were not able to take much with us, only what we could wear and some bundles, without food. We came out of the house, leaving our warm family home, never to return. We were loaded onto waiting sleighs and driven, crying and terrified, through the dark night to the railway station at Dąbrowica, about 7 km from our settlement. To this day I can hear how we were farewelled by neighing horses and howling dogs. The horror remained in my memory for all time.

There was a goods train at the station which stood there for a long time. We were loaded into cattle trucks like sardines in a can, without regard for age or sex. Children, not understanding this macabre situation, asked tearfully why we were taken from our homes and where we were going. The wagon was packed and smelly. There were no windows. A hole cut in the floor in the centre of the wagon — and not screened with anything — served as the toilet. Adults and children relieved themselves in full view of everyone. Through gaps in the boards forming the sides of the wagon we watched what was happening outside. All day they kept bringing more frightened and weeping people, loading them into those miserable wagons. As they finished loading they bolted the wagons closed from the outside and the train moved off. Peering through the gaps and reading off names of places as we passed, we were already sure that we were being taken to the Russian border. Along the way people came out of their homes to farewell us with tears because they knew we were being transported to Siberia.

Thus began our "removal" to a "safe place."[5]

Account of Maria Borkowska-Witkowska

A total of eight of us — Father, Mother, four sisters and two brothers — were taken at night on the 10th of February 1940.

The cause of our exile was the fact that Father had bought a piece of land from an army settler in 1938. They gave us thirty minutes to pack. My father was not allowed to move. The NKVD looked everywhere for weapons, even in the ashes in the stove which had gone out. My father was chairman of a rural co-operative and commandant of an army reserve called Krakus.

We were taken to the railway station Rozyszcze where there were trucks full of people. We rode through Kwierce and Zdolbunov to the border. At that time this was still Poland, but is now part of the Ukraine.[6]

Account of Ryszard Rzepczyński

At 4:00 A.M. on the 10th of February 1940 Russian soldiers with rifles came to our house. We asked them what they wanted and why they had come. They said they had come to search for weapons. They searched and took whatever they thought was of any value. They then told us we had one hour in which to pack and get ready to leave.

Some Ukrainian women from the village who knew what was happening came to our house and asked my mother for some sacks. When they were given some they took an axe and set about chopping the heads off our ducks and chickens. They filled two sacks with the birds with their feathers still on. Then they put these on our two sleds. We were also put on them and our journey began.

We were taken to Krzemieniec, about 24 km from Łosiatyń where we lived, some 4 km from the small town of Poczajów. There we were loaded onto cattle trucks and shipped off to Siberia.

I do not remember exactly how long we were on the train, but I think it was three weeks. Every now and then the train stopped and we were let out for toilet purposes and to get some *kipiatok,* which means hot water in Russian. During this journey we realised how grateful we should be to those women for killing and packing all those ducks and chickens for us. Those two sacks fed the whole wagon of people. There was a small stove made out of a 12 gallon drum in our wagon with a pipe for the chimney. This was used to boil the food for all of us. For a toilet we cut a hole in the wagon floor and put some blankets around it for privacy.[7]

Account of Marysia Pienta (née Wilgut)

My story begins when I was only ten years old. I can still remember the 10th of February 1940.

At 3:00 A.M., three Russian soldiers brutally invaded our home in Konstantynów, Poland. The demands were issued and we were to pack in thirty minutes, for we were going "elsewhere." I can still see them dragging my mother's limp, almost lifeless body out of the house. She must have known the dangers that awaited us, but as children, we had no idea. My father, oldest brother Adam, and oldest sister Jasia, packed us all into a sleigh. There were four other children: Zosia, Krysia, Ela, and Basia. We were like little birds gathered in a nest of *pierzyny* [down quilts] and pillows. My father, Adam, and Jasia were gathering all that we could take with us for immediate survival. They were watched very carefully by the soldiers. We were taken to the railroad station in Klewań. There were so many people there, so many frightened faces. We were packed in boxcars in groups of fifty. I can remember a stove in the middle of the boxcar and an opening in the floor, for hygiene purposes. There were only upper and lower ledges on either side of the boxcar. This is where we sat and slept.[8]

Account of Elaine Beres (née Nykiforuk)

On the 10th of February 1940 many Polish people were taken to forced labour in Siberia. At the time my dad and I were not at home, having gone to visit Dad's sister,

Aniela Beck, in the village of Lisowice and remaining there for five days. My dad's family, including his sister Aniela and brother Tom lived in that little town. There were also many uncles and cousins.

My brother John later told me what happened to the family while we were away visiting in Lisowice. Some policemen and civilians came to the house and told my mom to get ready. John was made to sit on the floor with his hands behind his back and was not allowed to move. Mother had to do all the packing herself. She didn't know where to start and what to do. She took whatever she could think of because no one could help her. The police put them all on a sleigh and it was very cold. All the families were taken to the school, where everyone had assembled. There were 72 families altogether. They were taken to the railway station at Stryj and were packed into wagons just like cattle. As many people as possible were crammed into each wagon. The people made for themselves a hole in the middle of the floor to use as a toilet.

As we were eating breakfast at my aunt's on Saturday morning, my cousin Ted Slupecki came up to my dad. The first words he said were: "Uncle, you are here but Auntie and the kids have been taken to Russia!" The news shocked us....

Dad and I stayed at Auntie's that Sunday discussing what to do. On Monday we went to the city of Stryj to the police and gave ourselves up. We asked them to reunite us with our family, but the police wouldn't do it. They put us in jail instead and they split us up. I was with another young girl in the same cell. We were there for two weeks, until the 26th of February 1940. They gave us food twice a day, one cup of soup and one piece of bread. The days were very long as there was nothing to do in jail.

They kept us in Stryj for another few days, then sent us to a larger prison in Lwów. We were there — all of us together — for three days. We were given soup twice a day but it smelt terrible, like dish slops, and we couldn't eat it. We only ate the bread, which kept us alive. From Lwów they took us to Sambor. That was on the 1st of March 1940. They put us together with another group which had already been there for a few weeks. We had to sleep on the floor. It was a big room. There were young, old, rich and poor — with guards who watched us all the time.

I had a chance to escape in Sambor. How? Because one of the group had money to pay the guard; he let them go to town to buy something to eat. The man gave me a pass to let me go to the city. He said: "If you go there, don't come back again. It is much worse where they are going to take you." I came back because my dad was there. How could I leave him? We were there until the 25th of March 1940.

On the 26th of March 1940 they put us on a cattle train. The train finally moved off towards Moscow....

The same things were happening every day. Whatever you heard and whatever you talked about, it was always the same. There were lots of people like us in the prison. They had been separated from their families and had gone to the prison to rejoin them there. They were sent to different parts of Russia.[9]

Account of Józefa Pucia-Zawada

We were awaked at 2:00 A.M. by loud knocking on the door and shouted demands to open up at once. My father open door and outside there were several Bolsheviks with rifles. They pushed Daddy back inside, yelling that we must get dressed to leave. Mum asked where to because we had two older sisters who were on holiday with our grannie. She wanted to bring them back, but her pleas fell on deaf ears. They wouldn't let us take much, saying there would be plenty of everything where we were going. In her rush, Mum pulled the tablecloth off the table and collected in it a few things such as spoons, soap, and other trifles .

Only those spoons have stuck in my memory because as soon as we sat down in the train I felt very hungry, crying that I want to eat. And I got smacked on my hand with one of the spoons to keep me quiet.

Once we were dressed to go out the Bolsheviks told us to get on the sleighs and took us to the railway station at Przemyśle. Mother cried a lot, perhaps from a foreboding that we would not see my sisters Marysia and Aniela again.

There were many people already there, also in tears and lost. Everyone feared what awaited them. The Bolsheviks' attempts to cheer us up by saying that where we were going things would be much better, did not help at all. They guarded us to ensure that no one ran away. Then, shouting and pushing us, ordered us to get into the goods trucks. The trucks were overcrowded and there was no more room. Then the doors were slid closed and bolted. With a great jerk and much whistling the train moved forward so suddenly that people fell onto one another. My father and another man knocked a hole in the floor because there was not even somewhere to relieve oneself. Someone gave a blanket to shield it, but in the morning someone had stolen it, so everyone had to relieve themselves in full sight of others. It was not long before people grew indifferent to such overt satisfying of physiological needs.

From time to time the train stopped at a station, the soldiers opened the doors and we could get out to stretch our legs. Whoever had something to sell exchanged it for bread, while others ran to the engine for hot water to make tea. When the train moved off again with a big jerk people fell against one another, scalding themselves. One could hear nothing but moaning and crying.

I remember the horrible whistling of the engine to this day. It was very cold in the train and some heating was needed, so the older people decided that when the train stopped two children, a boy and a girl, would be sent to pick up coal from the side of the track. Before they were able to collect any, a soldier struck the boy with his rifle and pushed the girl hard, so that they returned in tears with an empty bucket. Later people got wise and when the train stopped everyone put a piece of coal in their pocket so the soldiers would not see them and the truck got some heating.

Hunger tormented us a lot. The older and weaker ones began dying. At stations the soldiers carried out the dead people, laying them by the side of the track, then the train hurried on into the unknown.[10]

Account of Franciszka Skibicka-Smenda

My first memory is that of my dog, my only pet, howling. No one listened to my childish, plaintive questions as to why my dog was crying? It was early morning and strange men were urging my mother to pack her things onto a waiting lorry. My mother was holding me with one hand and I saw her touching the walls of her newly-built home with the other. She was crying. I saw those strange men pushing her towards the lorry.[11]

Account of Anita Paschwa (née Kozicka)

One night, in April 1940, our worst fears were realized. Six Russian soldiers with guns and rifles climbed up into the attic and began to read our names one by one. They told us to get ready within half an hour. We were ready anyway, but not for Siberia. We thought that somehow we would get to Warsaw to the house of the nobleman whom Walter [Anita's brother-in-law] had helped to escape. Maria [Anita's sister] began to cry and begged one of the soldiers, saying that I was not her family, that I was an orphan since the age of four and a half, but he just pushed her to one side and continued reading name after name. He said that everyone from this hiding place goes to the train. My sister insisted that I was just visiting her and that I go to school in Rokitno. "If she is with you here, she goes with us," they said.

After a few days of staying at the boxcar freight train station we began to move toward the Russian border via my birthplace, Rokitno. When the train stopped there my sister Maria begged another soldier to let me go, but he just said, "Be quiet and sit still." The reason for stopping was to fill up the locomotive with water and coal for the long journey to Siberia. In each boxcar there were from 50 to 70 people. Each of the cars had double benches to sleep on. There was straw on these benches as our mattresses. The children's toilet was the hole in the middle of the car, but the older people waited until the guards let them out once a day to go into the fields or bushes. It took two weeks to reach Novosibirsk, but at least we were not as cold as those that were taken in February. Those people in our group who were taken from their homes were lucky; at least they could take more clothes and food. We had nothing left. All the better clothes and the rest of the silver spoons, knives and forks were exchanged for goods at the city market in Włodzimierz. We had only one piece of bread and a cup of water each. Some people were very good to Nina [Anita's niece], who was almost six years old.[12]

Account of Eva [Ursula Sowińska]

Some may meet my words with a skeptical smile, for I know that to accept such a truth one has to experience it. Even to me, that remote, gloomy past of mine seems to be sometimes beyond my comprehension....

On April 13, 1940, at four o'clock in the morning, our house was surrounded by many soldiers. Six soldiers with an officer came inside to accuse us of various "crimes": of being the family of two army officers, of belonging to the wealthy class, and of pursuing the education of a "false" history of Europe and even the world, the latter being unmistakable signs of our being the deadly enemies of the "great, beneficial" October Revolution.

We had to get ready immediately. We did not think at first that such a terrifying change could occur. To leave our home, the peace of family life so suddenly, and to face the destruction of all this, which meant life to us, seemed like a hellish nightmare.

The farewell with our governess was unspeakably dramatic. Our last words sounded like the strange commandments of a persecuted and tragic love. She had been with us since my parents were married and had been the nurse of my sister and me. During the Russian occupation she offered my mother her help, which was officially forbidden by the Communists. As she packed our clothes, into which she smuggled some valuable pieces of jewelry, she spasmodically cried and fearlessly cursed Stalin aloud. She followed the three of us, my mother, sister, and me, through the garden — from which each of us took a handful of earth — to the gate.

The gate, through which I used to run from home to the mountains and woods with my happy illusions of childhood, was shut behind us in a hurry by a Communist, and we started to walk toward the open grave of a veritable purgatory on earth. At seven o'clock in the morning, our train left our town, destined for Siberia.

Cruelly stolen from the Motherland and home, each of us with a handful of holy earth bade farewell to our beloved country. At the station all the families had been separated, and I found myself in a deadly cold cattle car among country fellows whom I did not know. Before departure my mother told my sister and me never to give the Communists the opportunity to enjoy our tragedy, to pray with faith, and to remain spotless daughters of our homeland. As the train moved, the whole long serpent of wagons was full of patriotic songs, the songs which cemented our spirits. But we knew in our hearts that many would never return.[13]

Account of Anna Mineyko

We heard all sorts of news. I was terrified when I heard of arrests and deportations. Then, on 13 April 1940, our turn came. When they came for us, I was feeding Alek but when they entered I had my back to the cradle and the twins were sheltering at my side....

When I was arrested, I was asked how many children I had. On the spur of the moment, I decided to own up to two. I said that the youngest had died. I stared at Kolesnik as I said this, and he confirmed my story. I was given the order, "Go off, with your things," and I was closely watched to see whether I would look at or say goodbye to the baby lying there, but I ignored him. And so, I left Alek that he might live; I knew that my twins might not survive the journey we were to undertake, and that a five-month-old had no chance.

We were driven in manure carts through the market town. I rode with my head held high, almost in triumph, for we were following in the footsteps of our ancestors who had been exiled to Siberia, in chains, for fighting the Russians. My mother reminded me of Marie Antoinette. As we passed, people made the sign of the cross in the air and I realised how well loved was my mother. They were crying and saying their farewells to us. We, too, said our farewells to them, but without tears. I looked back once more to see the "palace" of Brzostowica. Halfway to the station, our carriage passed us, carrying some Bolshevik officials. They pushed the cart into the ditch.

We left the railway station of Brzostowica in cattle trucks, heading east all the time. There were bars on all doors and air vents; one could not see out unless one climbed up and squinted through the tiny windows. We had no food or water. In my sleep, I felt with my hand for Alek because my breasts were swollen with milk. Then I woke to the grim reality. I was going to an unknown country, somewhere far from Poland, far from Białystok.

Sometimes, by jumping up and holding on to the grate, I saw the gloomy mountains of the Urals, then the river Volga. On one occasion, I saw a huge sign that said in Russian "Europe." On the other side it was written "Asia." We spent twenty-eight days in the cattle trucks; how we survived it I shall never know. The temperature was often minus twenty degrees centigrade on this nightmare journey. The bodies of the children who died were simply thrown out of the train. I thought of Alek and rejoiced that he, at least, was safe with Buba [Tenia Malenicz, a neighbor].[14]

Account of Adela Konradczyńska-Piorkowska

The Russians filled our local government with Ukrainians, usually illiterates. One of them was a man my father employed for ploughing. Because my father had helped him and his large family during hard times, he now came to our aid, warning my father twice against being transported. It was winter and as early as January two transports were sent off to Siberia. The Russians burst into my uncle's home and shot him as he opened the door, while his oldest son disappeared without a trace. My aunt and two children were taken to Russia. Unfortunately, following the amnesty she was not able to join up with the Polish army and her descendants are in Russia to this day.

Our turn came. This happened at noon on the 12th of June 1940 when a truck drove up and four soldiers with rifles jumped down. My mother told them that my father was at the mill and two of them went for him. They gave us 25 minutes in which to pack. Incredible chaos followed. My mother jumped out of the window and hid in the garden. Unfortunately, they found her within five minutes. She had lost her head and was unable to do anything. The fact that we at least managed to take some clothes and food we owe to a neighbour who came to us. She put a sheet on the floor and threw whatever she could onto it. There was no bread as the dough had only just been made.

My father lifted me onto the truck together with our bundles. The soldiers threw my mother in like a sack of potatoes and she was badly beaten in the process as they avenged her attempted escape. We watched our home disappearing and I cried at the sight of our little, pregnant bitch running after the truck. They took us to Podwokoczysk, 12 km from the Russian border. We were put in prison where there were already many other families. They held us there for two weeks. When our neighbours found out they helped us with whatever they could, mostly with food. They told us that our home had been tightly locked up and no one could get inside.

When they had assembled a complete transport the Russians loaded us onto goods wagons like sardines into a can. There was a hole in the centre of the floor to serve as a toilet. A few of the men organised some rags or blankets to give an illusion of privacy. There were primitive wooden bunks on both sides of the wagon. The old and weak people and children lay on them in turn to straighten their bones and to rest a little. The rest of the passengers had only restricted standing room. The engine driver tormented them especially whenever the train stopped or started, when everyone fell on top of one another, sustaining various injuries. Young children fell from their mothers' arms. Twice a day a bucket of dirty water was put in and, of course, was for drinking only. We had no water for washing and we did not receive any food. We shared whatever anyone had. It was summer and the heat was incredible. When the train stopped at a station we called for water for the children. Sometimes someone would take pity and passed some water in a bottle. There were about fifty people in our wagon. People sang religious songs during the journey. It sounded very beautiful because everyone sang to God sincerely, straight from their hearts.

After a week's journey, deprived of any sort of hygiene, sweaty in the heat, with dirty clothes, we were infested by lice. Mothers cut their children's hair. My mother cut my long pigtails, so carefully nurtured by my beloved Granny, with a knife. I loved my Granny very much. She taught me everything good. I owe a lot to her today for shaping my young years to love God and my fellow-men. I built my life on these foundations.[15]

Account of Jerzy Wróblewski

On the 20th of June, 1940, I had intended to take a small boat out on a lake in search of sunken logs for which a nearby sawmill paid well. I was wakened by loud knocking, first at the door, then the window. Looking out, I saw a local Jew whom I knew and next to him an officer and a soldier of the NKVD. I knew the significance of this situation at once They had come to arrest us and send us to Siberia.

The officer ordered me to open the door. When he entered he read out an order as follows: "By decree of the Supreme Soviet you are sentenced to exile into the interior of the Soviet Union for five years as untrustworthy citizens towards the Soviet government."

He announced that they would search the house and all our possessions. There were four of us there — my mother, my little sister who was only six years old, and my mother's father. My father was already in a Soviet lager, having been caught while trying to cross the border between the Soviet Union and Poland in 1940.

Frightened by what was happening, my sister sobbed bitterly. Having carried out the search, the officer also had tears in his eyes as he whispered quietly in Russian: "There are beggars in Russia who have more possessions than you." The communist propaganda which was drummed into them about the wealth of Polish "gentlemen" and bourgeoisie could not be reconciled with what he saw here. He told us that we had half an hour in which to pack.

With great anger my mother told him: "For a hundred years tsarist governments sent Poles to Siberia and could not populate it. Even when they send us now they still won't do it!"

We were living from day to day and had no reserves of food. We packed a bit of clothing and bedding, whatever we could, in sacks. Grandfather had two trunks — one with his clothes and the other with his carpenter's tools. A cart came and our things were loaded on it. I ran to tell our neighbours what had happened and, having done so, stopped for a moment. I had a chance to escape, but my conscience and faith in God — that he will not abandon us — made me change my mind.

We were placed on the cart together with the driver and soldier, while the officer and the Jew followed on foot, unwilling to share in our distress. It was only a short distance to the little town of Phost-Zahorodzki where waited two Soviet trucks, already partly filled with others also sentenced to exile. I was surprised to find a number of Jewish families among them — some whom I knew....

We placed our entire faith in God, that He would not abandon us. We settled on a lower bunk close to the doors. More carts with families sentenced to exile kept coming up through the night.

The next day they locked the wagons, leaving a small gap where a makeshift toilet had been made out of two planks. I calculated that they had put 58 people with all their possessions in our truck. Within a very short time the truck became stuffy through lack of air as the sun began to heat it. Packed like sardines, everyone was very depressed. Crying and sobbing mingled with the words of prayers.

The train moved off. Through a small gap I could see the familiar route. We came through a number of railway stations which I knew and for the first time I saw what the border looked like. It continued to be patrolled by border guards. There was a cleared strip of about 100 metres with barbed wire entanglements on the Polish side and the same thing on the Russian side.

My heart was heavy because I was leaving my homeland and doubted if I would ever see it again. I remembered the thousands of exiles after the September and January Uprisings. And the thousands taken prisoner in the last war; those who had been exiled previously; those arrested later or caught while trying to cross the border to the west.

A similar fate awaited us and no one could say what the outcome would be....

As the train ran around a bend in the track I was able to see the composition of our transport. It was pulled by two diesel locomotives. There were 43 trucks, three of them different from the rest. One was situated behind the locomotives, a second was in the middle and the third at the rear. These carried the guards and I was sure that the conditions in them were better than in ours. There were little towers on the roof and protruding windows on both sides through which the guards could look out and observe the whole length of the train. No one was allowed to approach the train on any of the stations through which we passed.

On one of the stations we were issued with a salted herring each and afterwards we suffered terrible thirst when there was insufficient water to wash them down.

We had been on the train for three weeks before we reached Novosibirsk, where they didn't know where to send us next. After a long wait orders were received to proceed south. Eventually we halted on a branch line where there was a saw mill. Our guards left us and when the trucks were unlocked we were taken over by the local militia.[16]

Account of Wisia Reginella (née Danecka)

On the 29th of June 1940, at night, on the eve of St. Peter and Paul Day, we were awakened by the door being battered. I knew what awaited us. Impatient, they broke the door down with rifle butts and carried out a search. The children, frightened, cried and begged that they should not kill their mummy. After plundering and stealing whatever had value, they ordered us to get dressed. They lied hypocritically that we were going to my husband. The children calmed down and collected their toys for the journey. I knew that, together with my orphans, I was going to Siberia, that this was the end of my dreams of returning to normal life in a civilised world, that the hour of my suffering, wandering, ill-treatment and humiliation had struck.

I could not allow my breakdown to be seen by those who were committing this act of force and lawlessness, or by my children, who already understood that in me they had their mainstay and their hope. As best I could, I gave these frightened, torn from sleep children hope and calmed them as best I could.

For the rest of the night and the whole of the next day we waited at the railway station under NKVD guard. Kind people brought us bread and sausage despite the guards. And when at last the train arrived People held out their hands to us and invited us into the wagon, yet were without comfort themselves.

Looking at these helpless, lost people I was seized by some kind of real feeling that I was the only one here who was aware; that I must take control of these people. I believe that the belief in self and strong mental condition instilled in me during military instruction now came to the fore and I became resilient to all difficulties. When there were quarrels in the wagon over some trifle I talked to the unfortunates like a commanding officer to soldiers. I warned them of what awaited us. I was able to control the disgruntled ones and the journey continued in harmony, as in a family.

Since then I was given the nickname *generalicha* (a female general). Even when the commandant wanted me he gave orders to call the *generalicha*.

As the last rays of the setting sun penetrated the small, barred windows of the cattle truck people looked at one another with serious eyes. No one slept. Each was overcome by their personal tragedy and the fate of their nearest and dearest.

Terrified children, seeing the stony expressions on adults' faces, cuddled up to their mothers, some asking: "When are we going home? When is supper?"

Restless sleep was interrupted by the strident howling of the locomotive. Along the way still more trucks with exiles were joined on, together with an additional locomotive. The whole thing dragged ever deeper into Soviet Russia, to slave-labour camps. The journey lasted more than ten days in such inhumane conditions. At times the train stopped to throw out the corpses of children and old people. The remainder reached their destination, the coal mine "Barba" at Sieviero in Kazakhstan *Oblast* (country).[17]

Account of Maria Gabiniewicz

September 1939 had arrived. First, German armies marched into our land, then they withdrew and on September 17, quite unexpectedly, in came the Red Army. This marked the beginning of the repressions against the Poles and our family was not spared. Three terrible nights have imbedded themselves forever in my memory: the nights on which the NKVD arrested my brother Józef and later my father, and the night on which our family was deported.....

Life without father was very difficult. The entire burden of looking after the family fell on the shoulders of my mother. We had a premonition that a new tragedy was about to unfold and it did. On the night of June 19, 1941, the NKVD surrounded our house once more. We heard frantic knocking on our door and the pounding of fists against our window panes. We froze. We were unarmed. We all, not only our mother, knew what awaited us: it was our turn. A question rang out: "Is everyone at home?" A soldier grabbed my shoulder and shook me. My ten-year-old brother, Tadek, began to cry. Bronek, who was thirteen and helped Mother in various tasks, was pasturing the horses that night. Informed by the neighbors of what had transpired, he hid in the field of grain and later in the forest. The NKVD searched the area repeatedly but in vain; they did not find him. The hours went by. Dawn came — summer nights are short. During all this time my seventeen-year-old brother Stach was guarded by the NKVD; he was not allowed to move at all. Mother tried to gather some essential things together, including some food. The bread was in the kneading trough; she was going to bake it in the morning. Although it was summertime, she dressed us in winter clothes. In that terrible time of uncertainty she made us feel safe. We knew that she was vigilant, that she would not overlook anything.

A truck pulled up. Our things were loaded on. An NKVD man grabbed Tadek and threw him on as if he were some object. The vehicle began to roll. One more look at the home, the buildings, the fields, and the paths we knew so well leading up the hill called "Signal," where we loved to walk and play. Mother blessed everything that remained behind with the sign of the cross. We did not realize that when we would return, Siberia would be associated with our exile for the rest of our lives.

At the railway station in Sokółka there was a line of boxcars and 50 people—women, men, and children—were piled into each one of them. Each car had boards for beds, two small windows with bars, and a hole in the floor for a toilet.

It was tight. We sat down on our belongings. After many hours the train began to move. I remember that Mother made a sign of the cross on our foreheads. I saw that the other mothers were doing the same. Some began to weep out loud, others squeezed to the windows in order to see their loved ones once more. At the station in Białystok we learned that a war had broken out between the two occupiers. Germany had invaded the Soviet Union.

The trip was difficult. In addition to all the other inconveniences, we were plagued by constant air raids. At the sound of the siren we hid under the bed boards. Someone hung a white scarf out of the window. Some did not bother to hide believing that nothing worse could befall them. The number of air raids increased with each day. We were constantly tired.

Late at night Mother woke us and told us that in a little while we would be crossing the Polish border in Stołpce. She wanted us to be awake for this moment. I heard weeping in a corner of the boxcar. Most of the exiles, however, joined in prayer and then everyone began to sing: "Dearest Mother, protector of the people ... Eve's exiles call unto you ... have pity, have pity ... let us not be homeless." That hymn accompanied us throughout the years of our exile. Poland was behind us, before us stretched an immense territory ... unknown ... unbounded.[18]

Account of Jane [Janina] Żebrowski-Bulmahn

A knock on the door in the middle of the night is never a good omen, but in Poland in June of 1941 it struck fear into everyone. Two years earlier Poland had been divided by her two constant enemies, Russia and Germany. Our section of Poland fell under Russian occupation. In my school, there was talk of families disappearing suddenly. It always seemed to happen the same way—a knock on the door in the middle of the night.

We did have a forewarning of what might happen to us. The children of a Russian officer whose family lodged in our home hinted that because our father would not cooperate with the authorities, he was considered an undesirable. Also, my two oldest brothers, missing from home, were suspected by the authorities of being in the Polish underground. They had joined the underground shortly after Russian occupation of our part of Poland rather than serve in the Russian army, which they were ordered to do. We had minimal contact with them after that time, always in secret and only at night.

Awakening to the loud knock, a shiver went through my body. A terrifying thought ran through my mind, "It's our turn now." Part of me felt a subtle excitement about the unknown, but the other part foresaw the agony which lay ahead.

In one instant I realized that life as I knew it was over. As had happened to other families, this day we would leave all we had and everyone we knew and loved and be taken someplace called Siberia to live out our lives in want, sickness and, ultimately, death. No one sent to Siberia was ever known to come back.

In the living room two Russian soldiers, NKVD, fully armed, pointed rifles at my parents and gave orders in Russian. Father spoke fluent Russian and the rest of us understood it quite well. We were to get dressed quickly, pack only the possessions we could carry and be ready to leave at dawn.

Mother was sobbing quietly, just sitting there, seemingly unable to move. My older sister, Czeława, and my brother, Edmund, 14 at the time and I were busy trying to collect things we needed to take with us. But, how do you pack a whole way of life into a trunk? How do you decide in a few short moments what is important to carry to a life you do not know?

Father started protesting and asking questions, "Why? Why us?" He was pushed and hit with the rifle by one of the soldiers. The orders were clear; we must obey.

Czesława, wearing only night clothes, asked permission of the Russian soldiers to go to the outhouse. That was the last we saw of her. She knew what she was doing. By not changing her clothes she did not arouse suspicion. We lived in the country and the rye growing close to our home was already tall, and she intended to run for the fields. Since it was still dark, we thought she would be safe. We had many relatives in the area, and she would probably hide in the fields till nighttime and then approach one of them. We were happy for her that she would not have to face our fate, but how sad we felt knowing that we would be separated from her forever.

As dawn was breaking, I got dressed and quickly ran to the garden to get some vegetables. I had my own small plot and the vegetables were already ripening. One of the soldiers followed me and chased me away. At that moment I knew it was no longer my garden. I started crying.

I returned to the house, as ordered, to face the inevitable. Just then my four-year-old sister, Juzia, woke up and began to cry, or rather scream, uncontrollably. Since Mother was not capable of consoling her, I tried, but without success. She would continue crying for days through most of her waking hours.

The soldiers left us alone for a while and went to take inventory in our other buildings. I noticed my brother, Edmund, putting on several layers of clothing although it was quite warm. He showed my parents what he was doing and they nodded approval. He then went to the farthest room of the house, climbed through an open window, and made a dash into the fields. Now only my younger sister and I were left with our parents.

When the soldiers discovered what had happened, they started beating Father mercilessly. He kept repeating, "I didn't know" over and over, but in their rage they did not listen. I got so frightened I could not speak, but inside I was crying out, "Stop it, stop, do not kill him!" Finally, since it was already light, they stopped beating him and gave orders to be ready, adding that if anyone else was missing, they would kill the rest of us.

Just as we were ready to be put in the open wagon, Father took a watch out of his pocket to check the time. It was an expensive gold watch he had brought from the U.S. One of the Russian soldiers noticed the watch and ordered Father to hand it over to him. This my father did with tears in his eyes, and we all knew that from then on nothing belonged to us, not even our lives.

I prayed a prayer of despair as we pulled away, "Lord, how could you do this to us? How could you forsake us like this? Why did you not protect us? Why us?"

How can I describe the feeling of complete emptiness, no, desolation I felt as we pulled away? We knew our destination and what awaited us. In my young imagination, I could not perceive what it would be like to live in Siberia and to watch each other die far away from home....

At the railroad station we were packed like animals into freight cars with windows shut and boarded but one very small one left open for air. These boxcars were specially designed for deporting "criminals." On each side of the car there were two large platforms, an upper one and a lower one, to fit as many people as possible. Those who were on the upper platform had some degree of comfort since there was enough headroom to sit up. Those located on the lower platform could only lie down or sit on the floor in the middle of the car. We were on the upper platform. There were about 100 people in our car.

When the car was full and the door was shut, a feeling of anxiety came over me. The close quarters and people crying and wailing all around me were frightening. Our desperate situation became even more evident now. I had trouble sleeping because there were always voices around me, either talking or crying.

Our bathroom facility was an opening in the floor. For privacy, a bed sheet was hung hiding the area. There was little fresh air in the car with only one small window open, which made it very uncomfortable. Living in the country we were used to fresh air but even that was denied us. An armed guard was always standing outside each rail car.[19]

2. Soviet Union

Milewski family memoir

February 16, 1940 (Sabina) We crossed the Russian border and all we could see was the snow and the vast forest. After traveling all night we arrived in Minsk, where we were given one loaf of bread for three people. I am sick and have a sore throat.

February 17, 1940, Saturday. The train stopped in Orsha for 24 hours, continued on to Smolensk, and arrived in Moshaysk at nine o'clock in the evening. They did not let us out for three days. We were given some soup with grouts (*kasza jaglana*) but not enough firewood; we are extremely cold. The wagon is covered with white frost at night, which melts during the day. Our underwear and bedding will rot pretty soon. In the freight car it's dirty, smelly and damp beyond description. Teresa and I are sick. Andrzej and Staś [Stanisław] are holding out pretty well. We still do not know where are we going. Will we survive? It's been only a week since they took us.

February 18, 1940, Sunday. At 10:00 A.M. we arrived in Moscow where we were given more bread and soup. The train stops and starts so often that we are full of bruises from being tossed about and cannot even cook. If this continues I doubt very much that we will get to wherever we are going alive. We are short of wood and have to let the fire die out at night. They give us barely enough food to survive. A hole in the floor surrounded by a cloth partition serves as a toilet. Eight people sleep on one wooden bench; there is not even room to turn around.

February 19, 1940, Monday. We arrived in Yaroslav. Nothing new; the same Golgotha. Under escort they allowed us to go to the station to buy some bread, sugar and sweets (for the babies only). Just before noon the train left the station but they will not tell us where are we going.

February 20, 1940, Danilov. We stayed there for about 24 hours. The news spreads: we are going to the White Sea.

February 21, 1941, Wednesday, Vologda. We are guarded all the time and treated like criminals. We were given some bread and soup. In our transport are some people from Święta Wola: Mrs. Litwinowicz and Halszka Dypczyńska.

February 22, 1940, Konosha. We received more bread and soup.

February 23, 1940, Friday. We arrived in the city of Arkhangelsk. They will most likely unload us here. We are waiting with fear.

February 24, 1940, Saturday. We were taken to large wooden barracks with fireplaces seven miles outside the city of Arkhangelsk. We finally got some food. There are 50 people in each barracks. We sleep on the ground. We're surrounded by terrible noise and mess; plenty of children keep us awake at night. They separated us from our traveling companions. Now we are with the Bienkowskis. We are getting food once a day. In the morning and evening we cook what we have. We only have enough bread for two days; we still have some lard. There are Soviet cooperatives where one can buy bread, salt and coffee — and that's about it. We are not allowed to leave the barracks, but we sneak out whenever possible.

February 27, 1940 We were taken to the bathhouse. They disinfected our clothes because we have lice. They are taking a census. Every day people are departing on sledges pulled by reindeer. We are now with our friends: Bienkowski and Roszko.

February 30, 1940, Friday. Four sleds pulled by horses came for us. Only the first sled had a driver; we deportees drove the others. Our family and a Russian man were loaded onto one of the sleds. For us, a real Golgotha has begun. Twice a day we stop so that the horses can have a rest and we are traveling by day and night. Andrzej has to walk most of the time because the driver will not allow him to sit on the sled so as not to weigh it down. Poor child, he has no fur coat, his boots are always wet and his feet are frostbitten. The country is mountainous, and we have to descend down such steep hills that we are even afraid to look. On our breaks we only get boiled water (*kipiatok*) to drink.

March 2, 1940 to March 4, 1940 We have traveled 120 kilometers so far. On the 4th we arrived at the village of Rozna, where we changed horses and drivers. It is still very cold. We received ten rubles per person with which to buy bread and sugar. They let us rest for 24 hours. We are exhausted. Children are coughing.

March 4, 1940, Monday. We start traveling again in the evening. The sleds are slightly more comfortable but overturn more easily. The drivers are much nicer. Thick fog makes it impossible to see ahead. We travel all night with only two hours rest.

March 5, 1940, Tuesday. The previous night was horrible. Our train consisted of three sleds: on the first was the driver, our belongings were on the second one, and we were on the third. The night was foggy and cold and we lost our way. The sled overturned four times and although we called for help nobody answered. It overturned again on a steep and slippery hill just before we reached the rest area. That time all our belongings fell out and the horse ran off but, thank God, not too far before halting by a fence. We were following the Pinega River and arrived in the town of Pinega in the morning.

March 6, 1940, Wednesday. At noon we received some soup and bread and were allowed to rest.

(Stanisław) That night, after having something to eat, we slept in a local village. Although the horses and drivers would sometimes be changed, the soldiers that guarded us always remained with us. All the villages we encountered were similar, consisting of wooden houses with thatched roofs strung out along frozen dirt roads. Inside our house there was a large brick fireplace for warmth and cooking with a crawl space on top for sleeping. There was also a large wooden table with benches for sitting and sleeping. Such a dwelling could hold ten to fifteen people together with a caretaker family responsible for doing the cooking and cleaning. There was an outhouse. Water came from melted snow.

During our travel we encountered all kinds of weather: from beautiful days with clear, crisp air and temperatures plunging to -30°C, to fierce, blinding snowstorms when all one could do was to follow the horse and sled. To step off the beaten path was to find oneself shoulder-deep in snow. It sometimes happened that the sled would slip off the path as well. At such times, with much swearing from the drivers, the entire transport would halt until the sled could be righted. Such delays, of course, extended the time it took to get to the next area designated for rest and food.

Passing the town of Pinega we followed the Pinega and Yejuga rivers until we arrived at our destination: a small village-kolkhoz called Kokornaya lying about 300 kilometers southeast of the city of Arkhangelsk.

March 7, 1940 Thursday. (Sabina) The last 10 kilometers took us through a dense forest. We arrived at our destination, Kokornaya village, at midnight and had to wait on the road for an hour because no room could be found for us. They finally put us up for the night in a community hall. We placed ourselves near the stove with the Bienkowski and Tipelt families. We got nothing to eat.

March 8, 1940, Friday. In the morning we went to the *banya*, the communal sauna bath, on foot. They gave us five rubles per person for food. In the afternoon they assigned us our living quarters. We dreaded the thought of what the place might look like or how we were going to live there. Our belongings were placed on a sled, but we had to walk over three kilometers to get to our assigned hut. When we arrived there, the four of us were placed in one room with the Bienkowski-Roszko family (four persons) and the Tipelt family (three persons). The room is very small for 11 people. There's no way all of us are going to fit into it.

The neighbors came over to greet us. They are Ukrainians who were deported here ten years ago from their homeland. They told us their stories and were sympathetic to our plight. They took us to their houses for the night. The Tipelts are sleeping with an old couple and Teresa and I are bunked with an old lady. There are lice and bedbugs. We have no shoes, underwear or clothing. We are morally crushed. I feel sick and my face is swollen. There is no food. We are depressed. I may have a kidney infection, but how to treat it?

March 9, 1940, Saturday. We have unpacked our rags. I say rags because all our clothes are torn and dirty. We were given two kilograms of bread for four people, and we had to pay for it.

March 10, 1940, Sunday. The local authorities wrote down all our names and ages and counted everybody. At a meeting for young people at 5:00 P.M., they were told that they would be sent to work in the forest tomorrow as lumberjacks. From our group Mr. Roszko will be sent away.

March 17, 1940 Every day we walk three miles along a narrow pathway in the deep snow for rationed bread. A single moment of inattention lands us in the snowbank. For water we walk one kilometer down a steep hill to the river. It's an art to get the full buckets of water up the hill without spilling them. It happens often that we slip and fall on the icy pathway near the house and, my God, we have to go to that river all over again! Andrzej's frostbitten legs are worse and he has fever. Teresa has an eye infection. My health is not too good either. In the evening Mr. Roszko came back from the forest.

(Stanisław) Our settlement, surrounded by forests and fields, consisted of two sections, the section at the bottom of the hill near the river being wider than that at the top. We lived on top of the hill. The NKVD headquarters, the school, and the *banya* were located down below. The kolkhoz was built in 1933 by the Ukrainians who had been deported there by Stalin during the purges. They were simply left in the middle of the forest and had to fend for themselves. Cold and hunger killed most of them.

The second wave of deportees to land there were the Tatars from the Crimean Peninsula of the Black Sea.

When we came there we were allocated one gram of butter and two grams of bread per person per day along with a cup of watery soup. But who could survive on such rations? We managed to get through that winter because, from time to time, Mother would trade the things we had brought with us — a silver spoon, a knife, etc. — for some potatoes or other staples that the local peasants had put aside from the previous summer.

March 18, 1940, Sunday. (Sabina) Today is very windy and cold. A snowstorm covered our pathways. It is sheer torture to go for bread or fetch water. But we are elated because we have managed to get a kilogram of jam and we will have something to put on our bread for few days. Our diet consists of weak tea and dry bread for breakfast, potatoes — which we get from the Ukrainians — for lunch, and water and bread again for supper. The children are always hungry.

(Stanisław) That winter was very severe with many snowstorms and drifts two to three meters high. We had to walk a mile along an icy pathway down to the river for water. I still remember that agonizing walk up the hill while carrying two buckets of water in my frozen hands and the wind blowing me off the pathway. Because there were no vegetables in our diet, we all suffered from scurvy. Everybody in Russia had lice and the bedbugs were eating us alive at night. Once a week we went to the *banya.* Women and children bathed together. The bathhouse was filled with so much steam that one could hardly see inside. We sat on wooden benches and whipped ourselves with tree sprigs.

Hunger, starvation and lice produced typhus epidemics. We spent hours combing our hair; we boiled our clothes to kill the lice and bedbugs. I was the first to contract typhus, then Teresa and Mother. My illness, however, was not very severe. Teresa suffered the most for weeks at a time and was probably on the verge of death. Her symptoms consisted of extremely high fever, nightmares and delirium. I vividly remember the sleepless nights when she was tossing and fighting for breath while Mother sponged her with cold water to keep her body temperature down. There were no antibiotics or any other medicines. We fed her with soups and whatever other food was available. We knelt at her bedside and prayed. This is what saved her and us in that Russian hell. She recovered, but every day some of our friends died.

In the settlement I was enrolled in the second grade in a Russian elementary school. Coming from Polesie in Eastern Poland, and so being familiar with the Belorussian language, I had no problems learning Russian. In two months I was speaking like a native. The most difficult part for me was mastering the Cyrillic alphabet.

March 19, 1940 (Sabina) Andrzej is ill with a high temperature: 39°C. Teresa has an eye infection. It is very cold and snowing outside.

March 23, 1940 I am worried about Teresa's eye. It is swollen, inflamed and watering all the time. I cannot sleep at night because I am so afraid. No medicines. Arkhangelsk is 300 kilometers away. We cannot even dream that they will let us out of this prison. We are being guarded all the time.

March 24, 1940, Easter! What is in my heart I am unable to describe, but God answered my prayers and Teresa's eye is better. For that reason I will forget all the pain that we are suffering, both physical and mental, and we will be happy that her eye is saved. On this holy day we got up at 6:30 A.M. In Mrs. Tipelt's room we are preparing the *święcone,* the traditional Easter meal which consists of coffee (real coffee which we brought from Staniewicze), milk (provided by an old Ukrainian) which we have not seen since our departure from Poland, cakes baked from Nestle flour, *makojki* or barley pancakes, and a few slices of pork. Mrs. Wanda Roszko gave us bread and honey, leftovers saved just for this occasion. Teresa also received some bacon as a present from Mrs. Godecki. After so many dry days this feels like a royal feast. But I forgot the most important thing: we had two eggs, obtained with great difficulty and at great expense (three rubles). We are celebrating Easter with the Tipelts and Roszkos. After the *święcone,* I went with Mrs. Roszko to the shop (three kilometers away) because we heard that there were some goods for sale, like sweaters, soap, etc. Unfortunately we were too late and the shop was already empty! Usually there is nothing in the shop, so that when something arrives people just rush there and push and fight to get it. From the shop we went to the *stołówka,* a diner which was opened yesterday at school. I wanted to surprise the children and so we bought *gulasz,* meat stew, for which we paid nine rubles. But to our horror, when they filled the dish the portion turned out to be very small: just enough for one person. Our expedition was not successful. It is now 4:00 P.M. and only now we are gathering for our daily prayer. Heretics!

March 25, 1940, Monday. At 5:00 A.M. Mr. Roszko went to work in the forest. We had the usual breakfast: dry bread and watery tea. Then prayers. It is snowing and very cold. Teresa's eye is better. Jendruś Godecki is very ill.

April 7, 1940, Sunday. I became ill: skin rash, swollen eyelids, high fever. It's very cold and windy. Andrzej has a swollen leg which is very painful. They reduced our bread ration: we now get 500 grams per person. It is not enough. There's no answer to our letters to Father. Staś is also ill with swollen eyes. They reduced our rations again to 300 grams of bread per person. How am I going to feed the children?

April 14, 1940 Staś is better and went outside for the first time. Andrzej still has to stay at home. The card, which I sent to Mrs. Genia, came back undelivered. We are worried because we thought that our families would be informed of our whereabouts. I have exchanged window curtains, two brassieres and two head scarves for 33 kilograms of potatoes.

April 20, 1940 There is no answer to our postcards. The snow is melting. Whenever we go out our shoes get full of water. Our eyes are swollen and full of pus. A rash covers our bodies. Teresa has enlarged glands. Our strength is failing. We've been two months without fat, only water, potatoes and dry bread. If this does not end we will not return to our beloved country. Our clothing is torn and our shoes are worn out. What will happen if they send us to work in the forest? God save us! Yesterday, I brought wood from the forest on a sled and fetched water from the river; today I am sick. Andrzej's toe is oozing with pus; he cannot leave the house.

April 24, 1940 Today we received a postcard from Anna. Our aunts have left Staniewicze.

April 25, 1940 (Teresa) We are gluing together a broken statue of the Blessed Mother. Andrzej borrowed some glue made from horses' hoofs.

April 28, 1940 (Sabina) They took some young women to work in the forest, among them was Mrs. Roszko. It's cold and windy outside. I exchanged one meter of batiste cloth for one bucket of potatoes. The children are always hungry, there's not enough bread. Teresa is sick, her neck is full of swollen glands. We may not survive.

May 1, 1940 Today is a great communist holiday. They are organizing celebrations and a show in the club. The lumberjacks have two days off. We are cleaning the house and preparing an altar for May prayers and rosary.

May 3, 1940 Today is our holiday [Polish Constitution Day]. We pray the rosary and have services every day. Roman and Wanda Roszko went to work in the morning. It's spring and everything is melting. The mud is terrible, one can hardly pull one's legs out of it. Large streams of water have formed and are roaring down the mountain. The roads have washed out. We have great difficulty reaching the river to get drinking water. They are offering us land if we want it (0.25 hectares).

May 4, 1940 Spring at last. Everything is melting. Rivers of water everywhere. Large chunks of ice float down the river. There is so much ice that in some places large mountains of it have accumulated and had to be broken up by work crews.

May 5, 1940, Sunday. As always, we pray. In the evening an order came for Andrzej to present himself to the commandant. He will go to work where Mr. Roszko works, in the forest burning tree branches. They left in the evening.

May 7, 1940 Thick river ice continues to float downstream. I spent all day in the village trying to get some potatoes. No success. Knee deep in mud and water. When I returned at about 4:00 P.M. I received an order to present myself at the commandant's office. So I had to go back to the village again. I was asked whether I was fit enough to work to support my children. If I could not work, I would have to get a certificate from the *felczer* [physician's assisant] petitioning the Soviet council for a pension. What's behind all of this?

May 12, 1940, *Zielone Świątki* [Pentecost]. Andrzej came back from work with his clothes completely torn. I traded our last sheet and Teresa's blouse for 16 kilograms of potatoes. Twenty rubles for 16 kilograms of potatoes! It used to be five rubles. We are starving; they lowered our portions of bread to 250 grams.

May 15, 1940 They gave us 175 grams of bread for each person, but because the bread is made from prematurely harvested grain it is very heavy. For four people, that amounted to one small slice per person. Freezing again. Andrzej came back from the forest. They gave us a small parcel of land to cultivate. It is located 1.5 kilometers from our *posiolek*, the settlement in which we live. We have to cut the trees and clear the land ourselves. We live in *posiolek* Kokornaya, Pinezkyi rejon, Arkhangelskaya oblast.

May 17, 1940 (Teresa) Today went to cut the trees on our parcel of land. The plot looks horrible, a partially burned forest. We worked all day and came home terribly tired. It is extremely hard work. Some trees are gigantic. We have an ax and an old small saw. We can only work there in our spare time, when Mother is not working in the kolkhoz and Andrzej is home from the forest.

May 18, 1940 Great happiness! We received two postcards from our father, written on April 9, 1940, and April 20, 1940. He knows where we are! We work all day clearing the tree stumps off our parcel. It is getting hot. We have no summer clothes or shoes. Mom tailored her robe into a dress.

May 20, 1940 Staś got a job herding cattle. He takes them to the pasture at 6:00 A.M., brings them back to the barn at 11:00 A.M., then back to the pasture at 2:00 P.M. until evening. He will get 60 rubles a month and some milk from each cow at a discount. These cows belong to private individuals. The weather was beautiful in the morning and it snowed in the afternoon! That's the weather here.

(Stanisław) Looking after the cows was a very difficult task for me and a great responsibility. In our area each family was allowed to own one cow. I took care of about 12 cows and two horses belonging to the Ukrainians and Tatars. When the weather was nice and the cows and horses were grazing peacefully, I would sit by the river and occupy myself by whittling some object out of tree branches with my pocket knife. But it was not always so idyllic. Sometimes a horse fly would bite one of the cows and they would all go crazy and start running in all directions. When this happened it would take me a long time to collect them again. When I couldn't find a cow, I would have to ask the owner for help. The kolkhoz itself also owned a large herd of cows. In the evening, when we brought our herds into the barn for milking, my cows often got mixed up with those owned by the kolkhoz. It was then up to the owners to separate them out. The good news was that, being always hungry, I could get some free milk from time to time. That was a Godsend.

May 22, 1940 (Teresa) Every day the NKVD assistant commandant, we call him "*Rozdziawa*" [big mouth], comes to our house and checks on what we are doing. They really supervise us here. They know who is doing what. Everybody's name is in the book and what he's doing and where he walks and whom he visits, etc.

May 23, 1940, Thursday. Corpus Christi. Andrzej brought us a cot to sleep on.

May 24, 1940 We again received postcards from our father. Andrzej brought a second cot and two boards. We are elated because, after three months, we are finally going to sleep like kings. "*Rozdziawa*" was walking around again and making a list of all the young people who will be sent to work in the forest. Andrzej, Elzunia, Danuta and many others will be among them.

May 25, 1940 Andrzej went to work. As usual, the assistant commandant was checking whether anyone remained behind. He informed us that we could buy carrot, beetroot and turnip seeds to plant. Perhaps we might get potatoes from the kolkhoz.

May 28, 1940 It is almost June but there's still frost and it's snowing. Staś is tending the cows. We are still clearing our lot so we can plant potatoes.

June 1, 1940, Saturday. Today they are plowing our lot. After many months Staś has earned his first egg!

June 2, 1940 Mr. Romek Roszko attended a general meeting. He came back very depressed. They are sending him to work 80 kilometers away for two months.

June 3, 1940 We received a postcard from our father dated May 10, 1940.

June 7, 1940 They gave us some potatoes for planting and we are now preparing the land. Two good things happened: we got a postcard from Aunt Janina Milewska from Warsaw and 100 rubles from Mr. Kasprzak from Poland.

June 8, 1940 We planted 8 kilograms of potatoes and prepared the soil for vegetables. We are soaking wet because it was raining.

June 9, 1940, Sunday. Andrzej is being sent to work in a forest 25 kilometers away where he will be for about a month. He will be clearing meadows.

June 10, 1940, Monday. At 3:00 A.M. they came again to make a list of everybody in this settlement. Mrs. Dypczyńska has moved to another house with a Tatar woman. Elza and Jurek Dypczyński and Andrzej went to work in the forest.

June 11, 1940 Mrs. Dypczyńska is very ill. Her children are working in the forest and no one is there to give her even a glass of water. We spent the evening with her. We are planting potatoes; it's extremely hard work. I am writing this diary at 11.30 P.M. and the sun is still shining. We are covering the windows with blankets so that we can sleep.

June 15, 1940 We have been working on our plot for the last few days. We planted carrots. Andrzej came back from the forest for a visit. They have been getting 800 grams of bread per day and soup twice a day. They are always hungry.

June 17, 1940 We planted our last potatoes but do not know whether they will grow because we planted them late. A postcard has arrived from Romek with the news that there is going to be a war between Russia and Lithuania. That is why we are not getting any postcards from Father. We are depressed.

June 18, 1940, Tuesday. The assistant commandant was again making a list of where everybody works. We had a visit from the Gypsies. They were nasty and arrogant and we could not get rid of them. We received a postcard from Kasprzak from Staniewicze with information that our house had been disassembled and moved to the village where it now serves as a *dom oświaty* [cultural center]. We have nothing to go back to. Displaced persons!

June 19, 1940 Hot, beautiful day. Summer at last, but there are swarms of mosquitoes.

June 20, 1940, Thursday. Very hot day. We are washing our clothes in the river. Mrs. Makowa died today after a long illness and much suffering.

June 21, 1940 There are boots and jackets in the store, but they do not want to sell them to us. They are only for people working in the forest. With Lilka we picked quite a lot of sorrel. Here, they have the biggest mosquitoes that I have ever seen in my life. Today we had big storm with hail the size of peas. In the evening we went to the cemetery to bury Mrs. Makowa. It was a terrible cemetery with graves among the burned tree trunks.

June 22, 1940, Saturday. The chief of the forestry office came to Kokornaya. He inspected every house, including ours. Bald and fat as a bull, he spread himself out by our table and inquired about everything: about Father, how we live, and so on. He also informed us many times that Mother had to go to work, otherwise we would die from hunger.

June 25, 1940 Today children's boots are for sale in the store, but again they do not want to sell them to us. They are only for people working in the forest.

June 26, 1940, Wednesday. It's a terribly hot night and the mosquitoes are eating us alive. During the day we had our first swim in the river. We received a postcard from Aunt Janina Milewska from Warsaw.

June 27, 1940 We worked on our plot in the woods and seeded turnips. It is very hot with temperatures reaching 39°C, but we enjoy swimming in the river. It is impossible to sleep at night with the room temperature at 40°C. If we try to open the door a swarm of mosquitoes fly in and it's even worse.

June 28, 1940, Friday. Other people are receiving packages but not us. Mrs. Lila, who is one of them, sometimes shares her food with us. I was sent to the dining hall today but they do not want to give us anything; the food is only for the working people. If one of the lumberjacks does not take his portion then we can have it.

June 29, 1940, Saturday. St. Peter and Paul Day. We worked on our plot and picked some sorrel. A much-awaited postcard came from our father, dated June 8, 1940.

June 30, 1940, Sunday. After two months we were finally given some soap: two large pieces per family. Twice a day we walk to the water-powered mill to get some flour. Mom made *makojki*. For breakfast we had coffee and dry bread; for lunch potato soup mixed with sorrel; in the evening, flour and potatoes with sour milk. We get milk from Mr. Rydzyk.

July 1, 1940, Monday. Very cold again; rain and wind from the north. From hot to cold. This rapid change in weather can only happen in the far North. Still fighting lice and bedbugs. We rubbed everything—floors, beds and walls—with a strong salt solution to kill them, but to no avail; they are dropping from the ceiling. Andrzej went to work at Ust Pinega. There they sleep in the open at night and go back to the barracks on Sunday. They only get dry food, so they have to cook for themselves. We got some flour from the mill.

July 2, 1940, Tuesday. Encouraging news: Germany, Rumania and Turkey declared war on Russia. Probably lies! We worked on our plot trying to clear it from the weeds that grew among the potatoes. When we returned home we found a postcard from our father. This always gives us tremendous joy and hope.

July 4, 1940, Thursday. It's raining. We washed clothes in the river while swarms of mosquitoes were biting us.

July 5, 1940 It is impossible to sleep. I stayed in bed with a 38.7°C fever and upset stomach. Andrzej came home with some farmers' cheese (*twarog*), curds and the onion greens that grow wild near the river. It is hot and humid once more: temperature up to 40°C.

July 10, 1940, Wednesday. We were at our plot again trying to get rid of the weeds. They brought Mr. Cholda and Lola from Ust Yejuga. Both are very sick and there are no medicines with which to treat them. In the evening we received a postcard from Halina [Teresa's father's sister]. Today marks the fifth-month anniversary of our arrival in Russia.

July 11, 1940 Mr. Cholda died from starvation and sickness. In our group seven people have already died. They brought Andrzej back from Ust Yejuga. He is sick with severe diarrhea.

July 12, 1940, Friday. Today we buried Mr. Cholda.

July 14, 1940 Today is the funeral of Mr. Czerniakowski. They are selling boots but only to those on the list. Ms. Aldonka Wojciechowska did not buy any. Mom bought boots for Andrzej, size 42, for 37 rubles. He will have them for work in the forest.

July 17, 1940, Wednesday. Due to a bitter frost last night, our potatoes froze. We received a package from Poland from Mr. Kasprzak. What an incredibly good man. It included trousers for Andrzej, two kilos of butter and cheese, two pieces of soap, tobacco, wrapping paper for tobacco, two spools of threads, letter paper, and four candies. From the dining hall we bought burgers made from horsemeat.

July 21, 1940, Sunday. After a one-week rest at home Andrzej went back to work.

July 22, 1940 We received two letters: one from Aunt Janina Milewska from Warsaw and the other from our Grandmother Sicińska from Żelazno.

July 24, 1940 In the morning Mom went to the settlement. Meanwhile, a woman came to our house and I showed her the suit for which I wanted 100 rubles. She liked the suit but did not have enough money to buy it. It is a shame because we need the money badly.

July 25, 1940, Thursday. Mrs. Wilczakowa's two-month-old baby died; she will probably also die soon because she is very sick. For fruits we eat *kobylice* (miniature bitter plums that grow on shrubs and from which we also make tea) and *moroszka*, which look like blackberries but are bigger, yellow, juicy and grow in bogs.

July 28, 1940, Sunday. Andrzej came back from haymaking. We slept in the kitchen on the floor; it was impossible to sleep in our room because of the bedbugs!

July 29, 1940 The long-awaited postcard arrived from our father; it was dated June 30, 1940.

July 30, 1940, Tuesday. It has been raining all week, but we are happy because it is good for our potatoes. Mr. Nowak died. Mrs. Nowak went to the village for a coffin but was told that there were no wooden boards for people who are not working. Shame! Today they are distributing sugar, but only to working people. However, with God's help we also got some.

July 31, 1940, Wednesday. Today Mr. Nowak was buried. Mother went to the cemetery to help to dig the grave. Mr. Dypczyński arrived. He was arrested and deported to Russia with the Bienkowskis.

August 1, 1940 Commandant Frejman came over and told us that Mother will have to go pick blueberries and mushrooms in the forest. Supposedly, they will pay 1.20 rubles for each kilogram of berries and 6 rubles for a kilogram of dried mushrooms. She will also be entitled to get something to eat in the dining room.

August 2, 1940, Friday. We went with Lila for mushrooms. We also picked a lot of red berries and blueberries; so did Mom, who went in the other direction. We are going to sell them because we have no money at home. For cranberries, we had to walk up to our knees in water. I destroyed my shoes; I am going to buy sandals made out of willow bark. We went to the diner and sold the berries, which weighed 1.2 kilograms, for 1.43 rubles.

August 3, 1940, Saturday. We went 10 kilometers into the forest with Jadzia and Stasiu but we picked very little. It's so easy to get lost.

August 4, 1940 Went with Lilka for red berries which grow wild here. I picked a whole bucket.

August 5, 1940 We spent the whole day working on our plot.

August 8, 1940 We pick blueberries daily. Finally the price went up. We are now getting 1.20 rubles per kilogram.

August 11, 1940 Andrzej's birthday; he's 16 today. We went into the forest for berries again and picked a lot. Andrzej caught a beautiful pike in the river. It weighed about 1.5 kilogram.

August 15, 1940 Ascension of the Blessed Virgin. We pray for salvation from this hell.

August 16, 1940 We continue to pick cranberries every day. It's a nightmare: we have to walk knee-deep in the bogs and sometimes sink up to our armpits in the cold water, the mosquitoes and black flies eat us alive, our eyes are swollen, always running and fogged, and we cannot see.

August 17, 1940 Staś was signed up for third grade at school. I am sick in bed. Mom is picking berries in the forest.

August 17, 1940 Andrzej informed us that somebody received a letter which stated that Russia was given an ultimatum by Germany to return all the deported Poles between the 8th and 15th of September. The Belorussians can stay. If this is true, then the moment we have been dreaming of is near!

August 18, 1940, Sunday. We brought in the first crops from our plot of land: beetroots and young potatoes. Andrzej went to eat in the dining hall. From there the whole group is going to Ust Pinega; they do not allow walking there individually anymore.

August 21, 1940 The harvest has started. Only the women are working; they are cutting barley with sickles. We go to pick berries and mushrooms whenever we can. The only mushrooms that grow here are *kozaki* and *maślaki*. We take turnips from the government fields because we have nothing to eat.

August 28, 1940, Wednesday. The days are getting shorter: it is already completely dark at 9:00 P.M. We are preparing a kerosene lamp although we have no glass cylinder. It is getting cold and rainy. We brought some fresh potatoes from our field. Somebody is taking our potatoes! We are worried.

September 1, 1940 It is the first day of school for Staś. Mrs. Babiarz's father died. We will bury him tomorrow. Mom picked mushrooms and earned 6 rubles.

September 3, 1940, Tuesday. Mr. Ulak went to pick mushrooms, got lost in the forest and did not come back. He went early in the morning and now it is 10:00 P.M. and he is not back.

September 4, 1940 People formed a search party and found him. He was sitting under a tree exhausted, weak, confused and full of mosquito bites. It is extremely easy to get lost in the forest; several people die there every year. Staś came back from school and told us that the teacher told them that God does not exist; only old women believe in God.

September 5, 1940, Thursday. Staś has a very itchy rash, probably chicken pox, and is staying in bed.

September 6, 1940, Friday. Mom has been designated to pick blueberries for the commandant.

September 8, 1940, Sunday. The feast of the Annunciation. We stay at home and write letters. Andrzej went back to Ust Yula.

September 10, 1940 We picked blueberries and prepared them for winter. Fifteen people came from harvesting at Ust Yula, including Mr. Romek Roszko. Andrzej has large abscesses on his legs and will have to stay in bed. I have a sore throat. We received a letter, written in June, from Aunt Szulc-Rembowska.

September 15, 1940, Sunday. Early in the morning we all went to get wood. A large pine tree had fallen near the river. We cut the top off and brought it home.

September 22, 1940 We were told that we would be given a horse and a cart to bring the rest of the wood back to our home, so with the help of Andrzej and Staś we cut 20 logs. Mother got sick after picking mushrooms and is staying in bed. I have to get up at 5:00 A.M. to prepare dinner because we are not allowed to use the fireplace after that time. Staś takes the only pencil we have to school, so I have to write with chalk. We received some money from Aunt Paula Milewska by way of Berlin! We are writing letters to our father and Aunt Halina.

September 23, 1940, Monday. A postcard arrived from Aunt Paula from Warsaw asking us whether we received the money. If not, we were to let her know immediately.

September 26, 1940 It's raining and cold. We dug potatoes in the mud. We will try to buy more of them from Mr. Tiemnikov, otherwise we are going to starve during the winter.

September 30, 1940, Monday. The first real frost. Pools of water are covered with ice, but at least there is no mud. We are still digging potatoes; our hands are frozen and we are cold all over. The first snow falls in the evening. Staś received the last of his milk from Mr. Rydzyk for taking care of his cows.

October 3, 1940 Today is my [Teresa's] names day. Hopefully we will celebrate the next one in free Poland. Mrs. Arzajowa, who lives across the street, is leaving. The commandant came over and told us to move there with the Tipelts. We washed the beds with hot water and will relocate this evening. The accommodations are nice and warm.

October 4, 1940 There is news from Poland that the Germans have given Poland back to the Poles.

October 6, 1940 We have brought the last of the potatoes in from the field for a total of 246 kilograms; we stored them in the cellar. We are now frying some potato pancakes. To thicken the soup we added some shredded raw potatoes to the boiling water. We also got the paper, *Permuk Cebspa,* today and took apart an old woolen shawl to make socks.

October 11, 1940, Friday. Our neighbor Mrs. Arceptowa has pneumonia with a fever of 40°C. We made socks out of the yarn from the shawl.

October 12, 1940 Andrzej is working in the forest as a surveyor. In the evening he brought us some turnips.

October 15, 1940, Tuesday. We went to the *banya* with Mom and also managed to buy 33 kilograms of potatoes for 15 rubles in the village.

October 21, 1940, Monday. Mrs. Wanda Roszko brought us a postcard from Warsaw. The return address was: Polski Czerwony Krzyż [Polish Red Cross], Biuro Informacyjne, Warszawa, ul. Czerwonego Krzyża, 20.

October 22, 1940 We tried to get some of the cabbage leaves left in the field, now under snow, so we could pickle them and save them for winter, but they refused to grant us permission to do so. Better that they rot under the snow! Today, however, they let us do it and we retrieved 65 kilograms from under the snow. After a long bargaining session we also procured eight kilograms of barley from which we will make grouts.

October 23, 1940, Wednesday. Staś is sick in bed with temperature of 40°C. They say it's typhus. So many people are ill that they had to convert the school and the *banya* into hospitals. They are even bringing sick people here from Ust Yula.

October 26, 1940, Saturday. I am also ill. Staś has nightmares all night. Mother looks terrible from worry, sleepless nights and lack of food.

October 27, 1940, Sunday. Today is Mother's name day. In these terrible circumstances we are not celebrating. There are two women doctors inspecting everybody. They think that Staś has a severe case of influenza. Mother asked that they prescribe some milk for him. They said they will speak to the commandant and urge him to feed the people better!

(Sabina) Our situation now is hopeless. We live on borrowed money (from Ćwirko, 100 rubles). Our food reserves might last two more months. We do not have any flour and boil everything in water. We brought only one suitcase of clothes with us and everything is now torn. The children are very sick. Andrzej is still working but has boils and abscesses all over his body. My psychological state is terrible. Will I be able to carry on?

October 29, 1940 (Teresa) It's Mother's nineteenth wedding anniversary. It is very cold and snowing. We keep the fire going in the stove, but it is still cold in the house. Andrzej, Jurek and Marian are working in the forest cutting timber, putting up three cubic meters of wood daily for the kolkhoz.

October 31, 1940, Thursday. During the night Staś went though the critical part of his illness and is feeling better. We were given some bread from the kolkhoz, which we exchanged for barley to make kasha.

November 1, 1940, Friday, All Saints Day.

November 2, 1940 (Sabina) Staś is much better; he will live. The Blessed Mother has answered our prayers and my nerves have relaxed a little. The epidemic is spreading rapidly; is it typhus or severe influenza? Usually, children up to age 20 are affected. The reason is exhaustion from work and lack of food. Everybody over the age of 15 is taken for work. Executioners, torturers! God, when will you have mercy on us, give us strength not to doubt and carry on? It's bitterly cold outside and the snow is deep. We do not have warm clothes or money. What will happen to us? It is cold inside the house too because we do not have enough wood to keep the fire going. We are afraid to go to the forest in our light clothing for wood. By putting the trip off from day to day we are running out of firewood!

November 3, 1940 There's great panic in the settlement because three girls, all about 17 years of age, have died: Elżunia Dypczyńska, Bernarczykowa and Staś's teacher. They're taking the sick by sled, three at a time, in the freezing cold and snow storm, to the clubhouse in the second settlement. They took seventeen-year-old Irka Lugowska from our barracks. We went to see Elżunia with the wreath we made for her coffin.

November 4, 1940 Elżunia's funeral is today. I cannot go because Staś is still sick and cannot be left alone in the house. Mr. Bienkowski arrived at the *posiolek* and told us how he was tortured in the prison.

November 5, 1940, Tuesday. (Teresa) Mom sold the suit from Warsaw for 350 rubles and 16 kilograms of potatoes. It's a shame that it was sold for so little, but what could we do since we did not have any money.

November 7, 1940 Early in the morning we washed the floor and cleaned the house in preparation for a great Soviet feast day. The NKVD commandant came and praised us for keeping our house so clean. He then invited us to the meeting, where there will be a show, dancing and buffet. We will also be given 200 grams of bread with butter and one kilogram of sugar per family.

November 10, 1940 Staś got up for the first time. The *walonki* arrived at the store. These are boots made out of hardened wool, quite thick, excellent for deep, dry snow, but not waterproof. We hope to be able to get them.

November 15, 1940 (Sabina) The epidemic is spreading rapidly. They are taking the sick people away. Tita [diminutive of Teresa] became ill. The doctors check the houses every day and take away the sick. Clothing is disinfected.

November 17, 1940 Tita is much worse. Her temperature is 40.2°C and she is very weak. I am desperate. No doctors, no medicines. We pray to the Holy Mother for help. Will she listen to our prayers? Perhaps we are not worth it. Our help can only come from heaven. Staś is now better. We got some *walonki* for him and he went outside for the first time.

November 19, 1940 Tita is very ill. A package with clothes arrived from Warsaw.

November 23, 1940 For the last three days Tita has been near death. Every day Andrzej goes to the lower settlement and begs that they take her to the hospital and save her. They promise but nobody comes; no sled, no horses. "There is no room," is their constant reply. But that is not true. I went there myself and they lied to my face. I saw that there was room there and doctors as well, but they do not want us. Meanness without mercy! God, when will your justice come? For the last three days Tita has had nightmares. She shouts and talks aloud all night because her brain is affected. She is going into the malignant pre-death stage.

Terrible night between Tuesday and Wednesday. I am getting her ready for death. Can anyone know what I feel in my heart? We are praying at her bedside all night by the light of a candle. Tita sees shapes and figures on the ceiling. She shouts for help, for someone to save her. I think I am going mad; I am breaking down. The days are as frightening as nights; she suffers so much and there is nothing I can do. I think God is abandoning us, but I still pray day and night for help. Tonight at 10:00 P.M., when I am writing this, I think she may have passed through the crisis: she fell asleep for the first time and, after so many days of torture, this may save her. We feel abandoned. I need help with Teresa sometimes, but nobody can come to assist me because everybody is sick. Only Mrs. Lila and Mr. Bienkowski drop in now and then. Today Lila became ill.

The epidemic is spreading. In the other settlement they opened a hospital and brought two doctors from Arkhangelsk. The only medicines they have are aspirin and camphor. It is definitely typhus. The illness follows a predictable course. In the first three days the temperature stays at about 39°C. During the next three, it goes over 40°C and is accompanied by excruciating headaches and bone pain. In the next four to five days the brain is affected. Then the temperature lowers slightly and a crisis occurs which places the person in a live-or-die situation. If one survives, the temperature gradually goes down leaving one totally exhausted. There is no help either at home or in the hospital. We are practically starving; we have a few potatoes, some cabbage and 70 rubles. The prices are: 25 rubles for 15 kilograms of potatoes, two rubles for an egg and three rubles for one liter of milk.

November 24, 1940 Tita was taken to the hospital. I am going to work there as a nurse.

November 25, 1940 I am ill.

November 30, 1940 (Teresa) Mother is sick in bed at home.

December 2, 1940, Monday. They took Mother to the hospital. I am feeling much better. They are feeding us not too badly: in the morning we have tea with milk and sugar, a piece of a sour bun, bread and butter; for lunch there's soup with meat, macaroni and custard; in the evening we have milk, soup, manna, kasha or macaroni and, on occasion, sour milk. Mother was very sick for a few days but is now getting better. The boys visit us and are managing well at home.

December 9, 1940, Monday. I am still very weak but they are sending me home. I can hardly walk. Everything is always happening here at night, so I am leaving in the evening. Pani Włada and Staś came to pick me up because Andrzej is at work. It's extremely cold at home: there's five centimeters of ice on the windows. Pani Włada boiled some potatoes and I ate them with cabbage.

December 10, 1940 Włada is an absolutely wonderful woman. She came in the morning, cooked our dinner and washed our clothes because everything was dirty. Andrzej visits Mother in the hospital every day. Thank God she is getting better. Our money is running out; we don't know what to sell anymore. The days are very short: light at 9:00 A.M., dark at 2:00 P.M.

December 14, 1940, Saturday. Mother sold my sweater, the one from Warsaw, for 12 rubles. We had to do it because we had borrowed 15 rubles from Argarov.

December 16, 1940 We are trying to get some horsemeat, there is no other type here. It sells for three rubles per kilogram. Mr. Mazur will try to get us some.

December 17, 1940 We are very happy today because we received a letter from our father from Moscow. Andrzej took it to Mother in the hospital.

December 18, 1940, Wednesday. They brought Mother back from the hospital. She is very weak and can hardly walk. We do not have any food.

December 19, 1940 We are visited by a Jewish doctor who checks everybody for lice.

December 12, 1940, Saturday. We were visited by a Jewish *felczer* with whom Mother spoke in German. She asked him to prescribe some flour for us.

December 22, 1940, Sunday. Today, the commandant came over. We complained and asked for more bread, but to no avail.

December 23, 1940, Monday. Today we bought 4.5 kilograms of horsemeat. We will have it for Christmas. We are suffering from prurigo [an inflammatory skin disease]. We itch all over and look terrible.

December 24, 1940, Tuesday, Christmas Eve. Tonight we are having the *wigilia* [traditional Christmas Eve meal]. *Felczer* came for the last time; they are sending him back to Arkhangelsk. I obtained half a pint of milk and a spoon of butter from Rydzyk. At three o'clock we lit the fire and made *makojki* from the local wheat flour. They tasted very bad; we could hardly eat them. Then we had sauerkraut with mushrooms and potatoes, then soup from the same flour. It was thick and tasted excellent.

After the meal we took the *opłatek* [thin bread wafer] and shared it with our friends. Of course it was all so sad because we kept thinking about our father and the fact that we were not in Poland. Later Mr. and Mrs. Tipelt came with Pani Lila. We had a nice evening.

Andrzej took Father's ring to the Jewish doctor who promised to sell it for 300 rubles. We have misgivings about this venture but we have no choice. He gave us 100 rubles, some sugar, flour, kasha and a loaf of bread. He will send the rest of money to us from Arkhangelsk. We made some tea and ate bread with butter. What a feast! Our Christmas tree was decorated with cottonwool; there were no candles. Mr. and Mrs. Roszko had a very sad Christmas because their daughter, Bożenka, is ill and is lying unconscious.

December 27, 1940, Friday. Andrzej is ill; he is covered with skin abscesses. We do not have any ointment or bandages.

December 28, 1940 It is extremely cold outside: -40°C. Andrzej is very sick and abscesses are worse. We lit the fireplace but it does not heat the room. We are running out of wood. Mr. Usidus came and cut some wood for us. There is less and less water in the well. Soon we will have to go to the river for water, about a mile down a steep hill. When we have time, we sit on the stove. The water in the house is also freezing.

January 1, 1941, New Year! We are sitting on the stove in a niche singing Polish songs. Outside, it's -40°C. I went outdoors for water and got frostbite on my nose.

January 3, 1941 Bożenka Roszko is very sick and has a high temperature. Probably pneumonia. Andrzej went out for wood. His legs got frostbitten and we had to bring it in.

January 6, 1941 Bożenka is much worse; they took her to the hospital. She is the granddaughter of Mr. and Mrs. Bienkowski. Mrs. Roszko is not going to work; she is staying with her daughter in the hospital.

January 8, 1941 Tonight at midnight Bożenka Roszko died from pneumonia. At 1:00 A.M. Mrs. Wanda Roszko came over and we went to the hospital to prepare Bożenka for her funeral, scheduled for that afternoon.

(Stanisław) This death is firmly imprinted in my memory. She was my friend; I played with her and liked her very much. She was seven years old, blond and beautiful. I carried a wooden cross in front of her coffin during the procession to the place of burial and put earth on her coffin.

January 9, 1941, Thursday. (Teresa) Andrzej is very ill. Assistant Commandant *Rozdziawa* and *felczer* came over. We have scabies so they locked our house and forbade us to leave. We asked for some butter; received only 200 grams.

January 10, 1941, Saturday. The procurator arrived at the settlement. We complained to him that Andrzej is not getting any treatment. Mother finally was given medication (called *struptociki*) and he improved immediately: his temperature went down and his boils started to dry up. We thank the Mother of God for this help. We are now getting ointments and bandages. Tomorrow the doctors and *felczers* are going back to Arkhangelsk. We are still waiting for the money from the Jewish doctor for the ring so we can buy some food, but we are losing hope. They lowered our portion of bread to 300 grams. We are sending a letter to the doctor requesting the rest of money which we need desperately.

February 14, 1941 Just when we lost all hope and had no more money left to buy food, we received 250 rubles from our father. Where did he get the money from?

(Stanisław) As the winter progressed our supply of food dwindled and we began to suffer from vitamin deficiency. Sores and scabs covered my arms for an entire month. I held them in the sunshine coming through the window in the hope that it would help. I cleaned them and dressed them as much as possible. Gradually they healed. I attended school and that's what saved me because we received some food and milk there. I made skis from pine tree and attached reindeer skin to the bottoms so they would not slide backward. I also learned how to trap rabbits in the forest. One day as I was going to check on my traps, I happened to pass somebody else's trap with a rabbit in it. Suddenly a huge man bore down on me and beat me with a stick: a lesson for me to stay away from his traps.

The nights in the middle of winter were beautiful at times, with crisp snow and polar lights. The temperature would fall as low as -40°C; it was difficult to breathe. After school we sometimes skied with friends down the hill, with only leather straps holding the skis to our feet. I matured very quickly and became street-wise. I could fend for myself very well. But we survived because our mother was strong and wise. Everyone respected her, even the NKVD.

February 19, 1941 (Sabina) Through Mr. Kasprzak we obtained a package from Mrs. Mienicka and also one from Mr. Rachlewicz from Warsaw with some warm clothes. We are overwhelmed by the tremendous goodness of people, which saved our lives. God is good.

February 25, 1940 Andrzej is up for the first time since his illness.

March 1, 1941 We are sending a letter to the Jewish doctor with a request for the money he owes us. We sold Andrzej's suit, one of the last things we owned, for 200 rubles and 33 kilograms of potatoes.

March 25, 1941 (Teresa) There are rumors that they will take all the Poles from the settlement and move them to work in Krasny Bor. We sold a light coat and a scarf for 200 rubles.

April 1, 1941 At 6:00 A.M. they took all the starving children from the settlement to the orphanage in Pinega. The mothers, fearing that they would not see them again, wept and lamented. But what could they do? Their children were starving to death.

April 5, 1941, Saturday. Through the post office Mom received 50 rubles from a Dr. Baliński, whom we do not know. He must be a friend of the Szwejkowskis. Aunt Janina Milewska wrote that we are going to receive a package from them. Andrzej earned 78 rubles for a week's work. We bought 33 kilograms of turnips for 10 rubles. People who belong to the kolkhoz get them for nothing.

April 12, 1941, Saturday. Our Easter holidays are going to be sad because we cannot get any food. This evening I managed to get some carrots and one kilogram of horsemeat.

April 13, 1941, Easter Sunday. We spend this holy day with friends. Lila brought us a small piece of kielbasa and bacon.

April 18, 1941, Friday. Andrzej returned from work early. We went to the forest and cut down two pine trees. We also managed to get some bread on two occasions.

April 25, 1941, Friday. They allowed us to take some potatoes from the storage. It's a shame how, under kolkhoz management, so many of these potatoes turned rotten. Mr. Niedziułkowa was ordered to move in with us; now we have no room in the house.

April 28, 1941, Monday. The snow is melting rapidly. Mother and I are carting wood from the forest along a very muddy road. We are trying to get enough to last us until July.

April 30, 1941, Wednesday. We are cleaning the house for tomorrow's big communist holiday. The commandant is checking to make sure that everything is sparkling clean.

May 1, 1941, Thursday. Today is a big communist holiday. The commandant has been ordering us since early this morning to attend the meeting. They are selling sweets. Staś went early and returned at one o'clock in the afternoon with sweets, a bun and some bread — all of which cost him two rubles. The lumberjacks returned from Ust Yula for a three-day holiday. We played bridge in the evening with the Tipelts.

May 2, 1941, Friday. A movie was shown in the evening: "Girls from Kamchatka." This movie travels from village to village.

May 9, 1941, Friday. Strong winds and snowstorm. Our situation is getting worse. There are rumors of war with Germany, in which case we would starve to death. Nobody wants to buy anything any more, unless it's dirt cheap. For example, Mrs. Bienkowski was offered 20 rubles (which would buy 16 kilograms of potatoes) for her fur coat.

May 11, 1941 Andrzej has been out of work for five days. He was not paid because he has problems with Mr. Rudnicki, his supervisor.

May 12, 1941, Monday. Andrzej went to the kolkhoz to store wood. Tomorrow he will be sent to Ust Yula. We only have 50 rubles left.

May 14, 1941, Wednesday. Staś went to school without breakfast because today they are supposed to get tablets against bloody dysentery. We guess these tablets come from America. Is it possible that America is helping Russia? We certainly do not feel any effects of it. Just the opposite, prices are going up and nobody wants to buy anything. For example, 16 kilograms of barley sell for 53 rubles.

May 15, 1941, Thursday. Although it's the middle of May, the river ice has not melted and we still have snow. Something is happening: every house has been assigned two "elders" who have to report daily on what is going on to the commandant, who now arrives at the settlement at six o'clock in the morning.

May 18, 1941, Sunday. Happy news: Germany has attacked Finland and Russia is putting its armed forces on the western border.

May 21, 1941 Staś has abscesses on his legs. Our neighbor, Mrs. Nowakowska, is trying to cure them by incantations. What other means are there in our present situation?

May 23, 1941 The river has swollen and the floating of lumber has begun. Many people are engaged in pushing the lumber into the river.

May 24, 1941, Saturday. Andrzej is in debt in Ust Yula and is asking us for money. We are also in debt but fortunately we found a buyer for a man's shirt which brought us 40 rubles.

May 25, 1941 We went to the lower settlement for bread and took some things to sell. A lady *felczer* bought the stockings for eight rubles. We were lucky enough to buy a loaf of bread. In the evening Andrzej sent us half a loaf of bread with the message that he is going to be paid tomorrow.

May 26, 1941, Monday. (Sabina) There are constant rumors that we are going to be moved from here, but we do not know how much truth there is in that. Maybe it would be better because we can hardly continue to live here without money or provisions. We are starving and they give us only watery soup with dry bread three times a day; sometimes there is no bread. They sell us only 400 grams of bread daily, or 1.2 kilograms for the three of us. That's just enough for Staś before and after school. I try to buy food however and whenever possible; if I am successful then we eat and are satisfied. We talk and think about nothing else except food, how and where to get it. It is very hard; all day long it's Golgotha. God have mercy on us for we do not have any more strength. We now sell things that we absolutely need, retaining only a few essentials: one dress each and two nightdresses. What will happen to us in the future? The local people are exploiting us to the very end, buying very good things for practically nothing. For bread and barley they are asking exorbitant prices and there is nothing else to get here (16 kilograms of barley cost 72 rubles, one kilogram of potatoes goes for 1.50 rubles). I am sick after every walk through the settlement. Today we received a postcard from Marian Kubicz and 18.5 rubles from Pinega.

June 1, 1941, Sunday. First warm day; children are running outside barefooted.

June 2, 1941 (Teresa) Andrzej came back unexpectedly; he is being sent to Sultsa, 58 kilometers from us. It's very cold again and snowing. We sold a blue shirt for some potatoes. We received a long-awaited letter from our father.

June 6, 1941, Saturday. We went for the first time to pick cranberries and swore never to do it again because it would mean certain death: 12 hours knee-deep in cold water and ice underneath. (For one kilogram of cranberries we got one ruble.) Mother is sending letters to Father and Mrs. Baczyńska. Mr. Tipelt is surveying parcels for us where we can clear the trees.

June 9, 1941, Monday. We received a letter from Arkhangelsk informing us not to write to the Jewish doctor anymore because he is in prison. (We lost our 200 rubles.)

June 11, 1941, Wednesday. We went to pick cranberries once more; it's hard work but I made five rubles.

June 12, 1941, Thursday. It's Corpus Christi, a holy day, but our people went to clear the trees off their parcels anyway.

June 13, 1941 Sad news from Warsaw: our Grandmother Sicińska died on March 21, 1941. I went to pick cranberries again and earned six rubles. It was so tiring that I hardly had the strength to come back.

June 16, 1941 Baby Ćwirko died and we buried him today. In the afternoon we went to cultivate on our plot of land.

June 18, 1941 Andrzej sent us 70 rubles from his last pay through Mr. Tiemnikov. We bought small potatoes for planting at ten rubles per 16 kilograms. Those from the kolkhoz are all rotten.

June 19, 1941, Thursday. We planted our first basket of potatoes. Edek Nowak, age ten, drowned in our river. It is a great loss; he was so nice and good.

June 21, 1941, Saturday. We tried to sell Staś's sailor's blouse, but we could not.

June 22, 1941, Sunday. They were signing people up for work in the kolkhoz. Mother signed up for clearing the pastures.

June 23, 1941, Monday. Happy news and hopes of returning home: War!

June 24, 1941, Tuesday. Mother went to work at the kolkhoz. She came back tired. The work is not too bad but she has to walk very far.

June 25, 1941 I got up at 5:00 A.M. to prepare food for the entire day. We do not have anything anymore; we live on sorrel.

June 27, 1941 We received a package from Mr. Rachlewicz with oatmeal, grouts, onions, soap, small pieces of bacon or rather lard, and kielbasa.

July 2, 1941, Wednesday. (Sabina) We are very depressed because Andrzej has to leave at 4:00 A.M. to report for work somewhere far away; they did not tell us where. Are we going to see him again? We feel like we are losing our guardian.

July 6, 1941 We are without money and food, and we are starving. I work at the kolkhoz and they pay me 1.20 rubles per day, on which one person can barely survive. One really needs five rubles per day. That's what we earn at Kokornaya; in other regions they earn more.

August 3, 1941, Sunday. There's a long break in the diary because we did not have time to write. The last act of our tragedy has unfolded and we will perish. On Sunday, July 6, at eleven o'clock at night, Jurek Dypczyński came to our window and told us that at a meeting the commandant read out a list of names, including ours, of those who are to report tomorrow at 6:00 A.M. for work at Ust Yula (a forest substation), 12 kilometers away. I packed a few things at night, and at three o'clock in the morning I went to see the commandant to request that he let us stay at Kokornaya since it is a kolkhoz and I may still have a chance here to save my children from death (we are already starving). At Ust Yula we would perish because we would be solely dependant on food (and very poor food at that) in the communal dining room which costs six rubles per person per day for a total of 20 rubles a day for us all. The commandant told me that we had to go, and that he could care less about the children. As far as he was concerned we could all starve to death!

So we went to Ust Yula, where we are now living in communal barracks with women, men and children all together. Mosquitoes, lice, bedbugs and black beetles bite us constantly and because of that we cannot sleep. As soon as we arrived they immediately herded Teresa and me off to work: first to remove bark from the trees in the forest, then to cut grass with scythes in the fields, and then to rake hay.

End of August. We have been working now for four weeks and we still have not received any pay. We live on borrowed money. The first week they gave us, or rather sold us, 1.5 kilograms of bread per working person, and then they lowered the ration to 500 grams per day. This means starvation for us. They wake us at 3:30 A.M. for work, and we don't return until 9:00 P.M. We are totally exhausted and can hardly drag our feet. We have to walk to work about three to six kilometers. We take a small piece of bread along with us. For lunch they bring us watery soup, which costs seven kopecks. Staś and his friend got the job of bringing us cans of soup for lunch in a boat. They push the boat up the shallow river with long poles. For this they get some soup. In the evening Staś boils soup for us in a large pot. It consists mainly of sorrel, which he picks, and an occasional fish — if he manages to catch one. And that is what we eat. We live in the company of ignorant peasants who are unfriendly to us and deceitful. We are persecuted by the authorities in our barracks and by Mr. Skrzyński, our supervisor, at work. We are failing physically and psychologically. Thoughts of suicide tempt us. Our suffering is beyond description.

August 31, 1941, Sunday. Settlement of Korcha. Our wanderings have no end. On the 25th our work supervisor told us to pack our things and be ready to leave early in the morning on the 26th for Korcha, located 50 kilometers from Kokornaya. Teresa was ordered to stay. Our explanations, requests, petitions and cries did not help. For the sake of keeping the family together, I mustered the courage to act against the orders of the authorities with the full knowledge that I could be arrested for doing so. I was once arrested for asking Staś to fetch our things, which were left in Kokornaya, without the commandant's permission (he would not give it to us). I now told Teresa to go a few kilometers up the river and wait for us. We then put our belongings into a boat and pulled it with a rope from the shore. We met up with Teresa without being chased by anyone. On the way we slept in the workers' barracks in Tochca. They were full of young men and women who slept together like in a bordello. Would that have been Teresa's fate?

We arrived in Korcha on the 28th. Our barracks there were much cleaner and the diner was better and cheaper; but our earnings were smaller. At Ust Yula we received ten rubles for putting up one cubic meter of chopped wood, here we get four rubles. To reach the place of work we have to walk six kilometers in deep mud. It's very hard work, work beyond our strength. We feel handicapped because the other workers have the strength to earn from eight to ten rubles a day, and they do not get as tired as we do. I do not know how long we shall survive. The situation is hopeless: no food, our clothing is in rags, our shoes are destroyed. Although it is turning cold we must work barefooted. It is a miracle that we are still alive.

Beginning tomorrow Staś will be going to school in Sultsa, 2.5 kilometers away, where they are going to move us eventually. The authorities here are much more sympathetic.

This is our first Sunday in Korcha and we have the day off; it's a long time since we had a rest. Staś and I walked to Sultsa. This settlement is much more prosperous than ours. It is a forestry center and it's full of supervisors. I wanted to sell one of the quilts which we still have, but we could not get enough money for it. In the evening there will be a meeting of all the Polish people. Rumor has it that Polish delegates will be present. All Poles were given time off from work so they could attend this meeting, some of them having to walk 100 kilometers.

The meeting was adjourned till tomorrow.

September 1, 1941, Monday. The meeting took place at 9:00 A.M. and all the commandants were there. It was announced that Poland and Russia signed a treaty and that we are now free! Mr. Bienkowski made a beautiful speech. We are waiting for further developments. Will this save us from starvation, death and freezing? Everybody is applying for passports to the Polish consulate in Moscow. Andrzej is on his way back.

September 6, 1941, Monday. Break in the writing of the diary since September 1, 1941. We still are putting up cubic meters of chopped wood in the forest. When one of us becomes sick or develops abscesses on her legs she has the job of burning tree branches (earning 75 kopecks). Daily living costs us ten rubles. News reaches us that our men are returning from Ust Pinega, but it's not true because Andrzej has not returned. Now that they are free, the Poles are building rafts and floating down the river to be closer to civilization. In most cases they leave without money or provisions.

Pinega is 120 kilometers away and the journey takes five days. It is raining and very cold. The Jozga River flows right in front of the windows of our barracks. On some days one raft after another goes by. We continue to remain here waiting for Andrzej's return. He must know and see what is happening with our people. We have to decide whether to spend the winter here or leave. We have no provisions and little money.

September 24, 1941 We have received 100 rubles from Andrzej by telegraph. That means he is not on the way back yet.

September 26, 1941 This morning a lady informed us that a telegram addressed to Sabina Chmielewska arrived from the headquarters of the Polish army. I sent Staś to the post office but they would not give it to him because the last name was different. I went to the post office myself and asked them who signed the telegram. It was Alfred [Sabina's husband]. After a long argument they gave me the telegram. It took six days to get from Kokornaya to Sultsa and nobody here took any interest in finding out who the telegram was for. It was only by chance that we got it. I telegraphed back immediately that we are waiting for confirmation and money.

October 6, 1941 We do not have the answer to our telegram. The beginning of the end is here. It's freezing at night and snowing frequently. I cannot imagine traveling without provisions. If we do not get an answer in a few days the river will freeze. I am terribly afraid of this journey: five days on the raft with freezing water up the ankles on the Pinega River and then 700 kilometers on the Dvina River to Kotlas — a two-month journey in the middle of winter. What shall we do?

October 8, 1941 We received money from Mr. Wicher, mailed September 8, 1941, and we are exceedingly happy that Andrzej came back. It is good to be together. Andrzej looks good. They were fed well. At present he is delivering lunches to the workers in the forest and goods to Sultsa. He is also taking people across the river in a boat, brings bread, etc. Today we are building a bridge. We are in water up to the ankles and it is snowing. Tonight at a meeting the commandant asked us to donate woolen clothes to the Red Army. We do not have any news from the front.

October 9, 1941, Thursday. It was snowing all night. We are putting up cubic meters of wood in the forest. There's no news from our father. I am afraid we are going to spend the winter here.

October 15, 1941 Still no news from Father. Snowing every day. Andrzej carts wood in the forest but today he is cutting down trees. The work is very hard.

October 22, 1941 We went to Sultsa to inquire whether we could work inside. No results. We cannot live without work. We cannot work in the forest because we lack shoes and warm clothing. I have sent another telegram to Alfred. We work hard but earn too little to live on. Andrzej earns three rubles daily for delivering lunches. Teresa and I also earn three rubles, but we need 16 per day. We are running out of the money that we had earned haymaking and that Andrzej saved in Zapani. We only have one marble clock to sell but nobody wants it. Holy Mary have mercy on us and send us some help.

October 26, 1941, Sunday. Rain mixed with snow. Andrzej and Teresa were moved five kilometers from Korcha. Andrzej is going to work there as a lumberjack; Teresa, as a cleaning person. I tried to be transferred there with them but without success; maybe later when more workers will be needed. This is my first separation from Teresa. I am sad and there is emptiness without her. I am worried and hope that nothing bad will happen to her. At 15 years of age she has a well-balanced personality and a strong character. I pray to God that her eyes are not opened too early to the moral depravity all around us. We live in common barracks with one toilet and seven other families. 1) Cybulski: mother and son, husband and his father. He was an officer and a colonist in Polesie. 2) Borko: husband and wife. He was a bank accountant in Pinsk and had a small farm. 3) Czajka from a small farm near Lithuania: married couple with four grown children. 4) Świerczyński with his beloved and her daughter. 5) Holda with her mother and four almost-grown children; unclean, full of lice. 6) Bujak, who is slightly retarded, does not take care of himself, dirty and in rags. 7) A local family: grandmother and mother with three small children who cry and scream all the time depriving us of rest. Lice have spread to everybody. We feel terrible here. I cannot go on because I am running out of paper.

October 27, 1941, Monday. It's my birthday. Staś is lying in bed sick. It's snowing hard. Our situation is hopeless. There is no news from Alfred.

October 28, 1941 I went to Sultsa to ask the commandant of the forestry division for work inside because we have no shoes or clothes. He refused saying: "We only have work in the forest." In place of Teresa they are giving the job to a fifteen-year-old Belorussian girl. Teresa, a Polish girl, has to work in the forest. Manajenko, a real crook who tortured us in Ust Yula, has been appointed as the chief of the forestry division.

November 3, 1941 The river froze over and it is snowing. I am still not working, still begging all the various commandants to give me work that I can do inside. I found out that Teresa is working too hard: she cleans two large halls, looks after five large furnaces, chops and brings in wood, helps the cook in the kitchen, and carries lunch in deep snow two kilometers for the workers in the forest — this is too much for one person. I am asking them to transfer me so that I can help her even without pay. To no avail: she is Polish, she can perish. They are animals, not human beings.

November 15, 1941 I finally got a job with Teresa as a cleaning woman in the barracks in the forest. We are together again.[1]

Account of Vala Lewicki (née Miron)

All Poles were divided into two groups. One group with a very young boy was sent further away into the forest. We said our last goodbyes. We never saw them again. The remaining group, consisting of people mostly known to my father, were loaded onto a boat to be taken down the river to a base called Charnushka, 24 km from the Kama River and 29 km from Chormoz city, still in the Molotov district.

All people of working age (14 years and up) were employed in the forest, logging trees. Only two educated men, Mr. Siedlicki, who had held an important position in Poland in forestry, where my father worked, and another gentleman were given office jobs as accountants. My sister Ola and Yadzia Hornik worked in a restaurant.

School opened in September. Polish children had to attend with Russian students. Those who had to look after siblings while the mothers worked were exempt. Nadya was one of those. That is why Vala Zorko and I became best friends. Here, in grade 4 — the highest class on the base — were Janka K. and Lala Martynowska. We had a man teacher. He was not a bad fellow. When Russian pupils sang "Remember you dogs, *hetmany* (military commanders) and you Polish *pany* (bourgeois) our Red Army and battles," we sang back: "Remember you dogs, *hetmany* and you Russian *chamy* (boors) our Polish army and victories." The teacher just smiled. Yet it was not always like that. At the end of a school year we had our oral exam, probably for the purpose of sending children away for higher grades in town. In spite of bad conditions in the barracks and doing homework at night by dimmed light, I was a good student, so I did not expect anything disastrous to happen. I answered many questions correctly. Then came one about Stalin.

Through a difficulty in pronunciation I accidentally said: "Louse Comrade Stalin." All the examiners directed an intense, angry gaze at me. Their faces were creased up in fury and horror. Slowly I tried to still my fears which threatened to turn into panic. I heard the teacher's voice: "Say it again!" I repeated the sentence, this time omitting "tovarishch-comrade" and thinking that it will be fine now for Stalin is not my comrade. I was very wrong! All hell broke loose — one examiner stood up, grabbed me by the arm and threw me out into the anteroom. There, among the other children who were waiting to be called in, I began to feel an odd constricting sensation in my throat followed by dizziness and nausea. When this stopped a throbbing headache started to paralyse me. Perhaps growing up and the fact that I was suffering from scurvy contributed to some degree towards my feeling ill.

Not realising what I said or did wrong, I dragged myself home. But I could not explain my agony clearly to anybody. That night my father was summoned to the [NKVD] commandant's office for interrogation. This time it was Mr. Sergeyev as the previous one had been removed from the post. We spent the night in despair, waiting for news of father. After a few hours he came home and explained exactly what was the mistake I made in the classroom and how he convinced officials of my family's innocence.

It transpired that in Russian *voshch* means a leader, the head of a country; while *vosh* is a louse. When the first word, *voshch,* is pronounced quickly with consonants following, the "ch" is lost and the word "louse" is created. The question regarding Stalin required an answer beginning with *voshch* (leader). I began with *Vosh Tavarishch Stalin*.... Due to difficulty of pronunciation I accidentally said "Louse Comrade Stalin."[2]

Account of Stefania Buczak-Zarzycka

When the train had finally stopped at Murashi, we found more sleighs waiting for us. Here a tragic incident occurred. A young woman who had given birth on the train threw herself and her newborn under the wheels of an approaching train. She left behind her two older children. For two days we traveled by sleigh through forest land where there were no formal roads. We zigzagged around trees and our pathway was often obstructed by fallen pine and birch tree trunks. Our destination was the "Osmoy" Eighth Settlement *posiolok* in the Komi District of Siberia where the Ukrainians and Germans from pre-revolutionary days had established themselves. We were settled in large wooden cabins infested with bedbugs. Immediately, we were divided into groups; the able-bodied men and young women were sent to Michadzib, a forest district where they were required to build a new settlement; the older men and women remained to saw wood; children from the ages of eight to sixteen were sent to school; while children under eight were sent to state nurseries.

In the forest, the first group was required to clear the area of trees and build themselves a shelter. Until this was accomplished they slept in the open around a roaring fire.

In several months, the *posiolok* had been built; it was called Michadzib. Like all early Russian settlements, it was situated near a river, in this case, the Pryluskaya. (The river was of great importance because there were no road or rail links, therefore the river served as the principle means of transportation.) The forest group built five barracks, an office "*kantora*," and a first-aid station, which served as the only medical facility for many miles. Needless to say, there was no doctor present, only a medical assistant whom they called "*felczer*."

Upon the completion of this work, which took over five months, couples were reunited, but the children remained with their groups so that their education and the work of their parents would not be disturbed. Much hardship was experienced; people worked at least a ten-hour day, six days, sometimes seven days a week, and were poorly paid or fed. Any minor infringement of rules would result in the loss of pay (*prohul*). At school, the teachers insisted that we speak the Russian language at all times with each other. They allocated duties for us to perform as well as sporting activities after school. One activity I loathed was the run through snow. I would always detour through the forest which was laden with snow, often up to my waist, in order to avoid this "fun." However, one sport I did enjoy was kayaking, and I often challenged the Soviet and Samoyed children for races. Quite often I would win, and after one such success some Soviet boys tipped my kayak over, spilling me into the river. Splashing about I came to the surface and somehow managed to improvise swimming strokes to save myself. I had learnt to swim.

On the 1st of May (May Day) our teacher, Nina Yskarvionovna, presented us with a sweet and biscuit announcing that "Father Stalin loves all children without prejudice."

Taking her cue, a Russian girl rose and sang: "*Batko Stalin dayet confet, Yevo lubyt cilyj svyet*" (Papa Stalin gives us sweets, the whole world loves him).

In response, a fifteen-year-old Polish girl, Ludka Budar, declared: "*Batko Stalin dayty myla, bo vze vushy mayut skryla*" (Papa Stalin gives us soap, because all the lice have wings).

Upon hearing this, the members of the class either fell silent or began to giggle. The teacher removed Ludka to the office where she was questioned about the song.

Had her parents taught her these verses?

She replied that her ambition was to be a poetess and she was the authoress of the verse. That evening her father did not return home, and when he appeared six months later he told us he had been sent to a work camp in the far north of Siberia.

Some weeks later Staszek Wilk, who was about fourteen years of age, wished to improve the portrait of Stalin by drawing a pair of spectacles on him. The same fate befell his father. That year, on Christmas Eve, I drew an angel for our Christmas tree at school. We were told to remove the tree and for the person who drew the angel to come forward; that night my father did not come home. Six months later, affected by snow blindness and some frostbite, he returned. During these months I suffered with the guilt of having unwittingly caused this punishment. My father forgave me and reassured me that his treatment was no fault of mine. However, I have never forgotten this.

At the end of May spring made a brief appearance, followed almost immediately by the short Siberian summer. Great expanses of ice and snow began to melt causing the river to overflow and flood its banks. Many artificial tributaries appeared and the Siberian marshlands, the taiga, awoke from hibernation. Fields of flowers exploded into blooms, thousands of water birds made their nests and many stinging insects multiplied in order to irritate us it seemed. At night we slept in smoke-filled rooms, for the burning of birch tree branches repelled these insects. Bedbugs emerged from between the wood planks of walls and floors to plague us again and we all had ugly looking sores as a result.

During the summer holidays we were released from school and with our backpacks we paddled by kayak and other small craft back "home" to our parents. Here we were again divided into brigades and we were sent on various work expeditions. We cut young birch branches from which we made brooms and food bundles for animal winter feed. We also gathered moss for use as building material, but a more pleasant task was mushroom and berry picking.

My brigade leader, Janek K., was a young student from Zbaraż. Janek was very intelligent, possessed impressive orientation skills in the forest, and always traveled wearing a Polish student cap and carrying a balalaika on his back. He was a popular brigade leader because he showed us bears, reindeer and wolves in the wild. He was instructed to speak only Russian language to us, but as soon as we were out of the main settlement area we would all speak and sing in our native tongue. Once our baskets, made for us out of birch branches, were filled, he would make us promise we would not tell anyone about the songs he composed and sang for us....

Janek grew in heroic stature before our eyes. From these work parties we often returned quite late at night, but because of the "midnight sun" effect of the extreme North the night held no fear for us. At the end of the summer we returned to school, but Janek and his twin sister went to join the forest brigade. I was very unhappy that he left our brigade because I had become quite attached to him. I was eleven and Janek epitomised for me the qualities that an ideal young man should have.

In the spring of 1941 Janek went lumbering on the river and was crushed by logs while directing the float of trees down the river. He was found seriously injured and half-frozen in the cold water; a few days later he died. His brigade came to his funeral carrying a huge wreath we had plaited from pine branches. We all cried at his graveside. His sister died in unknown circumstances several months later, and in her extreme grief their mother was taken to a mental institution. Nothing more is known of her.

On a hillside under pine trees was the site of our cemetery. In the first six months only the graves of small children were dug, but later the number of graves increased with the deaths of adults in the prime of life who were killed outright or died as the result of serious accidents. Lack of adequate medical care compounded our problems. A small number had also suicided. At first, crosses on grave site were prohibited, but these always appeared overnight. After a few months the officials turned a blind eye to these.[3]

Account of Tadeusz Pieczko

We finally reached a small Siberian town where we were put on sleds and taken to a camp deep in the forest; the trip lasted almost the entire night. When we arrived there, we were housed in large log cabins with rooms measuring approximately 12' × 24' for each family. The cabins were crudely constructed. They were not insulated and the spaces between the logs were stuffed with moss. Each room had a tiny wood-burning stove and a wash basin on a stand, just like a prison cell. There was no running water or electricity. There were no guards in this camp because there was no place to escape to. We were in the middle of nowhere, far from towns and other villages. There were some Russians in charge and I think they had weapons, but they were not as cruel and abusive as the soldiers. At the camp, those that were able to work were put into work groups and most of them worked in the forests. These camps were similar to the German concentration camps, except that the Russians worked their prisoners to death whereas the Germans exterminated their prisoners for no reason at all (as happened with the Jews). There were also Jews in our camp but they were not Russian Jews. The Russian slogan was: those that worked, ate; those that did not work, did not eat. So their solution to the problem of the foreign Jews was somewhat different from that of the Germans: the Russians just wouldn't let the Jews work. At the beginning we tried to help these Jews in a small way, but this soon became forbidden and later the non-Jewish people themselves were dropping like flies for lack of food. Many of our relatives, neighbors and friends died during this time.

The small children were made to attend school. After a while, many of us did not have any shoes to wear. I often went to school keeping my torn shoes on by wrapping them in rags. In school, my feet became very cold as the snow on the rags slowly melted. It was miserable, but at least we stayed out of the blinding snowstorms and bone-chilling winds. The children were not fed in school, but some did bring pieces of bread with them when it was available. There was an exception however: at noon, those that belonged to the Red Pioneers would receive a roll and a glass of milk. Needless to say, it did not take us long to decide that we also wanted to be in the Red Pioneers. We did not want to give up the religious medals that we wore around our necks. Depending on the teacher, this at times prevented us from getting our snacks. Some teachers were sympathetic towards us.

The parents that worked outside in the forest had a very long and exhausting day. Because of poor nutrition, many became ill and passed away. Winter was very long. The snow melted in late April or early May and began falling again in September for another eight months. In the summer, the children would join their parents working in the forest and pick mushrooms or berries. My brother and I would trade these for other staples at the store. In this way we were able to contribute more to the upkeep of the family than our parents who were doing hard physical labor. Bread was very scarce, not very fresh and imbedded with roaches, hair and strings. But that did not bother us. When it was available we always made sure that we put some aside for leaner days. We would dry the bread and hide it in a cloth sack. When bread was not available, we would take out a slice of the dry bread and soak it in water to make it softer and more filling. People searched for food everywhere. To get provisions, some even sold their meager belongings to the Russians. Sanitary conditions were very primitive and there was no doctor, medicine or clinics....

I had a friend with whom I used to play. When they put a group of us in one room, he and I used to bunk together on the floor. One morning I awoke and found him dead right next to me. He died of tuberculosis. I was depressed and missed him for a while. His parents almost adopted me because I reminded them so much of him.

My cousin's wife had a baby which was born prematurely and died. The tiny infant was wrapped in a scarf and buried in a wooden coffin. We had a regular Catholic funeral for her. Since it was summer, we were able to bury her in a cemetery in the woods. I was chosen to carry a homemade cross at the head of the procession. I was so moved to have such a important assignment that at one point I fell flat on my face because I walked too fast.

Although religion was forbidden at this time in communist Russia, on occasion, when we visited a Russian home, we would see a religious picture or a statue hidden behind a curtain. Our camp director was a strict communist but when his child got sick he asked the Poles to pray for him. When the child passed away, he invited us to the wake and also to the burial. He asked us (on the side) to say prayers and sing church songs. His position would not allow him to display any religious feelings.

There was always a shortage of food. Occasionally, someone would bring a wagon full of vegetables for sale. Everything was frozen like a rock, but at home in a pot it all cooked just fine. Bedbugs and lice were always a nuisance to us. There was no soap either for washing oneself or for laundry. We were allowed a small plot of land for a garden. The summers were short, so we had to get the vegetables (mostly potatoes, carrots and cabbages) into the ground early. We dug the potatoes just before the snow fell and stored them under the floors of the barracks. There wasn't much, but it would last for a couple of months. Once a man stole a head of cabbage from a neighbor and got one year in jail.

In 1941 we, along with other survivors, were transferred to a labor camp in southern USSR..... After a few weeks of travel we arrived at our destination: Kazakhstan. The people here appeared more oriental. They were quite friendly but a little on the suspicious side. When we first arrived there some of the children went begging for food, and the local people would (if they had anything) share it with us. We were housed one family to a room. Again, the room was small (about 12' × 24') and had a dirt floor. There was no glass in the windows; rather, a wax-paper-like material served to let in the light and keep out the flies. Some of the local people kept their animals (e.g., cows or donkeys) in adjoining rooms. The buildings were made of sun-dried mud bricks laced with straw. They looked almost like the adobe bricks of the Pueblo Indians. Since there was little rain, the bricks lasted pretty long. Once in a while the buildings needed a fresh coat of mud to keep them standing.

The living conditions in Kazakhstan were worse than those in an American slum. The lice were as numerous as flies. We frequented a barbershop run by my cousin. Once, when a Kazakh received a haircut, he became the laughing stock of all the natives. They wore their hair long, like our Native Americans, or shaved it off leaving just a pigtail. They also had long, thin mustaches. The people here never heard of sanitation. There were no toilet facilities at all, not even an outhouse. The Poles received permission from the head commissioner to build a bathhouse and an outhouse near a creek. The natives never came to take a bath. The outhouse was simply an excavation in the ground covered with boards; around it were four walls of straw matting about four feet high for privacy. (Lumber was very scarce in this area; only some poplars grew along the streams.) Unfortunately, the outhouse became an object of curiosity to the Kazakhs who would gather and stare almost every time one of us went to the bathroom. They couldn't understand why anyone would go through all that trouble to relieve themselves when they could just use a ditch for that purpose. The nearby stream was our source of water for bathing, swimming, drinking and cooking. The animals also drank from it. Once in a while, when the water was diverted to irrigate the fields, we would find small fish trapped in the depressions of the streambed. Understandably, there were many health problems, such as dysentery, and quite a few people died not only from hunger but also from the lack of sanitation and polluted water....

The Jews in this part of the Soviet Union were kept in a single room in an abandoned school building. They were dying each day. We were forbidden to go there and they were forbidden to leave the building. Once in a while, however, one of them would wander off and go begging. At first we shared with them what we had but after a while, when nothing was left, we ourselves had to go begging from the Kazakhs. I used my younger brother for this purpose and it worked pretty well. He was old enough to walk but couldn't because of malnutrition. So I would carry him on my back as I went from one Kazakh to another. Usually they were sympathetic and gave us something to eat. Once a Jew came begging and we told him that we had nothing to eat. He was a terrifying sight and frightened us. He mumbled something and slowly moved on. Then he fell down. We all rushed over and just stared at him with fear. There were no adults nearby because they were all working in the fields. He died that day. Here, too, the Jews were not permitted to work, so they had absolutely no food. I think the whole group died out because at the end of my time in this area I don't remember seeing any of them....

At times, we went for days without eating anything. Once we saw a chicken walking back and forth in front of our quarters. We already pictured this chicken in the pot. Although we knew that stealing chickens was a serious offense, we took a chance anyway and made an effort to lure it inside. We pretended to throw seeds on the ground and the chicken started running toward us and ran right inside. We slammed the door shut and went after it. The inside of our living quarters had a dirt floor, so we dug a hole, buried the guts and feathers, put the chicken in a pot, and waited for our mother to return from work. At the end of the day, when we showed her what we had, she became frightened. But after a while she overcame her fear and we had the most wonderful meal.

One summer morning, while working in the fields cutting wheat, the men saw a horse eating wet alfalfa and knew exactly what would follow. Shortly thereafter, the horse went over to the creek, started drinking, and became so bloated that he could hardly move. That's when the men sneaked up on him, pulled him down, and kept his head submerged for a while. Then they went to the commissar and notified him that a bloated horse had drowned. We were allowed to slaughter the horse and keep the meat. That turned out to be both a blessing and a curse. On the first day everything was great but on the following days, since we had no refrigeration, some of us became extremely ill both from the shock to our systems (after having nothing to eat for some time) and also from the spoiled meat. I feasted on a liver and became so ill that for years thereafter I would get sick from just looking at liver.

One day, while working in the mountains, the men killed a wild boar. When they carried it back to the village with visions of having a great feast, the native Kazakhs — who were Moslems and could not stand the sight of the pig — ran away in disgust. Yet these same people would have their women search the seams of their clothes for lice and eat them. They believed that the lice took their blood and that by this practice they were getting it back. And the lice, just like the bedbugs, were very plentiful....

After noticing a huge flock of crows near the mill, we ran over to the commissar and asked him to shoot some for us. He obliged, and we had crows for supper....

On one occasion, as we moved from one settlement to another, we managed to get a ride on a regular passenger train. The cars were already packed with young people, probably students or some other young socialist pioneers. They were all engaged in loud and spirited singing. They were all dressed fairly well and some were eating their lunch and drinking. We just stood there in the aisle dressed in rags as the train sped through the villages and empty fields. And I kept wishing that at least one of them would offer me a piece of bread.[4]

Account of Sabina Kukla (née Lukasiewicz)

Most of the men were sent out to work in deep forest, some 70 km from the settlement, and they had to go there on foot. They usually worked in one place for three months. They came back to the settlement for a few days and returned again to their place of work. They cut down trees and shaped the wood for rifle butts. My father was one of those men.

The clothing and footwear which we were wearing when we left Poland were beginning to wear out. It was not possible to buy new ones because whenever the shop received a delivery a kilometre-long queue formed and there was only enough for the lucky ones who were in front. One usually went away with nothing. In many cases the sizes were also unsuitable. I was left without boots for the winter so I wrapped my legs in rags tied with string and went like that to work through the snow. I was not the only one. That was everyone's nightmare in this inhuman land. Hatred was born in these people as they pushed past one another in those queues to obtain something.

Legs and hands frost-bitten, constitutions drained from hard work, hunger and lack of vitamins.... My legs were ulcerated and covered in wounds which would not heal. In summer mosquitoes and flies entered these festering wounds during work. One wanted to cry. My wounds only healed in Tehran.[5]

Account of Maria Borkowska-Witkowska

We traveled north into the depths of Russia, all the way to Kotlas, changing trains once at Szepatowce. The train did not go beyond that. We were loaded onto lorries pulled by tractors. Thus we were driven 120 km to a small hamlet called Jol. The frost and winds were so severe that people began to fall ill and my youngest brother died soon after we arrived at our place of exile. My mother also fell ill....

I was the oldest of the children, being eighteen, and I was allocated to cutting down the forest. The commandant formed a brigade out of ten young girls, gave us saws and axes, and then sent us into the forest. The frost was cruel. We had no experience and did not know from which side to cut, and the pines were so thick that five girls holding hands could not surround one of them.

It took us all week to cut down one pine tree, which then had to be cut to various sizes. Each of us earned 250 gm of bread. My father asked the commandant to send the young girls to a men's brigade to relieve us from the hard labour — and this was done. From that time the work went faster. We worked at cutting wood in the forest through the whole winter while others carted the cut logs to a river called Vychegda. From there the river carried the timber to southern Russia. But the river was frozen over, so the timber waited for the spring thaw. In the spring our brigade was given large hooks with which to roll the logs into the river, right down to the bottom layer.

My friend Bronia and I were standing on one such pile of logs when the water took us, carrying us to the middle of the river while the commandant ran along the bank shouting for us to push the frozen timber away or we would block the whole river. And so my friend and I floated with the current far from everyone. It began to get dark and the timber to which we were holding on began to thaw and fall apart. We ended up on a single log. The river became fast running and we told each other that this was the end of us. But the water carried us closer to the bank. I saw a small birch growing in the river. My friend jumped in and grabbed a branch, then I caught her and gradually we reached the bank. It was very dark already and we didn't know which way to go. Suddenly a bearded man emerged from the thick forest and asked what we were doing there. We told him that the water had carried us down with the timber. He told us he would guide us out to a road, and only asked that we should tell no one that we had seen him. He was an escaped prisoner.

We walked 30 kilometres back to the hamlet and when we reached it we saw that no one was looking for us because the commandant had said that we had drowned. The Vychegda River is very wide and flows into the Dvina River. In that way the timber is floated down from Arkhangelsk into the depths of Russia.

My sister was fifteen, so she was not taken to the forest, but each day she had to walk 30 km with the mail.

We were not permitted to write to families in Poland for six months. Our family did not know what had happened to us. When we were allowed to write, uncles and aunts sent us food parcels — which helped greatly because for six months those who worked received one small dish of oats and 250 gm of bread. I used to give my portion to my father because I greatly feared that he may fall ill and die. I toasted my portion of bread on the fire, dug in the snow and collected berries. There were a lot of them in our area.

After my brother died my mother became very ill and the woman doctor said that nothing would save her. I wrote to the family in Poland. One day we felt that the end was close for Mama, but my father and I had to go to work in the forest and we were not allowed to stay by her. We thought that when we returned Mama would no longer be alive. But a miracle happened. When we returned to the hut Mama was sitting up in her bunk. Much later we learnt that after receiving the letter from Russia the family offered Mass in the cathedral at Lutsk for my Mama's return to health.[6]

Account of Ryszard Rzepczyński

We arrived in Kotlas after about three weeks and were transferred onto sleds again. This part of our journey lasted just over a week. We arrived at Ukhta, near the Ukhtimka River and were put in a camp in which we were permanently housed in barracks made of raw timber logs. There was ice outside and inside the barracks and everything was frozen or wet. That was how our life in Siberia began.

A few days after getting to the camp young men were separated from the old ones. The old men were given work in the camp sawing timber boards. The young men and women were taken to the forest to cut down trees. It was February, halfway through winter, with a great deal of snow and temperature of -60°C....

In the northern regions there is no night in summer. There is no sun, but it is still light enough to read a paper. It was hard to get used to it being light twenty-four hours a day, but we did. However, we could not get used to the bedbugs. Our barracks were made from logs with moss packed between them. This was a perfect breeding ground for bedbugs. Sometimes when we woke at night our arms and legs would be covered with them. We tried to get rid of them by burning fires inside, hoping the smoke would drive them out, but this was not successful.

We lived and worked in that camp through summer, autumn and winter. Part of the way through the winter I received a telegram. It was seven o'clock in the evening one day in February 1941. The message told me that my mother had died. The winter nights were long and dark, but I decided to walk the 25 kilometres to the camp where my family was. I packed some bread, matches and an axe in a sack and took off in the knee-deep snow. I walked all night and got to the outskirts of the camp at about 7:00 A.M. There, in the makeshift cemetery, I saw my father and younger brother digging a grave. I stopped and helped them and when we finished we went back to the camp. There a few people had gathered together and prayed. Then we carried the coffin with my mother's body in it to the cemetery. When the funeral was over we put up a wooden cross.[7]

Account of Marysia Pienta (née Wilgut)

After a long journey on the train, we reached our final destination in Russia. We exited the boxcar and were packed into sleighs. It was the only way to cross the frozen Dvina River which would lead us to Siberia. We arrived in Camp Reczuszka. The first night no one could sleep. We were in barracks filled with bugs living in the moss between the logs. I heard so much crying that night, not only from children, but from the adults as well. There was so much sorrow and so much fear. My father and brother worked at a logging camp. We saw them only on the weekends. Jasia and my mother had to work, while Zosia, Krysia and I went to school. Ela and Basia were at day-care. Because of the horrible conditions, my two youngest sisters did not survive. I'll never forget burying my sisters, Basia and Ela. My father and brother had to hold the tiny wooden boxes up with sticks so they would not turn over because the graves were filled with water. The image of my mother lying across their graves still remains frozen in my heart and mind.[8]

Account of Elaine Beres (née Nykiforuk)

They took Dad to the hospital at Dzujewka from there. The next day they put the rest of us in a different wagon and took us to Sverdlovsk. They wouldn't let me stay with my dad. In Sverdlovsk everybody was separated to go their own way. They sent me to Vrchaturia where I was told to get out of the wagon. I was told to walk along the railway tracks so that I could meet my family. I went by myself. I walked for two hours and finally reached a place called Unslak Leso Pilki. That was where people from my village were working, loading wagons with all kinds of boards. When they saw me they couldn't get over it that I had been walking all by myself. One man said to me: "Child, you have nothing here to come for." They then told me about my mom and sister passing away. One of them told me exactly where to find John [Elaine's brother] and the other children.

When I came into the room where my family lived John was out working. Someone told him that I had come and he came back from work. It was just before dinner. When we saw one another we couldn't even speak because we cried so much. For a very long time I couldn't talk about it with John. My mother was so young, just 39, and my sister was only 14.

John told me about the things that happened to the other children and himself after my mother passed away. They had nothing to eat and the neighbors had been sharing food with them. There was one lady who had been our neighbor in Poland. She now lives near me in Australia and she told me everything that happened after our mother passed away.

The four youngest children were taken to a Russian orphanage, where they had a better life, clean clothes, clean bedding and food. When I came to John I visited the children in the orphanage and saw that they didn't have it too bad in there. The Communists wanted them to become Communists also. I did not take them away from the orphanage at that time because John and I would not have been able to feed them with the small amount of money we earned. I would visit them often in the orphanage.

I remember Jim in the orphanage, but not Stanley. Jim didn't want much to do with me. Carol and Czesia spent a lot of time with me. Whenever I left Czesia would cry and beg me in Russian to take her back with me. She cried: "Please take me with you, don't leave me behind!" I can never forget her words.[9]

Account of Józefa Pucia-Zawada

There were quite a number of children in the orphanage in Aktimir, together with several adults who looked after them. We slept on the floor, next to one another. Things were not good in this orphanage and there was not much food. The reason was that the authorities wanted Polish children to go to their *Dzietdom* (orphanage). The Poles resisted as much as they could because they said that all traces of children who went there would disappear.

Russians came to the orphanage persuading the children to come under their authority. They promised that we would get lots of bread, milk and sweets. I was always terribly hungry so, naturally, I wanted to go with them. My brother Miecio begged me and them that I was only little and did not know what I was doing and that they should not take me. The Polish lady in charge also begged them, so they left me there.

Children who did go to the Russian orphanage died from hunger because Russian children stole everything from them. One little boy called Jasiu came back to our orphanage, but by then he was mentally ill. It turned out that in the night children had poured kerosene over his legs and set it alight because he would not give them his bread.

In our orphanage children contracted an eye disease and the Russian doctor, a good man, said: "What can I give you little fishes?" But he had a bottle of fish oil and gave us a teaspoonful each every day and the illness passed. Later on we had lesions in our mouths and the doctor said it was scurvy. They brought a sack of potatoes and onions. From then on we were not so hungry and the lesions in our mouths healed.

Father, who had been in the hospital again, was released — very weak and thin, but healthy. He brought a bag of biscuits with him. There was general joy when the lady supervisor gave some to all the children. Somehow Father attached himself to the orphanage, doing odd jobs. He made slippers out of blankets for our feet and woven sandals from jute. When news came that the orphanage was to be moved to Ashkhabad,

Father joined the army, telling Miecio to look after us. As he was leaving Father said that he would get abroad quicker with the army and would then take us. There was no other way out because they would not let him go with the orphanage. He said that he might meet our mother who had perhaps joined a women's army unit.

When the time came to leave Russia only children were allowed to go. Their adult caretakers had to remain in Russia. Later two ladies were allowed to go with us. It was said that it was thanks only to Gen. Sikorski that this small group of Poles was allowed to leave.

I remember that when we boarded the darkened ship together with the military we had to keep very quiet and were not allowed to show any lights because the captain was afraid that a German U-boat might torpedo us. Our beloved Miecio cuddled us to him at night, telling us stories about a boy from Warsaw called Wicuś. This Wicuś was in different places every night and had different adventures. Poor Miecio took care of us, yet was only 13 years old himself.[10]

Account of Władysława Bagińska-Polakiewicz

The ninth year of my life up to the time when we celebrated our first Christmas in that inhumane land included experience of the sudden storms of war — from September to February — and ten months of events in Siberia through which I lived. It is not easy to reach so far back in memory by myself. I am lucky, however, to have a mother and was able to ask her to tell me a little:

"Mummy, what was our Siberian Christmas Eve like?"

"Well, you see, that was a difficult experience ... there was nothing to eat.... At the table that evening all of us prayed together first and then sat quietly, deep in our own thoughts, drinking hot water. Albinek (my youngest uncle) was not there and we did not know where he was. Outside — frost far below zero. It was beautifully white, the snow glistening from the stars and the moon. Just beyond the barracks the mighty forest hummed, heavy with snow. And on such a night Albis returned from somewhere in shirt sleeves, but carrying bread for which he had exchanged his coat. We felt immediate relief and joy while Albis broke up the bread, handing a good-sized piece to each of us. And we shared the bread in place of the traditional wafer. After we had finished it we sang loudly: *Boże coś Polskę....* Perhaps there were also tears shed as a gift to the Holy Babe before sleep that evening."...

"Mummy, and at Auntie Stasia's — had everyone died by then?"

"All of them, or almost all ... eight people (the children died later in Kazakhstan).... Only Stasia's three-year-old Genia was saved and here, at our place, Józek and Mietek. And Genia, as you know, was already very anemic, extremely weak and covered in scabs, had lost her hair and could only whisper.... Stasia fed her for as long as she could with milk drawn from her after the death of little Romek, who had been born in Siberia — I have not told you that before...."

[T]he significance of that Christmas Eve was extremely profound and is etched forever in our hearts.... The holy, quiet evening was shared with us by a young Jewess with her four-year-old son, Witek. She found shelter and protection in Siberia with our family and stayed for a considerable time.[11]

Account of Władysław Jarnicki

We walked for several days through the snow drifts, sleeping in barns in villages along the way. When we asked for food we were given hot water, the so-called *kipiatok.* A woman who had been too late for the sled, and who marched with us with a baby at her breast, unwound the baby, already stiff and frozen. We cried over that baby but had to continue on our journey. We reached our destination after several days. There was a large building and outside there were already many people with luggage and children standing under the open sky in the snow.

There was a commission inside the building which had our papers. They divided us into groups and gave us provisions for three days. Some Communist youths came for us, wrapped in animal skins so that only their faces were visible. I was glad to be with my family and my brother, but I was sent to work on breaking rocks in the frost, without gloves. We then had to load them onto carts. Being without suitable clothing, people began to get sick and die.

We laid a complaint and the commission came and decided that this was work for prisoners and not for people in our category. They transported us to settlements and from there adults were selected for cutting down forests. Our single-room huts were built of timber, which was covered with moss serving as an environment for various insects which would not let us sleep at night. Our settlements had been built by exiles from the 1930s, probably Ukrainians, whom hunger and frost had killed. The same fate awaited us before long.

Around us there was nothing to be seen except the forest and the sky. Now and again we saw a polar bear. Had we wanted to escape there was no knowing in which direction to go, but without food there was no possibility of planning anything like that.

Our place of work in the forest was between three and six kilometers from the settlement. We had to be there by 7:00 A.M. Late arrival could mean a court appearance and the court was 30 km away from the village. One had to go there on foot. The court would deduct 25 percent of the wage for three months. If one was late a second time it meant a loss of 50 percent of the wage. We worked six days a week, eight hours a day, except Sundays.

We were able to buy one bottle of vodka and a packet of tobacco at Easter. The food was very poor and not enough of it. Twice a day we had some fish soup. Children received 300 grams of bread. There were two types of work. In one people were paid on results, while those on daily work were paid regardless of how much they worked. The former received 1200 grams of bread and the latter 800. We had to go to work even when the temperature was 40 degrees of frost [-40°C]. We were issued with boots made of blankets and lined with cotton wool. I also worked when there was 50 degrees of frost. At such times I was issued a padded long-sleeved jacket and a similar short-sleeved one.

Due to inadequate nutrition people were afflicted with snow blindness and on our way back from work at dusk we had to go in single file, holding on to those who could see. After some time the Soviets brought cod liver oil and following a week's treatment with this we recovered our sight.

During that time my wife also fell ill with a high fever. There was no other doctor in the vicinity except one Polish doctor, who told us he could not help because he had no medication—just a thermometer. I went to see a neighboring villager who had a cow. I gave him a feather pillow we had brought from Poland and he gave me a liter of milk. My wife felt a little better, but she was very weak. When I returned from work in the forest the next day I saw my wife crying. When I asked what was wrong she showed me an instruction that she was to go to court because she had not been to work. At that point a runner came up with a newspaper which had a large headline: AMNESTY FOR POLES. However, in our settlement no one had told us about this.

I went to work the next day, but the commandant still did not say anything. The day after only half the people went to work, the rest remaining in the barracks, but still receiving their bread. It was four days before the commission came and, in the presence of our NKVD, told us that under the amnesty we were free.[12]

Account of Anita Paschwa (née Kozicka)

We passed Novosibirsk, Tomsk, and Asino, and from here we were transferred from the boxcars to a horse and sleigh. Covering our faces with blankets, we arrived at the prison camp called Zalomnaya. This camp was used for the Russian prisoners and it still had barbed wire around it. We were told that soon they would take it down, because we couldn't escape from here even if we wanted to. This camp was located on the Chulym River, which was used for loading wood.

The minute we arrived in Zalomnaya, my niece Nina and I got a severe case of chicken pox. My sister had to go to work the next day cutting down trees so I, with high fever, had to be the nurse and doctor for both of us. I couldn't wait in line for bread and a cup of watery soup, so for the next two days my family was hungry. But somehow God was good to us and we survived this ordeal.

Sunday was the only day off from work. Being cold and hungry, some people were composing and singing songs about this horrible place. I remember just one of them: "Zalomnaya, Zalomnaya, you're a prisoners' camp where our Polish group has suffered so much!"

The children had to go to school in July and August which was at this time spring, summer and fall. Then in September it was winter again until late June. The winter lasted ten months and the temperature reached about 60 degrees below zero almost every few days. There was no water well so during July and August we used river water from Chulym. But for the other ten months we used snow and ice as our water for drinking, cooking and washing. To wash two pillowcases, I had to spend two hours to thaw the snow. There was no electricity, no radio or newspaper. We didn't know what was going on in the world. We had a small wood stove for cooking, warming the barracks, and lighting the cabin which had no wall at the top so the next-door family could hear us talk and we could hear them. We had no secrets at all.

After a year staying at Zalomnaya, we were moved to another camp a few miles away from there. We were moved to a huge barrack, and they showed us our cabin with an open top, the same kind as in Zalomnaya. When I went to explore this huge building in Guzary I almost fainted when I saw my two best friends from Tomaszgród where my sister Maria lived. They cried and cried and we hugged each other. They all thought that we went to Warsaw. They came here in February 1940, when we were also on the list.

In Siberia people were dying like flies, especially the oldest and the youngest. One man who rode with us in our boxcar was sent to Siberia for the second time. He was about 75 years old. Before he died he said, "This is God's will that my body will rest here in Siberia. I just don't know why God punishes me so severely. I have not done any crimes, I just worked very hard all my life by farming and improving my land, and look at me now! For that hard work I'm dying!" In two days he passed away and was buried in a shallow grave because the ground was frozen and we didn't have the machinery to dig the graves for those dying people. There was no food or medication for the survival of the very old and the very young.

At this time I was almost twelve and a half years old. Being raised in the woods almost on my own I was determined to survive no matter what. There were many pine trees so I tried to eat pine buds and sucked on the branches and this seemed to satisfy my hunger. Hunger is the most terrible thing. First your stomach growls, then you get a headache and feel very tired and weak, then you just lie down and don't care about the world around you. These were my symptoms in Siberia. My sister Maria always begged me not to give up because all of us would die of starvation.

You see, while the grownups were at work ten hours each day, the children and very old people stood in line outside the Russian kitchen for the cup of watery soup for each person and a piece of bread. So I had to wait in 50 or 60 below zero weather in line to get this precious food. On top of it all, I was a babysitter for Nina who was almost seven. Many times I was pushed out of line and had to go to the end of the line. When I got to the kitchen the cooks announced that they had no soup for us until tomorrow, but luckily we were to get our piece of bread. Many times I took little Nina with me so that when they would see this little girl they might give us a little more soup, but they didn't care. Finally I told Nina to stay in the barracks while I stood in line. This soup was made of fish bones and potatoes, if there were any. This was our meal for the day. The older people who tried to push me out of the line always told me that I'm young and I can survive this cold weather better, but they will freeze to death if they have to stand in line for 10 minutes longer. I just couldn't understand why our own people were so cruel to children.

One day a disaster happened to me. My brother-in-law, being a magician in Poland, somehow befriended a Russian food storage manager on the collective farm. Walter had mentioned to him that Maria still had two beautiful pillowcases from Poland and it would be nice if he would give those to his wife. Walter told the manager that all he wants is one kilo of grain in exchange for the pillowcases. So the Russian manager said yes. The next day I took those two pillowcases and left Nina with two of my friends, Sabina and Irene, whom Nina remembered from Tomaszgrod. I went alone to that storage place which was about two miles away from our camp. I gave the pillowcases to the storekeeper and he poured me one kilo of grain. I said thank you and left his storage place. I walked for a mile toward our camp and suddenly from nowhere an NKVD man began to follow me. The faster I walked, the faster he followed me, so I began to run but not for long because he screamed at me to stop or he would shoot me. So, shaking, I stopped and began to cry but he was very angry and asked me what I had in that bag. I told him that I had some grain. At this moment he grabbed it from me and ordered me to follow him to the headquarters. When I walked in he asked me who gave me that grain. I told him that I didn't know his name. "Oh, so he was a man."

I said yes. He grabbed my hat, pulled it from my head, pulled my hair and kicked me with his heavy leather boots, yelling, "Now if you want to live, tell me the name of this man or I will kill you!" At that moment he pressed his gun against my head and kicked me again. I was so scared that I thought it was the end of my life. Not knowing what was going to happen to me at that time I urinated so much on the floor that his shoes got wet from it. Then he jammed the gun into his pocket, pulled my hair again and pushed me with all his might into this urine. He stuffed a dirty rag into my hand and told me to wipe it or lick it, but the floor had to be clean. At this moment another NKVD man walked in and when he saw my face very red and my hair so messed up and my clothes all wet, he asked me what happened to me, but this bully would not let me talk because he showed him the grain bag and said, "She is stealing government food from the storage and won't tell me how she got it or who gave it to her." Then the other NKVD man who entered that office quietly put his arm on my shoulder and asked me if I paid for the grain. I said yes, with two pillowcases. He replied that he must see my sister Maria here in his office when she comes home from work. He sent me back to the barracks but kept the grain in his office. You see, my sister Maria was severely punished for giving me those pillowcases. She had to work one hour later every day for about two months. It was a crime for us to associate with the Russian people who were living there for many years.

Spring 1941 was a much happier time for me and my friends. As you know, spring starts at the end of June and lasts till the end of August in Siberia and after that again winter lasts for almost ten months.

We found out that there were Russian villages about four miles away from our camp. We would run on the bank of the Chulym River and take any clothing or bedding pieces and exchange them for food received from the Russian government, such as old potatoes left over from the last year. One potato a day made my stomach very happy. I always went with my friends, but never alone. You see, hunger forced me to overcome my great fear of the NKVD.[13]

Account of Eva [Ursula Sowińska]

After 42 days the long, macabre journey came to an end. We arrived in Siberia, the land so awfully well-known in history. We learned that our destiny was to be a concentration camp, whose main project was the building of a railway on the vast Siberian plains.

When I first entered the barracks I was still decently dressed and created a hateful atmosphere among the women in the room, for they guessed from my appearance that I was just at the very beginning of my Russian career. For a few hours I listened to spiteful remarks and maledictions. The very same evening, however, after my first contact with the NKVD (People's Commissariat for Internal Affairs) authorities, their poverty and abandonment deeply moved my heart with compassion and made me share with them everything I brought with me from home. Thus I won their hearts and became their favorite. Everything I did or said was accepted.

I was allowed many privileges, the highest of which many will think strange. I was given the right to use the room lavatory any time I wished. During the first few days I almost died from constipation because I was ashamed to use it in front of such a huge number of witnesses. Then too, the women never stole the bread I would save. None of them ever addressed me as Comrade, a common name given to all prisoners. Instead they called me Barishnia, which means "young lady."

But soon I was removed from their side as a destructive and undisciplined element.

Meanwhile I worked; with distress I took part in the railway work, which taxed my strength to the utmost. Carrying heavy stones and wood all day long extracted every bit of energy which bread, given once daily, and transparent watery soup, given twice daily, could give. Illnesses due to starvation and dirt such as typhoid fever, scabies, avitaminosis, and haemocolitis, were commonplace. The human machine was doomed to the last moment for work, and usually at night some poor souls were ready for departure to another world, bearing on their faces the expression of death, a warning addressed to their executioners.

Such experiences brought upon my mind the frightening shadow of doubt in those great things which our soul always seems to miss while we are alive — and strangely enough — the same experiences enlightened me with a priceless, however constantly disturbed, faith....

Unquestionably the technique of the Russian leaders to destroy a human being is slow and methodical. When the Communists realized that I was the youngest in my family, they felt sure that I would be easily frightened and would talk. How wrong they were!

My father was a great patriot of my nation. When the war started he thwarted the attempts of the German and Russian armies to exploit the land and the people. Therefore he was doomed by both the Germans and the Russians. Having the instinct of a persecuted animal, he used to hide himself successfully in towns and villages. His head was priced high.

One morning about three o'clock, in the horrid barracks of the concentration camp, there appeared the NKVD who gathered me as though I were a lifeless piece of scrap and took me far away to another prison, to a place I did not know. It was a distance of about four or five hours journey in a heavy track-car loaded with prisoners and covered all around to prevent observation, contact with civilians, or escape.

We arrived there quite late in the morning. After formal questioning I was sent to a collective prison cell, full of women from different nations, where we had nothing to do but curse, starve, and philosophize. Every night someone was summoned for the so-called questioning from which they sometimes returned, sometimes not.

In the first questioning session I was told that I was free and would be allowed to do whatever I pleased, provided that I would tell them where I thought my father was. Bravely I told them that he never returned. I was informed that very soon they would make me tell the truth and that my father was captured waiting for trial and execution.

In the second session I received a horrible beating and was told that my mother and sister were already among the angels, in whom we believed, and soon they were going to enable me to join my noble ancestors. I still believed in the optimism of my subconscious and in the parting words of my mother and gave their questions such idiotic answers I once taught myself that I nearly paid with my life for the joke.

In the following questionings, I stopped being a heroine. Having in mind the death of my mother and sister, I exposed myself with full resignation to death, by keeping to the story that I did not know, I did not know.... My determined stubbornness grew proportionally to their cruelty.

After many nights of grueling questioning, worn out, hungry, frightened, and ill, I was sentenced to solitary confinement, from which, to my strange joy, I was promised never to return alive.

I was taken far down to the basement by two swearing, most disgraceful, and disgusting women guards, in front of whom the most demoralized prostitute of Europe would create the pleasant contrast of an angel. I received painful kicks from both of them. Their final push sent me falling down the stairs. I hurt my body awfully while they laughed devilishly behind me. Finally they joined me and led me along the narrow corridor whose walls were covered with a thick, wet layer of something jelly-like, which promised the desperate longing for death. Meanwhile they informed me what a degenerate I was. We stood in front of a narrow, tall door. I could see that even they hesitated to open it. At last it stood wide open. The ghastly smell of something, like spoiled meat, attacked my nose. They stood behind me and with evil laughter wished me to survive, but in case I did not they asked me whether I wanted my dead body to be transported in an honor bag to my country and be buried among the kings. I was silent and I prayed.

Suddenly again I received a painful kick with which I entered the cell, falling down. The door closed behind me, and I remained motionless in the darkness full of the indescribable stench.

I was half alive from exhaustion, hunger, and pain. I was dreaming, half consciously, about strange things. It seemed that I rested comfortably and that somebody handed me many good things to eat. My ears were filled with heavenly music, which I am not able to express; the regions of my imagination were full of the strange kingdom of peace and happiness.

I did not know the length of these dreams. I always awoke to full consciousness, wet with vomit and urine.

From the small high window near the ceiling, anemic beams of light were falling. It must have been day already. My sight became gradually accustomed to the darkness, and with the help of the light I stared around the cell. I was dizzy and weak, for the smell became unbearable.

In the corner of the cell I noticed the shapeless heap of something.... I thought naively that it must be a bed. I was already partly poisoned by smell, and believed that I was in a gas chamber.

The thought of dying on a bed created an irresistible attraction. Crawling on the stone floor with great difficulty, I approached the imagined bed and touched it. To my inexpressible insane horror and disappointment, I recognized a corpse as the source of the stench. I understood then that I was sentenced not only to death but also to insanity.

The body was covered with rags, only a helpless hand showing as a sign of woe. It seemed of medium size and rested uncovered on the floor.

I exclaimed something and began screaming and actually screeched for a long time, calling my mother and God himself.

My throat pained terribly, and I was in a half-faint when in that deadly silence from the very corner where the body lay came a mysterious knocking...then silence...then knocking.... The body arose and, standing to its full height, approached me. Logic did not help me. I yelled again, for the body seemed to take a step forward. I implored it not to touch me.

Then a sane idea fully recovered my physical strength, and I thought of escaping through that small narrow window, the blessed little spot of fresh air which saved my life. Endlessly and crazily I jumped towards it, wearing down my nails until my fingers bled. My face, chest, ankles, and feet were cruelly hurt. Many times I fell down and still did not realize that I should never be able to reach the window, which was far too small even for my head. It was the despair of a bird in a cage.

Then finally I fell asleep — or perhaps fainted....

I awoke again in the room of questioning. They gave me something to drink. By this time I was losing my memory very frequently, but still I heard the questions. I did not know what they meant. I was continuously stammering but nobody was hurting me for it.

My wretched appearance must have created a slight pity even in their callous hearts. My brain was not responsible for anything I did. I had no control over any of my physiological actions, but this I found out later from my real friends.

The questioning did not stop, but it was without physical torture. But what did it matter? I was going to die anyway.

I was returned to the crowded room of political prisoners and remained under the tender care of those poor, bewildered women amongst whom a person could find real spiritual princesses. They convinced me that my mother and sister were alive. They kept me as clean as was possible and forced my ration of bread and soup into me.

After a long, long time, perhaps several months, an amnesty for all political prisoners from my country was declared. I did not meet the news with sane understanding. But those saintly women explained. Finally I understood....

I do not regret that I spent my youth in this great school of life. At the bottom of human existence I found, against the background of cruelty, the immense genius of life in tormented, enslaved hearts. In the shameless nakedness of human nature, in rottenness, poverty, and endless struggle, I found the treasure of altruism, understanding, and self-denial. Only this is what I learned to value.

The Russian people are the most helpful, honest, and kindest people I have ever met. For it is not easy to be good under those circumstances.[14]

Account of Anna Mineyko

We traveled by train from 13 April to 8 May 1940. Many thousands of people were off-loaded at Pavlodar. We all knelt down and sang with all our strength. We sang a hymn for the month of May called "Praise the May Meadows." The Russians were cross because we were singing. They asked who started it and we all said, "I did," pointing to ourselves. We were then taken in lorries to the gulags (camps). We crossed the Irtysh River by raft and went on to Ekibastuz No 1 and then by ox-cart to the "hungry steppes."

From the moment I heard my sentence of deportation, I knew I was responsible for my family of four persons: my mother, my sister and the twins. This was a new and heavy burden that I had not previously encountered. I knew that my mother and sister would not be able to help in any way and my twins were only five years old. I became porter and quartermaster, and was soon to be the only one who could earn a living. My mother, Lili and the children were my dependants and it was a well known saying that "He who does not work does not eat...."

At first, I looked after seven hundred grazing calves. I had to chase them on the steppes and I fed the youngest from a bucket when they sucked my fingers. They had no fear. Every evening, I brought my family a bucket of milk, which was illegal, although I did it openly. We lived thus until the nomads drove the cattle to the distant steppes. Summer was short and terribly hot.

After that, I worked on construction, I worked during the summer heat wave when the bottom of the river cracked into furrows large enough to bury huge lorries. I dug clay or I mixed it with chaff or chopped straw, trampling on it with bare feet for several hours a day. Then we made bricks from the mixture and baked them in the sun. I built the walls of enormous cattle sheds and renewed with clay bricks buildings that had dissolved after downpours of rain. All the work was done with bare hands, in summer as in winter, without tools such as trowels, etc.

In winter, we poured boiling water on the clay as it froze all the time. Then snow covered everything and our black and frozen barracks had to be dug out from the white ground from which nothing stuck out or was visible. We were eaten by bedbugs and millions of lice; the fumes and smell of the boiler filled our lungs; we had chronic indigestions from lack of nourishing food....

Praying was forbidden. Nonetheless, every evening we said our prayers with children kneeling down, and with feeling. We did not stop even if someone stood behind our backs. An old Kazakh woman asked us if the prayer was to God; she asked whether we realized that she could denounce us. When I said that we did know, she admitted that she, too, had faith and prayed. She was a Muslim.

On another occasion, Kyryllo, our overseer, went away for a few days as his wife, Natasha, gave birth to her third son. Natasha came to us asking if the "old holy woman" (my mother) would christen her child with the same name as the baby I had left behind in Poland. She said that she believed in God, but her husband did not, and that if he found out he would denounce her to the Party. But, when Kyryllo came home, he came ashamed and cap in hand to ask my mother the same favor, requesting that we should not tell his unbelieving wife!

One day, a crowd of workers saw children gathered round the well. They found that my little son, Michał, was being drowned by the others. The children lowered him deep into well in the bucket, threatening to drown him unless he would steal things from our home for them. He was lowered and pulled back up, but he did not agree to anything. After being rescued, he lost his speech for a long time. Another time, a gang of children threw stones at mine who had to take refuge in our barracks.

The well was deep, with a sweep (a counter-balanced bucket). In winter we melted snow or brought water from the well in buckets the rest of the year. To use buckets in winter was useless as the whole bucketful froze before it could be got indoors. Often, fellow-prisoners cut the bucket off the well rope. It was one sort of class hatred. When they saw me going to the well, they would say I had drunk sufficient wine in Poland.

I once fell while carrying water, and the bucket cut into my leg; because I was so thin, it broke the bone. A large wound formed and went septic because of the dirt; it swelled up and turned green. I had to limp on the other leg and Mother and the children brought half buckets of water. I was saved from gangrene by an old peasant woman who applied a hot brew of dung ash to my wound. We heard the same woman howling with grief on the steppe when her eldest son was found dead, frozen in the snow....

Money had no value: everything was bartered for food. The natives were poor and primitive. Sometimes they set dogs on me; one of them bit me quite hard when I went to sell my goods in the village. Bartering was odd; for example, for one needle I received one glass of milk for a month, but I was refused two eggs for my pearl earrings. I was told the earrings were worthless as they were colorless, i.e., ugly. I now wear them every day....

Unfortunately, our reserves of fuel ran out before the end of winter. I had to melt the snow in boilers belonging to others after they had finished using them. The fuel consisted of dried cow dung. I was not always welcome. Sometimes, I was filled with despair when I found human excreta in the melted snow because then everything had to be done again.

During the worst frost, I slept on my back with the children on top of me; that made it warmer and cosier. I tucked in the three of us with blankets and animal skins, but poor Mother and Lili froze separately.

One night, wolves tore to pieces a bitch which liked us and had taken refuge under our window. The struggle was bloodcurdling and very noisy. It was horrifying and also very dangerous as the window was at ground level and a small missing pane was stuffed with rags. The next day I inspected the signs of the struggle outside the window — blood and hair.

There were days when we were entirely covered by snow and we lay in darkness day and night. There was no electricity, oil or candles. My family hardly got up from beginning of autumn until spring. I had to teach the children to walk as if after a long illness. While we were lying in the darkness and hunger, I used to tell them never-ending tales and they forgot for a time about reality and hunger. My mother used to call me Szeherezade....

One day during the summer of 1942, I was returning, tired, from work. Some people ran out to meet me, telling me in a gabble about some newcomer. A man wearing a uniform who was not known to me was waiting in our abode. He saluted me in an unfamiliar manner, explained who he was and that he had searched for me for a long time. He handed me a letter from Andrzej Czajkowski and asked me if I would risk an escape from Russia. Without any hesitation I agreed. Then I exchanged a quilt for flour and cooked a delicious gruel and we all ate our fill. It was a real feast.... So we set off to freedom.[15]

Account of Adela Konradczyńska-Piorkowska

After three weeks of this arduous journey we reached a place called Viatka in Siberia....

From the first day they instilled into children that there was no God. There was only Father *(Backo)* Stalin. In order to prove it to the children they told them to pray to God to give them sweets. And, of course, they did not get any. Next they told them to ask *Backo* Stalin for sweets; when the teacher pulled on a very thin string sweets fell from the ceiling....

Our worst fear was that the NKVD would come in the night and take us for questioning. It was their habit to come between 2:00 and 3:00 A.M. Then one could hear shouts which tore through the night as mothers and wives cried, but it was for nothing. It was not necessary to be guilty of much. For instance, Mr. Jablonski, 30, was in the habit of singing the religious song "When the dawn rises." They burst in one night and took him away for questioning. It did not help at all that he had a wife and two small children. When he came back a few months later his own wife could not recognize him. He looked 60 years old. Some people never returned.[16]

Account of Wisia Reginella (née Danecka)

The shifts varied in the mine, depending on when the wagons to be filled with coal arrived. I had the afternoon shift. The distance from home to the mine was about four kilometers. I used to return from work late and everyone hurried, all the sooner to find themselves in warm accommodations. The night was cold and clear as, bundled up to the ears, I aimed for the barracks lights. It was late, so the lights had gone out and my eyes played tricks so that I got lost, turning this way and that on the spot, not knowing which way I should go and so tired and sleepy that I did not know what to do. And so I sat down under a small tree in order to rest a little, or to wait until daylight. I was just about to fall asleep when I heard a call: "Why are you so late, Mummy?" I jumped up. No children, silence all around, everything white. I ran straight ahead for some time but, in place of the barracks, I saw a small house, as if from a fairy tale, surrounded by forest. A moment later a dog started barking. Someone came out of the little house and I called for help, that I was at the end of my strength. It was a forester's house, a few kilometers from our settlement. We did not know of its existence because our movements were restricted. Someone gave me their hand and pulled me into the hut. A woman gave me something warm to drink and rubbed my frozen hands. I could not say a word to explain why I appeared there and what for. It was some time before I could tell those people what had happened. The forester had been transferred from Moscow. They knew that there were Poles in the nearby mine but they were not allowed to communicate with anyone. They helped me a lot despite the ban. He was afraid and did not speak much, while she was pleasant, intelligent and later invited me secretly and gave me a hunted-down hare or some wood, which was hard to obtain.

On New Year's Eve in 1941 I was scrubbing the floor in the preschool and it had to be as white as snow. I not only scrubbed with a brush, but also scraped with glass or a knife so as to satisfy the teacher. If she considered that the floor was not sufficiently clean she used to tip a bucket of water over it and I had to start again. And I had left a sick child in the care of a 10-year-old daughter of a neighbor. Through my tears I saw someone running from our barracks to the preschool. What has happened? My maternal heart knew that misfortune had struck. My son [Leszek] had died. Not caring whether anyone would allow it, I ran home. I thought the world was collapsing. Although I had known that he was seriously ill I still hoped that he would recover and recently it seemed that he was feeling better.

There were no holidays there, so the next day everyone was working. It was New Year's Day and Leszek's funeral. Someone made a small coffin, I was given a horse-drawn wagon and a driver, but who was there to dig the grave? There was more than 45° of frost [-45° C]. Again kind people were found and two young lads dug the grave with picks. I will never forget the sound of lumps of soil thrown up by those few people.

I was dejected, half-conscious and the hard labor contributed to the fact that some weeks later I contracted an ear complaint with a temperature of more than 39°C. I was taken unconscious to hospital. The doctor maintained that I had ulcers in my ears and wanted to carry out a skull trepanation. I did not agree to the operation. Despite suffering I believed that I would recover, for I had to live for Basia [Wisia's daughter]. Or who would take care of her? There was no one apart from me.

The Soviet system did not allow one to become accustomed to a place and job, to enrich oneself or become friendly with the local population. We were to be transported to cutting down forests. I joined Basia straight out of hospital, bandaged like a dummy. Once more they loaded us onto goods trucks, but this time in the midst of a severe Siberian winter. There was only one little stove for the whole large truck.

I obtained some relief on the train. The swaying and jerking caused matter to seep from my ears, my temperature came down and the pain eased. Good people changed my dressings.

More than ten days later the train stopped and through the little window I saw several sleighs, the horses up to their bellies in snow. The sick and the children were to travel on these while the others had to go on foot to a village 30 km distant. Basia rode with me and a 13-year-old girl to care for her. Some people cried, others knelt or prayed. Looking at them I was reminded of Grottger's painting "Transportation to Siberia." Six children died and one woman lost her sanity.[17]

Account of Maria Gabiniewicz

The train raced on day and night. Sometimes even now I hear in my sleep the clatter of the wheels as they roll along the track....

We passed the industrialized Ural Mountains and came to an area at the edge of the tundra and steppes which was desolate, where there were no farms. Through the small window I saw low mud huts that were being swallowed up by the earth and frightened poorly dressed people. After a few days the scenery changed — the train entered the Siberian taiga. We stopped at the Uzhur railway station in Krasnoyarsk. After three hours my feet touched the ground. On the platform I saw just how many people were crowded into those boxcars. Mother met some acquaintances from Poland. We were divided into groups and taken to kolkhozes throughout the taiga. Kolkhoz Yelnichna was about 40 kilometers from the town of Uzhur. We received orders not to leave our assigned places of exile. Mother and Stach worked from dawn to dusk for one kilogram of bread. Tadek and I had to attend a Russian school, thanks to which we received 250 grams of bread each day.[18]

Account of Jane [Janina] Żebrowski-Bulmahn

After about a month of traveling, our train started getting shorter. At each major station several cars were detached and left behind. After a few more days we, too, reached our destination. Two cars were detached at Barnaul. This was going to be our new place to live. Fortunately, there were several people we knew in the other car that was left with us. In fact, there was a family of distant relatives, with a little infant, bearing the same name as ours. As long as we stayed close to each other we would share the same fate and be a support to each other, no matter what. Hard work, sickness and, ultimately, death were our destiny. We had known for many years that this was what had happened to people sent to Siberia.

Soon we were ordered to leave our cars and get into the horse-drawn wagons. Several hours later we came to a small settlement, called kolkhoz (collective farm), in the middle of a wilderness. Our location was somewhere between Novosibirsk and Barnaul. From here there was no escape, we were told. This was early August.

Our family was given one room with one twin bed for the four of us. Two adults and two children did not fit very well in this one bed, but not being used to comfort as of late, we managed and in the winter we kept each other warm. We had little bedding with us and used coats and whatever we brought to cover ourselves. There was an iron stove in the middle of the room for cooking and heating in the winter, but no fuel of any kind.

Right from the start father had to report to work for 12 hours a day, six days a week. In Russia there was no unemployment. Work had to be done even if the next day it was undone. Father talked about having to dig ditches along a certain road only to have them covered up several days later for no apparent reason. Since there was always an armed guard present, no one dared to object or ask questions.

Since mother was going through the change of life and was in danger of hemorrhaging on several occasions, father was able to convince the authorities to leave her at home with the two of us until some later date. Our mother and the relative with an infant, were the only ones not forced to work for the time being.

I was actually old enough to attend school, but because I was of small stature, father made me two years younger so I would not have to go to school and be exposed to more communist propaganda. He decided to teach me, and later my sister, himself. This was difficult with no books and no school supplies available, and father working such long hours.

As a compensation for father's work, he was given enough coupons to buy milk and bread in the local commissary. There was no money for anything else and the supplies we brought with us were very meager. Since growing children could hardly survive on this diet, mother, my sister and I busied ourselves with gathering whatever was edible in the fields.

Now it was early September and we could find handfuls of grain in the fields that had been recently harvested. We could also find some wild fruits and edible weeds. Mother made soups out of the grain and edible weeds. In addition to the bread and milk we could buy with father's work coupons, we had some nourishment.

Several Polish children and I devised a method of providing some food for our families. We were allowed to play on the piles of grain that were just gathered, so we wore long boots and filled them to the top with grain. One by one, seemingly unnoticed, we ran home and emptied the boots and returned to repeat the process. I remember gathering a whole sack of grain that way. Sometimes I wondered if the guards knew what we were doing but closed their eyes to it since most of the grain was never shipped to the intended destination anyway because of the crippled Russian transportation system. Also, some guards in Siberia seemed somewhat sympathetic to us.[19]

3. Amnesty

Milewski family memoir

[The Sikorski-Maisky agreement — the "amnesty" — was signed on July 30, 1941. It provided for the release of the deportees as well as for the formation of a Polish army on Soviet soil. The first mention of this news appears in the Milewski diary on September 1, 1941: "It was announced that Poland and Russia signed a treaty and that we are now free!" However, it was not until January 6, 1942, that the Milewski family began their journey to freedom.]

> December 15, 1941 [and ff] (Sabina) The work is cruelly hard, and being Polish does not help. We serve 60 workers, bring water and wood in from the forest, and take lunch to the forest workers. They blame us for everything: a leak in the roof, not enough kerosene because the chief did not order it — everything is our fault. The work has become unbearable. We have to leave and go somewhere, but where? Andrzej fulfills his quota at work and earns 20 rubles a day; he can now partially support us. But thanks to the Blessed Virgin Mary, things turned out differently. On December 20, 1941, through the NKVD we received 1,000 rubles by telegraph from Alfred. At Christmas time a telegram came from the Polish consulate in Arkhangelsk informing us that our travel south to join our father and the Polish army that was forming there was all arranged.
>
> (Stanisław) We found out later that the money came from Colonel Jan Milewski, my father's cousin, who was a high official in the headquarters of the Polish army in London. He sent the money though British Military Attache in Moscow. This money saved our lives.
>
> (Sabina) While Andrzej continued to work until January 4, Teresa and I stopped working on December 30th and started our preparations for the journey. (We worked from 3:00 A.M. until 9:00 P.M. every day.) Our clothes are dirty and torn. We each have a patched-up suit and a change of underwear not in the best of conditions. After quitting work we moved to Korcha. We used most of the 1,000 rubles to buy warm outer garments — cotton-and-wool-padded trousers and jackets — so that we would have a chance at surviving the 320-kilometer journey to Arkhangelsk in temperatures of -40°C. God only knows if we will make it.
>
> January 6, 1942 [and ff] New stage in our life. Having spent two days trudging from office to office to settle financial matters with the forest management, we departed at noon for our first destination: the post-office town of Chakola. We traveled

on sleds which carried mail and were pulled by horses. We arrived at Chakola in the evening and slept on wooden benches. At sunrise (9:00 A.M.!) we left for Lojezierza, 13 kilometers away, and from there, with great luck, we managed to depart the same day for Trufanogorskaya. There, we were not allowed to sleep even on the wooden benches because they were reserved for the large number of army draftees. Our further journey looks hopeless. On the following day, after a long argument, we were sent to the next station at Pocza, where we slept once more on wooden benches in an unheated room. From there we went to Srednia Jozga through which whole transports of Lapplanders and reindeer happened to be passing just then. There may have been as many as 7,000 of them. We watched them at rest. The unhitched reindeer were allowed to go into the forest to feed on the moss, which lay sometimes at a depth of two meters and which they had to dig out with their hooves and antlers. The Eskimos carry raw, frozen meat under the seats of their sleds and eat it without cooking. We spent the night in a room packed with people, mainly Eskimos, who were very friendly and cheerful. Very early in the morning on the following day we left for Pinega, the provincial capital. We arrived there on January 10, 1942, and managed to get a room in a small hotel called Dom Kolkhoznika. It was our good fortune to share the room with Mr. Rapacki, our countryman, who before the war was the mayor of the Polish town Wysoko-Litewski. We remained in Pinega until January 14, 1942. We then received a reasonable amount of provisions along with a pass to Totskoye in south Russia.

We hitched a ride on a wagon carrying meat and hay to Chelmo. Traveling 25 kilometers a day we reached Kholmogory in four days. It was very cold: around -25ºC. We had a difficult time finding lodging for the night. On the following day we managed to get a ride in a truck to Arkhangelsk and arrived there in the afternoon of January 18, 1942. We carried our belongings from the truck stop to the town where we searched for the hotel for people from the kolkhoz farms. Walking through muddy streets with occasional wooden boards, we finally found the hotel and slept in the corridor with an unseemly crowd of people. The next morning we went to the Polish consulate and received a room with an old lady on 31 Svoboda Street. We had very little to eat for the first four days. From morning till night there were long lines of people in front of every diner. The consulate gave us clothes from England: suits, sweaters, socks, stockings and shoes. We were then informed that we would be sent to Arys, near the city of Tashkent, which is much further south than Totskoye. Because we were worried about our trip, we visited the consulate daily while waiting for the train. The consulate provided us with food for our journey. Mr. Józef Miron, a deportee from Syktyfkaru, also helped us. Like us, he came here to receive provisions and train tickets for his journey south, where he will join the Polish army. The tickets are extremely hard to get.

On January 28, 1942, we boarded a sleeping compartment of the train and departed for Yaroslav. Because the train moved at a snail's pace and stopped for hours at every station, on January 30th we were still 200 kilometers from the city. We began our journey on January 6th. Since that time we have traveled 1,200 kilometers and have 4,000 to go. Our food supplies will last only for one more week. May the Blessed Mother deliver us to our destination.

We arrived in Yaroslav on the evening of January 31, 1942, and had to spend two days and nights among the worst multitude of people imaginable: mostly released prisoners on their way to join the Red Army, some of whom were half-dead, starved, and even blind. They were all dressed in dirty rags and were full of lice. Thousands, crowding together like sardines, awaited the train for days at a time. We were totally exhausted both physically and mentally. Because people were stealing, we had to sit on our suitcases. We had to fight for floor space on which to sleep. There were trains but they were reserved mainly for troop transport. We finally managed to get the tickets and to board a train. After a two-hour ride we arrived at the station in Svanovo. It was similar to the one in Yaroslav with thousands of people inside. In order to clean the station they had to evict everyone outside into the freezing cold once a day. This happened to Teresa and Andrzej. As was the case with other mothers with small children, Staś and I were allowed to stay inside, in the train-station restrooms. We spent two days and nights in this station as well. This whole pattern repeated itself time and time again. Moreover, at every station we managed to miss at least one train. And if we did get on one it was often because it was very long and started off very slowly, thus allowing us to run after it and jump on. Our suffering is simply indescribable. We have spent weeks now sleeping in lice-infested dirty rags in train stations. We can only wash our hands once every three or four days. And on top of all of this, the package containing all the clothes we received from the consulate was stolen during our attempt to jump on a train in Novki. Now we really have nothing.

After many hardships and much deprivation, on February 14, 1942, we finally arrived at Kuybyshev, the town we had been dreaming about, the town with the Polish embassy. We hoped to be able to rest there for a few days and to get some new shoes to replace the ones stolen in Novki. All we had on our feet were the *walonki.* At the station, we were kept outdoors from the time of our arrival at 3:00 P.M. until 5:00 P.M., in temperature of -25°C. Leaving Teresa and Staś with our things at the station, I ran to the embassy thinking that I would be welcomed as a hero. But they welcomed us like dogs. We were put in a school: a nest of dirt, disease and starvation. We had to sleep on the floor. I heard that 47 children had already died there in the last two months. When the shoes arrived they refused to give them to us because I was an army major's wife. There, thousands of people, trying to get to the Polish army in the south of Russia, had to camp in old schools, in crumbling buildings without heat, in the railroad station, and even outside in the freezing cold — with very little help from the Polish ambassador Stanisław Kot.

At last, on February 23rd we were given three pairs of shoes, not the four that we needed; poor Staś had to continue to travel in his torn *walonki.* We went to the station every day trying to get out of this hell. Finally, with the help of the Polish military attaché we were put on a military train. This is our second day on that train, and we are very happy knowing that in a week we are going to be with Father.

(Stanisław) From Kuybyshev the train went through Orenburg, then through the Kazakhstan cities Novokozalinsk, Arys and Dzhambul, which was close to Lugovoy. It was a long and tedious journey and food was scarce. The soldiers wound up having to share their salaries and food with the civilians because only they received pay from the Soviets. The train stopped often on high embankments at small Kazakh villages for coal and water. These villages, usually located in wide-open spaces, consisted of a few mud-brick shacks and tents. Sometimes we slid down the embankment to these villages to obtain some food and milk. Once, I almost missed the train because I could not get back up the steep slope in time. Fortunately, I managed to jump on the last carriage just in the nick of time.

We arrived at the military camp of Lugovoy, where Father was the commander of an artillery regiment, at the end of March 1942. We were exhausted and starving, mere skin and bones. We spent the first few days resting, eating and trying to recover our strength. Andrzej joined the army, which was preparing to leave the Soviet Union. The camp consisted of thousands of tents pitched on a wide, muddy plain, above which towered the Pamir Mountains covered with snow. After recovering somewhat, we boarded a train and after several days reached the port of Krasnovodsk on the Caspian Sea. Early in the morning on March 28, 1942, we boarded a ship that would bring us that evening to the Persian port of Pahlavi. (Some of the civilians were smuggled aboard despite the lack of space.) Although the conditions on board ship were very bad — we sat on the deck packed like sardines, at midday, when it became extremely hot, we were given only water and salty herrings, and the motion of the ship made us sick — nevertheless, we were happy because we were leaving the Soviet hell.[1]

Account of Vala Lewicki (née Miron)

[After the declaration of "amnesty."] And so we boarded another cattle train which was to take us to Samarkand. Food which had been allocated by Stalin for the Polish army and civilians on Russian soil was not provided on the train. ID cards, though very important documents, were useless here.

Boiling water could be obtained at stations when the train stopped. But the problem was that this train would stop and start without warning. So those who had climbed down to get hot water or to look for food, or steal something such as grain, potatoes or linseed oil cakes from other goods trains, were often left behind. This was specially hard on small children whose parents had left to forage for provisions. Apart from loving their parents, these children thought of them in terms of the things which the parents did for their comfort, pleasure and security. Now they were deprived not only of those "privileges" but also of prospects of their very existence.

The train doors were never bolted and one could easily jump down any time if one wanted to do so. At night we had to sleep closely packed on bunks or floors. So closely in fact that the hordes of lice would easily march from one person to another. If the voyage on a ship could be compared to hell, the conditions on the train were beyond all comprehension.

Having left their place to do what is natural, a passenger would never be able to find it unoccupied on return. One late night I had to "go out." So when I returned I asked the lady next to me to move over. No answer. I repeated my plea several times — still no answer. Then, huffing and puffing, I took her hand in order to place it on her stomach so she could be turned over. The hand just flopped there. I paused, wondering what to do next. Then a fearful thought struck me — it couldn't be! ... Father was watching me as though expecting something. He asked me to turn her over. Instead, I lifted her hand again and flopped it back, heavy as lead. I tried to push her, but when I could not see or hear any sign of life in her I screamed loudly: "She is dead, she is dead!" My scream of horror woke up everyone in the wagon. Someone pushed me away and struck me across the face. Instantly I stopped being hysterical until Ola put my coat over my shoulders. The coat touched the body. The realisation that we shared the same parasites made me violently sick.

Before this took place the people in the wagon had not been sociable. Afterwards they became even more quiet and withdrawn....

Thus we arrived at Samarkand, the former capital of Uzbekistan. There we found that it was much colder than we expected. Heavy rain had fallen for much of the night. Not only did we humans feel the misery, but so did our parasites. They were not at all happy about the weather and fled from our heads to warmer and less exposed parts of our bodies. What a horrible sensation it was!...

Soon after Christmas 1941 my father Jan and other men joined the Polish army in Kermine hoping to save their lives and ours. Saying good-bye to them was a heart-rending scene. None of us knew whether we would see each other alive again.

Here in sovkhoz every family, including Poles, was given, free of charge, a plot for a garden. We also received some maize kernels and melon and pumpkin seeds which, thanks to Granny's strong will, were not eaten by us there and then. The land required a lot of energy, working and digging to make furrows. Ploughing would have spoilt the grooves for irrigation. Keeping it watered after working hours was the hardest part.

Ola was becoming more sick with each day. She did not actually complain of pain, but became lethargic. Mother and I had to manage the watering, opening many little *ariks* (creeks) and a large one which was almost a river. Later we had to close them, starting with the largest. One day under the bridge we saw Uzbeks beating a man to death — he allegedly killed and ate their dog. I saw his outstretched hand, grasping at the mud and unbelievably swollen. I shivered. What brutality!

Soon my mother received news that my father and Jan were sick with typhoid in the army hospital in Kermine, a few hundred kilometres away. She went there, leaving us "safe and sound." Nothing to worry about, with Grandmother and I minding the home! It turned out to be a very, very hard task for both of us. On the second night of Mother's absence, Ola burnt with fever, became red all over and delirious. We made cold compresses for her without success. Veronica, in a panic, upset a dish of water and started to cry. Ola noticed something shining on the clay floor where she was lying and cried out: "Vala, grab it, it is gold!" She tried to grab the water herself, thinking it really was gold. I became very frightened, more so when Grandma told me to go out into the night among the Uzbeks to get help from Comrade Popov. When I found myself outside in the dark with no one except God above me and Popov before me, there was no fear in me any more, only one thought: to get Ola to hospital, wherever it might be. This was Yuma Hospital, over 20 km away.

At home, Veronica clung to me even more closely than ever. She was very frightened and threw up whatever she ate, which made her terribly thin. Every time I looked at the shadowy figure of my little sister my heart went out to her. I would rush towards her in order to fling my arms around her to comfort her. However, I did not provide much comfort. Usually at moments like that we both broke up crying. I longed for someone braver to make me braver. Then I remembered: "God is here. He is with us." Yet I did not receive much help from above.

Actually my position became even more trying since Granny contracted severe dysentery and was losing her strength rapidly. After a week which seemed like ages to me, Mother returned home, only to find misery similar to that in Kermine. Leaving little Veronica with sick, old Grandmother, Mother and I set out on foot to Yuma to visit Ola and rescue her if she was still alive. She was alive, only her long, black hair had been shorn off and her skin was peeling off everywhere. The three of us just wept there in the hospital without saying a word to each other. We dragged Ola home to recuperate.

What cruel irony! Grandmother, who was quite well-off in Poland, and who saw the mystery of God in all its fullness — in every blade of grass, in the indescribable beauty of colours and shapes of flowers, in trees, in the singing of the magnificent birds and in the stars — died of starvation and was buried in unconsecrated ground without a priest, or last rites, or proper prayers. Only comrade Popov erected a small wooden cross on her grave.[2]

Account of Stefania Buczak-Zarzycka

In July of 1941 General Władysław Sikorski signed an amnesty pact with Joseph Stalin which allowed all Polish people who had been deported to the Soviet Union to leave their settlement of enforced labour. Immediately, generals Sikorski and Władysław Anders (who had just been released from the Lubianka prison) began forming a Polish army in Kuybyshev and Buzuluk. At first ex-prisoners or single men and women joined the army, and divisions sprang up in many other towns. The young, starving ex-prisoners arrived at these camps in torn rags, infested with lice or sores and poorly shod. So many had teeth missing, particularly the front ones, because of the beatings which they had been subjected to in prison.

In our settlement the news of amnesty caused great excitement: we had become "*volni grazdanie*," a free people once more. Single people and couples with older children quickly set about building makeshift rafts in order to take advantage of the summer river current, and left us to float down the river to the nearest railway station and then to Kirov. Many accidents befell these impatient adventurers. Couples with smaller children or aged parents waited for the snows of November when they could build sleighs.

When our two sleighs had been built we set off pulling our belongings. The terrain was not flat country so the going uphill was arduous, but once we reached the summits we would jump into our sleighs and toboggan downhill. We caught the train to Kirov and there we found ourselves surrounded by thousands of other tired and hungry Poles and thousands of Soviet soldiers and their families who were in retreat from the advancing Germans. We had just been set free by one enemy and yet, ironically, together we were facing another enemy. In three small waiting rooms thousands slept standing up, literally supporting each other in the crush. Antek became upset when his cap was stolen while he slept; thieving was rife, augmenting the confusion. Even here the queues for the canteen made every purchase difficult. Ola, suffering from scurvy, stood while her broken, blistered skin stuck to her clothing. Waiting all day outside in a queue, Marysia was buried up to her hips in the snow which had fallen while she waited. Everyone had been fearful to give up their place in the queue despite the conditions. The line of people covered in snow from head to toe looked like a row of misshapen Christmas trees. At the same time, my mother was waiting in another line for soup. She was more successful. That day, too, my father lined up for sugar while I guarded our belongings.

A few days later we climbed into a wagon in which the sleeping bunks were in three tiers. The room between the top bunk and the ceiling was so small that only children could crawl into this space. At the next station the men and young women left the wagons to obtain our provisions for the next stage of the journey. Shortly after they left the train began to move again. At first we were unconcerned because the train often detoured into a siding at stops. However, to our dismay the train continued on its way. Here we were without our kinfolk, food, water, or our amnesty papers. As the days passed the effects of privation began to show. Seven days later at a small station stop our wagon door was opened by a thin, bearded young man who, we could see by his torn clothes, was an ex-prisoner. He asked us to give him a place in the wagon, and although the older women were suspicious of him they nodded their heads in approval.

He introduced himself to us as Bolek Koniecki, then jumped out, and we could see him pulling up some of the wooden pickets from the station fence. We hid these while he went to fetch water. As we traveled on he lit the fire and made a soup, doling out a few tablespoons to each person like communion. Immediately the atmosphere warmed. He assumed a paternal role in the wagon and we welcomed his protection. However, he had one ghastly disadvantage: his lice, which we all dreaded catching.

One morning we heard a whimper from one of the top bunks. Stasia cried out that her brother had stopped moving, therefore I was sent up to see what was wrong because the space was too small for an adult. I touched the boy's arm but he did not respond, so I began to drag him towards the edge of the bunk for close inspection. Bolek helped me to bring him down, whereupon the women covered him with his coat and placed him by the wagon door. Anxiously, we waited for the train to stop so that we could give him a Christian burial. His family had already suffered unhappy circumstances. His mother and younger brother had died in Siberia, his father and older sister had been left behind with the others looking for food, so only his sister was present.

Two days passed without a stop and then on the third day it was decided that the body could no longer remain in the wagon. Bolek picked up the remains and stood near the door, ready to drop the body at a small railway station as we passed it. However, as we approached a small station tears welled up in his eyes, and shaking his head he put down the body. Going to the back of the wagon he whispered that he had already buried too many of his friends in prison. Pani Maria Frankiewicz took charge of the situation and ordered me to take the legs while she held the upper body. As the train slowed down at a signal box, we threw out the body of the boy trusting decency that he would receive a burial. I looked back to see his coat torn away from his face by the wind and each proceeding night, for many nights, his face would appear to me in nightmares and I would wake screaming.

Five weeks after we had left Kirov we passed over the Ural Mountains, covered in fir trees, to reach central Asia. I peered out of the wagon door to see my first desert. Miles and miles of sand led at last to Samarkand....

Three days of desert led to our next stop at the small town of Kamashy, where we were met by a Polish representative who informed us that the army could not accommodate families and we would have to journey on to the next kolkhoz. Disheartened and given a few provisions, we were promised that we would be informed when the army had fully organised. Our baggage was placed onto an arba pulled by bullocks while we followed our Uzbek guide in single file. We were unable to communicate with him because he was unable to speak Russian, therefore we followed him, not knowing clearly our direction or even how long our journey would take....

While at the kolkhoz we compared our lifestyle in Poland with that of the Uzbek people. This once nomadic tribe was forced to settle in this district by the Soviets, so they were also in the process of adapting many of their customs to their new circumstances. Tall, handsome and yellow-skinned, the people wore eastern clothing and were Islamic. They prayed in rows five times a day and had not Russified their language or culture. We could only communicate with their teacher and local shopkeeper. However, we could not purchase anything because the store supplied very little. We could not even barter for goods because our clothing and possessions did not interest these people. Our only currency were coloured buttons and hair ribbons with which we bartered for *lepioshka*. By the time we left the kolkhoz, our clothing was held together by strings and stitches....

Then, at the end of April, a Polish soldier rode into the kolkhoz, dismounted and with a cry of delight began hugging us in turn. Of course we were thrilled to see a soldier but could not quite understand his joy at seeing us until Ola shouted: "Bolek, it's Bolek."

We were amazed at his transformation into such a handsome man. Again, our salvation was brought about by him. He told us that the army had been formed for months and the evacuation of families was already taking place. We would have to hurry in order to catch the next transport. Bolek arranged our journey, then hastily hugged us goodbye. He was commissioned to travel to the various outlying kolkhozes to gather isolated families like ourselves, and we told him of families we knew to be in other collectives. He left us within an hour of his arrival because it was too dangerous for him to travel the steppe at night. His parting gift was a handful of salt and we hoped that we would all meet up again at the army's headquarters....

Ola, together with our teenage girls, joined the junior women's army corps (*junaczki*) and was sent to Kitabu, where she undertook a training programme. My mother and Marysia remained with the army, working with the units. Antek and I were sent to the orphanage very reluctantly, as we were told that this was the most secure way to ensure our departure from Russia. If for some reason our parents were forced to remain, our future would not be jeopardised. Of course, we did not accept adult logic and deeply resented our separation from the family.

The orphanage was situated in the town hall where we slept on the floor and ate porridge on the row of tables joined together in the centre of the room. The effects of illness and years of malnutrition were visible in the apathy and lethargy of the children. We were not continuously active as one would expect children to be; instead, we tended to be much more subdued. Some lessons and stories were organised but our concentration spans were short. More and more children joined us from *dyetdom* (Russian orphanages), children who had forgotten most of their Polish language. With us, too, were Ukrainians and Jewish children. Two-tiered bunks were built in order to accommodate the growing numbers. One day an Uzbek brought a two-year-old girl who became the youngest child there. The Uzbek told us that girl's name was Mayra and that her mother had died at his kolkhoz. One of the supervisors, Pani Kozak, adopted her immediately, providing her with at least a surname—some identity. Another new arrival, Bogdan, survived only four or five days. Unable to contact his parents, our supervisors arranged for his funeral. But only days later his mother turned up at the doorstep of the orphanage asking to see Bogdan in order to tell him that his father had just passed away. We all stood around the doorway to see our visitor and we witnessed the teacher telling the mother, rather coldly, that her son had died and she advised her to return to the kolkhoz. The teacher turned away from the woman but we stood there watching her reaction. The woman did not show emotion but remained frozen for about fifteen minutes. Thereupon she collapsed and died at once. No warning, no cry. Then the teachers took charge of her and we were hurried away from the scene.

The Uzbeks knew of the date of our departure before we did: our blankets were stolen as we slept on what would become our last night in the Soviet Union.

At last, in June 1942 our long-awaited departure was finally under way. Women and children were organised into the railway wagons first and then the army climbed aboard.

I caught a glimpse of my mother shivering with malaria, her legs so unbelievably swollen that she was being dragged towards the train by Marysia. Here I did not see either my father or Ola. At the next station, even more people crowded into the train while those who had died were being taken off from the coaches. I saw one such person being carried down in a stretcher followed by Marysia and her friend Basia, both sobbing loudly. Suddenly, I began to call out for my mother, realizing that she was the one on the stretcher. I began to shout and push my way through people to the door until, by some miracle, I heard her voice calling out to me from the next wagon, calling for me to be still.

The woman on the stretcher had been Basia's mother. During the following months, until the time we began our voyage to Africa, all the members of Basia's family died en route (four people).

The train moved off again and by morning we reached the port of Krasnovodsk. There, without protection from the intense sun and heat, we waited all day to board the ship. Heaven and earth created such intense heat that it became painful to breathe. Instead of a cool sea breeze, our lungs were filled with the foul odour of oil from the Baku oilfields. We could not reach the water itself because the shoreline and sea were covered in oil. We were even forced to buy drinking water from the Russians. Late in the afternoon we saw our transport, a fleet of fishing boats, and we lined up to go aboard these boats; our papers were checked yet again by the NKVD and Polish representatives. With a hoot of the whistle and the casting off from the wharf we looked forward to a better tomorrow, away from Russian jurisdiction.[3]

Account of Tadeusz Pieczko

The Polish government-in-exile in London was fully aware of the plight of its citizens enslaved by Russia but could do very little about it. When Hitler attacked the Soviet Union on June 22, 1941, the Polish government saw an opportunity to come to the assistance of its people. Eventually, Stalin allowed a Polish army to be formed in Russia to fight the Germans. He also agreed to release the deportees and to hand over Polish children to the International Red Cross. Be that as it may, he was in no great hurry to liberate the thousands of Polish laborers. They represented a free work force which would be difficult to replace because so many of his young and able-bodied men were conscripted into the armed forces. The Poles enlisted in their new army in droves; they were not as anxious to serve in the Russian army despite Soviet pressure. Since our labor camp was located quite far form the staging area, the men in our group were never able to join the Polish army.

The Polish government wanted to get as many of its children as it could out of the Soviet Union as soon as possible. After many days of painful deliberation, my parents decided to let me and my older brother take part in the evacuation; otherwise, we would have most certainly starved to death in a matter of weeks. Most of the men worked far away from the village and returned to their families only on weekends. And so, when the time came for my brother and I to leave, we never had a chance to say good-by to our father. We were loaded on wagons drawn by horses and camels and taken to the nearest town (Frunze), which took over a day to reach. Our mothers came with us to ease the shock of separation. When we arrived, there were already well over a thousand children at this meeting place. We were placed in a large building, fed, scrubbed and issued a cloth sack (about the size of a pillowcase), a spoon and a bowl. For clothes, we were given a pair of boxer underwear and a T-shirt. Then, our old rags were burned. Since this was summer there was no need for shoes.

Our mothers had to leave the next day and it was quite an emotional event. For some children this would be the last time that they would ever see their mothers. In a few months Stalin would not allow any more Poles to leave the Soviet Union and many of those that were left behind died of disease or starvation. With tears in her eyes our mother tried to explain to us that we would be better off with the other children. At least we would be clothed and fed and have a more promising future. Heartbroken, she remembered the many friends that we had already lost in Russia.

We stayed with the group for two days after she left but we couldn't take it. So we asked the people in charge to send us back to our parents and they agreed to do so. Since there were no buses or trains that traveled back and forth we had to wait until the next wagon was scheduled to go in that direction. The two of us were then turned over to a strange Kazakh who was told to take us back home. When we arrived at our settlement a day and a half later we were very happy to find our father at home.

After three days with nothing to eat we asked our mother to send us back again. (Our dad, meanwhile, had gone back to work in the mountains and would not return for a few days.) We were turned over to a Kazakh whom we knew slightly and from whom I remember begging once. He took us back to town. Our mother did not go with us this time and our father didn't even know we had left. I never saw him again. Shortly after we left he was ordered to serve in the Russian army. Since he refused, he was put in jail and died there on May 9, 1944.

By the time we returned, the original group of children that we were with had already departed. We were therefore added to another large group that was being formed. In a few days we were put on a train and taken to the city of Krasnovodsk on the Caspian Sea. This turned out to be the last group of children to leave Russia.[4]

Account of Sabina Kukla (née Lukasiewicz)

People from various settlements, from Turkestan and Uzbekistan, Tadzykistan, etc. began to travel. At first on trains, then on the Amu Darya River and back again. We stopped at various kolkhozes and picked cotton. Later we travelled in cattle trucks, though not as crowded as we had been during our exile to Siberia. In the course of such journeys many families fell victim to separation. When the train stopped at stations we would be told that it would stand for an hour, perhaps an hour and a half, or sometimes two hours. During that time people left the train in search of food and water. In the meantime the train would move off after a short stop, leaving people behind. Sometimes it was possible to catch up with it at the next stop, but mostly the situation was hopeless. Weeks passed before families found each other again, but not all of them. That was true despair. I also got left behind like that with two other people but after several hours of rapid march along the railway track we caught up with the train which was just about to continue its journey.

We were increasingly tormented by infectious diseases and lice. In the autumn we were returning from picking cotton in Uzbekistan on a barge sailing on the Amu Darya River. Cold rain and water soaked our bedding. My little brother Jureczek became ill and his temperature rose. He was not able to get out of his bedding at the bottom of the water-soaked barge. We were all frozen from the damp. When we arrived at some place, the name of which I do not remember, we were ordered to transfer to a train. We were told to leave Jureczek in the local hospital. We would not agree to that because the separation would have been forever, so we continued together on the train into the unknown. Once again we searched for food at stops. One day Jureczek asked me to find him some milk. I gave him that milk, he raised his little head, wet his lips and ... Oh, horror! That was the end. Jureczek died on the 5th of December 1941. We buried him the same day on a hill at the station Kitabu. There rests a Polish child which did not return to Poland. Why did this have to be?....

Sick people lay motionless and began to die one after another. We were at the end of our lives. I also became ill with typhoid, as did both my younger sisters and my father. Only Mother did not become ill until we reached Tehran. Mother nursed all of us. I do not know how long I was ill because I was unconscious for some of the time. When I regained consciousness I was told that I had been close to death. Whole families died out. Out of a family of five in our room only two daughters remained alive. In the Jewish family of seven people only two survived. By the time our stay in this kolkhoz ended only twelve people survived out of forty-eight. Each day several people were driven away on the arbas to a hillock close to the kolkhoz and were buried there. The Uzbeks grabbed the corpses by the legs and simply threw them onto the arba like blocks of wood, driving off without ceremony. That was a terrible sight. And then one day while we hopelessly awaited death, resigned and exhausted, a miracle happened.

My health was returning after the typhoid and I began to sit up on my bedding. One day two Polish soldiers in uniform came to us. We could not believe our eyes! They told us that a Polish army unit had been organised in this area and the soldiers were looking for Poles scattered among the kolkhozes. There was a chance of getting us out of Russia. They told us the whole story about generals Sikorski and Anders. They gave us some courage and hope, promising as they were leaving that they would return soon.

They came back a few days later and — a second miracle! They brought a loaf of bread! We had lost hope of seeing bread again in our lives and here was real, holy bread! When we were so hopelessly hungry and ill I prayed to God to let us see bread once more in our lives. I prayed: "Oh God, I don't even want to eat that bread if only I could see it just once more and then I can die." Since that time I never throw bread away.

And so the long awaited moment came and with it a glimmer of hope that we would get out of that hell....

To many people it was not given, however, to reach the shores of freedom. They continued to die and their bodies were thrown into the sea. Nonetheless the majority did get there although in the months which followed death continued to reap its harvest in hospitals and camps in Tehran.[5]

Account of Maria Borkowska-Witkowska

Amnesty was announced in July 1941. My father made a sleigh which we rode 120 km to Kotlas. We were allowed to embark on a goods train together with other Poles. Altogether there were 35 of us. We rode for two months to another kolkhoz in Kazakhstan. During the journey my second brother became ill with measles. He was four years old. At Chelyabinsk they took him to a hospital. My mother went with him but was not allowed to stay. She was told to return to the train or they would leave the whole family in Chelyabinsk. The train moved off as soon as she returned. Near Alma-Ata we were told to disembark at a kolkhoz. My father went at once to look for my brother in the hospital. By some miracle he found it and the hospital sister told him that my brother had lived only four days. Now I had lost two brothers who were buried in Russia. On returning, my father said goodbye to us and joined the Polish army then being formed in Russia.

In the kolkhoz we were given only 250 gm of barley. Mama found two stones and made flour during the whole time we lived in Kazakhstan. After enlisting in the army my father sent us bread from time to time. I went to work in the kitchen where an old Cossack called Babaj cooked meals for 15 young Polish men. Some were so exhausted that they could not get up and I carried the food to them. The poor boys lay on ground covered with straw, slowly dying. Typhoid is a very infectious disease and so I also contracted it and nearly died but, thank God, I recovered.

We thought that we would never leave that country. After a while I had to work on the steppes. Mama prayed her rosary every night, saying that only God could get us out of there.

Before my father left he registered us everywhere. Thanks to that we were able to leave the kolkhoz. I recall that very many families had to remain because they had no one in the army. In the kolkhoz they gave us a donkey, but he refused to move, so Mama bought a camel and thus we rode to Yangi-Yul. We got on the last transport from Russia to Krasnovodsk and the journey was very tedious.

We did not see my father again. After leaving Russia he reached England and was severely wounded during the bombing of London. He died at the age of 50. My mother with her four daughters left Iran via Tehran for Africa.[6]

Account of Ryszard Rzepczyński

There was an assembly in camp the next day and the commandant explained to us what had happened and that Stalin had said we were free to go wherever we wanted. That was wonderful news, but how were we to go anywhere? We were about 180 km from the town of Yarensk and the shipping lanes. How were we going to get all the people, children and belongings there? It was too much to carry.

It was suggested that we should make rafts out of the logs. There were burnt forests with plenty of trees, so we started to cut these down into about 7- or 8-metre lengths. We made a raft for each family out of 12 to 15 logs, depending on the size of the family. The young women and children gathered vines which the older women boiled and these were used to bind the logs together. It took us between one and two weeks to make the 75 rafts we needed. There were more than 75 families, but that was the number which decided to make the journey to Yarensk.

A few families stayed behind because they were not sure they could make the journey. When we had all the rafts we needed we brought them into our camp. The next day everyone started loading their belongings onto their rafts. Luckily we had some potatoes, dried bread and a few other provisions to take with us because the trip down river took about three weeks and we would have starved without them.

The journey was difficult. In places there were shallow waters where the rafts got stuck. Sometimes it took a whole day to get the raft off the sand banks. We all had the same problems and difficulties. When we arrived at the port we had to unload our rafts. I had 16 kilos of potatoes which were heavy to carry, but I could not leave them behind because they were our only source of food. We had to carry our belongings four kilometres to where the offices were. The men went in and obtained tickets for which they had to pay. We had some money which we had saved from the camps where we worked for about two years.

We loaded our families and belongings onto the ship and were on our way down river to Kotlas, from where there were trains running. Once there, we had to buy train tickets. The people who had no money had to sell whatever they could — clothes and valuables — to the Russians to get the few roubles they needed. The train took us south.

We arrived at Kuybyshev and there we met up with soldiers from the Polish army which was forming in Russia. We were told there that any men or boys over the age of 16 could join the army. So quite a lot of us joined up, and our journey as civilians across Russia ended there.

It took us over a month to get to the Polish army camp because our papers were stolen. Some men passed themselves off as officers, took our papers and disappeared. There were about 17 of us left without any official papers. Now we had to work out a way to get to Tatischevo where the Polish camp was.

We travelled by freight trains for a month, sitting wherever we could, on top of wheat or on top of the train. I do not want to complain too much about our hardships but the worst problem we had was with our personal hygiene. There was nowhere to wash and we were not able to change into clean clothes. On top of that the lice problem was atrocious. The men who were also on their way to join the Russian army were absolutely covered with lice.

We finally arrived in the Polish army camp and there, at last, life took on some semblance of normality. After a few days we were separated into units. Later we travelled from there to Persia, from Persia to Iraq, then Palestine and Italy and there our journey ended.[7]

Account of Irena Okulicz-Kozaryn (née Szunejko)

Amnesty ... we were now free to leave our camp Churga Arkhangelsk. But free to go where? Poland was ravaged by war, so we could not return to our home. Our only option was to travel to the south of Russia where the Polish army was forming.

The majority of able-bodied men had left the camp by this time to join the army. Only women, children and the elderly were left behind.

November 1941. The Russian winter was settling in already. Our group of 30, composed mainly of mothers and children, packed our belongings and we began our journey on foot to the railway station, Vologda.

After waiting for a week at the station to obtain our tickets we embarked on yet another journey. Little did we know that the next 14 weeks would be spent on the train as we experienced many moments of intense fear, relief, hunger and anticipation. The journey was very slow. The train was often side-lined to make way on the tracks for Russian soldiers making their way to war. At times we waited for an hour — at other times for up to a week.

Conditions on the train were appalling. We were cold, hungry and dirty. When the train stopped all of us raced to queue to buy bread. But, more often than not, we would leave with nothing and remained hungry. As we waited in the queues we often did not know when the train would be leaving. Many a time the train would depart, leaving behind people still waiting in queues, separating them from their families. Some managed to catch the train but many did not — and remained separated.

Mid-February 1942. The journey ended — or so it seemed. We arrived in Tashkent, Uzbekistan and were sent to a nearby collective farm. After months of travelling we were not prepared for what was to be our temporary home.

No trees or any other vegetation — a very macabre and eerie feeling. Only the endless cotton fields. The air was filled with cotton particles with a hot wind blowing and nowhere to escape.

Our food ration was of poor quality and very small. We had reached the end. No hope, as we felt imprisoned in this God-forsaken land. People were sick and dying. My mother exchanged her wedding ring for a small bag of carrots to be shared among our group. What a feast!

Being hungry day after day, one soon forgot the taste of ordinary food, including bread and potatoes. Oh, what it would have been like to have a slice of bread to myself.

We heard later that a Polish army was forming in Tashkent and civilian transports were leaving Russia. That was when we decided to leave the collective farm and to make our way to Tashkent.

Hundreds of soldiers in Polish uniforms, as well as civilians, were already there, waiting for transport to Persia. To be eligible to travel one had to have a member of one's family in the army.

In my own case, my father had been called up to the Polish army in 1939 and we never heard from him after that. One would think that we would be eligible to go. But some bureaucrat said that we were not a priority. They told us to go back to the farm from which we had come.

My mother decided that we would never go back. Our situation was very bleak and it could be expected that my story would end there.

Our next experience, however, was what I call "our Russian miracle." One of the passing Polish soldiers asked if anyone knew of his family, whom he had left behind in a Russian labour camp in Arkhangelsk? He had not heard of their fate since then.

The soldier was from Nowogrodek, our part of Poland. My mother explained our plight and he took her hand and said: "Come with me — you are my sister and you can live."

We never saw the man again, but we remembered him in our prayers for a long time. I believe that good deeds are never wasted.

We left Krasnovodsk, a Russian port, after travelling so many miles through strange cities and over unknown rivers, and after many tears and false hopes.

We arrived in Pahlavi, Persia, on Easter Saturday.

The above is a memoir of a ten-year-old girl, written 55 years later.[8]

Account of Anita Paschwa (née Kozicka)

An "amnesty" was declared in July 1941, and all those who were taken from Poland were free to leave Siberia. We were provided with no transportation. To leave the area, we were forced to use whatever material was available. Intending to use the river as our highway, a group of us built a raft of willow branches. It was late in the year and we worried that the Chulym River which flows into the Ob River would freeze. We had no time to waste. In one week Maria and I and others who were with us had built a raft of six logs. But we had no oars. We thought of asking some of the local people to help us make some, but we had no money to pay them, no clothes to give them and no time to wait, so we did without them. With the few rubles my sister had, Maria and I bought two loaves of bread and dried them. That was to be our nourishment for the long journey down the rivers. We all covered ourselves in hay to stay warm and prayed to God that the Chulym would not freeze.

We reached Asino, a small Siberian town, where we boarded a boxcar of a freight train for Tomsk, and then after a few days another train headed to Novosibirsk. When our bread and money ran out we gathered grass and dandelion roots, washed and ate them.

Once in Novosibirsk, we knew we needed to find a warmer climate before the cold set in and we wanted to find the place where the Polish army was being organized. But no one along the way had any specific information. We continued our journey and reached Tashkent. There our troubles really began. We found the warmer climate, but it was so hot there that many of us became sick from the contrast in temperature. People were dying like flies and there was no one willing to bury them. The local people, afraid of getting the diseases we had — cholera, typhus, diarrhea and dysentery — stayed away. The water was polluted and insects covered the dead bodies. This was even more horrible than what we had endured in Siberia.

The Russian authorities, anxious to get us out of the country, gave us each a loaf of bread and loaded us on freight trains which took us to Kerkichi, a seaport on the Amu Darya River. There we boarded eight empty grain barges. We were fed a soybean extract used as camel feed which was as hard as a rock. This and polluted water sustained us for two weeks until we reached Turtkul in the Uzbek USSR. Along the way many children took sick and died. Their bodies were thrown from the barge so the rest of us would be protected from disease.

From Turtkul, carrying our belongings in small bundles, we walked fifty miles to a town called Nukus. The few carts available were used to transport children under eight and dying elderly people. When we reached Nukus, two or three families were herded into small clay huts. We slept on cotton straw and were given a first handful of a grain called "jugara." To get any more grain we would have to work the cotton fields. We worked very hard for two months, and when all the cotton had been picked we were no longer needed in Nukus and were ordered to return, again on foot, to those dirty grain barges in Turtkul. Once again the young children rode whatever carts there were and the rest of us walked in the hot sun. Along the way, two army trucks with young drivers suddenly appeared. They offered to help us and allowed all the children to get into their trucks. When someone asked them if the older women could ride, they said they would take only children. I got on and, being very curious, paid close attention to the road. After about a half day's ride, I noticed the trucks turned off the road we had been walking. None of the children talked. We were all very happy just to be riding. At first I thought the soldiers had lost their way to Turtkul, but after it had gotten very dark we reached a small village. There they told us to get out of the trucks and go into a teahouse and sit on the floor. Then two husky local men with whips at their belts came in, gave each of us a dried pancake and a cup of water, and told us to go to sleep on the floor.

There were about fifty of us in that group of children. No one talked at all; we just did as we were told. I was so frightened that at first I could not sleep. Eventually sleep did come but about 3:00 A.M. I woke up and began to worry about those two husky men who were watching us, and why the truck had taken another road. Then I remembered hearing when we were still in Siberia that the Russian government wanted to enslave all the Polish orphans. It scared me then and even more now. I became convinced that was why we were in this teahouse. I decided to run away and try to find my sister and the others. I got up and tiptoed past the snoring guard. Outside the teahouse there was no sign of the two trucks we rode in or the two soldiers who drove them. I ran down the road, hoping to get back to where the trucks turned off. I needed directions to Turtkul. I finally met a shepherd to whom I said only one word: "Turtkul." He drew a line in the sand showing me which way to go. I kissed his old hand and ran without stopping to catch my breath. Finally I reached the intersection and was on the road to Turtkul. All along the way I prayed that God would not let me die in this desert wasteland alone. Here there was not even grass to eat or any water to drink. I had to get to the seaport by eight o'clock that night. I knew that the group was going to Tashkent from Turtkul to try to find the Polish army. If I didn't get there, I would never see my sister again and I would probably not survive. I just kept running. When I reached the barges, I collapsed. When I awoke, I was surrounded by the mothers of those other children I left behind. They were crying and screaming at me. Some were ready to beat me. They wanted to know what happened to their children and why I was there alone. I told them how to get to that village, where to look for the children, and about the guards. One member from each family of the kidnapped children left the barges — and their chance for freedom [the barge was to leave that night] — to look for their children.

At ten o'clock that night my sister [who remained on the barge] and I and the others began our two-week journey back to Kerkichi and then to Tashkent. When we arrived, we were placed on a Red Army collective farm. For two months we worked in the fields. Many more people died there. My sister and I got word that the Polish army and an orphanage were being organized in Guzar. We left the farm and traveled through Gizhduvan, Kagan and Bukhara. As we slept in a rail station in Bukhara waiting for the next freight train, our cooking pot and two spoons, our only possessions, were stolen from under our heads. When we reached Guzar, my sister left me in the orphanage station while she sought out the Polish army headquarters. After a time, I was taken to the orphanage about two miles from Guzar. It was a tent city of dying children. They shaved my head to eliminate the possibility of head lice and fed me only water-softened bread to reintroduce food into my stomach. When I awoke the next morning, the girl with whom I had slept was gone. The other girls in my room told me that she had passed away during the night.

After four days at the orphanage I began to worry that I would never see Maria again. But on the fifth day she came to my tent and told me that she had enlisted in the Polish army as a WAC [Women's Army Corps], that she would soon leave Russian soil and that, at thirteen-and-a-half, I would now have to take care of myself. We cried as we said good-bye hoping to some day reunite. The very next day I was on my way to the seaport of Krasnovodsk and eventually to real freedom. I knew then that God had listened to my prayers and spared me from death in this strange and horrible land.[9]

Account of Wisia Reginella (née Danecka)

It was here, in Kazakhstan, that the amnesty found us. We suddenly became comrades, brothers and allies who were to fight the Germans together with them. Some general from the NKVD told us that our situation was different now, that some fellow called Sikorski had signed a treaty with Stalin, whose titles he now recited in full. At this point a solicitor, a Jew from Poland, rose and said: "I beg your pardon, but that is not some fellow Sikorski, but the Commander-in-Chief and Prime Minister of the Polish Government in London." The Poles applauded and sang the Polish national anthem. Silence fell. The Russians were speechless. The NKVD men talked among themselves, then the general rose and commenced a speech of apology. A storm was averted. The solicitor left the next day and I met him later in Samarkand....

We arrived at Samarkand after great difficulties. People everywhere. The NKVD directed us to some narrow street where it was warm and we slept. Everyone settled down as best they could in order to look for some sort of accommodation in the morning. At that time there was no Polish outpost here and we were condemned to use our own initiative. We were watched by the NKVD and the militia. In the morning the NKVD men appeared and chased everyone into the rail trucks which would take us to distant kolkhozes to pick cotton. Together with a Jewish family of five I ran off to the nearest house. We would not go to a kolkhoz for anything in this world. A good woman had pity on us and allowed us to hide in a pigsty, where there were some pigs. The other people from our truck were driven away and we never saw them again. Our hostess was afraid of the militia and insisted that we should leave the pigsty in two days' time at the latest....

I had some roubles, a wedding band, ring and a gold chain. My fellow residents talked me into buying meat, frying some cutlets and selling them. I did this. However, when it came to selling my cutlets I looked at the poor, impoverished people and gave the cutlets away. That was my first business in Soviet Russia.

A Polish outpost opened in Samarkand. An orphanage, located in a former Orthodox church, was created and soup was being distributed.

There was someone now concerning themselves with Polish people. Food, medicines and clothing arrived from America. An epidemic of typhoid broke out....

The typhoid did not pass me by, either. I became feverish. And what a trip to hospital! They collected the sick from 9:00 A.M. They lay or sat on the *arba* until late afternoon. This was followed by hospital activities: cutting off hair, a bath in cold water—

and barely enough of that to cover the ankles. Despite my temperature which was rising with every moment, I begged God not to let me get pneumonia. My teeth chattered until I lost consciousness. Still in fever, it seemed to me that I was skating. As I was being taken to hospital I begged that the Polish outpost be informed that my child had been left without care. Aleksander Reginella quickly appeared and took Basia under his care, bringing me food until I returned from hospital.

There was a lot of talk that we would go to Tehran with the troops....

The last transport was about to leave and I was again ill with dysentery. At that time the political situation changed for the worse. Arrests of outpost personnel began as did difficulties regarding leaving.

Our guardian and friend was threatened with arrest, so he came to us and swore on everything that we must go, because this was the last transport.

It was thanks only to him that we left for Tehran. We reached Krasnovodsk after some adventures. The heat was extreme as we lay all day on the sand waiting for the ship which was to take us to Pahlavi. The NKVD never left us. The Polish-Soviet commission would not admit sick people and one could only take what one could carry. No money could be taken out. People abandoned their last possessions and money on the beach while speculators collected everything, haggling as though in a bazaar and taking money to Pahlavi where, it turned out, it could be exchanged. Everyone was fearful and wanted only to escape from that "Paradise."

As on the previous occasion when I had typhoid, Dr. Mogielnicki again came to my rescue. I looked like a disaster with my head shaved, weighing about 39 kg and could hardly stand on my feet. He obtained a bit of ice from somewhere and told me to swallow some from time to time as that would prevent frequent dashes for the toilets. Fortunately I got through the commission all right and we found ourselves on a ship. On the deck hundreds of people were suffering from dysentery. Everyone was using some sort of pots because there was no question of getting into a toilet. Everyone was soiled with excrement.[10]

Account of Maria Gabiniewicz

Autumn was approaching. The first snow fell towards the end of September. We had neither the clothes nor the food needed to survive the harsh Siberian winter. We then received news about the "amnesty" resulting from the Sikorski-Stalin agreement of July 30, 1941. The Poles were given *udostovierenya:* internal passports that enabled them to move about within the territory of the USSR. From labor camps, settlements, and the farthest places of exile the Poles flocked to the southern republics. They all gravitated to the place where General Władysław Anders was forming his Polish army and organizing Polish outposts. One very frosty morning Mother packed some articles in a wooden crate, filled a sack with dry bread, and together with others we headed southward. We camped for weeks on end in railway stations waiting for trains. Diseases beset us. My life was threatened in Novosibirsk but I did not go to the hospital. Mother did not want to part with me for fear that I would be placed in a children's home where I would be Russianized and then be stuck in Russia forever (many Polish children suffered such a fate). She kept in close contact with the Polish families whom she befriended with the conviction that if anything happened to her (everyone reckoned with the possibility of dying) they would look after us. At that time Tadek and I were still small children. Childhood is a fragile time of life, but in those circumstances we were turning into adults very rapidly. Together with our mother we learned to fight for survival, to mollify our hunger, and to deal with illnesses, often having to witness the death of close neighbors. At the same time, through her bearing Mother taught us to believe in our own survival and to have hope for the future. In the darkest hours she always saw the light. She never doubted that Divine Providence watched over us.

In the course of our journey we halted in Dzhambul, Kazakhstan. Hunger stared us in the face. We were running out of things to exchange for food. Our shoes were worn out and our clothes were very tattered. Together with other Poles, Mother went to distant kolkhozes (sometimes 50 kilometers away) from which she brought back some flower or porridge. But the food didn't last long.

To forget about my own hunger I used to walk two kilometers to the Dzhambul railway station. I counted the cars on passing trains, walked the streets, and waited for my mother who always returned from work along the same road. I knew that she would always have two slices of bread for Tadek and me. For lunch she would eat her soup, but save the bread for us. I was never disappointed.

Bread never tasted so good as in Russia. If someone were to have asked me then: "What is your fondest wish?" I would have answered: "To eat as much bread as I could."[11]

Account of Jane [Janina] Żebrowski-Bulmahn

About the middle of December of 1941, a small group of Polish people were permitted to go to Barnaul, which was several hours away, by a horse and buggy. They had to obtain permission and transportation from the kolkhoz administrator. When they came back late in the evening, we could not believe what we heard. The news spread like wildfire.

They reported that at the post office in the city they saw an amnesty notice for all Poles. When they inquired, they were told that since the Western countries — England, France and the United States — entered the war against Germany, any country which was part of the Western Alliance was included in the amnesty. Poland was part of this Alliance.

We found out later that an agreement was signed by the Polish General Władysław Sikorski, who was prime minister of the Polish government-in-exile located in England and commander-in-chief of the volunteer Polish army which escaped after the defeat of Poland in 1939. It was signed at the Kremlin with the Russian high command on July 30, 1941, granting amnesty to all Polish prisoners and deportees. The agreement was named the Sikorski-Maisky Pact. However, we were not informed about it but found out by accident in December of 1941.

The agreement also stated that a volunteer Polish army would be formed in Russia from the prisoners and deportees under the command of the Polish General Anders. Anders himself had been in a Russian prison in Moscow but was released as a result of the amnesty pact. Any man, woman, or youth 16 years or older, in good health, would qualify. The volunteer army would be trained in Russia and then shipped to the Allied front in Africa and Western Europe. The Polish army camps were located in the south of Russia, in Kirghistan and Uzbekistan.

Upon asking further, the Poles were told that we were free to travel anywhere within Russia, but could not return to Poland. They were also told that anyone who had a close relative in the volunteer Polish army would be able to leave Russia. Travel within Russia had to be done by our own means, of course. The Russian government would not help us....

The authorities, seeing us depart, were saying, "Some day we will regret letting you leave." They did not attempt to hold us back.

After traveling for about ten days we came to Tashkent in Uzbekistan. The Polish camp outside of Tashkent, called Dzalal-Abad, was our new destination. We were met, believe it or not, by Polish soldiers. What a welcome it was! We wanted to hug and kiss everyone, even strangers. We were one of the last trains to arrive. This was early January 1942....

After living in Uzbekistan for about eight months, we were notified by Polish authorities to report to Samarkand for a trip out of Russia. We said goodbye to our Uzbek friend and wished her a healthy and beautiful baby. After the war was over, I asked Father to write her and tell her about us as well as to inquire about her child, but he was afraid that it might put her in danger since Russia was still under communism.

In our joy at the prospect of leaving Russia, we did not give any thought to how we would get to Samarkand where we were to meet our train. As I mentioned before, the authorities considered us free to come and go but would not give us any help. We were brought to this settlement by Russians since they needed workers, but going back we were on our own.

We had no choice but to go on foot. Father estimated that if we made steady progress, it would take us about 10 hours because Mother, my sister and I could not walk as fast as he could. Nothing would discourage us, and we were prepared to face whatever discomfort and pain we had to endure to get there.

It was heartbreaking to realize that we were the only family from our area that could leave. All the others were prevented because of illness and the prospect of hours of walking which they could not do.

Early in the morning we gathered our meager possessions and put them in cotton sacks to throw over our shoulders. Each of us had a small bundle to carry. We walked and walked, it seemed, endlessly. We only stopped for a few minutes, here and there, when someone weakened, or to have something to eat. My sister had to be carried by Father quite frequently so Mother and I took their sacks to lighten Father's load.

Weariness was not the word for what we felt — more like total exhaustion and pain in every part of our bodies. Since we did not have shoes, our feet were bruised and bled. It took several weeks to heal them. But we never allowed ourselves to think about giving up. We were going to make it or die.

Finally in the evening we saw lights from a distant station. An end to our journey was in sight. The last few miles seemed the hardest because, for the first time that day, we allowed ourselves to think about how we felt.

Father went to report in, and we just put our heads down and rested. He came back shortly with some food and water and informed us that we could board the train. The next day the train left the station and proceeded to Krasnovodsk, a port city on the Caspian Sea. There we were to board a ship to cross over to Persia (now Iran) which, at that time, was under English jurisdiction. Now, we could almost feel the closeness of freedom. This was August of 1942.[12]

4. Near and Middle East

Introduction by Andrzej Szujecki

The evacuation of the Polish people from the USSR, together with the army units of General Władysław Anders, took place in three stages. The first lasted from March 24 until the first days of April 1942. In addition to the over 30,000 military personnel, about 11,000 children left Krasnovodsk by sea for Pahlavi. In Pahlavi, primitive transit camps were set up on the shore of the Caspian Sea for the military and civilians. A hospital was established in Kazvin and over 1,400 patients were placed therein. By April 25, 1942, the last of the refugees had left Pahlavi by truck via Kazvin for Tehran, where the Delegation of the Ministry of Labor and Social Welfare was engaged in establishing a series of temporary camps for the civilians since April 1, 1942.

The second stage of the evacuation from the USSR across the Caspian Sea to Iran lasted from August 10 to September 1, 1942. During that time over 43,000 military personnel and about 25,000 civilians came to Pahlavi. About one third of the civilians were children. The refugees were put up in tents along the beaches in five designated regions. After a month-long quarantine the civilians were sent via Kazvin to Tehran while the military personnel were sent mainly to Iraq and other countries in the Near East. The final liquidation of the Polish bases in Pahlavi took place on October 16, 1942.

A smaller-scale evacuation of the Polish people from the USSR took place through Ashkhabad-Mashhad. It included, in addition to military personnel, a large group of civilians, 1,936 of whom wound up in Tehran and 675 in India.

The Polish army that left the USSR was concentrated in central Iraq, northeast of Baghdad. In Palestine, yunak schools, a Women's Auxiliary Service, and some training centers were established. In Tehran, four Polish refugee camps were created (Nos. 1–3 and No. 5 which housed the orphanage). The Polish group (consisting mainly of orphans) in Isfahan was initially referred to as the Polish Refugee Camp No. 4; it housed 2,600 refugees in February 1943. Although the numbers fluctuated, between September and December 1942 there were about 25,000 Polish refugees in Iran. Isfahan was administered by the Polish Delegation of the Ministry of Labor and Social Welfare in Tehran and later by its agency in Isfahan. The Polish people were directed mainly via Ahvaz (in south Iran) and the ports of Khorramshahr and Basra to Africa and India. Small groups (mainly orphans) reached Mexico and New Zealand. By the end of 1943, about 33,000 civilians had left Iran (2,119 died there). There remained 3,933 refugees in Tehran, 2,388 in Isfahan, 2,834 in Ahvaz, and 66 in Mashhad. In October 1944, even with further transports to India and Africa, there still remained 4,531 persons in Iran.

At the end of 1945 the remaining group of Poles (about 4,300) were evacuated from Tehran and Isfahan to Ahvaz, and from there to Baghdad and Beirut. The last transport reached Beirut by train on November 26, 1945. About 300 Poles still remained in Iran. In Lebanon, after their stay in the temporary camp in San Simon, the Poles found refuge in settlements in Ghazir, Zauk Michael, Ajaltoun, and Boladoun. The emigration of Poles from Lebanon, and there were around 6,000 of them there in 1946, to Great Britain, Canada, Australia, Argentina, Poland, USA, and other countries lasted until 1950.

To be sure, political, organizational and economic factors weighed heavily on the Polish people in Iran during these difficult World War II days, but of greater importance to the children themselves were the twin institutions of school and scouting. In May 1942, on the initiative of the of the Delegation of the Ministry of Labor and Social Welfare, a Commission for Education was established in Tehran, whose tasks included the creation and supervision of schools. Led by Piotr Paluch the commission did what it could under the difficult circumstances. On August 1, 1943, the responsibility for the creation of Polish schools in Iran was placed in the hands of the Delegation of the Ministry of Religion and Public Education. At that time there were 24 schools in Iran, including nine primary schools and a secondary school in Tehran, eight primary schools and a secondary school in Isfahan, a primary and secondary school in Ahvaz, and one primary school in Mashaad. At the end of 1943 there were 246 children in six kindergartens and 2,434 children in all the elementary schools. The teaching staff consisted of 172 instructors and five priests. In the secondary schools and lyceums there were 532 students taught by 72 instructors and five priests. There were also technical schools: the Women's Secondary School of Tailoring (four year curriculum) in Isfahan, and the School of Commerce (one year curriculum) in Tehran. Numerous other courses were also available, e.g., English. The greatest impediment to education was the lack of textbooks. The problem was somewhat mitigated by having them printed in Palestine and later, in Iran. The intellectual needs, particularly of the teenagers, were met by the libraries, such as they were, and by the growing number of publications, such as *The Pole in Iran*, which had a circulation of 1,800 copies, and *The Scout*, a Polish Scouts' Association periodical in the Middle East.

Scouting played a major role in the lives of the exiles, especially in the difficult period after their exodus from the Soviet Union. The first Scout team was organized in the Civil Refugee Camp No. 1 on April 14, 1942. Soon others followed. A spontaneously organized Scout troop in Tehran consisted of five Girl Guide groups numbering 230 girls and one Boy Scout group of 60 boys. By May 29, 1942, the troop included six groups of junior Scouts. On June 29, 1942, a Girl Guide group, consisting of the sisters of the Polish Red Cross and the nurses, was organized in the Main Civil Hospital to care for the educational and sociocultural needs of the patients. At the end of July 1942 Scout groups were organized in Civil Camp No. 3 and on August 15, Scout leader Anna Lubieniecka (Scout commandant in Tehran since June 15, 1942) received the first Scout pledges in Iran.[1]

Iran

Pahlavi

Milewski family memoir

(Stanisław) On the beach at Pahlavi we were told to strip for disinfection. After our hair was shaved we were given a shower and issued new clothes by the Red Cross. Then, army trucks took us to a camp, located on the outskirts of the city, where we were put up in tents. Driving through Pahlavi we saw open shops with goods for sale — the first such sight since our deportation two years ago. Shops with dates and figs were everywhere. There were happy people walking around and laughing. Unfortunately, because we were so malnourished, the soup with large chunks of mutton that we were given made many of us sick. Many also died in Pahlavi from dysentery and various other diseases brought over from the Soviet Union. We were so emaciated that we all looked like skeletons, but thanks to the British army doctors and the soldiers who shared their food rations with us, many of us survived.[2]

Account of Vala Lewicki (née Miron)

On arrival at the port we were taken to the beach in trucks and stayed there for a few days. Sleeping on the sand did not worry us too much, though the sun was scorching. The lack of fresh water was the worst enemy.

Somehow I could not relax here. Soon I became sick with a high fever, shivers, darkness in my eyes and splitting headaches. As in a dream I knew that my mother had gone in search of some water for us. During her absence I was found and taken by the army health inspectors to the army hospital on a ship. When I woke up I was in Pahlavi, Iran, on the other side of the Caspian Sea. In a hospital there, a doctor told me that I was suffering from malaria, a phenomenon I had never heard of before.

It was a shattering experience. There I was with a "sophisticated" illness, pitchforked alone into a sea of unknown people. Suddenly all my former wishes and hopes rushed out of me like wild, frightened animals. I felt empty, lost, with nothing to look forward to. But as the days went by I began convalescing and was allowed to sit outside the tent. The dread of uncertainty and loneliness which gripped my heart and had been dormant for a while, now started growing more vicious with each day. I began to wonder and ask myself silently: "Where is my family? Are they here? If so, why don't they look for me?" Trying to penetrate the mist between me and the opposite shore to my family I was so overcome by sadness that many times I felt tears coming to my eyes. At such times I covered my face with my hands, determined that no one should see me cry. Often such sessions ended with headaches and shivers and I had to go inside before the symptoms of a malaria attack developed fully. The problem really got me down but I kept my vigil.

One morning, after receiving medication and dressed in my washed lime-colour batiste dress, I took up my usual position outside. From there I could watch people walking to and from the sea. I had seen a number of dwarfs previously, but none of them had aroused my curiosity as much as the one I saw now. He was jerking along beside a tall, uniformed man. They were coming towards the hospital tent. I could not take my eyes off the "Liliput," who looked so normal otherwise. Then I realised he had no legs. The Russian winter had claimed both of them above the knee....

In Pahlavi (Iran, Persia) Polish people, especially young girls of my own age, were dying by the hundred of dysentery, caused by a rich, heavy diet of mutton and rice on empty stomachs.[3]

Account of Stefania Buczak-Zarzycka

Once aboard, we were all so tense lest anything go wrong that our teachers ordered us not to move from our places. We were so close to freedom; nothing could go wrong. However, I pretended to go to the lavatory, but really I went to see my mother who was still very ill with malaria. She assured me that she was not seriously ill and that we would join her in Pahlavi. One of my teachers snapped at me so I returned to my position beside Antek. We all understood the seriousness of the situation; few children even spoke to each other. The waves pounded the small craft and as we rolled up and down Antek and I decided to strap ourselves together with the rope tied around our luggage. If one of us should over balance, the weight of the other would prevent us from falling overboard.

The sun was high as we coasted to the shoreline of Persia. Soldiers were standing in the water, waiting to carry each child across to land. Quite a few British troops and even journalists were observers standing around the transport trucks. We did not notice them at first. Instinctively everyone, even the children, upon reaching land would make the sign of the cross in thanksgiving, while most of the adults knelt down on the yellow sand in prayer. Later, when I was older and mixed with many of the English, I was told that these observers were shocked by the sight and felt that they were dealing with religious fanatics. At that time few outsiders knew of our experiences and how grateful we were to escape an ugly and early death through starvation.

Our next destination was another tent city divided into check points manned by guards. The first section was the medical division where we were checked, allowed to bathe and given new clothing. Our lice-ridden rags were thrown into incinerators which burned continuously for days.

Movement between the sectors was restricted in order to prevent the spread of disease, which again had erupted and reached epidemic proportions. Dysentery, hepatitis and typhoid claimed countless numbers. The dead were gathered by soldiers and were buried in mass graves, often unidentified. I was in an orphanage and suffered from hepatitis. My special diet was comprised of raw carrots and apples, which I could collect directly from the kitchen. This was quite a privilege.

Antek and I began to search for my mother by asking at each tent for information. There was no central office with information about where individuals could be located. I, along with thousands of others, poked my head into each tent in turn, looking for relations and friends....

Finally I found her, still very ill, and warned her that the orphanage group was due to be shifted to Tehran very soon. I was so concerned that I would be separated from her over even a further distance. However, she reassured me that as soon as she was well she would collect us from the orphanage. Marysia and Mother found, our next task was to locate Ola. Although the beach was warm and inviting, we did not dare to take time to enjoy any of this. Ola was found in much the same way. We had all changed, however, through the effects of illness, malnutrition and head shavings. In ill-fitting clothes very often the boys and girls were indistinguishable. At first, I didn't recognise Ola as she lay puffy-faced and ill. She called out to me and I had to look from face to face in order to decide which of the girls was my sister. This upset me greatly and I cried inconsolably for some time, in part because I was happy to see her but also because I had not recognised my own sister. News of the new arrival of army units from Guzar spurred us on in search of my father.

We spoke to the commanding officer who assured us that my father must be in the area, but we could see that they were disorganised for no one could tell us his location. It was decided that Marysia should keep looking, but Antek and I would have to go back to the orphanage. While we were searching, Marysia came face to face with her sweetheart from Poland. Both were so shocked that they stared at each other for some time before either made any sound or movement. Then Michał approached Marysia and embraced her.[4]

Account of Tadeusz Pieczko

We were taken across the Caspian Sea from Russia to Iran in a small ship, or rather a boat. It was packed with children but there were also a few adults. The children occupied every available space, including life rafts and boats. There were no sleeping, dining or sanitary facilities of any kind. My brother and I found a small area under some insulated pipes. We didn't want to leave this spot for fear that someone else would move in and we would have no space to sit or lie down. I don't know how many days it took to reach Pahlavi, Iran, and I don't remember eating at all on this trip. There was a cut-away section on one side of the ship which, I suppose, was intended for dumping refuse; and that's what we used for a toilet. The real toilets on the ship were reserved for the use of the crew only. The trip was very frightening; the possibility of falling off the ship as it swayed in the tall waves was very real. I heard that someone did fall off. I heard screaming but didn't leave my space for fear of losing it. I also had to guard my sack containing all my worldly possessions. When we reached Pahlavi we were housed in huge English army tents. Our first meal consisted of crackers and salty margarine. Many of us got sick from it. In a couple of days the most undernourished children were separated from the rest and sent to a special fattening-up camp. I and my brother were in this group. What a life: just eating, sleeping and swimming in the Caspian Sea. After a few weeks we were reunited with the rest of the children, who by then were in a special camp in Tehran. As we traveled by bus from Pahlavi to Tehran I thought that we were passing through the most beautiful place in the world. This must have been the Garden of Eden. The vegetation was lush and green and fruit grew all along the road.[5]

Account of Sabina Kukla (née Lukasiewicz)

English authorities surrounded us with care after we disembarked in Pahlavi. We were deloused right away. We were given boiled rice with tinned mutton or beef. There were also hard-boiled eggs which the Persians sold, calling out *Yaycy Varoni*! (boiled eggs). People fell upon these eggs and on food generally, becoming very ill. Starved stomachs could not accept so much nourishment at once, causing intestinal twisting and cramps. We were loaded on open trucks and taken to the public baths. We had to leave all our possessions on the beach and we were promised that they would not be lost and that we would find them there on our return.

We stripped naked in the baths — children and adults without exception. We were shaved in all areas where lice could lodge and multiply. Warm water was poured over us and we were "punished" with birches. Following such a bath we emerged as God had made us. While we were bathing all our clothes were burnt. We were given a blanket each with which to cover ourselves and were driven back to the beach like that. And here there was one more shock! All our possessions had also been burnt. Hardly anyone saved their documents and photographs or other memorabilia. Only things contained in trunks survived because our bundles had been burnt. Burning feathers from pillows were carried along the beach by the wind. An extraordinary sight — the flames were taking our last memorabilia from us.[6]

Account of Anita Paschwa (née Kozicka)

On March 24, 1942, we boarded a Russian ship called Zdanov to Pahlavi, Iran. The seas were very rough. Many people became sick and died on the way. I did not dare move from my blanket for fear of coming in contact with the smelly mess that covered the deck of the ship. In the four weeks that followed more than 30,000 Polish soldiers, their families, and 11,000 orphaned children left Russia using this route. When we arrived in Pahlavi we all screamed: "Freedom, freedom, freedom!" When we reached the shore our clothes and blankets were taken from us and burned. We were bathed and given brand new clothes. But the sandy beaches of Pahlavi, the polluted sea water, the very hot sun and the weakened condition of many of the children and older people took their toll. The fact that they were buried in free soil was some comfort, but the loss was almost unbearable.[7]

Account of Wisia Reginella (née Danecka)

We reached Pahlavi at last. We walked, or rather dragged ourselves, to a camp some distance from the port. The Persians helped and received us kindly. Children showered us with gifts of fruit and sweets. Finally we arrived at the camp. There were army tents on the beach and little shops which sold everything. In the meantime I treated myself as best I could, chewing tea, coal and anything else anyone advised me to chew. I did not eat anything fat, yet the bloody diarrhoea would not give way.[8]

Account of Jane [Janina] Żebrowski-Bulmahn

[The] trip only lasted a couple of days and soon we were in Pahlavi, a port city in Persia (now Iran) on the Caspian Sea. We were the last transport out of Russia and arrived in Pahlavi on August 31, 1942.

It all seemed so unreal, like a wonderful dream. We were out of the hands of communists and finally free.

Straight from the ship we were escorted to bath houses. We had to strip completely and leave all our possessions at the entrance. Our heads, underarms, etc. were shaved.

This was done to delouse us from our stay in Russia. Men were taken to one bath building and women to another.

As we proceeded to the showers, I noticed that the people looked like skeletons — living, walking skeletons. The long months of hunger took their toll and the results were visible on all of us.

When we came out of the showers, we were given a set of clothing as well as immunization shots and vaccination. The clothes did not fit, in most cases, and all the children looked like boys with our heads shaved. We did not care. We were alive and free.

All this was done by Polish and English soldiers stationed in Pahlavi. However, all the costs involved were defrayed by the Polish government-in-exile which escaped to France and then England after the German takeover of Poland. The Polish soldiers who traveled with us were immediately taken to the Polish army camp.

We were then taken to large tents where each one received a screened-in bed complete with bedding. This was the first time we had slept on a regular bed with a pillow and all the bedding since we had left Poland. Right from the start men and women were separated. But we could visit each other during the day and at mealtimes.

At mealtimes we were directed to an army mess hall and given food twice a day. At first we were given only liquids and bread for a couple of days and were told that many of us would probably come down with dysentery from long periods of hunger. And sure enough, most of us did. Here we also met people who had come out of Russia earlier. We had a lot to share together.

As our systems strengthened, we were gradually given solid food. Medical attention was also provided for us.

In addition to the dysentery, we came down with some sort of eye problems. Children, in particular, were affected. Our eyes got very sensitive to the light so that we could hardly see, and at night filled with pus. When we woke up, we could not open our eyes. Mother kept some water handy and washed our eyes each morning till we could open them. It was a strange feeling having our eyelids "glued" together, but what a small price to pay for freedom. We were also given eye drops each day by an army doctor until our eyes cleared.

Our camp was located right on a beautiful beach where we could play and bathe for hours. There were always a number of fishing boats in the area. Some of them offered us a fish in trade for an empty bottle. We kept busy collecting bottles and trading for fish which our mothers prepared on handmade grills. We certainly enjoyed eating the fish.[9]

Account of Ryszard Tyrk

We finally arrived at the end of the eagerly longed-for first stage on our road to freedom. The camp at Krasnovodsk was surrounded by a barbed-wire fence. On one side sand stretched to the horizon; on the other, the sea. We were quartered in huge barracks. In comparison to these, airport hangers were like chicken coops. One such barracks housed 500 of us. This human anthill was overseen by the Polish army. Soldiers with eagles on their field-caps dispensed the food and provided medical assistance. The army was evacuated first; the civilians, as space permitted. We were packed like sardines; a number of us wound up in the engine room where the temperature reached 50°C. Our transports were well-traveled, steel-clad cargo ships and it was a wonder that they remained afloat. We were assigned to a ship which bore the name "Zdanov." While in Krasnovodsk, since the relations between the Soviet and Polish authorities worsened by the hour, we spoke of nothing else but whether they would let us go, whether they would recall us from the docked ships or even ships at sea. We boarded on August 13, 1942. On August 15, 1942, at 4:30 A.M., just after sunrise, we saw the Persian port at Pahlavi. We remained for a few hours on board ship while awaiting the barges which were to take us ashore. But before that happened a great consternation, a veritable panic, seized us all because of a rumor to the effect that the ship would soon sail back, that such orders had already arrived. Two people jumped ship intending to swim ashore; fortunately they were rescued. To restore order several shots were fired and that was that. At last the barges arrived and my foot touched free Persian soil a few minutes past eleven o'clock. The shoreline, as far as the eye could see, was filled with people. As it turned out, after our departure from Krasnovodsk two other ships left the port and reached Pahlavi, but unfortunately the third one was recalled after several hours at sea.

Pahlavi, a medium-sized port, was located a few kilometers from where we were quartered. The sandy, undulating landscape was covered with clumps of some kind of bushes. Our camp consisted of one concrete barracks and near it were a few hundred strange buildings made of poles driven into the sand and covered with mats. Both the military and the civilian camps were divided into two sections. The first, called "dirty," was a quarantine section. There, whoever did not already have typhus, got it. Dysentery, malaria and God knows what else also took their toll. A significant number of those in the "dirty" camp remained forever in the sandy hillsides of Pahlavi. Those without evident signs of illness were transferred to the "clean" camp. I am certain that both my mother and I owe our lives to my grandmother. She made sure we were provided for. From the camp kettle we received mostly fatty soup with large chunks of lamb in it; but there was not much meat, and the rest was all fat. We threw ourselves at these delicacies but Grandmother guarded them like a lioness and would not allow us to get near them. Rather, she heated water on some bricks that served as our stove and added to it a few spoonfuls of broth and some diced lean meat — that was our fare. She was also vigilant over what fruits we ate, and they were countless. Many people, however, gulped everything down that was near at hand. The result: typhus, twisting of the bowels, a short stay in the hospital, and eternal rest. We were moved to the "clean" camp and remained in Pahlavi for about three weeks. The children occupied themselves with playing ball made of rags, collecting interesting rocks and shells, and bathing in the sea, but only in the morning, since later in the day huge oil slicks floated on the water. The Persians set up many booths in the vicinity of the camp and for a very good price one could purchase hard-boiled eggs, fruits, nuts, and sweetmeats of ground walnuts and honey of many tastes and colors. Many Persians understood enough Russian to communicate with us. They were well-wishing, very cordial and presented the Polish youth with sundry delicious tidbits. From Pahlavi we went by truck to Tehran. The road led over dangerous mountain trails so narrow in places that the wheels of the vehicles slid along edges of chasms. Every few kilometers there were turnouts. We spent the night in Kazvin, where we washed and were fed soup consisting of lamb, paprika and raisins.

On September 8, 1942, we began our descent and finally down below we beheld a large town over which towered spiry minarets and domes of masques. On the outskirts of Tehran we were greeted by children carrying shallow baskets filled with fruit. The transports were directed to the five camps situated around the town. Camp No. 5 housed the orphans and teachers with families. The distribution centers at Ahvaz and the port at Khorramshahr in the Persian Gulf constituted two other stages of our journey. Here the paths of the exiles diverged: some Poles, via Karachi, went to India and to many settlements in Africa; others went to New Zealand, Canada, the United States and Mexico.[10]

Tehran

Milewski family memoir

(Stanisław) We stayed in a tent city just outside Pahlavi for few days and then were loaded onto British army trucks and taken to Tehran. (The Polish army, meanwhile, was transferred to Iraq.) The trucks we were in were driven by Indian soldiers and Persian civilians. Our journey took us through the majestic Elburz Mountains. The serpentine road was very narrow and in some places the trucks had to make several attempts in order to negotiate the road's sharp bends. As we gazed into the chasm below we prayed that our truck would not fall off the mountain. The view, however, was magnificent and we could see picturesque Persian villages surrounded by date and olive trees in the valleys below us. The houses were made out of mud bricks and animals could be seen in the streets.

We were one of the first transports of Polish people to reach Tehran at the beginning of April 1942. I remember that we were warmly greeted by the Persian people with gifts of food, dates and clothes. We were simply amazed by the sight of smiling people and a bustling city full of open shops and traffic.

Our place of residence was to be Camp No. 1 on the outskirts of the city. It belonged to the Persian air force and consisted of two large red brick buildings surrounded by a high brick wall. Inside the buildings were cement platforms that served as beds. For privacy, blankets were hung to separate families. There were so many of us, however, that some of us wound up sleeping on the cement floor and even outside. Eventually, due to the constant stream of new arrivals, a tent city emerged outside the walls. The tents were later replaced by mud-brick barracks and surrounded by a barbed-wire fence. We were very crowded: at times there were 7,000 people in the camp with about 80 people in one barracks.

There were four civilian camps and one orphanage in Tehran. The smaller building in our camp was transformed into a hospital and also became a residence for the staff and their families. Since my mother was a hospital nurse, my sister and I lived there, as did some of our close friends: Mrs. Makowicz and her daughter Barbara, Mrs. Dulemba, Mrs. Nowicki with her two sons, and others. There was only one very good doctor, Dr. Telerman. Severely ill patients were transferred to the nearby British hospital staffed by many doctors from India. I spent a few days there being treated for dehydration and dysentery.

As in Pahlavi, many Polish people died in Tehran soon after their arrival. They were put on the ground against the wall and later buried in a Polish cemetery. A large cemetery with about 3,000 Polish graves remains near Tehran to this day.

Like other children, Teresa and I attended school. I finished my fourth and fifth grade in a year and a half. There was a shortage of teachers and teaching materials such as books or even paper. The books we used were printed in Palestine and later in Iran. At first, classes were held outside, then in tents, and later in barracks. There was a constant turnover in teachers and students. Scouting and sports played an important role in our education. I attained the rank of patrol leader and played soccer. Gradually, we recovered physically and emotionally. As the summer grew warmer, we sometimes slept on the roof of the hospital from where we had the most spectacular view of the sunrise over the snow-covered peak of Mt. Damavand, the highest peak in the Elburz chain of mountains. To get outside the camp we needed a pass, often however we managed to get out through the holes in the fence. The land at the foot of the mountains was flat and contained several small villages surrounded by olive groves. There were goats, chickens and donkeys wandering about. The houses were made out of mud bricks. The vegetation on the mountains was sparse. We explored the countryside and collected porcupine needles. In the evening we watched camel caravans coming down from the mountains bringing goods to Tehran. I often went into the city with my mother, Teresa, and friends. It was fascinating to see people dressed in Persian clothes milling around in a bustling bazaar with dark winding alleys where one could buy anything from Persian rugs to engraved silver boxes. We bought two silver, decorative, curved, Persian knives and several ivory elephants, which I still have. There were magnificent mosques decorated with beautiful ceramic mosaics.

It was a great treat for us to be picked up from time to time by Colonel Antoni Szymański, the Polish military attaché in Tehran, for an outing in the city or a ride to the beautiful suburb of Shemran at the foot of the mountains. He was a childhood friend of my parents. He was also a friend of Shah Reza Pahlavi with whom he went hunting tigers in the mountains on horseback. Besides being a great sportsman, the Shah also owned several small Polish planes in which he performed aerobatics above the city of Tehran. We loved to watch him do this. In May 1943 we were visited by the Shah and Colonel Szymański during a large Polish Scout jamboree held in Manzar je-Shemran.

Each time a transport of new people arrived, the camp became alive and new friendships were forged. However, as the refugees were reassigned to the camps of India, Africa, Palestine and other places, the camp became deserted. Since Mother was a nurse, we had to remain in the empty camp waiting for the new arrivals. It was very lonely. The last transport arrived at the beginning of September 1943.

Meanwhile, my father and brother were in Iraq with the Polish Carpathian Division. Father visited us once in Tehran and spent a few days with Mother in a city hotel. They decided that we should go to Palestine, where I would join the Polish cadet school in Barbara, Teresa would join the military school for girls in Nazareth, and Mother would be employed in Nazareth as a supervisor and a school nurse.[11]

Account of Vala Lewicki (née Miron)

Tehran was very beautiful, full of magnificent gardens and groves, rich people, pretty women, mostly dressed in European-style clothes. Their transparent silk scarves drooping from their heads were a great contrast to the cotton, floral, orange scarves given to Polish women in the camps. There were very rich shops, lots of them, both above and below the ground. Where the smaller shops were cramped, goods such as fruit, nuts, silks, gold and even Russian gold coins were displayed on the sidewalks. But Tehran was also a city of very poor people — beggars really. Every few meters there stood a beggar with some disability, or just unemployed and unpaid. There was no social security, no religious benefactors to help the poor in Iran.[12]

Account of Stefania Buczak-Zarzycka

[Having left Pahlavi] in trucks and lorries which were partly covered, we began to wind our way along the most precarious road I have ever seen. On one side of the road huge walls of rocks blocked the sunlight while the other side dropped into sheer cliff faces. The teachers tried to distract our attention from the Elburz Mountains route but it was obvious that they were more anxious than we were. One of the trucks went over the side which temporarily held up the convoy. As our wheels began to slide downhill our teachers agitated mannerisms revealed our danger, but we completed the journey without further misadventure and we arrived at our camp on the outskirts of the city of Tehran. The orphanage was allowed some buildings but many people were still housed in tents grouped into four sections. We were part of the first camp. At first we were provided with flannelette dresses which were totally unsuited to the climate. Later, we were provided with more appropriate clothing. Here, our diet improved greatly: we were given fresh fruit and vegetables daily.

Mothers began to appear in search of their children, and these frantic, sometimes disturbed, women often mistook other children to be their own. It so happened that one such coincidence involved Antek and myself. Our names and birth dates were identical to those of the children of one mother who came to our orphanage. We were confronted by a strange lady who embraced us declaring herself to be my mother. When I denied this she began crying and shouting angry abuse at me: that I had forgotten her or that I was being hurtful and spiteful. At first, the main orphanage supervisor did not believe me having already seen many children confused by such dislocation as we had experienced. Not until our teacher, Pani Trybuchowska, appeared were Antek or I believed.

I felt so sorry for this woman who left still crying, wandering from hall to hall, calling out her children's names. By the end of the day that same woman returned to me to show me her children whom she had found safe and well. Her whole manner changed. As she left I felt happy for those children, but at the same time this incident heightened my concern for my mother whom I had last seen gravely ill. We saw or heard of many women whose children had died become so grief-stricken that they claimed small children from the orphanage who were not their own at all. Often the authorities had great difficulty in verifying claims or in tracing these children once they had been taken from the orphanage.

Epidemics of malaria and a serious form of conjunctivitis plagued the orphanage; I was also taken to the hospital. This was an awkward time because my group was in the process of being transported to Africa and it took all my strength to convince the authorities that Antek and I should remain in Tehran so that my mother could reach us. Once the group had gone Antek had nowhere to sleep, so he curled up under my hospital bed until he was discovered by a doctor on night duty. This doctor arranged accommodation for him at a child-care centre for children awaiting their mothers. While in the hospital, I exacerbated my condition by constantly rubbing my eyes, for I was terrified that once I left the hospital I would be allotted to another orphanage and would be separated from Antek as well.

Two weeks after my admission to the hospital, my sister Marysia came for us as my mother was still too ill to travel far. Antek was visiting me, sitting on the window sill in his usual pose. Even though I had not yet fully recovered the three of us left the hospital and set about registering ourselves for ration cards and passes for unrestricted movement around the camps. As we had arrived at the office a little too late to receive our passes, we decided to brazen it out and take our chances by simply walking through the check points.

However, Antek's and my self control gave away as we approached the gate and we started to run through it. Of course, the two guards gave chase while another detained Marysia. We ducked into the shrubbery and after several hours, when the guards realised that we would not emerge, they allowed Marysia to go through the check point. Mud-splattered and scratched, we climbed out of the bushes to meet our sister further down the road.

At last we were reunited with our mother, and this time we vowed that we would never again be separated. Now all we needed to be complete was Father and Ola. Obtaining the address of my father's unit we wrote letter after letter but received no word from him. Most of our letters were returned signed or stamped "address unknown." We found out from the *junaczki* group that Ola was once again in hospital with pneumonia. The mortality rate of that organization was high and we decided to take her from the hospital immediately and care for her ourselves. Some of her friends arranged a lift for her to our tent and at last we were a family unit again, bar one very important member....

At about seven o'clock, into our tent walked a beautifully dressed, elegant woman. As she stood before us I could see that her head was unshaven and coifed, which was most unusual for that camp. We were all a little taken aback by this sophisticated lady; no one in camp had possessed fine clothes or worn makeup for three years.

"Are these your children?" the woman began. Her name was Burzacka and in introducing herself and her circumstances, she made a point of dropping the name of her aristocratic relations, the Dzieduszycki. I could see how my mother's face turned to the woman with interest at this point. She explained that she had been deported quite late in the war, that news of the amnesty had caught up with her in the train and so she was able to come directly to Tehran without ever having spent time in the Soviet Union. This explained her appearance. She had been traveling with her cousins and her stepdaughter, Isabella, who died of diphtheria two weeks earlier. Distress was evident in her voice as she admitted that she had not yet informed her husband of his daughter's death. A Polish army major, he was due in Tehran shortly on leave and she dreaded his reaction to the news, as he was devoted to Isabella. She feared that he would blame her for neglecting Isabella. Then she quickly came to the point of her visit. Would my mother give up one of her daughters for adoption? Suddenly, we began to listen intently to this woman. She promised to care for this child and give her every possible material and social advantage. She would even allow the girl to visit her family.

My mother did not, as a rule, demonstrate much emotion and kept her thoughts to herself. Without even thinking long she asked: "Which child?"

The woman turned and pointed to me. Then she squatted down in front of me and repeated her promises to me. I resembled her stepdaughter; perhaps another child would help her husband overcome the grief he would surely feel. I asked her whether our families would always travel together and she replied that this would not be possible. Bursting into tears I refused. My sister Marysia, nudged my ribs and encouraged me to go. I cried even more until finally my mother sighed: "Stop crying, no-one is sending you if you don't want to go."

The lady stood up but before she left she asked me to reconsider my decision. I shook my head to indicate no; even though I loved my mother I could not understand why she would have wished me to leave with that woman. I felt strangely alone within my own family circle for a time but then the day-to-day problems clouded this visit into the background. However, now I felt that this incident placed some kind of barrier between my mother and myself; our relationship was never quite the same.

While in Tehran, the revolution broke out and we were ordered to stay flat on the floor in our tents. For the rest of that day and night, we heard continuous explosions, mortar fire and shouts. Next morning, a silence fell so suddenly that it was eerie at first.

For three days, the city was under martial law, but then normality was reestablished. We left Tehran almost immediately.[13]

Account of Tadeusz Pieczko

In our camp in Tehran we saw many Polish and British soldiers. I found one of my paternal uncles there. I also met a lady who came from our village in Poland. She had a young daughter who was very friendly with the soldiers. As a result, she and her mother ate very well. The young girl also had a very nice bicycle. Many years later, I learned that this girl had died at a young age from V.D. I remember that her mother's husband was killed in an accident in the field and that I attended his wake. Whenever I visited this family I would always be given extra food. Since the daughter was also in charge of handing out bread in the kitchen lines, I was able to get an extra loaf now and then. This made me popular with the other children in my group. Once they gave me some coins, so I went to the market, where the merchants were selling their wares and food — mostly fruits and vegetables — and I bought a tomato. I was very hungry, but wanting to cherish the tomato a bit longer, I held it to my nose and smelled it. I remember that aroma to this day.

While we were there, an uprising occurred in Iran against the ruling Shah. Since he was in hiding, his royal palace, which was outside of Tehran, was unoccupied except for some servants, a maintenance crew and a few guards. We took this opportunity to visit the palace. What a sight! I never saw anything like it before or since anywhere in the world. I still remember the water cascading down one of the staircases leading to the palace and the two huge marble lions guarding the entrance. The grounds were immaculate. There were greenhouses and wild birds.

By this time we were beginning to look fairly prosperous and our sacks were pretty well filled. We were all issued a bar of soap, a washcloth, a towel, a toothbrush and tooth powder — in addition to the bowl and spoon which we brought with us from Russia.

Blankets were given to us later, as well as a fork and knife and a tin cup. Up to this time we didn't bother changing our clothes since all we had were the clothes on our backs. Things were different now.

In Tehran, we were able for the first time since leaving Poland to attend religious services. These were held outdoors. On All Souls' Day we went to a nearby cemetery and, in a section where Polish soldiers were buried, we found the grave of one of my uncles. We received special religious instructions and made our First Holy Communion. For this occasion all the boys received a clean pair of pants and a shirt and the girls got new dresses. After Communion we were treated to doughnuts and hot cocoa, and what a treat that was; we didn't remember what they tasted like anymore.

Our sleeping quarters were located in several large halls. Each child's space, which no one dared trespass, consisted of a blanket on the floor folded in half on top of which lay the sack with all our worldly possessions....

While there, I became seriously ill and ended up in the general hospital in Tehran. My symptoms consisted of choking and I had a difficult time breathing—a condition that repeated itself later in India. I entered the hospital in Tehran on the same day that my brother Eugene left. He was there for the removal of some kind of growth on his cheek.

We always observed the adults who arrived from time to time from Russia in the hope of finding our parents, relatives or neighbors. I remember standing by a public washing area one time and observing a man who resembled one of my cousins very much. As I stood there studying him while he shaved, he kept his eye on me, worrying that I might steal his soap.

I did find an uncle who looked much like my father. I visited him once in the army tent where he lived with his family. They treated me to a piece of fruit.

After spending a few months in Tehran, we were told to get our things together and prepare for departure. None of us children knew where we were going and we really didn't care ... as long as we were not separated from our brothers or sisters. We were taken to a nearby railroad station in army trucks. There, we boarded a train and headed south for the Persian Gulf. But only half of the original group of children made this trip; the other half was shipped to a different destination. It seemed that every time our group stopped somewhere for an indefinite period of time it would be split in half and sent in two different directions when the time came to move on.[14]

Account of Marysia Pienta (née Wilgut)

While in Tehran, my mother and oldest sister, Jasia, contracted Typhus. They were hospitalized in town and I was left to care for my two younger sisters, Zosia and Krysia. The only transportation to town was a bus that was always full. I needed to see my mother and Jasia, and perhaps more importantly, they needed to see me. My mother was always so happy to see me. She was glad to know that my younger sisters and I were all right.

Many times, the bus to town was full and the driver refused to open the door to let me on. I had to get to the hospital, so friends helped me and pushed me through the window so I could ride to town. Once I was at the hospital, it was very difficult to find my mother and sister. There were so many sick people and they all had their heads shaved. Then I heard my mother's voice as she sang the hymns I was so familiar with. I found her.

Getting back to camp was difficult and sometimes treacherous. I often missed the bus that was going back to camp and I had to walk. I was a young girl, alone in the dark. I trembled with fear. I knew there was no choice. I had to get back to my camp. I started walking and prayed very hard. I believe in angels and I know that my guardian angel was with me. I could feel her presence. I always made it back safely.[15]

Account of Anita Paschwa (née Kozicka)

From Pahlavi we were transferred to Tehran. From the windows of the camp orphanage I would watch the bodies being taken to the mortuary. I watched intently whenever I could looking for the face of my sister, Maria. She was very sick when I said good-bye to her in Guzar and I prayed that God would watch over her for me. She had been my mother since the death of my own mother in Poland.

There was a total of five camps of Polish refugees in various countries. There were about 8,000 people in our camp in Tehran. I tried to keep track of Maria through the authorities in our camp. After two months of no word of her, I was told that she had been located in Camp II in Iran, and that she would soon be shipping out to Palestine with the Polish army. God had once again answered my prayers, and we visited with each other each relieved that the other had not starved to death. We said good-bye a second time.

When the camp authorities began to organize a school for the orphans, I was asked to what grade I would like to be assigned. Before I left Poland I was in the fourth grade, but I had not been in school for two years and I was concerned that I had forgotten most of what I had learned. But once again I was a happy fourth grader. I loved school and was a very conscientious student.[16]

Account of Maria Gabiniewicz

We left the Soviet Union on the last transport. The thousands of despairing Poles left behind were sent back to the kolkhozes. I will never forget the dangerous trip by truck along the mountain range from Ashkhabad through Mashhad to Tehran. At 2,500 meters above sea level we crossed the border.

After the Gehenna through which we passed, Tehran was a completely different world. Camp life was orderly, there was a school, we had scouting, and priests ministered to our spiritual needs....

Poland was far away but so near the heart. Mother would sometimes take me into town, to Tehran. On the other side of the camp enclosure were signs that read: Warszawa 4,340 km, Tehran 2 km, Kraków ... Poznań ... Lwów ... Wilno ... From the moment we left the Soviet Union we were returning to Poland. Mother engraved the love of the fatherland on her heart and, together with my father, imparted that love to us.

Tehran was the gate through which we were sent in groups to different parts of the world. Our stay in Ahvaz in the Persian Gulf was short. I remember the unbearable heat. We slept in tight quarters, in the sultan's stables. But we rejoiced over our freedom. We were happy. Mother declined the tempting offer to go to Santa Rosa in Mexico. She volunteered for the transport to Africa through India. She figured that Africa was closer to Europe and that perhaps someday we would return to Poland.[17]

Account of Jane [Janina] Żebrowski-Bulmahn

Then came time to leave for our next destination. Early in the morning the British army trucks showed up to pick us up. From Pahlavi we were on the way to Tehran, the capital of Persia. There were about 100 trucks in our convoy.

I will never forget the trip. The narrow road that led through the Elburz canyon seemed so huge that it made me dizzy looking down. Our drivers, however, did not slow down but negotiated the turns and twists in the road at a great speed. Many times we held our breath, thinking that any moment we would either be hit by the truck behind us or, with the driver unable to control his vehicle, plunge to the bottom. We did a lot of praying that the trucks would not veer off the road.

We made one stop at a small oasis where we could get water and attend to our bathroom needs. We could not stay very long since other trucks were pulling in and we had to be on our way again. After many hours, we made it safely to Tehran.

Here, again, we were given shelter in tents next to an English/Polish army camp. By now food was no problem, and we were beginning to regain strength in body and spirit. We could also go to the city of Tehran anytime we wished since it was within walking distance. I remember going with Mother and standing in front of the Shah's beautiful white palace. I also remember many beggars sitting on the ground just outside the palace gates....

Now life went on as usual. We were again a family except that the men and women continued being separated with living quarters in different parts of the camp. I assume this was done to avoid pregnancies. We visited with each other, as before, during the day and at meal times.

Here, for the first time since we left Poland, children were gathered for schooling. I entered third grade since that was the grade I would have attended in Poland. Polish teachers were recruited from our group. We were given paper and pencils and had to sit on the ground since no desks were available. There were no textbooks, but the teachers did a very good job from memory, and we were making steady progress. Polish schooling continued all through the war years. It lasted all year long to make up for the time lost in Russia. The teachers were not paid but gladly contributed their skill and knowledge.

While still in Tehran, I came down with malaria. It was a dreaded illness and many people did not survive. Mother had it earlier in Uzbekistan and it took her a long time to regain strength. I remember being so very cold that my whole body shook. I was hospitalized, given some medication and then lost consciousness. When I woke up a few days later, I was completely drained of all energy. When finally released from the hospital I could barely walk. Mother had to help me.

Little by little I, too, recovered. However, for months afterwards I had severe pains in my middle back and was told that malaria had settled in my kidneys. The doctor was confident that eventually the pain would go away. Years later I was told that one of my kidneys was deformed, possibly due to malaria.

When my strength allowed, I returned to school again, and joined in other activities set up for us in the camp. A Scout troop was formed and I watched them often after school as they were drilling and marching. I longed to join them and I was old enough to do so, but my parents would not allow me since I still had severe back pains.

I remember sitting on a bench and watching their every move. I was there whenever they met. They knew how much I longed to join them and included me in some of their activities.

One activity I did join was target shooting. It was organized by one of the Polish soldiers in the military camp and any child 12 years or older could participate. The only guns available were real guns but loaded with blanks. After seeing so many guns in my life, it felt strange to have one in my hand. Our first instruction was on safety before we proceeded to target shooting. We all learned a lot from this experience.

As I look back, what was surprising was that no one from our family perished in Russia in spite of hunger, unsanitary conditions, and no medical help. We were an exception, however, since many people got sick and died in Russia, mostly from typhus and dysentery and, of course, malnutrition and hard work.[18]

Account of Andrzej Szujecki

The trip wore me out so much that I'm not exactly sure when and by what way we arrived in Tehran. I came to when the truck stopped near the Polish Camp No. 1. It was afternoon and the sun lit up the yellow wall surrounding the camp. A while later we found ourselves in an expansive yard surrounded by dark concrete buildings. We were then led through a gate in the wall to a row of unfired brick barracks. This was to be our "town" in which we would remain for over a year.

Our barracks was located in the first row nearest the wall and bore a number in the low twenties. Similar structures were located around a large water basin. There were about 100 of them in all, not counting the few dozen tents occupied by the military and yunak units which were taken down shortly after their departure. The barracks had four entrances, two on each side, which divided it into three sections. About 80 persons were quartered therein. The entire interior consisted of beds made of unfinished boards. Between the beds and the walls were narrow passageways hardly wide enough for two persons to pass. The quarters were so cramped that in trying to change one's sleeping position one would often awaken one's neighbors. In subsequent months, as people left for South Africa and India, it became less crowded and individual families found intimacy by separating themselves from their neighbors by means of blankets, boards and other materials.

Life's basic needs were met in the course of the daily routine of the military camp. Washrooms and showers were located about a hundred meters away, mostly under the open sky. A bit further was the field kitchen from which orderlies brought us three meals a day. The morning and evening meal consisted of coffee or tea, bread, margarine or butter from British military tins, and yellow cheese. Sometimes other things were served. The dinner menu consisted mostly of well-baked brown goulash and macaroni. The food, brought to the barracks in pails, was dished out into mess-tins and aluminum plates or poured into cups.

The camp, surrounded with barbed wire, was spacious: it took over ten minutes to walk from one end to the other. The primitive, smelly latrines, constantly being treated with quicklime, were located on the periphery of the camp. Dysentery was rife. In Camp No. 1, in addition to the barracks which could house about 7,000 persons, there were brick, storied buildings surrounded by a wall. They were located between the barracks and the road leading eastward to downtown Tehran. Formerly, Persian army officers were located in these buildings. Now, the building closest to the barracks served as a hospital and the one nearest the road housed the camp administrative offices, Scout clubroom and the Poles who arrived here before us in August or September 1942. Two other buildings served as a school and home for the Polish refugees from the USSR. There were, therefore, about 8,000 Poles in the entire camp.

At that time there were four other Polish camps in Tehran. Camp No. 2 was located about two kilometers from the first camp. Camp No. 3 was nicely situated 600 meters beyond Tehran at the foothills of some mountains. Both of these served the civilians who arrived here already in the spring of 1942. The camp we called No. 4, located by the road between Camp No. 2 and Tehran, was reserved chiefly for Polish officers awaiting assignment or discharge. Camp No. 5 was not really a camp but a building in Tehran that served as a Polish orphanage.

Shortly after arriving at Camp No. 1, I was assigned to the fourth grade on the testimony of my mother that that's the grade I was attending in Lwów. The school was located in several typical barracks which were not equipped for educational purposes. They were dark and dirty. There were about 30 boys and girls in our class. Many of the boys and even certain girls that came recently from Ashkhabad and Mashhad had shaven heads and sallow complexions. We were dressed in any old way, in ill-fitting suit coats and sweaters. The clothes which we received from the camp supply depot came mostly from the Polish-American community, the UNRRA [United Nations Relief and Rehabilitation Administration] and other sources. Some of us came to school in Scout uniforms sown in the camp tailor shops. These were made of light khaki-colored military materials. Our desks and benches came from kindergartens and we had a difficult time adjusting ourselves to them. Even though we were in the fourth grade, the majority of my classmates had a difficult time reading and wrote badly making very many mistakes. The few teachers we had tried mainly to bring us up to par with our own age group. I remember that we had so few textbooks that the teachers had to borrow them from each other for classes. We used graphite tablets and slate pencils. Being one of the oldest in my class and among those whose education was not neglected, I was in the beginning bored to tears and couldn't wait until recess to play a game we called "buttons." This game became very popular among the boys in 1942 and 1943 and was not without its hazards. Many of my contemporaries lost even the buttons off their own clothing and walked around holding up their pants with their hands or supporting them by means of a piece of string. The winners walked around with entire sacks of buttons of various shapes, colors and sizes. The popularity of that game ended as suddenly as it had begun, but suitable buttons continued to be used as "soccer balls" on miniature fields constructed on tables.

Toward the end of 1942 our school was moved to more suitably prepared barracks with school desks, a blackboard and much better conditions for studying. Our tutor was Helena Kurzejowa with whose son, Janusz, I became very friendly. Throughout the entire sojourn of the refugees the teaching staff and the students kept changing. The course of studies was therefore irregular. Nevertheless, I completed grades four and five in Tehran. Although school had an important influence on the development of the children and young people, in my case — and perhaps in that of many others — scouting played an even more important role.

My road to scouting in Tehran let through the Scout clubroom located in block 1 whose best section, as far as I was concerned, was the small library with Polish books printed mainly in Palestine but also in England. The library and scouting were under the watchful eyes of several older girls led by the adjutant troop leader Janina Zarębianka, and assisted by Adolfina Tillówna, the leader of the team II Girl Guides, and Danuta Pstrokońska, who had a funny way of pronouncing the letter "r" and whom I liked the best. Because I frequented the library often I was noticed and soon accepted to the St. Kinga scouting team.

The unit (under Wojciech Stroka) met almost daily; the team (under Zdzisław Dussil) met less often. We learned how to march, track, tie knots and provide first-aid assistance....

On November 1, 1942, I was assigned guard duty in the cemetery in which over 1,000 Poles were buried by this time. Among the fresh graves wound hundreds, perhaps thousands, of the residents of our camps. Candles burned, a few flowers were laid on the graves. The cemetery had two gates: one led to the main street near which a few trees grew, the other was a wide opening in the wall through which one could see a semi-desert with small mountains on the horizon. Standing near the gate on clear days one could see the distant, perpetually snow-covered Damavand, the tallest peak of the massive Elburz Mountains. When the festivities of All Souls' Day were over and several months went by, the cemetery became unexpectedly the location of nocturnal Scout-training exercises.[19]

Account of Stanisùawa Jutrzenka-Trzebiatowska

The transit to Tehran was carried out in trucks driven by experienced Persians. The road was quite narrow. On one side could be seen the distant chain of the Elburz Mountains with the extinct volcano Damavand. On the other side precipitous, deep valleys into which two trucks, heavily laden with people, had the misfortune to roll.

At several points immediately before Tehran there were medical commissions checking the sanitary condition of people, as well as suitcases and bundles. Many of the latter, considered unsuitable to cross the border, were burnt on an enormous bonfire. In almost 100% of cases lice- and tick-ridden hair was cut off. Both Danusia and I emerged still in possession of our hair and suitcases. Our suitcases were momentarily opened by the authorities and passed through the control without problems.

Our arrival in Tehran was full of surprises because it was Good Friday prior to Easter. All kinds of cakes, as well as hard boiled eggs in great baskets had been brought in large quantities to both the enormous barracks and the air-force buildings. These had been vacated for us — homeless and hungry people. As we made our way through the streets of the town, the Persians threw bunches of flowers from balconies into the trucks, accentuating the friendly welcome. It was not surprising, therefore, that there were tears of emotion and joy, discreetly wiped away, in that pleasant, friendly atmosphere.[20]

Isfahan

Account of Aniela Molek-Piotrowska

Pahlavi was a transit camp. After a short rest there we were ready for further travel to Tehran.

There our orphanage was moved to Isfahan, the former capital of Persia. Premises belonging to Persian magnates were put at the disposal of Polish children, personnel and social welfare. Our well-being was assured for a time. Children under six years of age were placed under special care. Our female establishment was located on a large area surrounded by a high wall. The two-storey building faced the garden, with French windows giving access to a balcony. It stood in the shade of fruit trees and large bushes and there were many beautiful trees including apples, pomegranates and many other fruit trees. The garden was a wonderful place in which to rest in the shade of the spreading trees. We had splendid conditions, thanks to the Persian magnates.

Before long schools were established — primary, general and professional — offering a variety of courses. There were many such establishments in Isfahan. In ours there were children up to primary school age. Normal lessons commenced as it was necessary to make up for lost time. We visited Persian heritage sites in our free time. In my memory I have preserved ancient Isfahan and many impressions — the famous slim minarets, Persian bazaars, eastern traditions and customs.[21]

Account of Anita Paschwa (née Kozicka)

In June of 1942 our group moved again, this time to the town of Isfahan in central Iran. It was later known as the "City of Polish Children." All the orphans were moved there because the climate was much more conducive to restoring health to children weakened by the struggle in Russia. There were 20 camps in Isfahan in all. I was in Camp IV at first and later moved to Camp XII. That camp was housed in a beautiful mansion. The first floor held school rooms and offices and the second, the dormitory where we slept. This was a very happy time for me, although there again I had a brush with death.

Some of my friends and I decided to go into the vineyards which were off-limits to us. There were no grapes left on the branches, so we began to eat those that had fallen to the ground. When the dinner bell rang I made my way to the bathroom to wash up, but before I got there I fainted and lay there until I was found after dinner. I woke up two weeks later in the hospital. I had been in a coma. I had very high fever, a rash, and what looked like bee stings all over my body. The doctors never examined what was in my stomach or did any other testing, so no one knew I had eaten those grapes, which turned out to have been infested with insects. I almost did not survive the ordeal. God had spared me once again.

In Isfahan, in addition to school, I was able to participate in scouting. I earned my scouting cross, "Czuwaj," and had lots of good times in the process. We hiked around the mountains with full stomachs and good friends. By December 1942 there were 25,000 Polish refugees in Isfahan.[22]

Account of Andrzej Czcibor-Piotrowski

I'm in the third section, in the field hospital staffed by the Fathers. My number is 57 (we were numbered according to our size from the shortest to the tallest, the tallest fellow was designated as "one hundred"). In this monastery, surrounded by a high wall, we are as if born again. Bathed, finally washed and clean, we stand as naked as God made us, and the caretakers in brown habits — there are five of them — hand us our bed linen, socks, bright linen clothes and suede summer loafers. We dress quickly and now are presentable. They feed us as much as we want; we eat mostly rice, variously prepared. It is delicious.

Our lessons will supposedly begin tomorrow. I will be in the fourth grade, skipping third grade entirely and having completed barely two grades in Warsaw before the war. During the Soviet occupation of Lwów I began my education in the first grade in the Ukrainian language, and while in exile, in Panina, I became a first grader again this time in a Russian school....

In Isfahan we studied two foreign languages, English and Persian, and in addition to doing manual labor we engraved. A Persian artist drew delicate patterns and ornaments (consisting mostly of motifs of birds of paradise and complicated arabesque forms) on variously shaped brass plates. The plates were connected by layers of a black substance resembling tar, and then — some with lesser, others with greater skill — we would tap a graver lightly with a hammer along the drawn patterns. To some of us — but unfortunately not to me — this seemed to be a splendid thing and we gazed with wonder at the forms that emerged. It was difficult to believe that our boys were capable of mastering so soon the secrets of this exotic art form.

I became quickly accustomed to the heat. I did not even sweat in the dry air — until I contracted malaria.... During the day we kept our clothing to a minimum, and at night we slept naked under bed covers.

In our Camp No. 3, supported as we found out by our Holy Father Pius XII, I received my first initiation.... One day two of my friends and I went to town with the pocket money we had saved up. A shopkeeper that we knew counted our money and in return handed us a full bottle with a Russian label that read: Żubrówka [a vodka flavored with the sweet-scented grass Hierchloe].

For Sunday Masses we went to Camp No. 2, the girls' camp. I will never forget *My Sunday Missal* or the celebrant, our catechist Fr. Franciszek Tomasik. I scanned the Latin text which was translated into Polish on the opposite page. With exceptional zeal, I prayed for the dead, naming in my mind my mother, who died there in the North being scarcely 35 years of age.

We prepared ourselves for our First Holy Communion. I already knew what sin was and that by committing it we offended God.... I could therefore go to confession and receive God's body. At the time all of this seemed mysterious and unusual to me.

About one year later I had another exciting experience: Confirmation. I did not have any trouble picking out a name for myself. I knew that when the priest would come to me I would whisper: Franciszek, the name of our catechist so loved by us all.... The clergyman who bestowed upon us the sacrament of Confirmation was Monsignore Alcido Marina, archbishop and apostolic legate.... During the solemn celebration of the Mass I stood right behind him and held his miter in my trembling hands. I loved not only our catechist priest; there was also Sister Maria, who took a great liking to me and to whom I showed great tenderness. On many occasions she would take me hand in hand to the sanatorium where, lying as quietly as a mouse in a corner bed, I would catch an afternoon siesta among the girls.

In Isfahan we were confronted by someone's death only once, when an automobile ran over one of our friends from Camp No. 15. I came there after leaving Camp No. 3 and then Camp No. 6, located in a one-storied building with offices in a beautiful, spacious park surrounded by a high wall.

I often walked by myself through this paradise of tall mulberry, fig, and quince trees and pistachio bushes. Sometimes I would hum a melody to myself about an orphan pasturing cows beyond the river and cry away pretending that I was that orphan....

We had our beloved games, pastimes, and sweets that we purchased with our pocket money and indulged in. I don't remember how much money we received, but it was enough to assure us of one hour's ride on a motorcycle. An enterprising Persian made quite a profit off us from that "wanderer" of his. He rented us that vehicle, held together by a miracle, and off we went for a ride, alone and naturally without a driver's license, along the less-traveled city streets. On other occasions we would rent bicycles, and as a group — boys and girls together — we would go on longer trips on the outskirts of Isfahan.

From among my Persian and Armenian friends I most fondly remember: Rahim, a Persian butcher by trade, but one who loved wrestling and taught us that sport, and who was as beautiful as a prince out of an eastern legend by Sartep; and Andranik, an Armenian who accompanied us on our outings and with us climbed Kuh-e Sefid, the Mountain of Wisdom over 3,000 meters high. We communicated by means of a strange and straightforward language consisting of Russian, English, and Persian words. As for the sweets, we delighted in the oriental sweetmeats consisting of ground walnuts and honey. We also loved roasted walnuts and raisins and always tried to have a handful of them in our pockets.

I sympathized with the Persian women who, irrespective of age, went about in loose garments and breeches and in wraps that hid the face leaving only one eye exposed. The only exception were the Europeanized dark-headed and plump wives of the military personnel. The officers constituted a separate caste here. They wore beautiful light-brown uniforms cut in the German fashion and also hats. They were an impressive sight. We were all envious of them and we looked at the rank and file soldiers with a certain forbearance and compassion since they often wore rags, were barefooted, carried their guns on a string, and for a few pennies were ready to part with their bayonets or rifle magazines.

I acquired oriental knowledge. I remember that I studied a long time how to snap my fingers in a variety of ways. It's not a simple matter to master this task and later to use it as an accompaniment to a song. I tried and tried until one day, in a math class being conducted by Bronisław Czopa, after repeated attempts all of a sudden I succeeded in bringing forth a loud snap. "Piotrowski," said the professor without much reflection, "get out!" Although I was reprimanded and punished, I felt proud of my accomplishment nonetheless. Now I could join the choir and together with Rahim, while snapping away, sang Persian songs about an evening escapade to Lalehzar and an encounter with a beautiful maiden....

Meanwhile, I was approaching my thirteenth birthday. I thought up a present for myself: I volunteered for the Polish Merchant Marine school which was to be opened in Great Britain. "Obi," as I called my Persian friend Albin, and I found ourselves on a list of the lucky ones. Along with them we set out on a long and distant road, but, as it turned out, not one free of dangers.[23]

Ahvaz

Account of Vala Lewicki (née Miron)

On the way to the Persian Gulf, our group stopped in Ahvaz, one of the hottest places on earth. Barracks here were built of concrete, so the heat in them was bearable. From noon until 6:00 P.M. no one was allowed to go outside without good reason, such as collecting buckets of food for distribution inside. We had lots of food and fruit and medicine. Since malaria was the worst sickness to be feared there, twice a day we were made to swallow Atebrin and salt tablets in front of the health inspectors. Children attended a school where English was taught.

Our camp was adjacent to an Indian army camp and hospital with mixed staff: Polish, English and mostly Indians, many of whom could speak Polish. But they had no Polish girls. This was forbidden by both European and Indian officials. Our girls gained rather than lost by this decree. About 6:00 P.M. an American invasion would pour into the Polish civilian camp from nearby camps and the city. This was also forbidden and the camp had barbed wire all round it, but the Americans found a way. They cut holes through the wire. But there was another obstacle to entering our camp. Hundreds of Polish children would always stand in those gaps and would not go away until the Americans had given them chewing gum. Veronica was among them. So we always had chewing gum in abundance. Children also looked out for the military police who were supposed to prevent the soldiers from coming to the camp. But the GIs had a strong sense of comradeship. If one soldier was caught by the MPs he would shout: "MPs — run for your lives!" This message was passed on by the children as well until every man had left our camp.[24]

Account of Stefania Buczak-Zarzycka

Our next stop was Ahvaz where we were housed in the army barracks and stables. The city was in the middle of seasonal sandstorms and a heat wave so we could only walk about if our faces were covered in wet towels. I heard someone remark that this must be hell on earth. This general sentiment was compounded by the news that General Sikorski and his daughter had died in a plane crash over Gibraltar (July 4, 1943). This was a disaster personally felt by all because we knew it was General Sikorski who had been responsible for our rescue from the Soviet Union. What would happen to us now? His Requiem Mass was attended by all at the camp and all mourned deeply....

On the 31st of March, 1943, we received notification that my father was now officially classified as "missing in action" and that my mother was now entitled to a pension. She refused to accept this news insisting to officials that her husband was alive, and she also refused the pension which she stated was implying his death.[25]

Account of Eugeniusz Knurek

I came to Ahvaz from the orphanage in Tehran. This was in September 1943. I stayed there until the end of 1945. The memories of that camp are a legion — both happy and sad.

As did so many others, I also contracted malaria, had terrible shivers and, later, attacks of fever. I was therefore taken to a hospital where I underwent a three-week cure. The worst part of it all was that although after a few days a person felt better, yet he had to lie there for weeks on end, and that was difficult to bear. My friends entertained themselves, played ball, watched films in the open air, and here one had to lie in bed. And so one day on a whim I decided to sneak out, got past the nurse without being observed, and went to watch a film. Naturally my absence was noted in spite of the fact that I had arranged my bed to make it seem as if I were still in it. The following day the doctor, as punishment, ordered that all my clothing and my pajamas be confiscated and so, being naked, I had to remain in my bed for the next 48 hours, And because there were women and girls in that place, I was mortified.

My second recollection had to do with learning how to ride a bicycle. We often snuck out of the camp without passes in order to go into town and rent a bicycle for an hour. For this privilege we bartered milk, Australian canned cheese, chocolates, etc. One day it was announced in the camp that no one should go into town because of the Muslim holiday, Ramadan, during which all the stores would be closed and because it would be unsafe. But the desire to ride a bicycle was stronger than the prohibition. Together with one of my friends I snuck out of the camp and went into town. Sure enough, everything was closed. We turned into an alley off the main street and froze with fear. Before us, at a distance of some 100 meters, was a group of men, some of whom were naked to the waist, who sang, shouted, and chastised their bodies with whips. We were seized by great fear and made tracks as fast as we could. After covering a few dozen meters I met an American military patrol and asked to be taken back to the Polish camp. My friend, who ran in the opposite direction, did not resurface for a long time. Rumors circulated that he was abducted by the Persians. Great was his mother's despair and emotions ran high in the camp. Suddenly, at sundown, an army jeep rode into camp with two American soldiers and between them sat the Polish boy. As we found out later, he too ran into a military patrol and was first taken to their own camp. There he was fed and given chocolates and chewing gum. But this was not the end of our escapades. The following day we had to stand before the camp commandant as well as listen to the reprimands of the director of the school and our teacher — never mind our mothers — but somehow we survived it all. In 1945 we were transferred from Ahvaz to Lebanon by way of Iraq (we spent two weeks in Baghdad) and Syria. I stayed in Ajaltoun, was moved in 1947 to Zauk Michael, and a year later left for Argentina.[26]

Lebanon

Zauk Michael

Account of Teresa Żurkowska-Wanat

Zauk Michael is a town located in a mountainous area north of Beirut with a beautiful view of the Mediterranean Sea.

A group of orphans from Isfahan was sent to this largest Polish settlement in Lebanon. However, before suitable arrangements were made, we had to live together in a building consisting of several rooms and had to fend for ourselves. The oldest girls there were not yet seventeen and they had to provide for our daily needs, go shopping, cook, wash clothes, clean, and take care of the finances — a task that was completely new to them. They had to do all of this in addition to their regular scholastic duties, which naturally suffered. It soon became apparent that these responsibilities were too much for them.

We received the news of the founding of a boarding school with great joy. Wanda Ustrzycka assumed this responsibility. She was a person with a great deal of pedagogical and administrative experience. She was a good organizer and was full of life and energy. She picked her own staff. For the boarding school we rented a building from the mayor of the town. It stood on the highest hill amid almond and olive trees that gave off a beautiful scent and bloomed fabulously in springtime. The entire property was surrounded by a high wall, but a tall metal gate was always left invitingly open. Near the gate was a spring which provided us with water. The orphans arrived at this school in February 1946 and lived there, as if in their own family home, until 1949.

I especially recall our first Christmas. The older girls took part in the preparations for the festivities and arranged for the arrival of Santa Claus together with the angels and devil. They assisted in preparing the traditional Christmas Eve dinner, dressed the Christmas tree, and organized the distribution of presents. They had a lot to do since there were about 100 orphans in the boarding school. The first anniversary of the founding of the school, February 1, 1947, was also a very festive occasion. After a splendid dinner the choir sang the following song:

After our arrival here in Lebanon
A decision was made to found this home
It was uncertain who would take up the task
Until the arrival of Ms. Ustrzycka.

There was much work with the children
Four Saturdays and three Sundays
Until clean, pretty, and in complete health
They began their new lives here.

A year has passed and everyone
Feels wonderful and is very happy
We give our thanks to our director
Our beloved Wanda Ustrzycka.[27]

PALESTINE

Jerusalem

Account of Grażyna Gołębicka-Płonka

The beginning of my stay in Jerusalem is connected with the old town. One entered it through the Jaffa Gate. On the right side were the walls of the Tower of David, straight ahead a small street led to the Grave, and on the left was the hotel "Petra" in which I lived together with my parents for over a year. Here I became acquainted with the hotel owner's son and with him got to know the environs of Old Jerusalem and attended children's parties of the local notables. Directly across from the windows of the hotel was the produce bazaar where I shopped for watermelons, picking out the ripe ones by feeling them with my fingers. I became quite an expert at it too.

Our next place of residence was Betsawawa on the outskirts of Jerusalem, near Bethlehem. This was the Arab quarter, the home of Maria and Emil Machsz from whom we rented a flat. Here I played with the two daughters of the proprietors, Hilda and Haida, both younger than I. On the crest of the hill lay a large garden full of grape vines surrounded by quince and fig trees on which I spent many hours. On one side of the house, on a hill, was a copse surrounded by a rock wall. There I searched for turtles and, when it rained, for mushrooms which we ate. On the opposite side of the house was a harem near which prowled a constant stream of children. One day, as I was returning home from school, I was pelted with rocks by them. Fortunately our proprietor happened to be in the garden at the time, saw the whole thing, and rescued me. It all ended well with apologies from the father of the children who from that moment became my friends. The trip to the school was long and at the same time interesting. I had to overcome a number of difficulties the first of which was the most interesting and absorbing. It was a patch of land with large stones. I would linger by snake eggs waiting for them to hatch, then I would jump from rock to rock and twinge with happiness as the snakes crawled out from under them. Large rats waited for me along the path also, but out of respect — and also because they looked threatening — I went around them.

My school was located in one of the central districts of Jerusalem. It was both an elementary and a secondary school. We were not many. I was then in the third grade. In one room there were two classes and a single teacher taught both sections at the same time. Even the blackboard was divided into two subjects. Of the teachers who took care of us I remember Stefania Kaikowa, Stefania Gołębicka, and Leopold Graff.

All students belonged to the Scouts. We attended the Scout meetings with great joy. At times Helena Sadowska would visit us. I will never forget our trip to Ain-Karem. We clambered over mountains on donkeys and along the way picked delicious fruits off bread trees. We all longingly awaited vacation time which we would spend in a Scout camp in Natanya near the Mediterranean Sea. Our spiritual caretaker, Fr. Stefan Pietruszka, prepared us for our first Holy Communion and Confirmation. Together with the army we participated in such celebrations as the Way of the Cross to Golgotha on Good Friday and the procession on Palm Sunday. I don't recall when our school was established. But after my departure to Poland in 1946 it was dissolved and the students were moved to Ain-Karem.[28]

Ain-Karem

Account of Hanna Lesser-Chmielewska

Ain-Karem is a beautiful town located in the mountains about ten kilometers from Jerusalem. St. John the Baptist was born here and his mother, St. Elisabeth, was visited by her cousin, the Blessed Mother. There are, therefore, two churches here: St. John the Baptist and Visitation. There is also a Franciscan monastery as well as a monastery of Orthodox nuns and a mosque from whose minaret a muezzin calls the faithful to prayer. The mountains are covered by cypresses, olive groves and quince and fig trees. In spring when the fruit trees are in blossom, the town drowns in flowers. Here in this oasis of peace a few hundred Polish girls found shelter thanks to the white fathers who gave them their living quarters for their school and boarding school.

I was ten years old in 1942 when I found myself in the Center for Polish Girls in Ain-Karem. Thin as a rail, my head shaved due to an infectious disease, I sat down for the first time at a desk in a Polish school. We learned how to read Polish from a copy of the Old and New Testament found in the Polish Home in Jerusalem. We did not receive real school books until several months later. Thanks to the Polish Ministry of Labor and Social Welfare, the Polish army, and the good will of many people, we received the necessary school equipment, scouting outfits, coats, shoes and dresses. We accepted it all as the most beautiful and expensive presents from Santa Claus. We studied like mad. In the course of the first six months we worked our way through two school grades. We were children, but being children who had lived through so much we took our responsibilities very seriously. Gradually we discarded the physical appearance and all the other deprivations connected with our Siberian slavery. In the large hall of the former monastery, now serving as a boarding-school dormitory, there appeared colorful blankets on the girls' beds and on them a variety of fluffy mascots purchased out of our own savings. Vases with hand-picked cyclamens and anemones graced our shelves. We also began to frequent the small Arabian store of Ibrachim, a hunchback, where we discovered the most delicious coconut candy bars in the world, as well as the store of the Arab, Maria, full of yarn and embroidery threads.

And so, amid our school responsibilities, Scout meetings, sporting and musical events, countless parties and games of youth, we passed these five years in Ain-Karem. We lived as a loving Polish family about which the foundress and school commandant, Julia Masłoń-Kicińska, was wont to say: "I have here a group of MY children." We were treated in the same way by all our teachers and caretakers who gave us the best that could be given to youth out of their own ingenuity and patriotic hearts. The level of education here was very high and the mutual understanding between students and teachers reached an optimum level.[29]

Barbara

Milewski family memoir

(Stanisław) We left Tehran for Bakhtaran in October 1943. The train ride took us through beautiful mountains and many tunnels. At Bakhtaran we were loaded onto trucks and taken to Baghdad, located in a beautiful green valley between the Tigris and Euphrates rivers. We admired the vegetation and especially the luscious, green palms. We spent several nights in the Polish military camps and then were transported by Pakistani soldiers in trucks through the black desert of western Iraq, so named because of its sand and the black boulders which extended up to the horizon. The temperature was extremely hot outside and even hotter inside the trucks, which had canvas roofs and were open in the back. Occasionally the trucks had to stop in the middle of the desert because of overheating. At these times we were unloaded and had to wait for the engines to cool and water to be added. I can just imagine what the temperature must have been like inside the tanks of the Polish Carpathian Division which was training here.

As we entered Jordan the topography became greener and we were greeted by rivers and grass meadows. We traveled though Amman, then north of Lake Galilee, over the Jordan River, into Palestine, and finally arrived in Jerusalem itself. There, we were separated: Mother and Teresa went to the Young Woman's School in Nazareth and I joined the Polish Cadet Corps in Barbara. By this time my father's regiment had already departed for Egypt, but he was able to obtain a leave and spent a few days with us in Tel Aviv. We did not see him again until the end of the war in 1945. As members of the Polish 2nd Corps, my father and brother Andrzej took part in the Italian campaign and fought in the battles of Monte Cassino, Ancona, Bologne, and others.

The Polish Cadet Corps was situated in Barbara, which lay 10 miles from the Mediterranean Sea, near the ruins of the old Roman fortress of Ashqelon, some 30 miles north of the Arab city of Gaza. When I joined the school in November 1943, the cadets lived in tents in the desert. Wooden barracks were constructed for the school and administration. There were some 500 boys in the five companies of cadets; about one-third of them were orphans. The youngest boys were in the 1st company, and that's the one I joined. I received special tutoring to enable me to enter the high school. After graduation (I graduated in 1947) the cadets went into the army or continued their education for two additional years of liberal arts schooling in Barbara or in the engineering school in Kiryat-Motzkin, located between Acre and Haifa. The main purpose of the cadet school was to prepare us to become officers in the Polish army. For that purpose strict discipline was enforced. We practiced marching, military drills, field exercises and training with guns. We rose at 6:00 A.M., did morning exercises, said prayers, ate breakfast, attended school, played sports and did our homework in the evenings. The camp was surrounded by barbed-wire fence on the other side of which were grape and orange groves. We used to buy such produce from Arab children through the fence. The rainy season extended from January to March. Sometimes it rained so hard that the tent pegs got washed out causing the tents to collapse on top of us. The dry hot season extended from May to December. We took every opportunity to swim in the sea and play in the ruins of the old Roman fort, Ashqelon. To get there we had to walk through Arab villages where we were constantly pestered by children to buy melons, dates, oranges or grapes. It was muggy and hot and we came back exhausted.

When I joined the Boy Scouts, our scoutmaster was Lieutenant Ignacy Plonka. We made many excursions to various places in Palestine, some following the footsteps of Christ: Jerusalem, the Dead Sea, and Tiberias (Teverya) on the Sea of Galilee. We climbed the Mount of Temptation with Lieutenant Zdzisław Peszkowski, a Scout leader, who later moved to India and eventually became a very well-known priest.

Many cultural activities were organized by the school. We had a choir and published a school magazine called "Junak." There was a good library at the school, and because I enjoyed reading I read almost every book there. Most of the books were published in Jerusalem. I joined the school orchestra, playing the clarinet. We played in Tel Aviv, Jerusalem, Nazareth and at dances which the school organized and to which the girls from Nazareth were invited. On Good Friday we participated in the procession on the Via Dolorosa, the way of the cross to the Basilica of Jesus's tomb in Jerusalem. We visited Bethlehem, the Church of Gethsemane and the famous Omar mosque, the Dome on the Rock. I often explored the city with my mother and sometimes with a friend of the family, Mr. Witold Pluciński, a retired officer who lived in Jerusalem. We also went to Egypt to see the Sphinx, pyramids and the Cairo museum.[30]

Nazareth

Milewski family memoir

(Stanisław) Some of my most joyful memories come from the time I spent with my mother and sister in Nazareth. In my mind's eye, this beautiful town in the mountains of Galilee probably looked about the same as when Christ lived there. It was populated by Christian and Moslem Arabs. In the center of the city was the Basilica of the Annunciation, and next to it was a Franciscan monastery which housed the Polish girls' military school (Szkola Młodszych Ochotniczek — SMO). To the north was a charming, old Arab city with winding, narrow streets and adjoining shops where one could buy everything. At the top of the hill there was a Polish elementary school for girls. From that hill one could see the entire town of Nazareth with its churches and mosques. Nazareth brimmed with life during the day. In the evening, its peace was only broken by the songs of muezzins from the top of mosque towers calling the faithful for prayers. We explored the Arab town of Kana and climbed Mt. Tabor where we prayed at the Church of the Transfiguration. We vacationed on Lake Galilee, swimming in its clear waters and exploring its shores. We prayed at octagonal Church of the Beatitudes with its magnificent view of the lake.

With the end of the war in 1945 some people decided to return to Poland, but we dared not because of my father's prewar anti-communist activities. Obtaining a leave of absence from the army, my father came to Nazareth, where he remained with Mother until 1947. The Polish armed forces, meanwhile, were transferred to England.

I graduated from the Polish cadet school in 1947 and was transferred to an engineering school in Kiryat-Motzkin. The girls' school in Nazareth closed its doors at the end of August 1947, and I hitchhiked there to say goodbye to my mother and sister. When I arrived there everybody was being loaded onto army trucks. I remember standing in the street, together with most of the Arabs of Nazareth, and waving goodbye. A feeling of loneliness engulfed me as the last truck left the city. My mother and sister were in one of those trucks on their way to far-off England, my father was in Egypt, and I was left all alone. Luckily, we were all eventually reunited. At the beginning of September we were put on a train in Haifa and taken to Port Said in Egypt, where we boarded a ship for England.[31]

5. India

Introduction by Wiesław Stypuła

The coming of the Polish refugees to India was made possible by the invitation of a young prince from Navanagar named Jam Saheb. Several months after the maharajah's declaration, a settlement was built in Balachadi, near the town of Jamnagar. The first group of children arrived there in July 1942, and from that date until 1946 about 1,000 of them lived there. For that entire period of time, Fr. Franciszek Pluta was the commandant of the settlement. At the end of 1942 construction began on a new settlement in Valivade, near the town of Kolhapur. The first group of refugees, mostly women and children, arrived there in June 1943. About 5,000 persons passed through this camp by 1948. The chief builder of the settlement and its first starost or elder was Capt. Władysław Jagiełłowicz. Despite the climate and the people's poor state of health, a school and some medical facilities were quickly set up. All the young people in the settlement went to school even though there was a shortage of teachers, programs, textbooks, and equipment. In Valivade, in less than a year, there were three kindergartens, four elementary schools, a secondary school, a lyceum, a trade school, a pedagogical lyceum, and a teachers' school for village agriculture. About 2,500 students attended these schools. There were also many technical courses for the teenagers and adults. There was a lack of medical staff, rooms, equipment, and medicine, but a few treatment units were nevertheless quickly established. A center was set up in Panchgani for those needing special care, especially those in danger of contracting tuberculosis. The local community offered a great deal of assistance; for example, in Balachadi, where malaria epidemics occurred often, the core of the medical personnel consisted of Hindu physicians.

Cultural life also flowered in the settlements. There were community centers, libraries, art studios, and amateur theaters for children, teenagers and adults, where classical and children's plays were performed and local events were celebrated. Several song-and-dance groups emerged and there was even a youth orchestra in Balachadi.

Sports were also important: soccer, volleyball, basketball, light athletics, field hockey, ping-pong and even tennis. Polish teams competed successfully with local ones in these events.

The Polish Scouts in India, to which belonged over a half of the refugee children and teenagers, clearly distinguished themselves in the history of Polish scouting in exile. Their training took place in harsh semidesert conditions as well as in the Deccan jungle.

The organizational achievements of the Polish settlements are also noteworthy. For example, in less than a year Valivade evolved from a small settlement to a dynamic town of several thousand residents with their own town council, fire brigade, civil security force, post office, church, many stores and offices, and the cooperative "Zgoda." In 1948 the last Polish settlement was liquidated and its residents were scattered throughout the world; only some of them returned to Poland. By virtue of their having spent so many years together in India, a special — almost a familial — bond has been created among the former residents of the Polish settlements. Despite their eventual dispersal they still maintain contact with one another. This is evident from the associations of Poles from India that currently exist in several countries, from the reunions that they hold, from the bulletin that they publish, and from their participation in various social activities.[1]

Bandra

Account of Wiesław Stypuła

The trek of many Poles to India, and in particular that of the Polish children gathered in the orphanage of Ashkhabad, led thousands of kilometers over dangerous mountain ranges separating Ashkhabad from the Persian town of Mashhad, as well as over the forbidding deserts bordering Afghanistan. In the winter of 1941–42 the so-called rescue expeditions of the Polish Red Cross under the leadership of vice-consul Tadeusz Lisiecki traveled that route in order to bring food and medicines from India to the Poles located in the southern regions of the USSR. The initiator and organizer of these expeditions was the Polish consul in Bombay, Eugeniusz Banasiński, assisted by his wife Kira. The first children's transport left Ashkhabad on March 12, 1942. One of the organizers of the Polish orphanage, the famous actress and singer Hanka Ordonówska, accompanied the transport as a caretaker.

It began like this. A rumor began to circulate that we would be leaving the following day. Where? Into the unknown, the distant South, the equator. On the one hand there was a pleasant anticipation of this exotic journey; on the other hand there was concern for our nearest and dearest. Where are they? What is happening to them? Will I ever see them again? Perhaps they are no longer alive. Then a long, long night troubled by anxious thoughts. Tossing from side to side. In the morning redeeming, restful sleep.

Reveille! And right away movement, nervous moods, nudges, laughter, and finally the morning assembly. We stood in twos, by blocks, and were counted several times. Toward the end of the roll call, big news: right after breakfast trucks will arrive and, in accordance with a prepared list, the first group will depart.

Nervous waiting and … relief when the name was read, the name which was pronounced correctly but sounded so strange. Is it really me? After roll call I must run to my caretaker and check, just to be sure it was me. The sick and those under quarantine remain at the orphanage. Gazing at the sad, tearful children I was filled with a profound sadness. I understood how they felt because only a few months ago I went through a similar disappointment when I came here from Kassan-Sai, near the Uzbek and Chinese border, and while the first group of about 100 children readied for departure I had to remain behind. At that time, separated from the rest by a low fence, we observed for hours on end our lucky contemporaries. How we envied them! Especially since wonderful things were happening on the other side of that fence. The settlement was brimming with life from daybreak onward: gymnastic exercises, marches, singing, playing, conversation, meals in common, races. Two young persons held sway over the children: the forever-smiling and energetic Jadzia Tarnogórska and the thin, forever-singing Hanka Ordonówna in the fantastic, large hat which she always wore.

The artist taught us various songs: "Sea, Our Sea," "Where the Brook Flows Slowly," "Hail the Dawn of May," and the national anthem. When she got tired of singing, marching in step with each first foursome, she whistled nicely. On the evening before the departure she also organized a farewell party featuring choral singing, a few readings, and her own lengthy recital.

And late that night, at the request of some of the adults, she sang the immortal "Love Will Make All Things Right." She put such passion, expression and heart into her performances as if she had a premonition that soon she would leave forever this land of eternal shadows. That was my first and last encounter with the legendary singer because on the following day, in a sorrowful frame of mind, I hid in some nook so as not to watch those departing.

But now that I, together with over a hundred others, was to begin the next stage in my journey through the world, I was in an entirely different mood. The first transport having crossed half of India, through Quetta and Delhi, arrived at Bandra, a suburb of Bombay. The children's stay in Bandra lasted several months. Those who were weak or were infected with tuberculosis, together with Hanka Ordonówna, were sent to the health resort in Panchgani. The rest went to the first stationary Polish settlement in India, that of Balachadi near Jamnagar, which was just then being completed.

Later transports to India came by way of the Caspian Sea, through the temporary camps in Iran, and then by water to Karachi where the main temporary camps, Country Club and Malir, were located.

In all, between 1942 and 1948 over 6,000 Polish refugees — the majority of whom were children — found shelter in stationary settlements in India.[2]

Balachadi

Account of Wiesław Stypuła

The evacuation of the Polish people from the southern regions of the USSR met with a great deal of trouble right from the very beginning. In this dramatic situation the breaking of the impasse came from an unexpected quarter: a young Hindu prince from Navanagar, the Maharaja Jam Saheb, spontaneously offered to take in a thousand Polish children. Commenting on his motives for doing so in an interview in the weekly "Polska" (Nov. 25, 1942) he said: "Being deeply moved by the suffering of the Polish people, and in particular by the fate of those whose childhood and youth were caught up in the tragic circumstances of the worst of all wars, I longed in some way to improve their situation. And so I offered them a welcome on lands far removed from the turmoil of war.... I am trying to do whatever I can to rescue the children who, after these terrible trials and tribulations, will have to gain the strength and stamina to cope with the future tasks which will confront them in liberated Poland."

The invitation was accepted with gratitude and there quickly began the construction of a settlement for 1,000 persons near the summer ocean-side residence of the prince located by the village of Balachadi which lay a few dozen kilometers from Jamnagar (presently in the state of Gujarat). After a few months of very intensive work the settlement was ready to receive the Polish children. In June 1942 children arrived from the temporary center in Bandra near Bombay and raised the red and white flag given to them by the Polish sailors on the ship "Kościuszko." After the first group other transports, each carrying hundreds of Polish children, arrived until the end of 1942. The office of the commandant of this camp for the entire length of its four to five year existence was held by the chaplain, Fr. Franciszek Pluta from Równe.

In spite of the difficult subtropical weather conditions, financial troubles, the lack of qualified personnel, significant differences in the ages of the children (from two to sixteen years of age), the lack of Polish books and textbooks, and so on, life in the settlement became completely organized in a very short period of time. A kindergarten and grammar school were established consisting of 14 sections. A hospital with a medical team was founded. Culture, education, and extracurricular activities also flourished. Numerous cultural groups were established: choral-recitational, theatrical, and orchestral. An entire line of art courses was developed featuring drawing, embroidery, decorative art, paper cut-outs, and so on. The animating spirit of the cultural life in the two centers of the settlement was at first Jadwiga Tarnogórska and later Janina Dobrostańska.

Much attention was given in the settlement to the physical education of the children. In addition to the daily obligatory gymnastic exercises, the majority of the youth also participated in other sporting events (soccer, basketball, field hockey, and light athletics). Numerous games and tournaments were organized in which we often competed successfully with local teams. Our capable trainer and at the same time our "torturer" was Antoni Maniak, a former member of the Lwów-based "Pogoń."

The residents of the settlement maintained constant contacts with the local people. The representatives of the local authorities participated in all settlement festivities. The technical staff as well as a part of the medical staff consisted of Hindus who were extremely well-disposed towards the children. Aside from the credit that rightfully belongs to the Polish personnel, the Maharaja Jam Saheb himself— through his personal engagement and almost fatherly concern for the Polish children — should be credited for the great organizational and educational achievements of the settlement. Not only did he constantly and generously replenish the perpetually empty coffers of the settlement, he also took a lively interest in Polish art and culture. Reymont's *Peasants* figured among his best-loved pieces of literature. He never omitted any of the festivities of the settlement and surveyed the artistic accomplishments of our groups with great interest, often inviting them to perform their pieces in his palace in Jamnagar. He was a great sport enthusiast and rooted for our teams when they competed against the local ones. In November 1946, when the last group of children left the settlement, he personally escorted us to the railway station and, without concealing his tears, lovingly and at length clutched the youngest ones to his bosom. He will remain in our hearts until the end of our lives as an exceptionally pleasant, kind-hearted, and sincere friend of the Polish children. He was a truly good man from the "Good Land," as this corner of the Hindu continent was called — the land of Jamnagar.[3]

Valivade

Account of Wiesław Stypuła

In February 1943, after the temporary camp for Polish refugees was established in Malir near Karachi, Capt. Władysław Jagiełłowicz was assigned an unusually difficult mission. He was ordered to go to the land of the Marathas (presently, Maharashtra state) where, near the village of Valivade, he was to assume the functions of a starost and be in charge of constructing a stationary settlement for about 5,000 Polish refugees.

Although the land of the Marathas was not the richest region of India, it was an exceptionally beautiful one. It embraced the vast seacoast areas of the Deccan plateau located in the central and northern sections of the Indian peninsula. These predominantly mountainous territories with sprawling jungles were not conducive to farming. The local population was poor and was characterized by a certain rawness, pride, a warlike disposition, and patriotism. Here in the 17th century Shivaii, the legendary leader who would later become king, was born and spent his life attempting to liberate the Marathas from the control and influence of the Moslems and especially the sultanate in Bijapur. The capital of the kingdom was initially the powerful fortress of Panhala and later, the well-fortified and rich in relics of the past, Kolhapur.

The founding of the settlement, lying a few kilometers from Kolhapur, proceeded at an unusually rapid pace. The work began with the arrival of the first major transport in June 1943. The biweekly "Polak w Indiach" (September 15, 1944, no. 29) described at length the organizational efforts and dynamism of the Polish community which consisted predominantly of women with children and children without parents. The following were organized in the course of a single year: the administrative apparatus of the settlement and five separate districts, permanent and volunteer fire brigades, a civil security force, a unit for unattached children, a hospital, a post office, four elementary schools for children and one for adults, a secondary school, a lyceum, a teachers' school for village agriculture together with a small commercial farming industry, a pedagogical lyceum, a trade school, three kindergartens, a six-month sewing course, a knitting course, a course in bee-keeping, a workshop for adults and teenagers, a six-month course for store workers, a three month course on Polish Red Cross health procedures, and an English language class.

Later other courses were added, including automotive, book binding, and radio repair courses. There were 24 school sport teams and 4 extracurricular ones all of which participated in 29 official sporting events. There were many outings both by car and bicycle. A large church with a steeple was erected and provisioned. With donations from the residents and with their labor force a thousand trees and bushes were planted and 3 public and 12 school playgrounds were made. The English as well as the Hindu authorities took note of and admired these impressive accomplishments. The settlement at Valivade was regarded as one of the best organized and dynamic Polish settlement of refugees in the world.

And all this was due to the selfless and supremely dedicated efforts of people such as the starost Capt. Władysław Jagiełłowicz, the directors of education Żerebecki and M. Borońska, Scout instructors B. Pancewicz, Z. Peszkowski and A. Handerek, those in charge of extracurricular activities A. Skomorowski and J. Dobrostańska, as well as O. Sasadeusz from the educational section and the spiritual director of the Poles in Valivade, Fr. L. Dallinger.[4]

Karachi

Account of Vala Lewicki (née Miron)

[W]e reached Karachi on a very stormy and rainy day. Not a good omen for a shipload of new arrivals. The tent camp located on grey desert sand outside the city made a very unpleasant impression on us.

But a few days later I felt happy for I was lucky enough to be chosen by ballot for a place in an English convent school in the city. This was the fairest way to choose as there was very limited room for the thousands of school-age Polish children. I remember when an official opened the door and stood aside for us to go in, my heart missed a beat or two and my stomach did a strange leap. When my name was called out I was overcome by the feeling of being lucky and by determination to be worthy.

We still lived in the camp, where no lights were lit at night, and attended school only in the mornings. The convent had a long stretch of parkland with huge trees flapping with birds and multi-coloured bougainvillea everywhere. The buildings sat proud and erect on the rising ground behind the misty trees. The school was a showplace with gleaming rooms and very well equipped bathrooms.

At first we were put in a classroom with English children. The room was divided down the middle: English children on one side and we, Polish teenagers, on the other. Each morning a nun would stand up in front of the class and begin religious instruction from the Bible. She usually selected passages from Genesis. Had we understood English well we would have gladly listened to her, as attentively as the English children. But we were different. Although we wanted to learn, we were frustrated to the point of tears.[5]

Account of Stefania Buczak-Zarzycka

We climbed aboard the ship taking us to our next transit camp at Karachi, which was then part of India. In order to reach the Persian Gulf we glided slowly down the Tigris River.

In groups we stood leaning on the rails and showing one another the comical antics of the monkeys which we could clearly see on the river banks. These monkeys, the first we had ever seen in the wild, were sitting or jumping about small apple trees whose unusual fruits were the size of plums. The humidity was so high that our clothes clung to our bodies. The birds flew up and over the ship as it moved further into their territory. An older man who stood with us described this place as the Garden of Eden, and we looked out at the orchards of unusual apple trees thrown in amongst the jungle and decided that he must be right. To himself he muttered that if Eve had not tempted Adam we might not be wandering the globe at this moment. As we were only four meters from shore, we cast a careful glance at the trees lest the biblical snake of evil strike out at us.

Several days later we reached Karachi and were amazed to see the town situated well below sea level. The wharf was an artificially constructed wall of rocks, and as the ship berthed the site created an unfamiliar perceptual phenomenon. I felt as if I could touch the wharf with my fingers. After I had disembarked and walked down many steps to our transport lorries, I looked back to see our huge ship rocking back and forth like a toy high above me. Occasionally, a wave of water would wash over the sides of the wharf to the town below. On the outskirts of this city we set up another camp site. The administrators of the new camp were English and the organisation of our welfare was commendable. From here, all refugees were destined to be transported to East Africa, Mexico or South Africa. Encircled by barbed wire, the camp looked out onto desert country sprinkled with small bushes. Hyenas and Jackals were the only animals we saw. One night, a jackal wandered into my tent after food and I reached out to pat what I thought was a dog. This animal took flight immediately. Because our stay was to be so brief, schools weren't organised; rather discussion groups (*pogadanki)* were formed for different age levels. In the groups we were informed about India, its rich culture, complicated social structure and many religions. We admired the saris and attempted to learn how to dress ourselves in them.[6]

Account of Tadeusz Pieczko

Aboard the ship heading for Karachi, I noticed a small rash between my fingers. I knew that this meant quarantine, and so I walked around with my hands in my pockets. But a doctor spotted me on deck and ordered me to show him my hands. I started crying as he dragged me off to sickbay. The quarantine section on one of the open decks was separated from the rest of the ship only by a wire fence; it looked like a cage. There were five of us in it.

One day, we were told to stay calm and not get alarmed while the ship's crew practiced firing their big guns. When they went off, the whole ship shook. In fact, the entire convoy of ships started firing toward a small island in the gulf. What an impressive display of firepower! Our ship with all the children stayed farther back of the other ships. Some of them were quite small but others were large and all were steaming back and forth. As part of the exercise, the children were told to put on their life jackets and stand on deck. The five of us in the quarantine cage also put on our jackets. After it was all over we realized that it was no practice; it was the real thing! As we came closer to the island we saw a German ship on fire.

No one was allowed in the quarantine section except the ship's hospital staff. One hospital aide was a huge Hindu man in military uniform. He struck me funny because of his large size, his red beard and traces of red hair under the edges of his turban. Occasionally he would come out on deck, bring me a treat, and talk to me while pointing to the islands that we passed. I didn't understand him of course, but it didn't matter. I suppose he felt sorry for me because midway to our destination the other children were released from quarantine while I had to remain there. A day or two before reaching Karachi I made such a fuss about being separated from my brother that they put him in quarantine also.

Once we reached Karachi my brother was returned to his group but I was kept in a hospital tent for a while. After a few days the whole group of children was moved a few miles from Karachi and housed in army tents. I finally rejoined my group. Occasionally we saw British soldiers. Once they showed us a movie: their version of Laurel and Hardy in the army. Although I don't remember the names of the actors, I remember that they were funny and that the fat guy had a nose shaped like a kaiser roll.

We were now well taken care of. The food was good and for our meals we always got some fruit or a tomato. I had a habit of smelling the fruit or the tomato before eating it because I cherished it so much. Each boy had at least two pairs of pants and two undershirts. We slept on cots that had ropes for springs. This was better than sleeping on the sand. Unfortunately, the ropes were an ideal nesting place for bedbugs and they would bite us every night. Every so often we would have to debug the cots by soaking them in a boiling solution that smelled like creosote. Each one of us was responsible for debugging his own cot. This meant that one had to get a buddy to help carry the heavy frame and carefully lower it into the vat. A Hindu laborer would usually help. That got rid of the bedbugs, but I got headaches from sleeping on my smelly cot.

We had to wash our own clothes on the cement floor in the public shower area. Once, my brother asked me to wash his clothes for him, so I took his and my dirty clothes and started washing them. A Hindu attendant saw me and offered to help. Since their clothing consists mainly of cloth sheets, they wash it by beating it against a large rock. The Hindu did the same with ours. When I brought the clothes back to the tent to hang them up, I discovered that he had smashed all our buttons. I got some new buttons from one of the adults and sewed them back on.

Since we had a lot of time on our hands, the adults decided to hold classes. Pencils and paper were scarce, so we used slate boards instead. We all enjoyed going to these classes, provided they did not last too long. Some of us had never gone to school before and didn't even know how to write our names. Since I began my first grade in Russia, I signed my name in Russian. My schooling there lasted only a few weeks; the lack of shoes and warm clothes prevented me from continuing.[7]

Account of Jane [Janina] Żebrowski-Bulmahn

We stayed in Tehran for only several months and time came to move on. We were told that we were going to India for a longer stay. This was February of 1943. We were put in army trucks and taken to a train and then a ship in the Persian port of Khorramshahr on Persian Bay. The ship went very slowly and we had drill several times a day. We never knew which one could have been the real one because of German submarines roaming the area.

As we approached the Strait of Oman, we were given an escort of about 20 smaller ships to accompany us. We stayed there for two days, then began to move with our ship in the middle and the convoy around us to keep us safe. It was very interesting to watch all the ships moving at the same speed with ours in the middle. When we entered the Arabian Sea, the convoy left us and we were on our own.

About ten days later, we approached India and our ship anchored in the Port of Karachi. Army trucks were ready here also to take us to our camp close to the city of Karachi. The British and Polish army camps were located just outside the city. Our camp was next to theirs.

The civilian camps consisted mostly of women, children, older men, and some younger men with physical or mental handicaps. All young men and single women were in the Polish military. But now they were dressed properly, well fed and well trained. Soon they would be shipped to the front someplace in North Africa, fighting under Polish command but as part of the British forces.

Here, too, we were given tents and resumed our "normal" routine, two meals a day, schooling and other activities provided for us.

Shortly after we got to Karachi, there was a very hot spell in India, normal for that part of the country. We had to stay in the shade to survive. It was a dry heat so as long as we stayed in the shade, we were somewhat comfortable. But when we stepped outside, it was like walking into an oven. We were warned that it was dangerous to be in the sun for any length of time since we were not used to it. We also had to drink a lot of water. The problem was that the water pump was located quite a distance away from us. By the time we came back, we were thirsty again.

One thing I always associate with India is halvah. The Indian women would bring buckets of halvah to the camp to sell. It looked like taffy but had a distinctive sesame taste. I very much enjoyed it and ate quite a bit of it since it only cost pennies. Years later I was able to get some in supermarkets in Chicago and, although it had different texture, it tasted just as good.

The English administration provided the school children with some sightseeing trips. One such trip was into the city of Karachi which I remember as being very big and very attractive. There was a stream running through the city and it was filled with huge crocodiles. We stopped to watch them but were afraid to get very close since they looked so ferocious. There was also a lot of greenery wherever we looked in the city.

On the way back we took a country road and passed by several grave sites. Most of them seemed to have pottery on them. We were told that people brought food for the dead to feed on. We found this to be a strange custom.

We stayed about seven months in Karachi and I was promoted to fourth grade. Here we received some books and other school supplies as well as more clothing. Our next destination, we were told, would be Africa, again where England had colonies. Africa was to become our permanent residence until some future date after the war when we could return to a free Poland....

In August 1943, while still in India, Father found out that a small group of about 700 people were being screened for relocation to Mexico. The Mexican government offered to give refuge to 15,000 Polish people for the duration of the war, according to the agreement signed with General Sikorski and the Mexican government. After the war when Poland became free, we would return to our homeland.

Father, of course, signed up immediately.[8]

Malir

Account of Tadeusz Pieczko

Our stay in Malir was a pleasant one. It was here that I tasted toothpaste for the first time. Until then we used powder, but only when it was available. Toothpaste tasted so good that we ate most of it.

I joined the Cub Scouts and really enjoyed it. The adults in charge always tried to keep us busy. In that way we stayed out of trouble. For example, we made soccer fields by clearing the land of all rocks. We also played games. One game consisted of someone tossing a button against a wall and letting it land on the ground. His opponent would do the same with another button in an attempt to land as close as possible to the first one. If he could touch the buttons with his thumb and little finger, he would keep them both. If not, the other party would have his chance to do the same. Once, someone spread a false rumor to the effect that some of our clothes would be sent to poorer children. With our game in mind, we got busy and ripped off all the buttons from our clothes. Boy, were we ever busy sewing them back on.

Every time we had to walk from one place to another, the adults in charge had us march in twos and sing marching songs. I enjoyed doing this. After a while we marched with greater precision than seasoned troops. We were also busy collecting lizards and red spiders. These usually came out after a heavy rain. The ground would be all red from so many of them. We'd pick them up and throw them at the girls. A major effort was made to get the children interested in scouting and almost everyone joined up. Among other things, joining the Scouts also meant that one would get another pair of pants and a shirt. Once, when I went in a truck to visit my brother in the hospital in Karachi, I was dressed in my gray Cub Scout uniform with all the fancy trimmings, including a hunting knife suspended from my belt. I felt like a big shot; in fact, I felt like a general. I even got the attention of the British soldiers riding with me....

After a few months in Malir we were put on trucks and taken back to Karachi, where we boarded a British warship. After being assigned our places, we stood on the deck for almost half a day and watched the Hindu laborers, who were almost totally naked, load the ship with provisions. They walked back and forth over a plank and carried huge boxes and crates. The day was almost over before the ship slipped away from the docks. Our next stop was Bombay, India. There, we were put on board a large American battleship. Someone told me it was named the Hermitage.[9]

Account of Anita Paschwa (née Kozicka)

At the beginning of 1943 we traveled by train through the tunnels in the mountains to Ahvaz, where we stayed only about a week while we waited for passports. From there we took a ship across the Persian Gulf to Karachi, India, where we boarded English army trucks to a new camp, Malir. There we continued our education and scouting activities. We were being brought up following Polish traditions including folk dancing, singing, marching, religion and doing good deeds. From time to time we went on a sightseeing tour, and once a week we saw outdoor English movies sponsored by the English soldiers stationed there. One of the things I really disliked was eating a lime dipped in sugar at lunch every day.

I remember an incident in Malir which really frightened us all. One of the older girls who had gotten up to use the outdoor bathroom during the night was kidnapped by cooks working in our camp. Although she was found unharmed, we were no longer allowed to go anywhere alone and always had to watch out for each other.

Because of all we had been through we became a group of very close friends. But friendship was not a luxury afforded to a group of orphan refugees. We were constantly on the move. In September 1943 our group was split up again. Some of us went to Mexico and others to Africa. That September was spent gathering autographs in a book. Each was accompanied by a date and place as well as a few good wishes. It was our only memento of the time we spent together. Those of us destined for Mexico boarded a small ship in Karachi which took us to Bombay, where we embarked on The USS Hermitage, a huge ship carrying wounded American soldiers. Of the 726 Polish refugees who boarded, 408 were children.[10]

6. Africa

Introduction by Zdzisława Wójcik

Of the more than 37,000 civilians who managed to leave the USSR with the Polish army, more than a half found refuge in Africa, mostly in the countries of former British East Africa: Uganda, Kenya, Tanganyika (now Tanzania), both Rhodesias (North Rhodesia, now Zambia, and South Rhodesia, now Zimbabwe), and the Cape Country in the South African Union (now the Republic of South Africa).

According to available information almost 18,000 Poles wound up in African settlements, although more refugees than that passed through Africa—about 20,000. To begin with, until 1945 there was an influx of Poles from the refugee camps that ceased to exist in different parts of the world, for example, in India. Then, there were population movements from camp to camp; for example, when people changed locations to become reunited with their families or when teenagers were sent to the secondary schools in the larger settlements. Such considerations made it difficult to produce reliable demographic statistics.

Transports of Poles from Tehran (the first lengthy stopover for the refugees after leaving the USSR) came to Africa by sea from May 1942 to the end of 1943. They came mostly on British ships to Mombasa in Kenya, Dar es Salaam and Tenga in Tanganyika, as well as to the ports of Mozambique. The refugees were then scattered throughout Africa, at times in areas very far from the ports of landing. They were housed either in former POW buildings or in settlements built specifically for that purpose. The location of the settlements was determined by the local British authorities.

The Polish camps had British commanders, mostly former army officers, who were responsible for making contacts with the local authorities. They made decisions regarding the construction and further expansion of the settlements as well as the provisioning of the camps with food and clothing supplies. The British authorities in those tropical territories mandated certain standards for the Polish health services and helped to uphold them. Life in "Polish Africa" depended on the Polish emigration authorities in London. At the head of the Polish administration stood the delegate of the Ministry of Labor and Social Welfare of the Polish Government in London. The first delegate was Kazimierz Kazimierczak; he was followed by Kazimierz Chodzikiewicz. The delegate's office was located in Nairobi, the capital of Kenya. Several dozen employees worked in that office, including several persons who visited the settlement for various reasons, for example, Dr. Wiktor Bincer, who visited the camps and supervised the health services and the overall conditions of health therein. Initially, the office of the delegate oversaw the entire life of the settlements; for example, Deputy Delegate Tadeusz Kopeć was in charge of education. In the fall of 1943, however, the Delegation of the Ministry of Religion and Public Education began to operate in Nairobi with Seweryn Szczepański at its head. This institution was established to oversee both the secular and religious (we were not all of the same faith) education in the camps. In the educational sphere it fulfilled the functions of a superintendent's office. Our secondary school certificates were therefore meaningful and were respected in various countries.

In addition to these two main Polish bureaus in Nairobi, two others assisted the refugees. First, the Polish Red Cross under the directorship of Eustachy Sapiecha. This bureau was in charge of the important wartime and postwar task of making sure that letters reached the people to whom they were addressed and who were often scattered throughout the world. The Polish Red Cross also attempted to locate the whereabouts of family members — parents, children, siblings — lost during the war. The bureau was inundated with such requests because during the war everyone lost someone and was looking for someone.

In addition to the Polish Red Cross, there was also a Polish consulate in Nairobi which supplied the refugees with Polish passports. These were needed by everyone who traveled as an individual rather than as part of the larger refugee transports. The bureau also facilitated the procurement of visas to countries other than those in which the refugees were staying. Nairobi was therefore truly the capital of "Polish Africa" during the war years.

Because the Polish camps in Africa were scattered far and wide — there being hundreds and even thousands of kilometers between them — they were difficult to manage. Deputy delegate positions were therefore established in Uganda (with the center in Kampala) under Dr. M. Szyszkowski, in Tanganyika (with the center in Dar es Salaam) under W. W. Kuczyński, and in both Rhodesias and Cape Country (with the center in Lusaka) under Dr. W. Korabiewicz. The vast majority of the Polish refugees were settled within these three large territories, but some also remained for a time in Kenya. There was a temporary camp in Makindu, near the Mombasa (the port of arrival)—Nairobi—Kampala railroad line, where many Polish transports halted for a time before moving on to the stationary settlements in Uganda and Tangyanika. Sometimes they had to wait there for a few weeks or even months until the houses in the settlements to which they were to be sent were completed. Moreover, in 1945 Polish children were transferred to Rongai in western Kenya from the very humid and malarious settlement of Morogoro in Tanganyika.

There were 19 settlements in Africa but not all of them functioned for the entire duration of the Poles' stay on the continent. At the beginning of 1942 settlements were established in Tanganyika, Uganda, and Kenya. A while later, in 1943, camps emerged both in North Rhodesia and South Rhodesia. And finally, a children's center was set up in Oudtshoorn in the Cape Country. The number of residents in any one settlement varied over time. Initially the camps grew as new transports arrived. Between 1944 and 1946 there was little change. From 1947 onward, however, a decline set in as the refugees began to depart for Poland and other countries, especially Great Britain.

The settlements were divided into variously named units: blocks, groups, and villages. Most of life's necessities, including the distribution of food and clothing, were taken care of within these administrative units. The camp commandant was able to conduct his affairs through various group leaders. People who traveled to Africa together were usually placed within the same block or village.

The settlements also operated their own businesses: farms, canteens, butcher shops, bakeries, and fabric-weaving, sewing and shoemaking shops. This provided some people with work and money. This was important because, aside from the administrative sector, the schools, orphanage, and the hospital for which special training was required, there was very little work in the settlement. And there were many people eager to work, and their numbers were increasing as the younger generation grew older.

The population in the Polish settlements had a specific demographic profile: about 47 percent were women, over 41.5 percent were teenagers and children, and only 11.5 percent were men. To the last category belonged those who were old or ill, and therefore unfit for military service, and the specialists sent to the camps to perform some needed task. The teenagers were also predominantly female; the older boys were mostly in the military schools in Palestine or Egypt.

The high percentage of children and teenagers in the refugee camps made schools, orphanages, and the Polish Scouts' Association important components of the camps and added to their specific character. Young people could be seen everywhere, especially early in the morning, when they ran off to school, and in the afternoon, when they returned. The youth played an active role in the life of the settlements, appearing in school or Scout uniforms or in native costumes in camp productions and celebrations. Although there were specifically children's centers, like those in Oudtshoorn or Morogoro, all the African camps were filled with the youth and their affairs — our settlements were young.

Each settlement had a significant number of children and teenagers in the Scouts. In the larger settlements, there were entire troops and even separate girls' and boys' divisions. In the small ones, there were only separate Scout and junior Scout units.

The Catholic Church was another very important institution in the Polish settlements. In the beginning the work of the Catholic priests was difficult and there were very few of them. The parish priests had to fulfill all the pastoral duties, including religious instruction. Small settlements sought pastoral assistance from the clergy of nearby missions who were learning Polish as they were working with our people. In time more priests arrived so much so that in the larger settlements the middle schools had their own religious teachers. Catholic churches were constructed as well as they could have been, given the circumstances. Well-equipped Catholic community centers were founded and there was a Marian Society in the schools. Other, less numerous religious groups were in a more difficult situation and had no pastors. But there were some exceptions, e.g., in Tengeru, where an Orthodox priest came and after a while set up a parish.

The Polish settlements were liquidated beginning in 1947; the last one was closed at the end of 1949. A few of the residents decided to remain in Africa. Those who did not have families outside Poland and who did not wish to return to Poland were sent by the British authorities to Western Australia.[1]

Kenya

Makindu

Account of Vala Lewicki (née Miron)

The Polish delegate, Father Slapa, from the Polish Consulate in Nairobi, welcomed us to Africa, wished us well and informed us about the African way of life: what to eat, where to go and of whom to beware. In the camp we did not need a lecture about where to go as there was nowhere except an African village which, I must say, was very clean. Neither did we worry about wild, ferocious animals roaming nearby. The camp was fenced in with barbed wire. Nothing to be afraid of.

But it was not so. One night I took my lantern and walked to the toilet just a couple of barracks away, near the station. When I reached my destination I noticed a lantern burning in the doorway. That was unusual! I had never seen a lantern there before. I looked in every cubicle but found nobody. There was a train in the station. For a moment I was puzzled why anyone would leave their lantern and walk back in the dark. On the way back, when approaching the first barracks — Oh, heavens! — I saw a figure dressed in white running towards me. It was a black man. He stopped, stretching out his arms. I stood sill, frozen and engulfed by extreme fear. I tried to open my mouth to scream but no sound came out. I wanted to fight the intruder by swinging my lamp but my arms were limp and my legs as heavy as lead. Suddenly I flung my lantern at him and screamed and screamed.

I can say with certainty that there are different screams at times of great emotion, but those screams of immense fear are the loudest and the most desperate of all. My head whirled, and in place of all the colours of the rainbow everything turned black. As I tried to fight my way out of the blackness I heard as in a dream Polish being spoken. Two fully-dressed Poles, Mr. Kuczyński and Mr. Lipiński, both in their thirties and not fit for the army for some reason, grabbed me and brought me back to our barracks. My shouts had woken up everyone in the camp including my parents, who stood in the doorway with others but did not come out.

I could not speak for some days — my voice seemed to have left me. And I resented my parents for a while. But as the weeks moved on I began again to appreciate the value of their love and to have a great joy in their presence.[2]

Account of Zdzisława Wójcik

Through this temporary camp in Kenya passed a significant portion of the Polish refugees who landed on the African continent in the port of Mombasa and were transferred to the Polish settlements in the former British East Africa (Uganda, Kenya, Tanganyika). To the British who ruled this territory and to their well-to-do guests, this was an ideal place in which to observe African wildlife, particularly lions, from pulpits built for that very reason. To the Polish refugees this was the last stop on their journey to a more stationary settlement on the Dark Continent, the place of the final division into groups which were then sent in various directions, the place of unexpected meetings and exchanges of information — both joyful, that we somehow managed to live through it all, and sad, because not everyone was so fortunate as to find asylum in Africa.

I chanced upon Makindu in the first days of my assignment in Africa. I was sent to the African Delegation of the Ministry of Labor and Social Welfare of the Polish Government in London to work with the youth (mainly the Scouts) and to make sure that the teachers were paid their wages. We must remember that the teachers, both the professionals and the self-styled ones, belonged to that group of Polish people who were deported to the USSR and were miraculously rescued and who now worked tirelessly — at least from the moment that they crossed the Soviet border. They taught in temporary camps, on trains, on boats tossed by the waves and pursued by German submarines. Everywhere they went they spontaneously gathered children and teenagers about them, whether in classes or not, and conducted their lessons, be it even the reading of books in common, thereby not leaving any time for either follies or fear. The Polish educational authorities, aware of their work, treated them as working professionals — hence my mission.

There were actually very many — mostly female — teachers available, especially for the elementary schools, but there was a lack of qualified personnel for the middle schools. And that's when I met Wanda Dorosz and became acquainted with her exceptional, for Polish Africa, qualifications for teaching in middle schools. I did not know at that time that in the future she would direct the secondary school and the lyceum in which I myself was to make my debut as a teacher.[3]

UGANDA

Masindi

Account of Vala Lewicki (née Miron)

All youngsters except students in secondary education attended school locally. Because of a shortage of high school teachers I had to be sent to the Polish boarding school in Masindi, 400 kilometres away, together with 20 other girls. There we were assigned to 20-bed dormitories in the orphanage situated 3 km from the premises of the humanistic high school which was the professional gateway to all branches of tertiary education. Rain or shine we shuffled along the muddy roads 6 days a week, leaving home at 7:00 A.M. and returning at 2:00 P.M. loaded with homework such as memorising Latin and English vocabulary and grammar, Polish, history, geography, science and mathematics. All equally important. To fail one of them would mean no promotion to the next grade.

Fortunately for us, our heavy washing, including the unfeminine khaki denim uniforms provided by the orphanage, was done by laundry staff. At night the troughs in the laundry with running cold water and coppers of hot water served us as bath tubs.

Meals were never elaborate affairs. The quick breakfast varied only between a plate of baked beans and a slice of bread with tea and coffee one day, and two slices of sparingly-buttered bread with cocoa or tea the next day. Occasionally we had powdered eggs which tasted like ... powder.

We had sandwiches for lunch, while dinner consisted of bean soup, a slice of meat and baked beans. Always baked beans! Dessert was usually made of paw-paw and condensed milk and we regarded this as something special. We always felt hungry but we were not starving. Actually we all looked quite well fed. And we were happy. I liked school and was good, if not best, at all subjects. The teachers — like Mrs. Markowska (Latin), Mrs. Hawling (English) and Mrs. Michniewich (history) — were very nice ladies. I respected them and I think they liked me. My classmates were a wonderful bunch too.

We also had some social life in Masindi. Every three weeks there was a school dance with gramophone music. We had a lot of fun, regardless of the shortage of boys. Once a month we were allowed out of the orphanage to go to the movies in the camp. And there were beautiful letters from our pen friends in the army to fill the vacuum and cheer us up. None of us thought that the letters might stop coming.

The war was over. The enemy was defeated and Russia and the Allies were victorious! And Poland? Out of that war, Poland was not a winner. A Polish Communist state, comprising the territory west of the Bug and San rivers up to the Odra (Oder) River was proclaimed.

Eastern Poland, which had been partitioned by the line drawn along the Bug and San rivers in 1939, still remained under the Soviet regime in 1945.

Our home and the homes of many, many pre-war inhabitants were still not free, despite the fact that for six years the Polish army had fought for the freedom of the whole country, on all fronts, including the final and decisive battle at Monte Casino. A few Polish families from Africa returned to Poland and resettled in the western part of the country near Odra River. The majority of us decided to stay abroad.[4]

Account of Adela Konradczyńska-Piorkowska

Trucks were awaiting us in Kampala and these took us 80 km to Masindi. The camp was situated close to the slopes of a mountain which the Poles named Mount Wanda. Native Africans cut down the beautiful jungle and in its place built our huts. There were five thousand of us. One day there were shouts and panic and we started to run and hide when we saw a mass of natives armed with spears running noisily into our camp. The situation was saved by the camp commandant who explained to us that this was traditional ceremonial dress and that they wanted to welcome us officially to Africa. We were never afraid again after that.

Our huts were made of clay and covered with straw. They were rectangular and each accommodated two families. Entering a common dining room each family would proceed to its own accommodation. The kitchen was separate in case of possible fire. The nearby toilet was just a hole in the ground shielded with bamboo. One had to walk a long way to the nearest water tap and we had to carry water for ourselves, the old people and the children. We received food daily, but there was not always sufficient amount of it. The young people were growing fast and there was no clothing. For that reason when the first elementary school opened our mothers went out to work so as to earn money for some sort of clothes and additional food. Not long afterwards parcels of used clothing arrived from America. Unfortunately those in charge of distribution took the best for themselves, but there were cases where the pocket of a dress contained a gold ring wrapped in a handkerchief with the address of the donor in America.

After two years in the camp many youths, including girls, went as volunteers to

England to join the Polish army in order to fight with England against the Germans. I was too young for the army and went to a commercial college. In our camp there was a grammar school, a commercial school and also a tailoring crafts school. Unfortunately there were very few professional teachers so we were taught by people such as engineers, clerks, etc. The discipline was good and we were taught all subjects as well as social etiquette. Unfortunately we were not trained in something practical which could give us a direction in life.

The only entertainment which all the young people liked was the Scout movement. Belonging to it was of the greatest help in regaining some equilibrium in life, comradeship, good habits and all that which had been lacking in our young lives. The movement organised excursions and holidays in the country. We visited rubber plantations, Lake Albert, etc. There were also games, sport and campfires where we could feel alive.

There was a hospital and four doctors in our camp. The principal plague was sand flies which established themselves under toenails. There they laid their eggs, infecting the leg because the sand flies lived on human blood. They ceased to worry us after a while because everyone inspected their feet and we somehow became acclimated. Malaria was the most troublesome illness and almost everyone in the camp suffered from it. Personally, I was so ill that even quinine was powerless. Dr. Sadowski in our hospital managed to obtain six injections for me and these effected a cure. The dentist treated and extracted teeth live, without anaesthetic.

We built a beautiful church on top of Mount Wanda with the help of the natives. After a few years' residence we left a large cemetery there. Among the graves are those of two hospital sisters killed by lightning during one of the storms characteristic of that part of Africa.[5]

Account of Zdzisława Wójcik

The Polish refugee camp of Masindi was located in Uganda halfway between the northern shore of Lake Kioga and Lake Albert, through which the White Nile flows. The first director of the settlement, engineer Jerzy Skolimowski, planned it out and supervised its construction. The main street was laid out so that it ran in the direction of Warsaw. Masindi was the second largest Polish settlement in Africa (over 3,000 residents). It consisted of several villages each with a central plaza toward which led various streets lined with rectangular houses. Not only the roofs but also the walls of these two-room houses were made of straw or, more precisely, dry elephant grass. Near the plazas were located kitchens, water pumps, washrooms, and usually some object of importance to the life of the entire settlement, such as a community center, school, or store. Each village had a chief administrator who reported to the director and looked after the affairs of the residents.

In my capacity as director of the Scouts in "Polish Africa," this was the second settlement I visited and it was still in the initial stages of development. It was here that I had my most memorable experiences: a moving reunion after years of exile, a serious illness, real difficulties in directing a large organization for the first time in my life, a beautiful outing into the heart of equatorial Africa with its pristine environment untouched by human hand. My stay in this camp was very eventful. At the beginning of

1943 it was not easy to get to the settlement in Masindi: two nights on the Nairobi-Kampala train, then from the Jinja port 24 hours by boat along the Nile and Lake Kioga to the port in Masindi, from there by bus to the town of Masindi, and finally by car which belonged to the leadership of the settlement. I was brought to one of the villages in the camp. There on the plaza, empty at this time of day, stood a lone figure: the delicate, frail, red-headed Kazia Skórska — my friend from school and the Scout troop in Poznań. A master of philosophy in Polish philology, a master of law, and a graduate of the school of journalism — all rolled into one — she moved just before the war to Lwów. It was she who provided my fiancé, Mietek, and me with shelter during our wartime exile. I was at her house when the deportation at the end of June 1940 took place. They first took the Skórski family: Kazia, her parents, and her younger brother Przemek — the rest fled. Later the same fate met us on the street. I searched for Kazia in the Polish embassy in Kuybyshev and in Tehran — but in vain; she left earlier. I didn't realize then that she would be the only one to survive the Soviet hell. Her parents died in one of the [Soviet] settlements; Przemek died after joining the [Polish] army.

In Masindi, she headed up the educational department. She was the director of the settlement community center with the library and radio which, placed on the window sill, especially during the evening news, attracted the camp residents who wanted to hear the news from the various fronts of the world. This was followed by a camp-wide discussion. To be sure, the phrase "community center" was a grandiose term for such a small straw house and its meager contents. I lived at that center for a few months together with Kazia and I know that in spite of its modest circumstances it was truly a great hub of cultural life of the settlement. We had a regular theater as well as a puppet theater, there were presentations, and what's most important, there were courses in the English language with English teachers. And Kazia taught English in the secondary school. How she was able to manage it all no one knows. After two years she left Masindi and went to Tengeru.

I also had a chance to observe how the health services functioned in Masindi, where the doctors made the rounds either on foot or by transport. I have personal knowledge of this. One day I became very feverish (it turned out to have been an acute attack of malaria) and having returned "home," rather than eat my dinner, I lay down. Seeing me in this condition, Kazia left the community center and halted the vehicle in which Dr. Grygierowa, the camp pediatrist, was making her rounds of homes with sick children. The doctor checked me out, immediately called for an ambulance, and reserved a place for me in the hospital. Dr. Jadwiga Zielińska, the camp health officer, made her rounds on foot. She poked her head into everything and was merciless in condemning all manifestations of dirt. She made sure that the rules of hygiene, so different from our own because they were tailored to tropical conditions, were observed. Dr. Saks was the head doctor of the hospital and Dr. Sadowski, a surgeon, was second in command. There was also an impressive and well-managed laboratory (especially important because of the constant threat of tropical illnesses) and a pharmacy connected with it and directed by Mr. Swarowski. I spent several weeks in that hospital and emerged full of admiration for the order and cleanliness within those barracks made of straw, for the solicitous nursing care, and for the efficient operation of the whole organization. On the other hand, I experienced great difficulties in the scouting work for which I had been sent to Africa. This place was totally unlike the idyllic Tengeru, where the Scout troop was led by an intelligent individual experienced in organizational work and knowledgeable in how to raise our youth in the tropics during the war. Here it was different. A power-hungry, applause-seeking person who was full of herself gained control over scouting work. She was also the director of the secondary school (after finishing only two years of Polish studies). And what did she say to the youth? "You have suffered so much, now study and rest." She did not want the school children and Scouts to do any work in the settlement. While old men and women cleaned the children's playground, the youth passed by without shame. The elders also built the sets for a forthcoming play, and again the youth did nothing. I was young and radical. I could not stand it. I sent a report to the Delegation of the Ministry of Labor and Social Welfare in Nairobi, but I did not expect such a reaction. The next day a telegraph message arrived dismissing this director and troop leader from her duties and a truck took her, her child, and her belongings to another camp. Never again in my life did I take such a drastic step.

When the new troop leader called for an assembly, no one showed up. They were still the "army" of the former troop leader. This happened exactly at the time when the ambulance was taking me to the hospital. The new, young troop leader had to begin work alone and she managed just fine. When my fever broke a few days later, she was already in control of the situation. She was the best troop leader in Africa for as long as our settlements continued to exist there. Wanda Swarowska should be remembered even though she is no longer alive.

The outing to Murchison Falls was organized by Jurek Skolimowski, the director of the settlement. Six or seven of us went there including myself, Jurek, Kazia Skórska, and Mikołaj Szyszkowski, the deputy delegate of the Ministry of Labor and Social Welfare in Uganda. In the port of Butiaba we got on a boat and traveled by night over Lake Alberta in order to be on the Nile at dawn and see the awakening life along the bank of this great river. Beyond the floating leaves of water lilies, lotus plants, and thick papyrus rushes grew huge sprawling trees. Large water birds awakened on their drooping branches and prepared for flight. Troops of monkeys jumped from one tree to the next and even to distant ones. Next to our boat swam crocodiles, not very interested in us but our skin curled at their sight. They also lounged on the bank where we were to disembark. Fortunately the short- and unshapely-legged crocodiles were not dangerous on land. Then we followed a serpentine, steep path in the mountains to Murchison Falls where we saw a mass of churning water glistening in the sun with all the colors of the rainbow. We returned along the same road that evening and were greeted by elephants. The sight of these huge animals, dark against the background of the rosy heavens, was unforgettable. They walked slowly, extracting with difficulty their heavy feet from the deep mud. On their shoulders, heads, and ears sat large birds, rosy in the setting sun, and cleaned them of the swarm of bugs. We returned at dusk, which in the tropics begins early, and suddenly it was dark. This trip was the only one that someone else had organized for me in Africa. I never went on another trip that I didn't have to organize myself or one in the course of which I had to perform some vital function. I will always remember it.[6]

Account of Henryka Utnik-Łappo

I was brought to the settlement of Masindi in Uganda by the first transport. This must have been in early fall of 1942. My report card from my first year of secondary school in Tehran carries the date July 7, 1942; the report card for the second year in Masindi carries the date September 30, 1943. Every three months a new school year! No doubt a great deal of compression of course material was needed to make up for lost time.

Africa greeted us with a scorching sun and a cloud of mosquitos from which we were protected at night by a mosquito net. As I recall, our first impressions did not fill us with happiness. There were four "roads" in my first village — dirt roads that led from the centrally located well with a pump to the four corners of the world. On both sides of these roads were houses, about five of them on each side, raised on wooden posts and covered with elephant grass, which was also used to reinforce the walls. The beds consisted of boards covered with elephant grass; above them were mosquito nets suspended from slender bamboo poles. That grass, especially on the first night, produced a strange rustling sound with every body movement, and in the silence of the night one could hear the whispering of the people as they moved about. For the next six years those houses and beds, later modified for the better by our own ingenuity, were to serve as our homes, our resting places during the turmoil of the war. In quick order other villages were erected under the supervision of engineer Jerzy Skolimowski, who could be seen everywhere in his overalls and cork helmet. New arrivals were coming.

We began our first lessons a few weeks after our arrival, when the second village was populated. There was also a transit camp to which people were brought only to be resettled among the other villages. By 1943 a secondary school was functioning very well. Kazimierz Arnold, a fine instructor of Polish, became its director.

On the third-year secondary school report card, dated December 22, 1943, the following signatures appear: Director of the school, K. L. Arnold; instructor, E. Michniewicz; director of the settlement, Engineer Hawling; and school administrator, Kinasz-Surowiecki....

In this short summary of events from our coming to the settlement of Masindi in 1942 until its liquidation in 1948, I wanted to comment on the secondary school, and how it emerged as a school of high caliber in spite of beginning in such primitive conditions. Our history is also a testimonial to the longevity of our nation. Despite our falls we quickly stand at attention.

After the sad and nightmarish experiences in the "inhuman land," our time on the dark continent can be said to have been idyllic. "Someone" built our houses, "someone" provided us with food, "someone" clothed us, and "someone" filled our heads with knowledge. To all these people, and in particular to our former teachers, on the 44th anniversary of our departure from Masindi I send the following magical words: *thank you*![7]

Koya

Account of Vala Lewicki (née Miron)

It was a magnificent early afternoon when we arrived at Koya. The first impression was good. The houses, built of clay and covered with elephant grass (no ceilings) were rectangular in shape and contained three rooms furnished with single beds, linen, towels, blankets and, of course, mosquito nets. The nets also came in handy in making temporary curtains for the windows made of hessian, in movable frames.

In most cases, regardless of its size, each family was assigned to one room. There were 10 people — three families — in our house situated a short distance from schools, administration buildings and hospitals.

Some people, such as the camp Polish officers as well as the English commandant, Mr. Mannering, doctors, teachers and people close to them had their own, much better, houses with proper wooden floors. The kitchens, one to every house, and the toilets were outside at the back of the house and very well built. In order to have a shower or to do our washing in cold, running water we had to walk to the end of the street where those amenities were placed.

Koya Camp was most beautifully situated and planned. It was a little peninsula on Lake Victoria, surrounded on three sides by water which glittered in the sun, with quite a high mountain on the fourth side. The small space between the lake and the mountain held a gate with Polish and African police constantly standing there. It was a perfect position for defense.

Apart from Mr. Mannering and, later on, one representative from the International Refugee Organisation (IRO) who was American, the settlement was run by Poles. Four Polish army doctors had the big tasks of looking after the sick and constantly training new staff. But, remembering what a high price was paid in young lives in Pahlavi and Tehran, they did everything they could as well as they could. If a patient needed an operation or complex treatment he or she would be sent to the European Hospital in Kampala....

Uganda was full of pitfalls. There were millions of malaria mosquitoes. For protection we had to wear long pants after 6:00 P.M. and cork or straw hats earlier, for the sun was merciless. Termites were the most unexpected destroyers. One day clothes in a suitcase looked nice and safe, and the next day they might disappear, leaving only dust. Everything had to be ironed because of some invisible worms which could burrow under the skin like ringworm and give a person hell.[8]

Account of Teresa Rogińska-Słomińska

I came to Koya in October 1943. The settlement was nicely situated on a small hill bounded on three sides by the waters of Lake Victoria. Koya was not yet ready to receive the new residents; homes were just being built. We were housed, therefore, temporarily in the school buildings. Bunk beds were placed in the classrooms and there we stayed until the construction was completed.

Africa did not greet me kindly. I was immediately attacked by "land fleas." They were probably attracted by the sores on my feet which were the result of my illness in India. The situation was truly worthy of pity. My legs were so swollen and painful that I could not walk. And before I regained my health again, I came down with malaria.

After a few weeks the new village was ready. The houses were made of reeds, whitewashed inside and out; the roof was covered with elephant grass. There were no attics or floors. Screens were installed in the windows which were covered at night with mats or shutters. There was no water, no electricity, and no sewage disposal. The kitchens, for reasons of health, were located in separate buildings. In spite of these primitive conditions, I thought that little house was very beautiful and pleasant because I still remembered the dugouts of [Siberian] exile and the tents, cabins, and barracks in which we lived in Iran and India.

The days passed and our life became more and more normal. We came to realize that Koya was not just another transit camp but a place in which we would remain probably until the end of the war. I was 14 years old at the time and had taken the exam for middle school twice. The school was in the process of being established in Koya. There were many problems associated with this because we lacked teachers. Eventually a curriculum was worked out and the date for the entrance exam was announced. So I had to take it once more. I passed without any difficulty. My studies in level I, however, were short. The émigré Polish educational authorities did not agree to accord the school in Koya the status of a state middle school. An exceptionally difficult situation arose for the youth who wanted to study but found that they could only receive a grammar school education. We were rescued by the arrival from Tehran of a new transport carrying several teachers with advanced training. Soon levels II and III of secondary school were established. After much effort a state secondary school and a lyceum of the humanities were founded in Koya. Its director was Jadwiga Delawska, whom we called "Pulchra." She was, in fact, very beautiful and elegant and exceptionally dedicated to the youth. She was the true "spirit" of the school. She taught us the Polish language. Math was taught by Bolesław Latawiec, called "Kite" after the English equivalent of his surname. The youth embraced their studies wholeheartedly. The difficulties having to do with the shortage of textbooks and the complete lack of other educational materials were overcome by both the professors and students inasmuch as it was possible.

An amateur theater, run by the female teachers, also operated in Koya. I remember most of all: "Jaś i Małgosia [John and Margaret], "Wisła do morza" [Vistula River to the Sea], "Śluby panieńskie" [Maidens' Weddings], "Zemsta" [Vengeance], and Rydel's "Jasełka" [Nativity Play]. The play "Wisła do morza" featured folk dances from various regions of Poland, beginning with those of the highland robbers and ending with the Kashubian ones. It was very popular not only among the Poles residing in Koya but also among the English living in Uganda. The creators of this show as well as many others were Maria Gładyszowa and Barbara Dulębina.

I spent my free time mainly reading books, which increased in number with each passing year, and also on handcrafts and swimming. The last was severely forbidden by the camp authorities. That rule was the least obeyed, particularly by the youth. It was difficult to restrain oneself from cooling off when the heat poured out of the sky and at the same time clear, beautiful water bordered the settlement on three sides. I went swimming often, heedless of the threat of incurring tropical diseases or of the threat of encountering a crocodile — and there were many of them in Victoria. I somehow got away with it, but others were not so lucky. One day during swimming a crocodile grabbed one of the boys. This happened in the presence of many people who were completely helpless. Every motorboat and sailboat searched the lake, but the body was never found.

My life took a new turn from the moment that the Scouts were organized in Koya. Gen. Anders' 2nd Corps helped in this by sending us instructors. To our settlement came Wiktor Szyryński, Ignacy Kozioł, and Romuald Rzędzian.

The children in the younger classes had a fantastic time in the Cub Scouts led by the sub-scoutmaster, Roman Rzędzian. The older children and the teenagers, which included me, spent our time in the regular Scouts. Frequent gatherings, bivouacking in the jungle, campfires, and training camps for assistants provided us with a great deal of satisfaction and joy. I learned a lot in scouting, including respect for the flora and fauna and camping skills. To this very day I profess the principle learned in scouting that the only thing that should remain after a camping trip is crumpled grass.

Camping was a great adventure. The residents of Koya were not wealthy. The majority of the parents could not afford to cover the costs associated with camping. We had to raise the money ourselves. To this end the Scouts sponsored dances with refreshments and lottery prizes. The girls sowed napkins and blouses which the English women bought readily. The boys took pictures and developed the prints and made covers for books out of bark. The money collected from such enterprises sufficed to cover the costs associated with camping.

The Catholic missions gave us a lot of help by letting us use mission facilities in exchange for a mere "God bless." Fireside stories taught us to love and sacrifice for our Fatherland, equanimity of the spirit in spite of setbacks, and the principle that we should live in such a way as to make others enjoy being with us.

The years passed by, the war continued on, and I thought that when it finally ended I would go back to the home from which I had been so brutally torn and exiled to Siberia. And I was not the only one who thought that way.

Being in level IV we founded the Club of Old Maidens. We took on new and unpopular names such as Agrypina, Ksantypa, Prudencjanna, etc. From among the resolutions made by the club members the two most important were: never to marry and to meet at Our Lady of Ostra Brama [in Wilno] at 5:00 P.M. on May 5, 1955. Neither resolution was kept. We all married and we were not able to meet in Ostra Brama for obvious reasons [i.e., the border changes after the war]. May 1945 arrived. The war with Germany ended. There was no euphoria in Koya. We already knew that the lands from which we hailed would not belong to Poland or, in other words, that we had nowhere to return to. The bubble of the myth of return had burst; only sorrow and great bitterness remained. But life went on. Koya was selected as one of those camps whose liquidation was to be delayed. Transports came to us from the settlements of Valivade and Jamnagar in India as well as from Masindi in Africa. Our class was being reduced in size at lightening speed as transports left for Poland and England. July 1948 arrived in Koya and brought with it a great event: the first and only graduation. Scarcely nine people participated since most of the members of our class had left for England earlier. We were grown up now. The first-year class organized a graduation ball in our honor. We had a good time but a constant theme emerged in our discussions: What now? After two weeks I, together with my parents and sister, departed for Mombasa where I waited for two and a half months for a ship back to Poland.[9]

TANGANYIKA

Tengeru

Account of Stefania Buczak-Zarzycka

In the middle of 1943 we left Karachi, and I looked forward to our next and more permanent home in Tanganyika (Tanzania)....

In just over a fortnight we approached the shores of the "*Czarny Ląd*" (Black Land). Our first glimpses of this land on the horizon were of the cocos palms stretching into the sky. As we came nearer to the port of Tanga I realized that I was actually in the strange land that our *babunia* [grandmother] had described years ago. Never in my wildest imagination did I ever think that I would make such a country my temporary home.

Moored at the dock, our luggage was removed from the ship and taken to the train by Africans who moved and sang in rhythmic unison. It was already evening at the station and Africans carrying large baskets of oranges offered these to us with the greeting: "*Jumbo, lazungu*" (Hello, white people).

We smiled and waved hello, relieved that we had encountered such a friendly people. Then our train journey began to the settlement of Tengeru, near Arusha.

In the valley of the Meru Mountain, near Kilimanjaro, and stretching out for miles nested our bustling camp. This area had just been recently cleared for our habitation; only the tallest trees remained inside our settlement and these provided shade and a home for birds. The campsite looked like a splendid park with the most beautiful, stunning tropical plants. Our freshly painted round huts were constructed of clay, while the roof was made of banana or palm leaves. Windows were covered only by shutters, not glass, which served to keep out insects and wild animals. These huts were covered by a roof but did not have a ceiling. Inside we found beds with mosquito nets, a small, roughly-made table, four stools and a kerosene lamp, as electricity was unavailable in these settlement huts at first.

"You know, this camp reminds me of our orchard and beehives in Poland," remarked Ola. "I hope these human bees treat their drones more tolerantly."

We all laughed realizing that the camp of seven thousand consisted mainly of women, children and the orphanage. Very few men were present — only young boys and men with physical disabilities. Most of our fathers and brothers were in the army under the command of General W. Anders at the side of Allied Powers.

After unpacking quickly we rushed out to explore and discovered that our two huts were nearest the river which divided us from the jungle. At first we couldn't see the river, only hear its roar because its banks were so high and hidden from view by the jungle. We walked through vines and ferns until we reached the bottom of the river bank and discovered the river bed lined with shiny stones that glittered like diamonds. By sundown, monkeys came down to the river, some with their babies on their backs, socialising and playing tricks on each other. We couldn't believe that there could be so many monkeys. A group of about ten Africans crossing the river passed by us and we eyed each other cautiously. The corn-rows of the women intrigued us as did their sparse apparel. These women balanced a basket of bananas on their heads while babies were tied on their backs.

Just as in all tropical countries, nightfall came suddenly and we returned to our huts. The night was so black that the stars appeared to be doubly bright, like silver discs suspended in the sky. Thousands of glowworms flew about and the warm evening was, at first, silent except for the clicking noises of insects. People had completed their cooking quickly and moved indoors, closing their shutters. Although we retired early, sleep did not come easily as we listened to strange, disturbing sounds and the occasional chanting in a strange language accompanied by rhythmic drumming.

In the morning, I bent down to put on my shoes and there under my bed was a gigantic reptile.

"Help, a crocodile!" I screamed, tearing out of the hut.

People gathered around as I kept shouting for help until an African askari (policeman) arrived, carrying a panga. He laughed, calling out that the creature was a lizard not a crocodile, and he pushed it towards the door, whereupon it ran away into the jungle.

My friend Danka laughed, "You know that a crocodile lives in the river, not under your bed."

The incident became one of our family jokes.

The settlement was divided into seven groups; we were in the sixth group and were fortunate to be allowed two huts. Here at last a sense of calm and security gradually crept into our lives and our relationships. After years spent crowded together on floors, in stables and tents, we often reacted by expressing extremes of emotions. Often our emotions were difficult to control. Here, we came to experience and, in turn, give each other more tolerance and respect. Even though these huts appear very primitive today, we experienced in them the first normalisation of everyday life. As the basic services of the community were organised we felt like pioneers. First, the hospital and dental clinics were established. Second, the building of schools was to be completed. At Tengeru a number of technical schools were established alongside the pre-primary, primary and secondary schools (*Gimnazjum i Liceum Ogólnokształcące*) .

There were schools for the training of motor-mechanics, dressmaking and designing, domestic science, agriculture and handicrafts. Initially, difficulties arose from our unfamiliarity with the African climate and produce.

A communal effort also took place with the construction of our church and its landscaped gardens. The church was designed along the African, not European model. The Polish priests who had been released from prisons and Father Jan Śliwowski, who came from North America, fostered the development of a number of religious sodalities. After a few months in the settlement it was noticeable that we hadn't been idle. Outside each hut could be seen delightful flowerbeds; I even saw roses in some which I imagined to be Polish roses. Soon the settlement took on the character of a small town with streets, street signs and even Polish national symbols visible on public buildings and huts. Inside the huts the women expended much energy decorating and personalising their huts into homes with kilims, embroidered coverslips, bedspreads, doilies and floor coverings from stitched bagging materials.

Our interrupted education had to be completed and classes called *skoczki* or make-up classes were organised. These were organised on a six-month rotation and rigorous exams had to be successfully completed in order for each candidate to proceed to the next *skoczki*. Again, there was a great shortage of textbooks, so a student supplied with a text was required to complete her or his study or reading overnight so that the text could be passed onto the next student. We studied late into the night and we were very motivated to complete the gaps in our education. On some of these marathon reading sessions I would place my feet into a basin of cold water so that I would keep awake. At times, I had only two or three hours sleep before my next school day. In 1944 the lending library was built and we had greater access to reading material.

Our cultural life expanded with the creation of the choirs, theatre circle, and musical and literary societies. Other organisations were the RKO, Catholic Action, YMCA, and the Scouts Hall (*Izba Harcerska*). Sporting groups emerged and social life flourished. Although our health and strength returned, new tropical diseases began to take their toll; yellow fever, malaria, and tropical ulcers were the most common problems. Also, a number of parasites and insects caused discomfort. A kind of sand flea called *dzin-dzingry* crawled under the skin of nails and hatched its eggs there. These became very itchy and painful if the egg sacs were not removed; if they were broken on contact, tropical ulcers would develop. These were difficult to treat and often people were forced to have their nails removed. However, we found that the Africans were most skillful in removing these sacs....

Within the settlement, more and more families received the news of the deaths of husbands, fathers and sons. [Stefania's father had also died by this time.] Letters came from such places as Monte Casino, Tobruk, Norway and Palestine. Each evening in the recreation hall crowds gathered around the wireless to listen to the BBC broadcasts concerning the progress of the war. Young women were recruited to work at the British Air Force maintenance and ammunition factories in Nairobi. Often girls increased their age in order to be recruited there as trainees. Others, like Marysia, found employment in Arusha or Dar es Salaam in private industry. The remainder in camp slowly made themselves at home, creating gardens and keeping pets. Not only were the traditional cats and dogs adopted, but many also befriended monkeys, exotic birds, native dogs and penned chickens.

However, chickens were often a risky and unprofitable proposition because the monkeys loved to rob their nests of eggs and snakes coiled themselves quite happily in their nests in order to be warmed by brooding chickens.

After school, boys received further education from the natives in the art of cockfighting, and Antek with his friends reared his champion cockerel without Mama's knowledge. His champion fought regularly at the bazaar and in the surrounding native villages, and Antek often returned with another rooster as spoils from these competitions. However, when he lost a challenge, he lost the rooster as well as our dog, Simba. Fortunately, Simba was so hostile to strangers that the winners preferred to give Simba back to Antek.

Nearby the settlement was situated the bazaar to which everyone bought their produce. Often, we would watch the parade of a family group going to sell their produce. The husband would be in front followed by his dogs and older children, while behind them plodded his wife carrying on her head an enormous basket filled with fruit, vegetables or even a live chicken. She might also be toting a baby in a sling on her back, and it was fascinating to see an African woman "throw" a long, thin breast onto her shoulder for her baby to suck.

We all went to the bazaar not only to buy goods, mainly fruit, but also because it was a central meeting place for the exchange of news and gossip. One afternoon an amusing incident occurred. Two friends who had not seen each other since Russia accidently met. Pani Buniec cried out after an initial exchange of hugs: "*Kuma* (Godmother), how did you get here?"

"*Kuma*, it's wonderful to see you again. I came from Ifunda," answered her friend.

Whereupon the Africans within earshot burst out laughing so hard that some threw their children, baskets of fruit or chickens in the air. Others were supporting themselves, as they almost doubled over with laughter. All the Polish people watching this spontaneous outburst were astounded.

"They've gone wild," people began whispering.

One small Polish boy ran up to the women and attempted to tell them not to use the word *cuma,* but before he could explain properly, the women told him off for interrupting their reunion. A Polish askari then approached and told them that *cuma* in Swahili was a colloquialism for a part of the female anatomy. "I never heard of such a thing. Why are the natives twisting around our language?"

The embarrassed ladies beat a hasty retreat. The episode helped to explain why children are always the first to learn a new language....

Through the BBC broadcasts we learnt of the Yalta Conference held on the 13th February, 1945, involving President Roosevelt of the USA, Marshall Stalin of the USSR, and Prime Minister Churchill of Great Britain. Here, it was decided that the eastern sector of Poland should be incorporated into the Soviet Union; thus around my homeland dropped the "Iron Curtain." For my family and most others the dream of returning home to Poland, a dream to which we had pinned all of our hopes during our trek through the Soviet Union and the Middle East, was now shattered. Initially, the general reaction was that of great sadness, then some began to display intense fear. "What will become of us? Where will we go?" These questions were repeatedly asked and heard everywhere. Others vented their anger and bitter disappointment. We had been sold out by our Allies: Britain and the United States. Most of us had relatives or had lost relatives who had been fighting alongside these Allies, relatives who had fled to England to join Polish forces there. The Yalta Conference was described as a deceit and a betrayal.

On the 7th May 1945, the war ended in Europe. After the prime minister's speech had been broadcast the strains of the last post ushered in a moment of silence, and even though our tears fell for all those who had fallen we were thankful that no one else would have to die. Celebrations of victory broke out spontaneously in every part of our settlement. In spite of the ecstatic atmosphere we grew more and more concerned for our future and rumours began to fly around the camp. One of these rumours was that Polish government-in-exile would purchase land in Africa in which a Polish settlement would be created. Another possible settlement place was one of the British Pacific Islands. But the most important outcome of the news was the fervor with which everyone began to learn English, only taught as an extra second language option hitherto. Academic Poles preferred to learn Latin or French before English. Everyone began to undertake vocational courses at the agricultural or the commercial colleges.

Representatives of the UNRRA (United Nations Relief and Rehabilitation Administration), and IRO (International Refugee Organization) came to visit us and expressed their concern for our future. They discussed the possibilities open to us: families of those in the armed forces would be reunited in England; some would be repatriated to Poland; and others would have to apply for immigration to other lands. As yet it had not been decided which countries would accept us. These visitors were followed closely by representatives of the Polish government of Warsaw who staged an open-air meeting encouraging people to return to Poland because she sorely needed people for postwar reconstruction. Even though Poland had lost her eastern sector, she had gained land to the west (Wrocław and Szczecin) and we were urged to settle in these areas.

During the meeting Father Rogiński and his altar boys suddenly appeared on stage dressed in rags and carrying picks and shovels typical of prisoners. Spontaneously people gasped aloud as if in pain. We all reflected on our time in Siberia and some stood up singing "*sto lat*" (hundred years) in support of the demonstration the priest was making. Others in the audience produced rotten tomatoes and other missiles forcing the representatives to quit. Later that night they quietly slipped out of the settlement. In the days that followed concern for the future was expressed in many ways. Quite a few single women became engaged, many to non-Polish men. The majority of these hasty engagements ended in marriage, but some experienced disappointment. The white Africans had for years formed a strong clique in the community and were very reluctant to accept sons-in-law and daughters-in-law of other nationalities. Also, up to this time very few people were lucky enough to be permitted to work outside our settlement. But now, permission to work in other African cities was obtained much more easily.

During this troublesome period when our future was in jeopardy our own administrators added to our fears. Knowing that only a few people wanted to be repatriated to Poland, some unscrupulous administrators threatened and blackmailed us. They openly stated that we could be blacklisted and deported to Poland if we broke even the most trivial of rules. The adults reacted strangely to this pressure. Some bowed before these treats and became very passive and cautious, while others became very quarrelsome and aggressive towards these officious figures. Time proved that these were not just idle threats; some people were transferred out to other camps and some were actually deported....

On the 2nd February 1950, about 1,500 Polish refugees, mainly widows with older or adolescent children, but also some single people and young couples, stood on the deck of the American troop carrier, General W. C. Langfitt in the port of Kilindini. I had been here so many, many times to bid farewell to my friends, but I hadn't imagined that I would one day say farewell to this Dark Continent which had so generously opened its arms to shelter us during those war years....

The whistle blew and the pilot boat pulled the ship away from the wharf. It was almost evening and the lighthouse was already blinking its message out to sea. I turned back to the shoreline of tropical trees disappearing over the horizon and whispered: "*Kwaheri Africa.*"[10]

Account of Aniela Molek-Piotrowska

The main road led into the camp [Tengeru] and on both sides there stood round huts covered with banana leaves and commonly called "bee hives." The settlement lay at the foot of Meru Mountain. It was large and had the character of a village. The huts were lost among the greenery of trees and multi-coloured flowers. The picturesque appearance of the camp made a pleasant impression on me. Africa holds rich memories of very young years when each day was filled with many duties. Most of the time was spent at school, while free time was used for excursions — such as to monasteries at Kilemy and Kiboshe as well as many others. We also spent time in libraries, held Scout meetings and so on. Films were also shown in the camp. We attended these with pleasure, although only those which were permitted for children. On Sundays there were walks by Duluti Lake and occasional boat rides on this wide, seemingly bottomless lake covered with water lilies.

One should not forget our beautiful little church, always filled with faithful inhabitants of the settlement and, each Sunday, with youth attending a school Mass. Scouting, which arranged Scout bonfires, was a large organisation attracting hundreds of youths. Among dense greenery the moon stole into the clearing where the Girl Guides lit a fire. In the distance could be heard the beating wings of a startled bird, then the roar of a wild animal followed by momentary fear, then silence once more. Time passed quickly by the fire — stories ended, Scout songs were sung — and the fire died down. In the evening silence, under the light of the moon, a circle of Scouts and Guides joined hands and the evening ended with the singing of the traditional song "Night Approaches." One sings progressively more quietly, then hums and finally only thinks.

That stays in one's heart forever. One can endlessly weave many memorable moments about growing up under the African sun, about the communal camp life, about the last stage, the liquidation of the camp, about the way more than one mother had to make decisions regarding their children's future, the sad partings from friends to whom one said goodbye perhaps forever, the moon which always shone brightly for us, and the summertimes filled with the scent of exotic plants. At times of solitary silence I often look back. There have remained only recollections of carefree African days of long ago, innocent romances, impressions — there, in Africa, where once we dreamt of a future.

When the camp closed we had to look once more for somewhere to live in a foreign land such as England, Canada or Australia. The end of the war in 1945 did not restore the ability to return to a free Poland for us.[11]

Account of Wisia Reginella (née Danecka)

We reached the port of Tanga safely, then, following a rail journey of several days, Tengeru station and, finally, by truck, the settlement of Tengeru at the foot of Mount Meru. Above us was a mixed forest and the peak covered with ice....

Our first impressions of the settlement were not happy ones. Round huts shaped like beehives and covered with banana leaves. Floors of beaten sand and windows without glass, although there were shutters. Four beds with string in place of springs, a small storage cupboard, a little table, four stools, some mugs, spoons, a bowl, a bucket. Water had to be carried from a central tap. Four persons were allocated to each hut.

How and where to cook? We had to cook on stones. The pot kept toppling over and water put out the fire. We cried and laughed in turn. Well, the war would end soon and we would go home. Such forecasts kept us alive.

All posts were already taken up by people from earlier transports. I only received 10 shillings a month from an officers' fund. It was true that we were issued dry goods, but it was always necessary to buy extras.

Fleas were our worst tormentors, laying their eggs under our toenails. This itched terribly, the toes swelled and ulcers formed. Whole herds of termites attacked the huts. We were troubled by malaria and other tropical illnesses. There were five thousand people in our settlement and a hospital with only a few doctors. With the passage of time, schools, a chapel, kitchen-diners and a bakery were established. There was milk from cows, cream, cheese and butter. A church was built as there were several clergymen there.

The whole looked like a large African village, except that whites lived there. A Polish YMCA, financed by America, was formed. Olek [Wisia's friend and future husband] and I both found work. He established trade schools in all settlements in Tanganyika and I worked in the chapel initially, then took over management of the YMCA. I liked this work. I established literary, musical, and sports circles and organised activities for adults, youths and children. I tended carefully to the preschool, visited the sick, supplying them with newspapers and books. We organised musical mornings at the church on Sundays with illustrated fairy tales with a musical background. We played netball and tennis....

The liquidation of our camp grew near. Following an UNRRA Commission some people were going to Canada, some to Australia and a small group to England. A few families decided to remain in Tanganyika.[12]

Account of Zdzisława Wójcik

This [Tengeru] was the largest Polish refugee settlement in Africa. It was located in the Arusha region at the foothills of the dormant volcano of Mt. Meru (4,565 meters above sea level) near the cratered Lake Duluti. From afar one could see the snowy stack of Mt. Kilimanjaro (5,895 meters above sea level), rosy at sunset, silvery-blue at sunrise. The settlement was surrounded by an African savanna. Umbrella-like acacias with masses of white flowers as well as other types of related flowering trees grew from ten to one hundred meters apart, and here and there, especially in rocky places, huge baobab trees and candelabra-like spurges that resembled cactuses could be found. All this was spread about on a grassy carpet, rust-colored or grey-yellow during the dry season, greening rapidly at the onset of the rainy season. The flowers of the savanna appeared at that time also: red, delicate, bullet-shaped varieties and foxgloves two to three meters high with crowning clusters of large, delicate, white flowers. All along the streams and lake shores lay dark and perpetually green tropical forests. And near Arusha, the capital of the region, in the fertile, black, volcanic soil, stretched cultivated fields of corn, barley, peanuts, and plantations with various trees and shrubs, such as papayas, coffee, sisals, and others.

The settlement lay on a somewhat rolling terrain. Consisting of small houses, it occupied quite a large area. The houses were round, made of black volcanic mud, and covered with either elephant grass or thatch from palm or banana leaves. They were whitewashed inside and out. Such a small house without a ceiling or floor had but one window and one door. The window did not have a glass pane but only a screen, to keep the bugs out, and a wooden shutter. There was no electricity, water, or septic disposal in the houses. These things existed outside the premises. Cooking was not done in the houses either. Oil lamps provided light. Generally one or two families lived in such a house, designed to accommodate four people. The new homes stood in areas cleared of weeds and in time beautiful gardens flowered near them year round in this climate without winters. The settlement functioned as a cohesive whole although it was divided administratively into so-called groups. It had an English commandant (a retired British officer) who was in contact with the outside world and in particular with the British authorities of Tanganyika who were responsible for the further expansion of the settlement and for providing it with the necessary food rations. The internal life of the settlement was left in the hands of a Polish director who was in charge of distributing the food and clothing and who oversaw the needs of the hospitals and schools.

In time the settlement expanded and acquired a certain infrastructure. The school was moved into specially built barracks. They were long and each one accommodated two classes. There were no windows but good lighting was assured by the space between the top of the wall and the roof which extended beyond the building itself and provided both shade and protection from the rain. Textile, tailor, shoe and other workshops came into existence along with a nearby farm, butcher shop, and a well-stocked canteen. A Catholic church was built and, later, an Orthodox church and three community centers: Scout, Catholic, and Polish YMCA.

What struck one most about this settlement was its exotic location in contrast to its unfinished sanitation facilities and lack of supplies especially in the hospital and schools. Due to the high level of organization in the settlement, life resumed its normal pace. Textbooks were lacking, but primers were copied by hand and materials gleaned from foreign-language textbooks and the popular press served as texts for the older classes. An orphanage was functioning, the camp hospital operated at full steam, Scout life flourished. The scouting organization embraced the majority of children and teenagers and was the only entity that could get along without community centers, sports equipment, libraries, and even qualified instructors. It worked thanks to the memories of the adults and a handful of teenagers. The Scout oath, the rules, and many scouting songs were remembered. Scout uniforms were sown in accordance with prewar patterns.

Of all the people that I met in Tengeru, I was most impressed by Eugenia Grosicka, who directed the large orphanage and the small adjacent old age home. She was also one of the Scout leaders in the settlement. The scouting troop in Tengeru, especially the girls' division, was large. The troop was divided into two basic units: one for Girl Guides and Brownies, the other for Boy Scouts and Cub Scouts. These were headed by Madzia Jarosz and Witek Kozak, respectively. This was a genuine scouting troop. It functioned even in the earliest times when there was a total lack of equipment and, most important, a lack of tents. We managed, however, by using blankets for tents, at least in dry weather.

I returned to Tengeru several times, if only in passing while on my way to the settlements in southern Tanganyika. I was sent there as an official to oversee scouting and the youth on behalf of the Delegation of the Ministry of Labor and Social Welfare of the Polish Government in London with its headquarters in Nairobi. I was also a commandant of the Girl Guides in Africa. I never expected that after two years of making the rounds of Polish African settlements I would finally end up in Tengeru and remain there until the end of my stay on the Dark Continent.

In February 1945 I began teaching natural sciences in the secondary school and the lyceum. Without textbooks, atlases or laboratories, I began to lecture on the most diverse subjects not only in biology, in which I had a theoretical background, and geography, which I loved and knew as well, but also other subjects like chemistry, physics, astronomy, and introductory philosophy. There were no middle school teachers. They said: "You're the youngest. It will be the easiest for you to learn what you need to know." I never expected that one day I would replace Ms. Grosicka as troop leader in Tengeru and follow in her footsteps — which was not easy to do. Or that, after many years, I would come to regard this period of my life, in which the workday began at seven o'clock in the morning and ended around 2:00 A.M., as the most beautiful and happiest. Or that I would carry constantly before me, even after almost 50 years, the image of the youth whom I tried to teach and the faces of the girls who placed their hands in mine and took the Scout oath.[13]

Account of Jadwiga Morawiecka-Zaborowska

The composition of even a few sentences about the stay of the Polish exiles in East Africa necessitates, in my case, a return to Tengeru. A return? But was there really a separation? No, there was not. Otherwise, I would have had to first become separated from my own memory and even from my own identity.

Our settlement consisted of homes built in the "African style." Their conical roofs covered with aprons of banana leaves or elephant grass were chewed day and night by tireless termites. This produced a distinct sound effect (which was actually rather pleasant). The interior contained but a few things: beds, table, stools, and something resembling a wardrobe — a rack covered by blanket-like fabric. The kitchen — actually only a stove — was located in the open air under a roof which warded off the sun and rain. The sanitation facilities were communal. They were not up to the highest standards.

However, almost every house was surrounded by a flower garden wherein grew nostalgic mallows, zinnias, impatiens and roses, but also the more exotic canna lilies, star-of-Bethlehem bushes, fragrant thorn apples, papaya trees, and creepers whose names I do not know. There was great concern for aesthetics in the settlement and also for the maintenance of Polish ambiance. When eucalypti trees rustled in the wind we dreamt of birch-tree groves and pine forests back home.

A sizeable group of Polish people (the first transports arrived in June 1942 — about 4,000 in all, including mainly women but also about 1,700 children and youth) found shelter, work and rest here. This became their home for the next few years; in my case it was for five years. This was a stationary settlement.

For administrative purposes the settlement was divided into groups. This term was used to designate a certain number of adjacent houses or a certain number of people living in those houses. Almost all of life's necessities — food, clothing, medical care (for example, the treatment of malaria) — were taken care of in these groups. The sound of a special gong signaled the dispensation of all these provisions. After a while even our dog, Simba, came to understand the meaning of the gong and hurried for his rations. The commandant of the settlement was an Englishman, Capt. Minory, a Polonophile. There were also Poles in the administration —first Józef Mądrzak, later Mikołaj Korzeniewski. The administrative functionaries were almost exclusively Poles. Only a few of us residents of the settlement knew the English language at the time and only a few managed to learn it during our several-year stay there. Perhaps the motivation was missing. The knowledge of the English language was not essential and we were, after all, bound for our homeland. The settlement had its own farm, bakery, cooperative, movie house and, what's important, a hospital headed by Dr. Tworkowski. Its personnel were almost exclusively Polish. A Roman Catholic church was erected with an image of Our Lady of Ostra Brama in the main nave, and the local Greek farmers sponsored the erection of an Orthodox church.

Our social and cultural life revolved around the community centers. It was there that the Tengeru community would gather during the news hour so as to be in touch with the rest of the world. We listened to the news together (no one that I knew owned a personal radio) and together we despaired, as for instance when we heard that the Warsaw Uprising had failed. The true current of life, however, ran in the church, school, and Scouts. This triad supervised our spiritual, intellectual, and recreational life diligently and effectively. The holidays of the church and its ceremonies marked the progression of the year. The impact of this on the life of the settlement was due in part to the efforts of Fr. Jan Śliwowski, our pastor of many years, a person of great energy and an efficient organizer.

The community center was the most developed sphere of life in Tengeru. There were classes for older people who were illiterate (I know this because my mother conducted these classes for a certain period of time) as well as a secondary school and a lyceum named in honor of Stefan Batory. In addition there were three elementary schools, a school of mechanics, secondary schools of commerce, tailoring, and agriculture, and dozens of other courses. The educational program was therefore very diversified and important. To be sure, given such a great need and in spite of the rigorous selection process, not everyone possessed the professional qualifications for teaching. In the course of my educational career in Tengeru there were three or four sequential directors of the lyceum. All the community centers and all the school, religious, and scouting organizations manifested a Polish character.

Many intelligent and noble people who were dedicated and concerned took care of us youth and imbued us with those values that they considered most important in their own lives. Everyone of us could produce a long list of their names. It is difficult to name them all. With great emotion I would like to mention Ms. S. Jagielska, the wife of the school inspector in Tengeru. She was an exemplary woman, mother, and human being. I never again met anyone like her.

I would also like to name a few of my professors. K. Skórska was our Polish language teacher. Wanda Dorosz, the director of the lyceum was the most formidable. She taught history, unquestioningly the number one subject that everyone studied. The young biology professor, Zdzisia Wójcik, continually embarrassed and so easily abashed because of her age and so highly regarded as a leader in the scouting hierarchy, was wholly dedicated to her mission which was at the same time her passion.

Many other significant people could be named but the dynamism of those times cannot be easily conveyed. What words can describe what had been Tengeru? To me, it was my young mother, my small round house, my class, the "monkey grove" between the "office" and movie theater, and the place of tender confessions and loving enchantments. It was the rustling of the leaves in the eucalypti-lined lane, the vibration of the heated air, the endless "safari" escapades with the Besarabian Misha and the fear that eventually they would throw him out of the school. It was the monotonous spatter of the rain falling for weeks on end during the rainy season on the parched earth. My Tengeru was also the tall trees, whose names I do not know, that wept so profusely during the flowering season. And the tropical night under the vast canopy of the sky bathed in millions of stars. And the uncommonly strong feeling of a secret union of everything with everything, the oneness of life and eternal harmony with the cosmos which revealed itself to me so plainly only there. It was also the life led in common: sociable, joyous, active. And the passing of the locusts. And the quaking of the earth during which a wall split in our house and everything suddenly became unstable and wobbly, and I was overcome with an indescribable fear that at any moment the earth's shell would crack under my feet and I would be forever separated from my loved ones. It was also the ambiance of the Scout camps and campfires, when hand in hand under the Southern Cross we sang:

In silent sleep peacefully lie,
God is nigh, God is nigh.

And beyond every shadow of a doubt we knew that He was. But what words can describe the indescribable? I know not.[14]

Kondoa

Account of Irena Bartkowiak-Drobek

This settlement, located in central Tanganyika, lay about two kilometers from the town by the same name. It's September 1942. After a several-day quarantine in port Dar es Salaam, where we were outfitted with clothes and cork sun helmets (which we are supposed to wear from morning till night), we are loaded onto lorries and proceed once more into the unknown. After about six hours of travel, which included a short stopover in the town of Dodoma, we reach the Kondoa settlement. We are greeted by 24 mud barracks whose roofs are covered with banana leaves; instead of windows, only shutters, no ceiling, dirt floor.

Before we are assigned to specific barracks, I go to investigate whether they are all the same. Suddenly I hear a voice. I turn and see a ghost. Something white is moving directly towards me and calling. I tear out of there as fast as I can on my ten-year-old legs, but the ghost is quicker and I am caught. It's a nun, Sister Giliana, who wants me to put on my sun helmet.

Twenty people move into every barracks. Finally everyone has a bed of their own as well as sheets, a blanket, and a mosquito net. So we are sitting in our own barracks No. 14 and wondering what's next. Suddenly we see about a three-meter-long snake slither down the middle of the room. In a twinkle of an eye all of us wind up on our beds, screaming at the top of our lungs. It's difficult to foretell how this visit would have ended had it not been for Ms. Łebowska from the neighboring barracks. Where she got the axe from I don't know, but with it she cut the viper in half. After that episode even my face-to-face encounters with cobras were not all that frightening.

Four hundred Poles, mostly women with small children, were brought to the settlement. The barracks into which we were placed were once used to house Italian prisoners of war during the First World War. In time they were remodeled so that each family could have its own room. The view here is sad and wild. There's a lack of greenery, except for the elephant grass in which, oblivious of danger, we play hide-and-seek, and the narrow mango-lined lane that separates the settlement from the strange Bubu River — strange because its 25-meter-wide riverbed is dry and reminds one of a beautiful plaza, but becomes very dangerous during the rainy season, its mighty current sweeping away even very large trucks. Several baobab trees are still visible on the horizon. The earth is so parched that nothing wants to grow. On the other side of the road stands a small church and an Italian mission run by the Passionist Fathers. About two kilometers away there's a town by the same name as the settlement. The stores, operated by Arabs and Hindus, are dirty.

The commandant of the settlement was an Englishman; Poles carried out the rest of the functions. Janina Kramin organized the grade school. We went to Tengeru for secondary-school education. Dr. J. Zamenhoff watched over our health. He set up a nursing curriculum for the older girls who, after taking exams, worked in the hospital. They could not complain about a lack of work because we were hounded not only by the tropical diseases but also by those brought over from other lands. The most frightening of all was black malaria for which there was no cure. We did not have a Polish priest. We were taken care of by one of the Italian missionaries, Fr. Benedetto Barbaranelli, who learned the Polish language and became our pastor. Our life began to return to normal: Scout and junior Scout troops emerged, embroidery shops were founded, and there was a theater troupe. The settlement was quiet. We did not need any locks because there was no thievery or hooliganism. We constituted a single family unit and we supported each other. The residents got along very well and we still maintain contact with one another. At the end of 1948 the settlement was liquidated. The local populace remembered the Poles living in the settlement with the following words: "Those who lived here were good people. They gave food to our children and were on friendly terms with the whole village."[15]

Kidugala

Account of Jadwiga Piotrowska-Truchanowicz and Włodzimierz Pełczyński

Kidugala, a Polish refugee settlement established in 1942, was located in the southern part of Tanganyika near the town of Njombe. It was regarded as one of the most isolated Polish settlements in Africa. Because it was situated on two hills separated by a river, the residents referred to these two parts of the settlement as the "first side" and the "second side," respectively. In spite of the proximity of the equator, the climate here was not typically tropical — there was only one rainy season. About 1,000 people lived in Kidugala (this number fluctuated from year to year) — mainly women with children — the families of the soldiers of the 2nd Corps. The English commandant was Mr. Fisher; the Polish director was Kazimierz Chodzikiewicz, appointed commandant of the settlement in 1943 — probably the only Pole to hold such an office in the Polish camps of British South Africa.

An elementary school, a middle school, and a music school were founded. The Scouts also operated here and undertakings were launched in the theatrical and musical arenas. Various workshops also existed specializing in tailoring, embroidery, metalwork, carpentry, and the like. The settlement in Kidugala was liquidated in 1948. Some of the refugees returned to Poland, others joined their fathers and brothers who were discharged from the armed forces and left with them for various destinations throughout the world.[16]

Ifunda

Account of Filomena Michałowska-Bykowska

The settlement of Ifunda was one of the smaller African camps set up for the Polish exiles by the British authorities. In all, 800 people lived there, mainly women and children. An area was cleared practically in the middle of the African bush and clay houses were built there and covered with reeds. The settlement, divided into so-called blocks, was situated on both sides of a dirt road. Every block was equipped with a canteen, kitchen, laundry, washroom, and bathroom. There were two large houses, which served as quarters for several families, and 18 two-room houses each accommodating two families. There were all together six blocks in Ifunda, designated by the first six letters of the alphabet. We ate our meals in the canteen. There was also a hospital and a church built by the Poles. Outside the settlement on a hill were the buildings of the administrators, including an office building, a warehouse, and the house of the commandant. The commandant of the settlement was an Englishman; the director was a Pole. The house in which I lived was located on the perimeter of block B, and across the way grew an old African tree whose sprawling canopy constituted a natural umbrella that protected us from the sun. How often I would sit under our tree in Ifunda and weave girlish dreams full of longing for the weeping willows, birches, oaks, fields and meadows of our homeland!

Our time in Ifunda stretched on. We received food, the necessary furnishings for the house, and even clothes, but we did not have anything concrete to do. The Poles could not live this way while awaiting their return to their fatherland. After a short time a kindergarten, an elementary school, and a technical school were established, embroidery classes were organized, and work was found in the kitchen, canteen, hospital, and the YMCA community center. The center was the focus of our cultural, educational, and charitable activities and it was there that the youth found its place in our community by engaging in collective social undertakings. The chief figures in the settlement were: the director Aleksander Czerny, Fr. Jan Sajewicz, the settlement doctor Irena Brzozowska, and the director of the settlement headquarters, Krystyna Godowska, who also functioned as a translator of the English language.

Life in the African bush was not easy. After our difficult stay in Siberia followed by our long and arduous journey by land and sea, and being unaccustomed to the tropical climate here, we were both physically and psychologically worn out. The blacks were recruited to do the heavy work in the settlement, such as chopping wood for the kitchen, carrying water, and maintaining the grounds in the vicinity of the houses. Initially they looked at us as if we occupied an inferior status position, but after a little while we got to know each other and our daily contacts became rather cordial. Actually the obligatory regimen of the settlement clearly forbade a display of friendship toward the natives, but having gone through the Siberian Gehenna we did not always understand the reason for this prohibition and explained our behavior by our felt need to treat everyone equally no mater what the color of their skin. Moved by pity for the poor black mothers, we gave them our clothing, blankets and some home furnishings as well. We even began to purchase chickens, eggs and fruits from them — an activity that was forbidden. Unfortunately, as they got to know us better they began to covet our own possessions. They simply attacked individual homes during the night and stole everything in sight. I remember such a restless night when three black men with javelins broke into our home. Four of us lived on our side of the house and four in the room on the other side of the wall: Mrs. Sawicka with her daughter Marysia, and Mrs. Majewska with her cousin Adela. We were all sleeping in our own beds under mosquito nets held up by tall sticks and tucked under our mattresses in such a way that no bug would be able to reach us. A black man opened the wooden latch on the door with his sharp spear, entered the house followed by two others, and they grabbed whatever they found: clothes, shoes and toilet articles. Mrs. Anna, who lived with us, awoke first and began to scream: "Help! Help! Thieves! They will kill us!" To be sure, the blacks, spooked by the screams, ran off, but they still managed to take my new shoes and dress which I planned to wear on our nature hike the following day. I don't know why but we continued to yell and cry for some time. Our terrible shouts for help evidently had such an effect on our neighbors that they also began to scream. No one, however, dared to go outside in the night. Little wonder — these were women and children. Panic seized some of the residents of our block B. From that time on the practice of maintaining a night watch was introduced in order to prevent the natives from illegally entering the settlement at night. I did go on the outing the next day, but I was so hoarse from all that screaming that I could not participate in the singing. More serious episodes included encountering a poisonous snake or a wild beast of the African bush. A person might fall asleep under the mosquito net, but not before he or she is gripped by fear of the possibility of a scorpion slithering in between the sheets.

I can recall several tragic events that happened in Ifunda. Not far from the settlement two friends of the English commandant came across a herd of elephants while out walking. One of the men was trampled to death, the other survived evidently because he lay down and pretended to be dead. This event was discussed for a long time in the settlement and it served as a warning against the unauthorized leaving of the settlement. At another time a farmer, who brought fruits and vegetables to the settlement, met a tragic end. Driving along the serpentine road from Iringa to Ifunda he fell off a cliff and was killed instantly. The same thing happened to the son of our dentist, Mr. Wajs. Every one of these tragic events affected the residents of Ifunda profoundly. We lived there as one large Polish family.[17]

Morogoro

Account of Zdzisława Wójcik

The settlement of Morogoro was the smallest of all the Polish refugee settlements in Tanganyika; scarcely 400 people lived there. It was located near a town by the same name, at the same latitude as Dar es Salaam, the capital of Tanganyika. It lay 200 kilometers from the ocean at the foothills of the South Nguru Mountains, not that tall by African standards, but towering some 1,500 meters above the settlement. The scenery surrounding the settlement was beautiful: clear, fast-flowing streams from the mountains and luxuriant tropical vegetation. Only the climate was unbearable and unhealthy: warm and always humid. The settlement was established rather late, in mid-1944, and consisted of ready-made buildings once used to house Italian prisoners of war. After a year or two it was liquidated and the residents were moved to other settlements.

The orphanage, operated by nuns in white habits, accounted for almost half of the residents — hence the high percentage of children and teenagers in Morogoro. Because of this, the second most important institution in the settlement was the school. Due to the small number of residents, however, this was only a grammar school. Several of the somewhat older children awaited transfer to a larger settlement that had a middle school. It was in this small, out-of-the-way settlement that I encountered, for the first time in my life, someone suffering from a loss of social status: a sickly, weak, but also a bright boy. He complained: "I'm 15 years of age and still in grammar school. My father was an engineer and what will I be? I can't even be a manual laborer on account of my poor health. And why does it have to be this way? After all, we're not in Russia anymore." There were other such individuals in Africa but in other settlements; for example, in Ifunda or Kondoa. There the youth confronted these problems in smaller or larger group settings and it was easier for them to gain entrance to middle schools outside their settlements. But this boy was by himself. Fortunately, the oversolicitous concern of the nuns in charge of the orphanage was overcome rather quickly and he was transferred to a school in Tengeru from which he managed to graduate before the Polish settlements were liquidated. Later, in Poland, he received a degree in higher education. With a great deal of emotion and joy we met again at the World Reunion of African Refugees, which took place in Wrocław in 1993.

The orphanage of Morogoro was transferred to Rongai in the northern part of Kenya. The older children and the adult residents, together with their families, were moved to other settlements such as Tengeru. Later, I recognized some of the children while teaching at the Stefan Batory secondary school in Tengeru. It was in Morogoro that I heard, on the radio placed in the window of the settlement community center, about the failure of the Warsaw Uprising. There was a brief mention of this event on the evening news followed immediately by the song "With smoke of fires," which the residents took up and wept as they sang. It was not easy to find words of encouragement and hope that evening around the campfire.

I visited the settlement of Morogoro in 1944, that is, at a time when the Scout instructors sent by the army were already working in Africa. Together we planned to offer a course for prospective Scout leaders from three settlements: Ifunda, Kidugala, and Morogoro. This program would be similar to the one we offered in Tengeru for the Scouts of that settlement and nearby Kondoa. My task was to become acquainted with the scouting organization of Morogoro and the youth leading it, to choose the candidates for the training course, to arrange for the necessary transportation, and to deliver the chosen Scouts on time to where the course was being offered. Someone else, probably Staszka Adamska, the troop leader in Kidugala, was to deliver the candidates from that settlement. To our joy, the transports bringing the youth from two different and distant parts of Tanganyika arrived almost simultaneously. The course, which had the character of an inter-settlement jamboree, went extremely well. We had a large number of instructors: those who were sent by the army, a number of troop leaders who were working in Africa, and also Fr. Jan Sajewicz, the pastor of Ifunda who, in his capacity of a sub-scoutmaster, assumed a leadership role in organizing various games and events not only indoors but also on the playgrounds and in the field. No other course had such an instructor. And all of this transpired at a time when the whole world was engaged in the most fearsome of wars.[18]

North Rhodesia

Lusaka

Accounts of Andrzej Szujecki

(1) The settlement was located about 1.5 kilometers from the British district of a small town which was the state capital, namely, Lusaka. Small houses, measuring 4 × 5 meters, were constructed for the Poles. They were covered with elephant grass, were without ceilings, and had three screened windows with shutters. Only certain important buildings were larger. With the exception of the kitchen and hospital, these were erected during the existence of the settlement. There was no electricity in the majority of the households; oil lamps and candles provided the light. Lanterns were placed along the main streets as well. Trees, of the same variety as in the surrounding African bush, also grew in the settlement.

The Polish directors of the settlement were: Kazimierz Skwierczyński (in 1943), Mikołaj Wagner (in 1944), followed by R. Wilczek. In all, about 1,300 refugees came from the Soviet Union to Lusaka in five transports, mainly through the Beira port in Mozambique: 5 persons on January 1, 1943; 513 persons on February 16, 1943; 430 persons on March 29, 1943; 48 persons on April 27, 1944; and 205 persons on June 20, 1945. At the end of 1944 there were 106 men, 495 women, 317 children and 50 teenagers — all together 968 persons — in Lusaka. In addition, at various times and especially after the end of the war, members of the so-called Cyprian group quartered in Livingstone also came there.

The first grammar school, consisting of six grades, opened its doors in May 1943 under the directorship of Stanisława Firleyowa. During this period of time a church and a community center were built and various craft shops were instituted. In November 1944 construction began on 38 buildings which were meant to serve as a secondary school, a lyceum, and a boarding school. It was here that the youth of North and South Rhodesia were to receive their training. Schooling began on February 7, 1945. Dr. Witold Eichler, a recognized entomologist from Pabianice, deserves special credit for his role in teaching natural history. He was also the founder of a small museum of natural history in the settlement. Scout work was begun in Lusaka on March 23, 1943, by Lidia Krasińska.... The Polish settlement of Lusaka was liquidated in 1948.

(2) From the station we were taken by trucks along a beautiful road to the Polish settlement. The road, running through the residential quarters of the English colonists who were mostly employed as civil servants in North Rhodesia, was flanked by trees with "fiery flowers" and mango trees. A red-and-white flag waved over the settlement and the Polish YMCA provided us with doughnuts for the sake — as someone quipped — of making a good first impression. Families were placed in their own houses but, because there were so few of them available, my mother and I had to share one with my friend Adam Mickiewicz and his mother.

The house was the size of a British army tent measuring about 4 × 5 meters, constructed from unfired brick, whitewashed, without a ceiling, with a thatched roof, an asphalt floor, and three screened windows without panes but with shutters. The furnishings consisted of four beds with mattresses, two bureaus and two tables. It all seemed very dismal, but later, when our baggage arrived and we received an additional two bureaus along with sheets, towels, and mosquito nets, and when we got used to our new surroundings, everything was O.K.!

For dinner and other refreshments we went to the canteen or brought the food from there to our houses. The settlement was located in the midst of trees. It had a grammar school, a secondary school and a level I lyceum class. It also had a dormitory for the students, a community center, a fairly good library, and a soccer field on which representatives from our settlement competed against local British and Italian teams (there was still a camp in Lusaka for Italian POWs).

The years 16–18 are very difficult ones in a person's life cycle. One is neither a child nor an adult. Teachers have problems with us, and we in turn do not regard them — with some exceptions — as our ideal heroes. Perhaps this is because so many of them became teachers by accident, or because of their squabbles, or because after all their wartime ordeals and deportation they felt wronged and deprived of a future. For example, our director Mr. J. simply did not understand our need to participate in soccer, bicycling, film watching, and social gatherings with our friends and even girlfriends. Quite the contrary: the students did not have the right to play ball games; watching films in the town of Lusaka was forbidden; and bicycling irritated the director so much that on more than one occasion, during his visits to our class, he reproached those that he saw riding bicycles. For example: "Męcner, your bicycle will fly out from under you to the sky. Sit down, sit down you poor devil." Or: "You, Szujecki, I'll teach you to wear that crop of hair! Don't pretend to be Adonis. I'll confiscate your bicycle."

Dr. Witold Eichler, the entomologist, was completely different. He won my admiration soon after my arrival in Lusaka, when I discovered his display of insects, identification manuals, and the equipment for collecting beetles and butterflies. I was determined to memorize every word in his biology lectures. I even decided to become an entomologist myself and began to gather insects — and there were a lot of them. At the end of the dry season I caught plump plant-eating insects which alighted on the leafless trees whose trunks were covered with flowers. After a rain, when the plants unfurled their leaves in the African bush, I gathered metallic-colored beetles. At the beginning of the rainy season, however, a veritable legion of insects could be found under the settlement lanterns and hundreds of multi-colored dung beetles crawled on the wet ground while the moist air teemed with variously shaded beetles and membrane-winged insects. Of course my collection could not match that of Dr. Eichler, a part of which could be admired in the tiny but accessible museum. Dr. Eichler was unstinting when it came to the probably meager savings that he managed to accumulate by helping the so-called Cyprian group. For example, one day he bought an enormous python for 15 pounds and displayed it in his museum. The snake was viewed by many of the residents of the settlement since the news of the five-meter monster evidently excited the imagination even of those who were not interested in African plant and animal life. Dr. Eichler, it seemed to me, was stand-offish and unapproachable, but the class respected him and did not disturb him during his lectures as was often the case with other teachers.

Besides my passion for entomology, volleyball, nature hikes, and reading everything in sight, my "hobby" included the dances, organized both overtly and covertly, both in the school hall and in the boarding-school houses in celebration of our girlfriends' birthdays. On such occasions the concrete floor was smeared with soap and dancing was superb. After a while the dances were moved to the Polish YMCA community center where there was a good floor and a better record player. We danced the tango, foxtrot, waltz, *kujawiak* [a folk dance], and polka. On such occasions we dressed well; birthday celebrations naturally required coats and ties. Although there was more freedom at the YMCA, it was also more difficult to carry on conversations there. In mixed company the boys stayed by one wall, the girls by the other. No one ever knew when Director J. would show up and take the opportunity to give us a lecture on what he saw. The walks back to our homes were the best part of the evening, when the warmth of the bodies of our partners radiating through their thin silk dresses was hotter than the warm air of the sultry African nights. We said our good-byes far from the houses where our sympathies lay and only on the following day at school did we exchange those meaningful glances with each other which spurred us on to the next get-together.

The first meeting of the older Beniowski Scout group organized by Dr. Wacław Korabiewicz, whom we called "Kilometer," took place on August 25, 1946. He was not only a great storyteller but also was able to conduct discussions on topics of interest to young males plainly and without prudery. One of the very first discussions touched upon the matter of boy-girl relations. Those that followed addressed such topics as ambition, materialism, and good and evil. Echoes of those discussions, conducted according to the principle of free thinking, had to reach our school superiors and especially the priests. Hardly a Sunday Mass went by without words from the pulpit aimed at the person who was raising us according to the principles of rational freedom of choice, that is, in opposition to canonical principles. Worshiping "Kilometer" as we did, we took those church invectives badly because behind them lurked anger, hatred, and envy directed at the authority of the person who was not affiliated with the church. "Kilometer" had only one aim: to teach us to want and to know how to think for ourselves. Unfortunately, "Kilometer" was with us for just over a month. My discussions with Mr. Korabiewicz, and later with Mr. Wawerkiewicz, did not weaken my faith, and I bravely continued to attend the Marian Sodality meetings as well as to participate in the school choir whose repertoire consisted mainly of religious hymns.

One morning, and here in Lusaka the grey dawn irrespective of the season comes at 5:30 A.M., I got on my bicycle and, together with my friends, set out for Fort Jameson. Eighteen miles down the road, in Kasisi, was a Polish Catholic mission established 40 years ago. It was May and so the climate was dry and quite cool. The brisk air was crystal clear. Our pants were wet up to our belts from the dew drops that glistened on the tall grasses. The sun announced its imminent appearance with a profusion of crimson rays and then suddenly sprang over the horizon like a giant ball. It sprang because here, unlike in Poland, there are no leisurely sunrises or sunsets. Four miles later we pass our settlement's farm, then an African village spread out among the trees of a dense forest. We turn onto a narrow road leading through the bush. We again encounter wet grass even taller than before and become completely drenched because of it and our sweat. We arrive at a stream without a bridge on the other side of which grow strange palm trees with bottle-like bulges halfway up their absolutely smooth trunks. My observations of beautiful mother nature end up in a spill, and I am immersed completely in the wet elephant grass — but here we are in Kasisi. A Mass is being celebrated in the chapel. We enter. The chapel is small but nice. Over the altar looms a figure of a monk performing the rites of baptism on two Negroes. Statues of the Blessed Mother and Our Lord Jesus stand on both sides. The altar itself is made of dark wood and sheet copper, materials which are readily obtainable in Rhodesia. But more than by the appearance of the chapel we are astounded by the fact that the church songs are being sung in the original tempo in Polish by the black congregation. This was the work of our missionaries. It was truly beautiful and worthy of admiration. As Brother Żak told us, more than one of the first missionaries was torn apart by a lion or a leopard; others succumbed to fever. It's safe here now, but in the deeper corners of Africa where similar missions exist the conditions of life are very primitive.

The year 1947 began with a rumor that the Polish settlements of Africa were going to be liquidated. The commandant of the Scout flag, Z. Słowikowski, appointed me as leader of the gymnastic troop. I was scarcely able to demonstrate my abilities in this responsible position when my mother decided to return to Poland. A representative of the administration in Warsaw, Mr. Jakobson, arrived and opened his doors to those interested in finding out more about their fatherland and the possibility of returning there and finding employment. Our Latinist, M. Gonet, agreed to serve as a so-called repatriation officer and thereby earned a universal condemnation.

After several delays we left Lusaka on May 22, 1947. Ten Poles who decided to return to Poland rode on that train, and three hours later 67 persons boarded the next one. We halted in Gatooma for three weeks and later reached Mombasa through Beira. Along the way, thanks to W. Korabiewicz, Adam Mickiewicz and I were able to disembark in Dar es Salaam and visit that town and in particular the natural history museum where "Kilometer" happened to be working at the time. Later he bid us farewell from the landing dock by crossing his uplifted arms in the form of an X symbolizing the unknown. There were other short stops: on the road fragrant with carnations in Zanzibar and in the port of Tanga, where sisal hemp and coffee were being loaded onto ships. In Mombasa, I was filled with fresh African impressions before leaving the Dark Continent on July 29, 1947, on the Dutch ship "Tabinta."[19]

Bwana M'Kubwa

Account of Jadwiga Sokołowska-Galas

There were a lot of refugee camps scattered all over East Africa, established by the United Nations Organisation. Once again we were loaded onto a cargo ship and after three to four weeks arrived in the Mozambique port of Beira. From there we travelled by train to Northern Rhodesia (now Zambia) to a camp in the middle of a jungle called Bwana M'Kubwa in the Swahili language (Big Boss).

What a sight it was! The darkest continent on earth. We had seen Arabs, Chinese, Mongolians and here we saw for the first time beautiful but poor black children running and waving to us and screaming as we passed through some of their villages. We felt a lot of compassion for these people because in many ways we related to their way of life. From the railway station we were loaded onto trucks and taken to our camp. This remained our "home" for the next seven years.

The first thing I noticed as we drove through the gates was a row of beautiful jacaranda trees in full bloom. The lovely lilac, bell-shaped flowers dropped on our heads and shoulders as we stood on the back of the truck. There were a lot of native plants and trees such as bananas, guavas and mangoes. Once we were all allocated our little mud huts we discovered that we were not the first ones there. The camp was divided into two: Camp I and Camp II. At first we were cordoned off from Camp I by a wire fence because we had to be kept in quarantine and were not allowed to have any contact with them for six weeks. As education was our main priority, temporary classrooms were set up in some of the vacant huts until, at the end of the six weeks, we were allowed to join the people from Camp I. My mother, as usual, went looking for Stenia, but to no avail.

The camp commander lived with his family in a lovely house surrounded by beautiful, tropical gardens. Only high-ranking British officers were appointed to these positions. I remember we used to sneak around the back of their garden and steal mangoes because they were better tasting than the ones growing within the camp. Perhaps this was because they were better cared for by the many servants.

The camp life became progressively better. Apart from school there were Scouts, Girl Guides, clubs, lots of hikes and excursions and social dances, among many other things. At least it was nice and warm and we didn't have to worry about warm clothes. My mother had a job in the camp kitchen and my second oldest sister Wanda worked in the dining room before she enlisted to work for the Royal Air Force in Southern Rhodesia, in a city called Bulawayo. There was no high school in Bwana M'Kubwa and once we had completed primary school we had to go to a boarding school in Lusaka, the capital of Northern Rhodesia, only coming home for school holidays.[20]

Account of Maria Gabiniewicz

Bwana M'Kubwa, meaning "Big Man" in the local dialect, is situated in North Rhodesia (now Zambia), south of the equator, near the town of Ndola, which plays a vital role in the communication and trade routes. It was the discovery of copper deposits at the beginning of the twentieth century that was responsible for the emergence of both Bwana M'Kubwa and Ndola. The settlement at Bwana M'Kubwa actually rests on the foundations of an earlier settlement by that same name. The destiny of this rather large town was tied closely to the destiny of the copper mine. When the ore deposits were exhausted the entire workforce wandered off, and the abandoned houses were destroyed by termites and overgrown by subtropical foliage.

The concrete floors of the elegant villas that once existed here became the foundations for single- and two-family homes with "elephant grass" roofs. The beds inside consisted of frames, each resting on four evenly cut logs, and netting made from straps of African animal hide. The mattresses were stuffed with seaweed. The beds were outfitted with sheets, blankets, and a mosquito net. Three dressers, a table and stools completed the entire stock of furnishings.

Bwana had the appearance of a beautiful garden. Mango and banana trees, heavy with their bounty, grew here. A lane, flanked by acacia trees and leading to the community center, became a place for taking walks and a meeting place. Palms opened their wide umbrellas over the school playground. There were many shrubs here with spreading crimson leaves known in Europe as potted "stars of Bethlehem." They were Bwana's main adornment. Two policemen guarded the gate: a Pole and a Negro. One night the Negro defended himself against approaching lions by hurling flaming torches and live embers from the campfire at them with his bare hands. He thereby saved his own life and that of the Polish policeman but lost both of his arms up to the elbow.

In the center of the settlement, in front of the headquarters or the "office," a red-and-white flag waved on a flagpole. It was lowered to half-mast and covered with a pall only once: on July 4, 1943, as a sign of mourning after the tragic death of General Władysław Sikorski.

Between April 25, 1943, and June 26, 1945, 1,461 persons arrived at the settlement of Bwana M'Kubwa traveling in four transports from Tehran through Ahvaz in Iran, Karachi in India, but mainly through the Beira port in Mozambique. Capt. S. Grills, the British commandant of the settlement known also as "Chop" (a shortened form of lamb or pork chop), who was married to Irena Paszkiewicz, a Pole, was especially well-disposed toward the Poles. The Polish directors were, in order of their appointment: A. Olszewski, R. Wilczek, and R. Zaborowski. An elementary school and two vocational schools — for mechanics and sewing — were set up in the settlement. In all, 350 children and 65 teenagers attended these schools. The kindergarten, directed by Ms. Maria Turczańska, accommodated 22 children from ages 3 to 5.

In 1943 two teachers, Helena Łyczakowa and Teresa Kuczyńska, organized the first Scout and junior Scout troops. Scout camps and outings provided many pleasant diversions, including a two-week camping trip in the Nkana area, a several-day outing to Livingstone and the Lake Victoria waterfall, evening outings by the light of the moon, and outings to a lake lying several miles from Bwana. The Scout jamboree in North Rhodesia, involving both Polish and British Scout troops, helped in the formation of unique ties of friendship. Campfires, attended by the entire community, including the administration, featured songs, recitations, skits and stories most often connected thematically with what occupied Poland and our colleagues in the armed forces were going through.

The prior weakening of our bodies due to hunger and our subsequent exposure to the African climate resulted in an increase of illnesses, mainly of the tropical kind. A need arose in the settlement for a hospital and medical staff. A British doctor from Ndola was put in charge of the delivery of medical care. Polish doctors — Dr. Czesława Alter, Dr. Waliczko, Dr. Bierzuński and for a short time, Dr. M. Ruciński and Dr. Perykładowska, a somatologist — gave generously of themselves. The hospital was always overcrowded and there was a dearth of qualified personnel in spite of the fact that training was provided in medical intervention and assistance. Malaria reaped a plentiful harvest. There were also incidents of sunstroke. The mosquito nets over the beds and the wearing of cork sun helmets did not always prevent illnesses. Failure to observe these regulations was punishable by a reduction in the already meager monthly allowance (10 shillings). Patients with the most serious illnesses were transferred to the hospital in Ndola. In the course of my five years in Africa, I succumbed to malaria 14 times.

The Roman Catholic parish in Ndola also embraced the settlement of Bwana

M'Kubwa. The ministry was under the supervision of the apostolic prefect, Monsignore Franciszek Mazzieri, a Franciscan of Italian descent. Fr. Artur Staroborski, a Polish Franciscan, was the pastor of the settlement. At first the settlement did not have a church. Upon arriving in Bwana we celebrated our first Mass outdoors on a temporary altar set up in the middle of the settlement under a massive fig tree. Toward the end of the Mass, a mamba measuring a meter and a half fell out of the tree and landed on the altar. Panic followed. The men immediately grabbed sticks to kill the poisonous tree-viper. Fortunately nothing happened to anyone. Later, the children conducted a funeral for the huge snake, burying it deep in the ground because of a Negro superstition that after sunset even a killed snake could come alive again.

In June 1943 Fr. Artur moved into a small house: his rectory. The services took place in a small chapel. The faithful took their places on bamboo benches arranged under the trees in such a way that everyone would be able to see the altar through the open doors of the chapel. Sometimes it was difficult to collect oneself for prayers, especially for the children, because the monkeys, for some strange reason, took a fancy to this place, jumping from tree to tree overhead and often sitting on the benches. There was close cooperation between the Polish and Negro parishes. I recall most vividly a meeting that took place on the feast of Corpus Christi. Several trucks come to Bwana bringing Negro children and teenagers. All are dressed in white. The Negroes bring to church all the riches of their culture, customs and temperament. The liturgy is sung. The swaying and dancing silhouettes of our black sisters and brothers in keeping with the rhythm of the song detract not one iota from the gravity of the procession and church service. In turn, we gladly go to the Negro parish in Ndola. We marvel at their resourcefulness and skill. Instead of building four altars — as is the custom in Poland — they build only two portable ones which they set up in turn along the processional route in four designated places. The British authorities forbid the Negroes to enter the settlements. The settlement gate is opened in welcome only on Christmas and Easter. The Negroes come with a handful of flowers from the bush, bow, offer their seasonal greetings, sometimes dance in front of the house, and depart happily with the gifts they receive. Their visits on other occasions, unfortunately, often end up with things that had been left outside the houses gone missing. On one occasion, even a pot with boiling broth was removed from a field kitchen.

The construction of the church began at the very end of 1943 and was completed in 1945. Unfired bricks were used for the walls and reeds, as was the custom here, for the roof.

The cultural life of the community, which embraced one and all, was geared to helping people return to a normal life after all their trials and tribulations. Thanks to the efforts of Fr. Artur Staroborski, the Catholic Action Center, built with the help of the American War Relief Services, opened its doors on April 15, 1945. The spacious, well-equipped hall with a stage, canteen, radio, and its own broadcasting station becomes an important hub of cultural life. An actors' circle is formed and talks are scheduled for the general public. At the same time a special educational unit, initially under the leadership of Ludwik Pietras, is formed to promote the cultural life of the community. Edmund Strzygowski takes over next and organizes a mixed choir. A drama society is founded. A radio station is launched. (In the 1940s the possession of a radio in Africa, never mind a radio station, was a great comfort.) A library with a circulation desk is founded in 1945 and houses over 3,000 books. Books are printed in London and in the Near East. The school also contributes to the cultural life of the community: English language classes are offered, there's a training course in the grammar school curriculum, and cutting and sewing courses are available. In its Sunday program, the People's University includes lectures about Poland. The school has its own library with over 2,000 books, a hall, an actors' circle, and a choir. Performances, presentations, and Nativity plays are organized. From time to time the British people in the area come to the community center in order to participate in Polish events and even to dance. There was also a Polish Red Cross in the settlement whose mission was to be an intermediary between the residents and the main branch of the Polish Red Cross in the search for missing relatives. The Polish Red Cross also handled the mail. Matters of safety and security rested in the hands of the British commandant. He was in charge of both the police force, consisting of the local Negroes, and of the guards, who were recruited from among the Poles. Negro guards, however, were stationed outside the settlement. The Polish guards were in charge of maintaining internal order, patrolling the escape routes, and checking passes. The first commandant of the guards was Józef Selwanowicz. He was followed by Franciszek Środziński and Sebastjan Łukasik.[21]

Abercorn

Account of Wanda Nowosiad-Ostrowska

The settlement of Abercorn was built near a town by the same name. The town had a hotel, bar, post office, one English shop, and several Negro ones. The first refugee transport, consisting of 355 persons, came to the settlement on August 13, 1943; the second, consisting of 229 persons, arrived on September 15, 1943. In all 561 persons lived in Abercorn: 82 men, 242 women, 216 children, and 21 teenagers. The directors of the settlement were Julian Jakutowicz (until February 10, 1944), Mr. Otrząsek, Antoni Zych, and Mr. Werakasos (from April 1945). The climate here was tolerable. The rainy season lasted from May to mid-November, and that's probably why the school year ended on December 15 and resumed again on February 1. Five days after her arrival, Ms. Burdzina began to organize the school. There were four buildings in the settlement which were divided into six, and later into seven, grammar-school grades. The older youth were sent to Lusaka for middle school. Ms. Bobotek was the next director of the school, and after her it was R. Machcewicz.

Our settlement was divided into six sections of single-room houses constructed of thick posts driven into the ground then lightly plastered and whitewashed. These small houses were covered with thatched roofs. The floor consisted of packed clay, and in the windows, instead of panes, there were screens which were covered by straw mats at night. A large all-purpose kitchen stood among four of the sections. The food was brought to the kitchen from a farm 250 miles away. Supper usually consisted of corn gruel; the butter was always liquified and had a strange smell. Pigs were raised within the settlement area, and the owner of the business made wonderful pork meats. There was also a washing area with cement bathtubs, a laundry, and stoves with built in brick storage areas, where water could be warmed or boiled.

The hospital consisted of an out-patient unit and three buildings which housed the patients. The hospital buildings had cement floors and ceilings. Dr. Eichler came there at the beginning of 1944 and founded an herbal-healing information unit. The doctors were: Dr. Bierzuński, then Dr. Józef Grutz, followed by Dr. Turski. In the building occupied by the elementary-school administrators one hall served as a community center where parties were held, films were shown, and theater performances were given. The same building housed the camp administrative offices and the post office. In the settlement there was a photography workshop directed by Franciszka Wiruń.

On December 8, 1944, a new church was dedicated. It measured 21.5 × 6.5 meters and was built by the residents of the settlement with their own hands. The camp also had a Catholic Association of Young Women, organized by Fr. Jan Waligóra, our first pastor. Fr. Waligóra, who was from Kraków, had been working as a missionary in Africa for 15 years. He knew several languages and dialects of the native population and was delighted to meet his compatriots this far away from home. He was greatly respected by the refugees. After four months he was replaced by Fr. Antony Wierzbiński, who came to us from the USA, and he was followed by Fr. Włodzimierz Olszewski, who remained with us until the liquidation of the camp.

The Polish people, being interested in world events, would congregate in the evenings near the only radio in the Catholic community center to hear the news from Poland and the world. Life in the settlement was enriched by the Scouts who organized campfires and outings and who participated in all holiday festivities, including the religious ones. They were the soul of the entire settlement, and each day before evening prayers the entire camp resounded with Scout songs. The women would meet in the evenings to crochet, knit and embroider; their handicrafts were extraordinarily beautiful. From Abercorn packages were sent on a regular basis to POW camps and help was organized for fighting Warsaw. Everything that was accomplished in this settlement, located in the deepest and most primitive corner of Africa and isolated from all cultural centers, was the fruit of our own initiative and the work of our own hands. Contacts with the local native population were friendly. Many Negro children visited the Scout campfires and tried to sing the Polish songs along with us.

One time we experienced a rather strong earthquake so much so that the people, fearing that the buildings would collapse on top of them, went outside. Fortunately, after several minutes the tremors ceased. And furthermore, we were visited by various plagues; for example, locusts and large black biting ants which, on their march through a given section, would blacken an entire house and yard. Left alone they would continue on peacefully, but disturbed, they would fight aggressively. Besides this, scorpions and, from time to time, baboons would appear in the settlement.

The war in Europe reached an end, and the time came for everyone to make a decision as to what they were going to do next: return to Poland; go to America, Australia, or England; or remain in Africa. There were many possibilities. People were most often encouraged to go to Poland. We chose Poland and returned to our homeland in June 1943. I was nine years old at the time.[22]

South Rhodesia

Rusape

Account of Marta Marczewska-Jankówska

Located in the bush not far from Rusape itself, the settlement consisted of some 70 brick houses with metal-clad roofs and small gardens. In the middle of the settlement was a singularly curious object: a chapel consisting of three Negro round houses in a row — Fr. Zygmunt Siemaszko's idea. The settlement must have had some very energetic individuals given its many surprising accomplishments despite its small population (726, including 258 children).

Rusape had an elementary school whose director, Ms. Szpakowska, I remember to this day as a person who was unusually strict and energetic. There was also a School of Household Management for Girls attended by those who completed the elementary school but did not go to the Polish secondary school in Digglefold. This school was organized and directed by my mother, Helena Marczewska. The girls studied home management and agriculture and trained in the settlement café as well as on the very prosperous farm with its cattle, pigs and chickens which provided meat not only for the three settlement canteens but also for area farmers as well. There was also a tailor shop serving the needs of the settlement and local inhabitants. It's important to add, given the circumstances, that the camp was organized superbly. It had three canteens, a café, shower facilities in separate buildings, and a hospital.[23]

Digglefold

Account of Bohdan Ławiński

Digglefold was located on the railway line about 15 kilometers northwest of Marandellas and about 70 kilometers southeast of Salisbury. It was named after Mr. & Mrs. Diggle, the British owners of a farm which they left in 1943 and which was subsequently converted into the Polish School Center. The British commandant of the center was Major F. J. Bagshawe, a friend of the Poles, and the quartermaster was M. E. Rutherford. The Polish director of the settlement was W. Kadow from Marandellas. He was often represented in Digglefold by T. Siuda, the director of the elementary school in the Marandellas settlement. The Polish School Center was directed by Gen. Dr. Ferdynand Zarzycki. He was the founder of the center, the director of the middle school, an educator, and the person thanks to whom Digglefold became a school of life.

Being responsible for the children's welfare and education, the center was under the Delegation of the Ministry of Religion and Public Education headquartered in Nairobi. The farm buildings had to be quickly converted to serve the needs of the school and boarding school. Old school desks were brought from the school in Marandellas and set up in rooms from which baskets of castor-oil plants had been removed. In the evening, by the light of oil lamps, textbooks were copied by hand. There was always a need for new buildings and provisions. This situation lasted until July 1945. In all that time everything that was possible to achieve in Digglefold was achieved. The school library contained 300 publications. The main building housed six classrooms, an office, chapel, kitchen, and the teachers' quarters. Among the coniferous trees and fruit orchards as well as in the open areas there were 17 other structures, including a community center, refectory, sleeping quarters, baths, laundry, hospital, and farm buildings. Places were set aside for sports and recreation. But there was a lack of electricity and a good system of communication. The rooms, which also served as sleeping quarters, were confining; there was a lack of storage space.

The Polish School Center in Digglefold operated from 1944 to 1946. The schoolgirls came primarily from Marandellas, Rusape, and Digglefold. Initially girls from the settlements in North Rhodesia — Bwana M'Kubwa, Fort Jameson, and Lusaka — also lived in the boarding school and studied there. There were also a few schoolgirls from the distant Oudtshoorn settlement in South Africa. In the final year, Digglefold became the home and school for the girls from the Polish refugee camps in India. In 1946 there were 152 girls in the secondary school and 37 in the lyceum. There were ten teachers, three schoolmasters, and 28 assistants. A doctor, two nurses, and an orderly worked in the center. In order to bridge the gaps in their education resulting from over four years of exile, preparatory and remedial classes were offered to students before the opening of the school and during its existence. Midway through the school year students were passed to the next grade. In 1945, 15 students were advanced in this way. At the end of 1943 a preparatory course for entrance into the third year of secondary school was made available to 20 students who were unable to document their completion of the second year. A public school for girls was established and opened its doors with great ceremony at the end of 1943. By 1945 it had achieved the status of a secondary school and lyceum. In December 1946, 18 students of Prof. Wacław Stefański received secondary-school certificates. In all, 23 girls completed the secondary school. For shorter or longer periods of time during their operation in Digglefold, the schools were staffed by 28 instructors, including four priests who were also known in the African settlements. Most often mentioned was Dr. Ferdynand Zarzycki, who taught Latin, contemporary issues, introductory philosophy, and bookbinding. The all-around well-liked teacher was the prefect of the center, Fr. Zbigniew Burgielski. Prof. Zofia Rzewuska taught Polish language and geography but was remembered as the choir director and the organizer of school festivities. Prof. Jadwiga Otwinowska was in charge of the declamations. Prof. Maria Mazurówna taught history and from the beginning was in charge of the school troop of the Polish Scouts' Association.

Scouting in Digglefold was organized by a student, Zofia Wierzbicka from Marandellas. Due to favorable circumstances — thanks to the personal interest of the commandant of the Scout Flag of South Rhodesia, Scoutmaster Stanisława Staszewska-Barska from Salisbury — from a team of 15 Girl Guides emerged one of the best Scout troops in Africa. In 1944 Scoutmaster J. Brzeziński and Sub-Scoutmaster Z. Słowikowski conducted a two-week session in Digglefold on scouting methodology and practice. In 1945 the Girl Guide troop of the Polish Scouts' Association in Digglefold consisted of three teams and numbered 117 Girl Guides. Sub-Scoutmaster Irena Sobocka, who directed them, was recognized as the best Girl Guide in South Rhodesia. The center served as the base for courses offered to the young cadre of Scouts and junior Scouts. Contacts were maintained with the British Scouts in Marandellas and Salisbury; the local press covered a campfire organized in Digglefold in which these Scouts participated. Aside from the Girl Guides, a Marian Sodality existed in Digglefold as well as a community center with a student store sponsored by the Polish YMCA. High artistic and publishing activities prevailed: there was a newspaper, people wrote poetry, embroidered. The schools enjoyed the same good standing as the prewar Polish schools. In addition to their classroom lessons the girls were taught everything that was traditionally taught in Polish homes.

The activities of the Catholic Polish School Center in Digglefold are very well documented. After the liquidation of the settlement, in drastically worse technical, organizational, and staffing circumstances, the schools continued to function for a time in the temporary camp in Gatooma.[24]

Marandellas

Account of Bohdan Ławiński

Marandellas — situated among Rusape (about 120 kilometers to the southwest), Digglefold (about 15 kilometers away), and Salisbury (about 90 kilometers to the northwest) — unfolded alongside a Rhodesian railway station and was an answer to the needs of the local farmers. A warehouse stood on the opposite side of the station and cattle ramps and enclosures bordered the tracks. The town and its important social institutions — school, post office, hospital, stores, court house, prison — had adapted to function in a racially segregated environment. The colored people engaged in commerce and in the service sector. There was no church or movie theater. A road to the north of the station led to the Polish refugee settlement about a kilometer away. On the right side of the road were the cattle baths; on the left, an airport with light airplanes and a racetrack for horses. Steers were raised on the local farms. Only as many milk cows as were needed were kept. Horses were maintained only for recreation and sport.

At the edge of the settlement, on the side facing the town, a small sign read: "Polish Settlement Camp of Marandellas." The settlement was not enclosed; at night it was guarded by black policemen from the town and guards from among the refugees. Only once did large animals trespass onto the territory of the settlement and cause damage. The offenders were the badly guarded cattle being pastured nearby during the day. On the north, west, and south the settlement was separated from the bush only by an antifire belt. The burning of the grasslands to the north endangered the settlement, but charcoal-heated irons, kerosene lamps, and kerosene stoves could also be a source of fire.

The terrain in the vicinity of the settlement, cleared, burnt and leveled, revealed a clayey soil. Trees and the remnants of ant hills were left on the perimeter of playing fields. The land sloped gently northwest toward a stream. A huge slab of granite hid the stream from the settlement and snakes of such great size as are found only in South Rhodesia rested on the slab. They also inhabited the settlement gardens. From the top of the slab one had a panoramic view of the entire settlement. This perspective was interrupted to the south by a building housing the British and Polish administrative offices of the settlement. Standing directly in front of the office building and facing the granite slab, now lying to the north, one beheld the center of the settlement: the Polish Home, canteens I and II with the kitchen and firewood between them, two buildings housing the baths and laundry, the parade ground with the flower beds containing Polish and South Rhodesian emblems, the church, and the grammar school.

The Polish Home was built by the residents of the settlement with their own funds and the assistance of the American Polonia. It contained a hall with a stage and also served as a community center with recessed shelving for books, a store, a tailor and shoemaker shop, a barber shop, and eight guest rooms. The Polish Home was used for meetings, concerts, theater performances, children's plays, and national, settlement, and family celebrations. There was a functioning library. The classic façade of the Polish Home, with its four columns, was clearly visible from the road leading from Marandellas to the settlement. On the right, that is, at the east entrance to the settlement, stood the section IV houses; to the north stood the houses of section III. Both sections contained 60 square six-room units.

The outhouses, frequently cleaned and disinfected, stood all along the east, west and north perimeters of the settlement. To the northwest stood two other large round buildings containing a sick bay, a small hospital with 12 beds, a delivery room, and the living quarters of the medical personnel. It was in the vicinity of these buildings that preparations were made for a park. Except for the eucalypti in the home gardens and the flora along the roads, the territory of the settlement was rather barren. There was a water pipe and reservoir at one end of the settlement. It also had a sewage disposal system. Water was obtained from faucets distributed throughout the camp. There were three laundry and bath facilities with showers. On the left, or west side, were the houses of sections I and II. The first consisted of 40 round two-person homes. All 136 residential units were made of brick and had thatched roofs. The floors were cement, the windows were small and placed high, the doors were made so that the upper half could be left open. This assured the residents of at least a minimum of comfort and security.

Marandellas lay 1,500 meters above sea level. It was airy and sunny. The evenings were cool and the mornings were cold. The day-night and seasonal differences in temperature necessitated proper attire. The refugees were required to cover their heads from 10:00 A.M. until 4:00 P.M. and to avoid being out in the sun during the "white" afternoon hours. One could sleep without mosquito nets from May to October. There was no indigenous malaria here and such as was brought from elsewhere was cured. Swimming or even wading, especially in standing water, was forbidden, as was going barefoot.

On the west, section I bordered a recreational area with two storage buildings, playing fields, athletic equipment, and swings. Across the way stood a large round building which housed the kindergarten. Near the settlement was a farm where pigs, chickens, and rabbits were raised. The farm was fenced in. A stream flowed through the vegetable gardens. In back of the settlement offices, which were flanked by warehouses, there was a mess hall. The location, organization and operation of the settlement was excellent.

The settlement in Marandellas, built at the end of 1942, was occupied for the first time, and filled almost to capacity by the first refugee transport, at the end of February 1943. The last transport with its 12 officers and their families arrived in November 1944. In December 1944 there were 622 persons in the Marandellas camp, including 266 women, 224 children, 78 teenagers, and 54, mostly older, men. Some of the residents, mostly the youth, studied in the middle schools of Digglefold (56–91 students) and Livingstone; others studied aviation in Bulawayo; still others served in the RAF's Army Auxiliary Service of the Women of Rhodesia and England. The residents were supported by funds from the Polish government's Ministry of Labor and Social Welfare, whose delegate was headquartered in Salisbury, and also by the funds of Catholic and other charitable organizations. The refugees reduced their expenses by working and the proper management of resources. Each person received ten shillings per month for pocket money.

In time, everyone felt the need to "do something," but only some were in a position to make this happen. All adults were obliged to work gratis for the good of the settlement. The women raised children and conducted the affairs of their homes but did not cook. They worked for pay in the kitchen, mess halls and canteens, in the gardens and on the farm, in the kindergarten, school, and health services. They enrolled in various courses: English language, typewriting, health services, home management, and hat weaving. They organized junior Scout and Scout teams and formed groups interested in folk songs and dances. They organized performances that also involved the children and the teenagers. They struggled with their loneliness and worried over the need to make a decision to return.

From the beginning the children had a kindergarten and the junior Scout group. The older children and the teenagers had school and the Scouts (there were 55 Girl Guides and 35 Boy Scouts). There was an artists' circle, a church choir, and training for acolytes. One could participate in sports, go on outings, learn carpentry. The men worked as camp administrators or in the kitchen or on the farm or in order maintenance. They served as Scout leaders. The natives considered us as friendly whites capable of physical labor. The British farmers came to the church, attended the performances, and bought meat products. The director of the settlement was the considerate, polite, and hard-working Władysław Kadow, a lawyer by profession. The British commandant, Major F. J. Bagshawe, not only grew accustomed to us but also befriended us.

The first group of refugees, along with those returning from North Rhodesia, left for Poland in September 1946. A transport of about 500 persons was formed and left the port of Beira on the ship "Mantola" for the temporary camp in Mombasa, Kenya. The settlement at Marandellas was liquidated toward the end of 1946 and the remaining residents were transferred to the temporary camp in Gatooma.[25]

South Africa

Oudtshoorn

Account of Bożena Masojadówna-Piłacka

The town of Oudtshoorn lies on the Cape of Good Hope halfway between Port Elizabeth on the Indian Ocean and Cape Town (Kaapstad) on the Atlantic Ocean. In the years of World War II this beautiful town of flowers and greenery had 10,000 to 15,000 inhabitants. Despite its modest size the town was known throughout the world, thanks to its ostriches and the ostrich feathers which, especially at the turn of the nineteenth century, were in fashion and in great demand. During the war there was an army camp near Oudtshoorn. The directors of that camp set aside about 40 brick buildings for 500 Polish children and teenagers (200 girls and 300 boys) from ages four to twenty (15 percent of them were orphans and 40 percent had only one parent). The negotiations with the premier of the South African Union (now the Republic of South Africa), Marshal J. C. W. Smuts, were undertaken in the name of the Polish government in London by Dr. Łepkowski, Consul General of Poland in Pretoria. The talks were successful.

It was decided that the funds necessary to cover the cost of upkeep would be provided by the Ministry of Labor and Social Welfare of the Polish Government in London through the Polish Consulate in Cape Town. The delegate of the Ministry of Religion and Public Education in Nairobi, Mr. S. Szczepański, was to be in charge of the school system. And that's how the Polish Children's Home in Oudtshoorn, named "Southern Cross" under the patronage of St. Andrew Bobola, came to be. It functioned from 1943 until 1947.

The first director of the camp was Mr. Tarnowicz, followed by Dr. Zygmunt Skowroński. The superintendent in behalf of South Africa was at first Mr. Van der Merwe and later, H. Farrell. The 500 children and their caretakers who were to come to Oudtshoorn were united by a common fate on the deck of the British ship "Duner." We sailed from Basra on the Persian Gulf on March 3, 1943, and arrived at Port Elizabeth on April 2. For the next seven days we rode at anchor under strict quarantine.

We arrived in Oudtshoorn on April 10. We were greeted very warmly. We began to live in comfortable barracks under the watchful eyes of our caretakers, who resided among us in the barracks in special rooms. Around the barracks we planted castor-oil plants. When they matured and bore fruit we immediately set out to taste them. We did not have to wait long for the consequences... At first we ate off delicate porcelain, but that was soon taken away no doubt because of our table manners which probably left much to be desired.

Three of the barracks were significantly larger than the rest. One served as the chapel. Both fear and respect were inspired in that chapel by the imposing figure of Canon Kubieński, assisted in his pastoral duties by Fr. Czarnecki and later by Fr. Łomiński. Their faithful allies were the members of our sodalities. Surrounded by saintly halos and wearing blue sashes they were understandably the objects of envy. The second barracks was the mess hall. The third was the kitchen staffed by our Negroes who very quickly mastered the Polish language and became our translators. Their linguistic capabilities were a source of amazement to us all. Other buildings contained washrooms, clothes dryers, and showers. There was also a hospital wherein Dr. Tadeusz Wilczkiewicz and Ms. Stanisława Sawko cured our old and new diseases, chiefly rheumatism, tuberculosis, malaria, and scabies. Dr. Józef Gondzik took care of and extracted our teeth. The most imposing building in the camp was the YMCA. Our occasional productions were held there. There was a kindergarten and five schools in the settlement: two primary schools and three secondary technical schools, namely, commercial, tailoring and shirt-making, and mechanical. About 60 teachers and caretakers stood watch over us. We exercised daily and played volleyball or "two fires" by the hours. On certain Saturdays we danced frantically in the community center.

The Scouts flourished under the leadership of Lt. Romuald Rzędzian, sent here specifically for that purpose. Scoutmaster Rzędzian was very handsome and all the Girl Guides irrespective of age (and not only the Girl Guides) fell madly in love with him. One day he made a blunder. During a visit of the royal family to the Union, the queen offered him her hand at a reception ceremony and he, Oh horror, kissed it. She became flustered and her blush was clearly visible right through the thick coat of face powder. In the course of that same ceremony, the Queen Mother, who is now grey-haired being over 90 years old, gave my mother her first lesson in the English language. In answer to the queen's question of whether she spoke English, my mother responded "very small," instead of "very little." She was corrected.

In the camp various interest groups were formed around such enterprises as sewing, artistic metal-work, photography, leather-work, and the making of musical instruments. At times timid complaints emanated from the town; for example, that the suspension bridge was being used by us for a swing, that the boys were playing with unexploded shells from the nearby firing range, or that they cut holes in the display cases and took what they needed, like mandolin strings or tools with which to engrave leather. Yet there was never a serious conflict along the town-camp border. The town was well disposed towards us, as could be seen from the many gifts, invitations, visits, etc.

We took part in various local and national events which, in turn, enabled us to spread the word about the heroic Polish people living among the populace of the Union of South Africa. That publicity campaign was initiated by my mother, Elżbieta Masojadowa, who was the commandant of the girl yunaks in Iran, and in Oudtshoorn was a Scout troop leader, the editor of the weekly "Southern Cross," and the director of the secondary technical school of tailoring and shirt-making. Thanks to her extraordinary dedication, the girls in Oudtshoorn made almost 7,000 sizeable embroidered works of art patterned after those of Kraków, Krupie, Kaszuby, Polesie, Wołyń, the Hucul region, and Buczacz. Under the guidance of J. Barański, M. de Malherbe and S. Radczak, the boys made beautiful leather goods, metal lamps, photo frames, school implements, and interesting photographs and montages (Stefan Adamski's domain) dedicated to Poland. They also made musical instruments.

These magnificent works made by the hands of the youth of Oudtshoorn elicited universal admiration in all 28 exhibits in 14 Union towns. They were featured in such prestigious wartime exhibits as "Liberty Cavalcade" in Cape Town, "Speed the Victory Fair" in Johannesburg, "Pinelands Allied Unity Fair" in Pretoria, "Warsaw Appeal" in Pietermaritzburg, as well as "We Have Existed for 1,000 Years," "War Fund," "Polish Relief Fund," and "Thanksgiving Cavalcade." All exhibits were accompanied by Polish songs and dances directed expertly by Stefania Marciniakowa, the education-cultural director. The costumes sewn by the girls for the large song-and-dance and theater troupes enchanted everyone. The reporters of that day raced to outdo each other in their use of superlatives when writing about the artistic accomplishments of the youth of Oudtshoorn. The proceeds from all these events were used to sponsor various worthy causes, for example: to erect a monument in Northolt in honor of Polish aviators; to assist fighting Warsaw, the civilians in the Pruszków concentration camp and other camps on German soil, injured soldiers and war invalids; to aid the Red Cross; to organize outings and Scout camps; and to conduct the publicity campaign. Five hundred thirty beautiful works were presented to the people to whom the youth of Oudtshoorn owed so much; among the recipients were Polish soldiers who fought on various fronts and were now convalescing in hospitals. Wonderful works also wound up in the museums of Oudtshoorn, Cape Town and Johannesburg.

Unfortunately we were sprouting like beans in Oudtshoorn and the time had come for our exodus. We were sent to various schools with advanced levels of study. In the beginning these were Polish schools in North and South Rhodesia. Later they were British schools in South Africa. Then, as a result of the shameful treaties of Yalta and Potsdam, the decision was made to eliminate the Polish Children's Home in Oudtshoorn altogether. It must be pointed out that the overall policy of the local authorities was aimed at retaining the youth of Poland in the Union on a permanent basis. These young people were regarded as unusually valuable assets; they were talented, enterprising, competent, upright and beautiful. The fact that we had white skin was certainly to our great advantage as well.

After the war some of the young people, in conjunction with the effort to reunite families, were scattered throughout the world. About 50 others, responding to familial and patriotic feelings, returned to Poland. The majority, however, remained in Africa. Their Poland lay beyond the Bug River and so they had nowhere to return to. The promotional campaign begun by the youth of Oudtshoorn (and continued to this day by the Polish community in the Republic of South Africa) left a deep impression on the consciousness of the local population, enriching it with knowledge about the people of Poland.[26]

7. New Zealand

Introduction by Anna Bednarska-Załuska

In 1944 New Zealand's Prime Minister Peter Fraser offered asylum to the Polish children, mainly orphans and those with one parent, whose parents had perished in the Soviet Union and Tehran or whose fathers fought at the front. The youngest of these children was about three years old. A team of teachers, caretakers, administrators, and medical and domestic personnel—105 persons in all—was organized in Isfahan. Fr. Michał Wilniewczyc, Sister Maria Aleksandrowicz, and Sister Anna Tobolska provided the children with pastoral care. On November 1, 1944, the ship General Randall anchored at Wellington with 733 children on board. The children were housed on the North Island near the town of Pahiatua (about 150 kilometers from the capital of New Zealand: Wellington). The place was called the Polish Children's Camp—Pahiatua. To the army buildings which were already there, only barracks for schools were added to accommodate the needs of the children. There was also a chapel, an auditorium, a recreation hall, and a small hospital. The main street was named in honor of General Tadeusz Bór-Komorowski. The settlement had a kindergarten, a boys' school, a girls' school, and a secondary school. Scout groups were also organized. The Polish Children's Home was maintained by the government of New Zealand and subsidized by the Polish government in London. The local authorities took an interest in the life of the Polish children in Pahiatua, as was evident from the numerous visits, and the people of New Zealand were generous and kind to them. After the war the adults and some children left the camp to become reunited with their families; only a few returned to Poland. The older children were placed either in Catholic schools associated with monasteries or in technical schools. Hostels were also organized for the youth: on Island Bay for the boys; on Lyall Bay near Wellington for the girls.

The last group of children left Pahiatua on April 15, 1949. Most of the children, however, remained in New Zealand. In the future, there would be marriages between the former inhabitants of the camp. Today they belong to a large Polish community and are active in Polish organizations. In November 1969, in commemoration of the 25th anniversary of their arrival in New Zealand, the former students of the Polish Children's Camp held a reunion. About 600 of them—mostly from New Zealand and Australia—participated. The 50th anniversary was also celebrated with great fanfare as they met again on the last Sunday of October in Pahiatua and at the beginning of November in Auckland. A small six-person group of "New Zealanders" also organized a meeting in Warsaw on November 3, 1994.[1]

Pahiatua

From the diary of Anna Bednarska

Tuesday, October 31, 1944. The next stage of our journey is coming to an end. Five weeks after leaving Isfahan in Persia we arrive in New Zealand. The view is beautiful. Wellington is the capital of New Zealand. The entire town stands on a hilly terrain. The houses have green and red roofs and there's greenery everywhere. New Zealand press reporters have appeared on deck and they are taking pictures of the prime minister and soldiers with our children. New Zealand soldiers are returning from the front and today they are disembarking while we, the Polish children and adults, are spending our last night on the ship U.S.S. Randall.

Wednesday, November 1, 1944. Today is All Saints Day. Fr. Wilniewczyc celebrated the Mass on the upper deck and right after that we arranged ourselves into groups. The children walked slowly off the ship. A train was waiting at the port and we boarded it. As we proceeded to our camp, children stood along the track and waved to us with handkerchiefs; in the stations where the train halted, we were greeted and given small presents. Sisters of the Red Cross treated us to sandwiches and ice cream. At the Palmerston North station, Girl Guides held a Polish flag aloft and sang. We exchanged addresses and everything was so nice and pleasant. We arrived in Pahiatua around 2:30 p.m. There, group leaders awaited us and after a few minutes we were already in the camp which was called the Polish Children's Camp — Pahiatua. Many buildings and barracks were there. A Girl Guide who spoke Polish, Monika Wodzicka, led us to one of them. It turned out that she was the daughter of the Polish consul. After an hour another transport of children arrived, and at 6:00 p.m. we went to the refectory for supper and then to sleep after so many emotions.

Sunday, November 5, 1944. We have been in the camp for four days now. Everything is very nice here — so much greenery. The barracks are clean, everyone has their own wooden bed with a soft mattress, two clean sheets, and six blankets. There are also bureaus with drawers and mirrors. We have central heating, wash basins and showers with hot and cold water, toilets, laundry rooms and clothes driers, and also tables and irons. The dining-room tables are covered with tablecloths, there are new plates and entire table settings, and … a sympathetic cook. After dinner we gathered in the auditorium to hear the delegate from London, Major Foxley — the commandant of the camp — and the captain of the Polish ship "Narvik" who, together with a part of the Polish crew, came to visit us in the camp. One of the sailors gave us a brief history of the ship and presented us — Polish children — with a flag, the most precious thing they had.

Tuesday, November 7, 1944. Today after lunch we bid farewell to the New Zealand soldiers who had been helping out in our dining rooms during the first week. In the afternoon we gathered together in the theater. First Delegate Śledziński spoke, then the wife of the consul, Mrs. Wodzicka, and Tenia Czochańska (a lyceum student) said good bye to them in behalf of the children. Next, the girls danced and the choir sang Polish songs. Then, at our request, the soldiers got up on the stage and sang English songs. They also did a Scottish and a Maori dance. The Maori were the earliest people to inhabit the New Zealand islands. It was fun, but now I have to think about my studies because school has begun.

Thursday, November 16, 1944. It's been two years since my father died in Tehran. He was very thin due to hunger. I am sad.

Saturday, November 25, 1944. I'm second in command of our Girl-Guide team. We had our first campfire in New Zealand. It was dedicated to the Scouts who died in the defense of Warsaw. The discussion was led by the troop leader.

Thursday, December 7, 1944. Today they showed us another Polish film, actually a documentary on General Władysław Sikorski while he was still alive and later, his funeral. In the next film Ewa Curie, the daughter of Marie Skłodowska-Curie, gave a talk on her mother's homeland which was followed by images of various towns: first Gdynia, then fields and forests, Bydgoszcz, Poznań, Częstochowa, Chorzów, Zakopane, Kraków, the Hucul region, Lwów, Wilno, and Warszawa. These beautiful images brought tears to my eyes. I have already traversed so many lands, but the most beautiful one of all is our beloved fatherland.

Thursday, December 21, 1944. We are trembling all morning. The second lesson — Latin and a test. All those terrible indicatives and ablatives become more frightening each minute. The test was easy. During the fourth lesson the director, Ms. Zięciakowa, came and informed us that our class (there were nine of us) would go to an English school. She said: "Young ladies, only remember this, that you are Poles and that you are not going there in order to fall in love with someone but to gain knowledge. Once more remember this, that you are Poles." Saying this she had tears in her eyes, and we began to cry as well. The journals had to be written, but we also added the statement that we wanted to finish our studies in our Polish secondary school. We said this during our lessons to all of our professors and the priest, and they supported us. The mathematician said that he was happy because we "do not sleep."

Monday, December 25, 1944. Christmas. We celebrated the *wigilia* [a Christmas Eve tradition] last night. We shared the wafer. Fortunately, I eat in the same dining room as my mother, Ela and Ula, but Olek is in the adjoining dining room. Our thoughts were with those who remained in Poland and with Tadzio, who was in the yunaks, and with Father and Józek who are no longer with us... I attended midnight Mass for the first time in my life. It's hard to believe that it's Christmas. It's a strange feeling because in Poland there's frost, snow — and here it's hot summer.

Saturday, February 3, 1945. Today marks the end of the school year. After Mass we went to our classes and our grades were read off. I'm already in the fourth year of secondary school. We are to remain in the camp. We rejoice.

Thursday, February 16, 1945. After dinner the entire choir and the dancing girls went to Palmerston North. We rode on a truck along a beautiful mountain road bordering the Monavat River. There was a concert and afterwards we sang in a radio studio. Ms. Żerebecka directed. Our recorded national hymn and two folk songs were played back to us. We were moved deeply. At the end we were given ice cream and returned to camp.

Saturday, February 18, 1945. We formed a lane to greet the prime minister, and the children — dressed in colorful Polish costumes — welcomed him. After visiting the small hospital the entire delegation — 21 persons — attended our English language class. Everything went smoothly and Miss Neligan was happy. Afterwards, there were performances by the children and in the evening we put on a Nativity play. I participated in the latter: I was the angel in the fourth act. Our director gave wholly of herself. Then we had supper in common, and the prime minister shook everyone's hand good bye.

May 1, 2 and 3, 1945. We have been giving concerts in Wellington for the last three days. We thought it rather funny to put on the Nativity play in May, but they liked it. The third of May celebration was preceded by a Mass during which the sermon was about fighting Poles.

Tuesday, May 8, 1945. Word has it since early this morning that the war is over. The Germans are beaten! Finally it's the end of the war in Europe.

Thursday, May 17, 1945. It's another sad anniversary. How difficult it is for Mother to bear the death of Józek who perished at Monte Cassino a year ago. He was only 21.

Saturday, June 13, 1945. Today we were visited by a New Zealand soldier who escaped German captivity and, together with some Poles, reached Poland. He fought in the Home Army. He told us about the suffering of the Poles during the occupation, about the Warsaw Uprising, and about how the Lublin Committee was not recognized as being legitimate.

Friday, August 17, 1945. Today begins our two-week spring vacation. We go to various towns and stay with New Zealand families. A sizeable group goes to Napier. Saturday we participated in performances and dances because of the end of the war with Japan. How everyone is rejoicing! In Napier, the Maori invited our entire group to their school, which is associated with a monastery, for a snack. In greeting we sang our Polish hymn, "Poland is not yet lost while we live." We were moved deeply.

Monday, December 17, 1945. We received holiday greetings from Mother's sisters in America and the happy news that our oldest brother survived a German concentration camp and that our home is only partially damaged.

Friday, December 21, 1945. We completed the fourth year, took a qualifying exam, and after vacation we'll go to English schools.

Tuesday, February 8, 1946. Seventy of us depart for the English schools. Hela, Władzia, Józka, and I ride, or rather sail, to Christchurch, where we will live and study in a school associated with a monastery. My mother is saddened by the fact that I'm going to another island. Oh, how our family is scattered throughout the world: Marynia and Edek are in Poland, Tadek is in Palestine with the yunaks, now I am leaving, and in a little while Olek will also leave. Only Ela and Ula will remain with Mother. Such is our fate in exile.

April 1946. We are studying together with New Zealanders. Our teachers are nuns. Additionally, one of them is teaching us English. On Sunday we went for a walk in pairs and spoke, of course, in Polish. Later, Mother Superior asked us to come to the guest room where an elderly lady was sitting. With a strange brand of the Polish language she began to greet and kiss us and invited us to her house for Easter. This was Mrs. Gdaniec who, as a small child, together with her parents, settled in New Zealand and also married a Pole. They were very friendly and invited us there on our free Sundays. We emptied their pantry, but they were only glad to have someone to speak to in Polish.

May 1946. We went to the camp in Pahiatua for our fall vacation. I missed my family. Perhaps we'll go to America because my aunt is making inquiries. But we must return to the school in the monastery and study and work a little because everyone of us — from the youngest to the oldest — has our share of work.

October 1946. I was transferred to the school in Masterton — closer to the camp, which I visit once a month. Great changes have taken place. The teenagers are gone; there are fewer and fewer children in the kindergarten — they are growing. Only the primary school remains. Priests come from Italy and England. An envoy of the Warsaw government appeared in the camp. The boys run away from her. She was accompanied by Delegate Zaleski, commandant of the camp.

Thursday, February 6, 1947. The summer vacation, which drew so many to the camp, is coming to an end. Today we had another visit by eminent guests: Apostolic Delegate Panico, Archbishop of Wellington O'Shea, and Prime Minister P. Fraser, who said that he was inviting about 100 former Polish soldiers to New Zealand with the prospects for work and starting up families.

Monday, February 10, 1947. We returned to our schools, to regular studies, and to planned undertakings. During my free time I read Polish books which I borrow from the camp library. Mainly, they are books by Żeromski, Prus, Reymont, and Kraszewski. I want to know their works so that I won't be embarrassed someday when I return to Poland by the fact that I don't know them.

Wednesday, May 21, 1947. We are in the camp on recess and find out that five persons had signed up to return to Poland. I asked my mother when would we make up our minds. Where will we go: to America, because my aunt sent us an invitation, or to Poland? Mother asked us where we wanted to go, and all four of us replied: Mom, we want to go to Poland!

June 1947. I did not return to school. I went to work in a small factory in Masterton and am living with some kind-hearted people. They treat me like their daughter. With the money that we earn, Mother and I buy various things that we will need in Poland. Although two years have elapsed since the end of the war, it's still difficult to buy anything here.

Monday, September 8, 1947. We became acquainted with many people at work. Because I'm leaving in two weeks, my girlfriends arranged a farewell party — 17 persons attended. They handed me small but useful presents. They were so good-hearted and were saddened by the fact that I was leaving for Poland. And I, I simply cannot wait until I stand on the soil of my homeland.

Saturday, September 20, 1947. Sixteen of us are leaving. All the formalities are taken care of and we are leaving welcoming New Zealand and many well-wishing and good people. The reporters exchanged a few words with us, took a few pictures, and ... we're off! It's 12:15.[2]

Account of Krystyna Skwarko

After a month of sea travel we sailed into Wellington harbour on November 1, 1944. The sun burst through the clouds and shone on the new country.

Everybody tried to squeeze in as near to the rails as possible to get a better view. We saw masses of tiny, colourful houses perched on the green hills surrounding the harbour with the taller buildings of the city lower down on the flat.

After the dry, barren and yellow countryside of Persia, New Zealand appeared a real fairyland.

The New Zealand prime minister, Mr. Fraser, the Polish consul-general, Count K. Wodzicki and his wife, Countess Wodzicka, who was the Polish Red Cross delegate in New Zealand, all came on board to welcome the children....

The following day there was a surprise awaiting us at the Wellington railway station. There were hundreds of smiling Wellington school children waving New Zealand and Polish flags as a gesture of welcome on the platform from which we were to leave for Pahiatua. The singing of the national anthems and gifts of flowers made the occasion even more moving. It was the first direct contact between the children of the two nations, a brief meeting which was to change into a deep and lasting friendship over the years.

There was another big, friendly welcome at Palmerston North, and all down the line, even at places where the train did not stop, there were groups of children gaily waving flags and handkerchiefs.

We had a final welcome on the platform of Pahiatua Station. Then the New Zealand soldiers helped us onto some army trucks and took us to our new home.

The official name at the entrance, "Polish Children's Camp in Pahiatua," cheered our hearts enormously. A place of our own in a distant land.

We were met at the gate by the camp commandant, Major P. Foxley, as well as Count and Countess Wodzicki and their two children.

The camp was run at the expense of the Ministry of Defence and was under its supervision. It was divided by tar-sealed streets into four main sections.

The first section contained the administrative building, four dormitories for the boys, a canteen, a recreation hall for the army staff and a dining hall for the younger boys.

The second section had detached family cottages for the staff with families, a dormitory for the pre-school children and another for the younger school boys. Further down there was a library, a large recreation hall with a small chapel (used on Sundays for church services), a gymnasium, a hospital and another dining hall for the older boys.

The third section contained the dormitories and a dining hall for the girls and some more family cottages for the staff.

The school buildings were in the final section. This also contained a long building divided into separate rooms for the single staff, some huts for the army staff and a clothing store.

Altogether, it was a well-planned place....

As far as the eye could see all round the camp there were paddocks, bush, hills and a river. It was enough space to satisfy even the most demanding boys. It was the sort of place where the children would be able to forget their unhappy childhood.

The girls were satisfied with the Girl Guide activities organized by their chief guide, Mrs. S. Kozera, as well as sports, netball, embroidery and singing. But for the boys that was not enough.

They needed more room to spend their energy. After being cooped up for several years in buildings surrounded by high walls and then close confinement on the boats, they were bursting with eagerness to rush into the open.

They organised their own kind of amusement with one craze after another.

It was slings first of all with the girls' ankles as the target for the missiles. Then they had fun rushing around as they pushed an iron hoop with a stick. Next they began to build all kinds of little huts in various distant corners of the camp and on tall trees. This was followed by the construction of homemade guns and before long there was escapades out to the river and onto the neighbouring farms. Some fascinating things, such as tractors, could be found there and the temptation was too great. They just had to find out how those things worked. So one tractor was partially dismantled by the boys — screws, nuts, bolts, everything. It was easy work but how to put it all together again?....

At first the change of climate adversely affected some of the children. They had left Persia during the hot season and arrived in New Zealand during a damp, rainy month. It was not surprising that many became ill with influenza. But to everyone's joy the New Zealand climate completely cured all those suffering from malaria.

After a few days' rest we resumed our school work from 9:00 a.m. to noon and from 1:30 p.m. to 3:30 p.m. We began our work with eagerness because both staff and the children were longing for a normal, regulated life.

We had to get used to the rules and regulations of the camp's administration, acquaint ourselves with the customs and traditions of the land to which we had come and get used to our new environment.

On the one hand the camp was under the authority of the New Zealand army, with Major Foxley as the commandant and all the army administrative and domestic staff took orders from him. In parallel with this there was the Polish administration with Mr. Śledziński, the Polish delegate, as its head. The Polish staff, including the school teachers, received their instructions from him.

The New Zealand government assured the children and the staff a place to live and their keep for the duration of the war. On the other hand the Polish government was to pay the salaries of the Polish staff and provide pocket money for the children. This was to be paid into their post office savings accounts....

It was intended that after the war all the children and staff were to return to Poland. But when the political situation of Poland unexpectedly deteriorated on the world scene, we became more and more dependent on the government and people of New Zealand....

Subsequent events were to cancel any plans of returning to Poland for a long time to come.

Poland did not regain her independence completely after the war but became a satellite of the Soviet Union. The Polish government in London was no longer recognized.

It was because of this that the delegate of the government, Mr. Śledziński, asked the adult community in the camp at a special meeting held on July 10, 1945, for support to continue to act not only on behalf of the government-in-exile but on their behalf as well. He told us that he had received an assurance from the Polish minister of education, Mr. Folkierski, that the necessary money for the care of the children would be supplied.

Mr. Śledziński's view was that the best way to become independent was to purchase a farm. This would not only support the people but provide work for some of the staff and the older children....

[O]n August 16, Mr. Śledziński gave us some depressing news. He had received instructions from the Polish social welfare office in London that every Polish settlement outside Poland had to become self-supporting. Our camp was to organise itself accordingly....

In spite of all the worries and uncertainties about the future there were many gay and happy occasions in our life at the camp.

There were the Scout activities organized by the chief scout, Mrs. S. Kozera. These included singing by the campfire, parades, the taking of the Scout oath, and the blessing of the flag.

Then there were the commemorative concerts, the Christmas plays and other shows put on by the teachers. The "choinka" [Christmas tree party] on Christmas Eve was popular not only with the children at the camp but with the local population as well. In 1944 all the children and the staff had presents sent to them through the Red Cross from numerous people and private firms.

The boys played mainly cricket in 1945 and 1946 but by 1948 rugby and basketball had caught on in the camp. It did not take the children long to learn that though they should play to win it was the game that mattered rather than the result.

In their first year of play they did so well at rugby that they had a series of triumphs.

Sporting activities brought them into constant and happy contact with New Zealand children on Saturday afternoons and during the inter-school matches. The enthusiasm arising from hard-won victories and the training in teamwork coupled with their association with New Zealand boys and girls benefited them physically, morally and socially.

The Red Cross Society in Pahiatua arranged a few entertainments and quite a lot of outings for the children.

Often on Sundays the young people gathered together in the recreation hall for games, table tennis, singing and dancing, accompanied on the piano by the lovable and tireless Mrs. Watson from Pahiatua.

The visits from hundreds of New Zealanders continued during the weekends.

In order to help the children get acquainted with the New Zealand way of life and to tighten the bond of friendship, the Catholic hierarchy and the New Zealand army collected 830 invitations from New Zealand families for the Polish children and adults to spend a two-week holiday with them in August 1945 and in January 1946.

So the Poles dispersed over both islands where they formed many close friendships that frequently continued to last to the present day....

The Polish high school was closed in August 1946 and the students dispersed to convents throughout both islands....

Another large group of children left the camp with the beginning of the new school year in 1947. Some went to convent boarding schools, others boarded privately, while attending the same schools....

The last group of children left the camp on April 15, 1949. It consisted of 45 boys and 45 girls.

The girls went to the Polish girls' hostel at Lyall Bay and the boys were taken to a special hostel in Hawera. Mrs. Tietze was in charge of the boys' hostel and Mr. R. Tietze was its housemaster....

The New Zealand government had kept its promise as far as the education of the

Polish children was concerned. Every orphan student who really wanted to continue with secondary or higher education was given the opportunity to do so. The government gave generous allowances to pay for the board, clothing and education of these students....

In the years immediately after the end of the war many of the Polish children remembered the Russian terror too well to want to fall its victims a second time. When the dreaded Russian Secret Police, the NKVD, took charge of the Polish police they knew that Poland was not free.

It was for these reasons that the young Polish people did not return to their homeland when they became of age and were able to decide their own future. Even some of those who had parents in Poland preferred to stay in New Zealand.

They grew up in the free, democratic land of New Zealand and became a part of it.[3]

Account of Maria van der Linden

The Polish Children's Camp was located a few kilometres from the Pahiatua township. Here the Skwarko family extended a very warm welcome to us in their small home unit. The healthy appearance of the Polish orphans at the camp impressed us immensely, as did the friendliness of the staff there. The food was excellent; rich, creamy milk, butter, cheese, plentiful meat, fresh fruit and vegetables were in abundance. This was surely the "land of milk and honey" we had been dreaming of! We were unaccustomed to such a rich diet. On arrival we were extremely thin, having been seasick during much of our long voyage and we really enjoyed the wholesome new diet provided at the camp. We remained with the Skwarko family for a week. This enabled us to adjust to our environment and made the transition to a new life less traumatic.

We were introduced to various staff members at the camp, including Major Finney [Foxley?], who was then in charge of the Polish camp. Since we spoke fluent English, it was decided to send us to New Zealand schools in Pahiatua. Alek, now 12 years old, attended the St. Joseph's Catholic Primary School there, while I was enrolled at the Pahiatua District High School. At 16 years of age I was placed in form 5 to become accustomed to a New Zealand school. As it was now mid-October I was not expected to sit the School Certificate Examinations scheduled for November. Indeed, the following two months were to be a period of readjustment for us both, from an English education system in India to a new New Zealand syllabus.

We traveled to Pahiatua on a school bus which picked up children from the nearby rural area. I can still recall the first comment of a New Zealand boy on the bus. He looked me up and down, then shook his head saying, "You're much too thin for my liking." Indeed, both Alek and I looked emaciated on our arrival in this country. We lacked the robust healthy appearance of the New Zealanders. It was to take us about six months to regain our strength and increase weight.

The Polish Camp was very well organised, clean and comfortable. There was much laughter everywhere. The children seemed happy and well-adjusted. In the primary school at the camp, instruction was in Polish. English was taught as a second language by New Zealand-trained teachers. This equipped the older students for secondary schools beyond the camp. Indeed, all senior Polish pupils attended New Zealand high schools, usually Catholic boarding colleges scattered throughout the land. Each of these schools took a number of Polish students. Mr. and Mrs. Skwarko's daughter Krysia was at one such college in Wanganui, so we were unable to meet straight away.

The Pahiatua Polish Camp had a happy family atmosphere. Many had shared experiences in the USSR, Isfahan in Iran, and in New Zealand since their arrival in 1944 as invited guests of Peter Fraser's Labour Government. We eagerly exchanged memories of our exile in the USSR and our subsequent experiences with Mr. and Mrs. Skwarko. So much had happened to us all since our pathways had parted over eight years ago in Poland in Sokółka. We learned of Mr. Skwarko's arrest by the Soviets in Poland in April 1940, and his deportation with other Polish prisoners to the USSR to work in a mine. Mr. Stanisław Skwarko had been a judge in Sokółka in Poland. On 19th June 1941 Mrs. Krystyna Skwarko and their two children Krysia and Stach had also been deported to the USSR, as we had been over a year earlier. They had been resettled on a collective farm in the Krasnoyarsk region. We compared details of our experiences....

We envied the Skwarkos' secure family unit, though we counted our own blessings. Many wonderful people had assisted us to arrive safely in New Zealand. There was so much to relate to our old friends.

After only a week at the Pahiatua Camp, Mother left for Auckland to undertake a three month refresher course at St. Helen's Hospital, in order to become a registered midwife in New Zealand. Both the Waikato and the North Canterbury Hospital Boards guaranteed Mother's employment following her registration as a midwife and a general nurse in New Zealand. After her departure for Auckland I continued living with the Skwarkos, while attending the District High School at Pahiatua. Alek however, transferred to a boys' dormitory at the camp. He made many friends among the Polish boys with whom he shared his life at Pahiatua. Some of these friendships deepened and continued into his later life. As all the young people of my age were at secondary schools outside the Pahiatua Camp, I remained an outsider, unable for some time to penetrate the close-knit group of Polish adolescents of my age. Alek and I continued to travel to school in Pahiatua until the end of November 1947.

Only six weeks after our enrollment at the schools there, a severe epidemic of poliomyelitis broke out in New Zealand. This necessitated the closure of all schools until after Easter 1948. The children at the Pahiatua Camp were isolated from outside contact to prevent an outbreak of polio there. Polish high school students scattered throughout New Zealand were found homes in their respective areas to spend their long summer vacation in. Similarly, Krysia Skwarko was unable to join her family at the camp. Several older children of the Polish staff there were also in the same position. Mr. and Mrs. Skwarko and a small group of other Polish adults and secondary school age children obtained permission to camp in a wooded area in the vicinity of the camp, yet beyond its confines. They lived there in the *lasek* (small forest) in tents for several summer months.

I found employment as a nurses' aide at the Pahiatua Hospital. While I worked there and resided at the nurses' home, I often visited the Skwarko family in the woods. I had no contact with Alek, who remained at the camp. My mother continued her work and the refresher nursing course at St. Helen's Hospital in Auckland, so we were separated yet again. For me it was a time of readjustment to a very new culture. I had much to learn. In India, at Kimmins High School, all the chores had been done by Indian servants. During my brief stay with the Skwarkos at the Polish camp I had only tidied up my room and helped with the dishes. At the Pahiatua Hospital I was suddenly "thrown into the deep end." Here I was required to clean the wards and all utility rooms. Ironing, washing, panning and sponging patients were new skills I had to acquire immediately. I felt embarrassed when asked to sponge men and to attend to their toilet needs. At the age of 16 I was very shy, having led a sheltered life in boarding institutions. I was shocked to learn of the lesbian relationship between two English nurses resident at the nurses' home.

Many of the nurses were kind to me. They donated clothing for me to wear as I had no money to buy new clothes and had outgrown my clothes from India. Moreover, fashions in New Zealand were different. When Christmas came I received several gifts from my nursing colleagues. Christmas in the middle of the summer in New Zealand was a new experience for me. The hospital wards were brightly decorated and the Christmas tree reminded me of our home in Poland. New Zealand Christmas dinner at midday on 25th December was also different from the Polish celebrations on Christmas Eve. Roast lamb with mint sauce, accompanied by roast potatoes, pumpkin, kumara and peas, was followed by rich Christmas pudding and Christmas fruit cake. Although I enjoyed this delicious food among many friendly New Zealanders, I felt alone with my thoughts of the past, unable to share these festivities with my brother and Mother, with whom I had no contact at that time. I always looked forward on my days off to a visit to the woods, where I could speak Polish with my friends camping there.

On the completion of her refresher course at St. Helen's Hospital in Auckland, Mother was appointed as a midwife at the Burwood Maternity Annex in Christchurch. Meanwhile, I was transferred to a private hospital for the elderly, many of whom were disabled after strokes or afflicted with senility. There I remained as a nurses' aide until after Easter in April 1948, when the New Zealand schools reopened. The polio epidemic was over by then.

That April Mother arranged for Alek's and my transfer to schools in Christchurch. Mrs. Maureen Baker, an old friend of Uncle Lovat, lived in Wellington. She kindly met me at the Wellington railway station and directed me onto the inter-island ship bound for Lyttelton. Mrs. Baker had helped us to obtain our entry permit to New Zealand and had kept in touch with us after our arrival in this country. Alek arrived in Christchurch a few days before me with a group of Polish boys from the Pahiatua Camp. He was already enrolled at St. Bede's College when I arrived. Mother met me at Lyttelton, from where we traveled by train together to Christchurch. I was allowed to spend the weekend with her at the nurses' home at Burwood Hospital. On the following Monday I was enrolled at Sacred Heart College as a fifth form student. Shortly after this Mother was transferred to a small maternity hospital at Amuri in North Canterbury, where we spent our May school holidays.

Unfortunately, Mother was unhappy in this isolated, rural community hospital, so she requested a transfer to Wellington. This occurred towards the end of our school holidays. A kind local couple, Mr. and Mrs. Croft, took us into their home when Mother left Amuri for Wellington. They were friends of Mother's acquaintances, Mr. and Mrs. Munro, who farmed nearby. A few days later the Morrison family from Christchurch visited their friends, the Munros, in Amuri. On hearing about our plight they offered to take us to their home in Christchurch. When the May holidays ended

Alek returned to St. Bede's College, but I remained at Spreydon with the Morrison family. Mother could not afford to pay school fees for both of us, so I had to leave school without any qualifications after six weeks' attendance at Sacred Heart College in Christchurch. That short period, and another of the same length at the Pahiatua District High School in 1947, was my only opportunity for secondary education in these early years in this new country.

I managed to obtain employment in the mail-order office of Ballantynes, a large department store in Christchurch. My task was to attend to mail orders received from rural customers. My net weekly wage was 30 shillings and sixpence. Out of that amount I paid 25 shillings board weekly to Mr. and Mrs. Morrison. My weekly concession tram ticket cost five shillings, so I was left with a sixpence to spend on myself every pay day. I desperately needed warm clothes for the winter in Christchurch, which was extremely cold in comparison with the Indian winter. Mrs. Morrison and a kind neighbour with two daughters of her own, Mrs. Ryan, gave me various essential items of clothing. Somehow, with their assistance I managed to get by. With the Morrison's encouragement I enrolled at night school to learn shorthand and typing.

My first social encounters in New Zealand were the Sunday evening Catholic youth meetings, which I very much enjoyed. I attended these socials with Shirley and Bev Ryan and the Morrison's two elder sons, Mervyn and Kevin. Their youngest son Brendon was still in primary school then. Now at 17 years of age, exposed to a new culture and with only occasional contact with my mother and brother, I missed the stability of my own family dreadfully. I had had no father since the age of eight and now I missed him more than ever. Although I was fortunate to have the friendship of the Morrison and the Ryan families, I felt like an outsider without my own family. I recall a very happy evening spent with them all at Mrs. Ryan's house across the road from the Morrison's home, where we all enjoyed singing by the piano in the warmth of their home. This was followed by a splendid supper and a friendly talk before I returned to the privacy of my room at Mr. and Mrs. Morrison's residence. That night I was very upset and cried myself to sleep. After experiencing that happy family atmosphere, I felt more than ever the lack of a close family bond, with the love and security that was part of it. I should have counted my blessings, but as an immature adolescent with strong suppressed emotions in a new cultural environment, I was incapable of an impartial, objective assessment of my situation.

Finally, Mother managed to settle down in her new position as a midwife at the Wellington Public Hospital. She obtained a couple of rooms in a house in Berhampore. I was then able to join her in Wellington, while my brother Alek remained at St. Bede's College in Christchurch as a boarder.[4]

8 Mexico

Introduction by Elżbieta Wróbel and Janusz Wróbel

The problem of finding a place for the civilian refugees from the USSR was very complicated. There was, after all, a war going on that embraced almost the entire world. The German armies had already conquered almost all of Europe and were threatening the Middle East from the west and north while the Japanese also threatened it from the east. It became imperative therefore to find a place where the people could spend the remainder of the war years in tolerable conditions of existence and, what is more important, in a place where they would be safe.

This undertaking was spearheaded by the Polish authorities in conjunction with their western Allies: the British and the Americans. The coordinated action of these three countries also embraced Mexico, whose government showed a great deal of understanding in regard to the difficult situation of the Poles and expressed a willingness to allow a certain number of them to come into the country. The official agreement regarding the transfer of the refugees was transacted by General W. Sikorski, during his visit to Mexico at the end of 1942, and President Manuel Avila Camacho. As a result, 50 years ago, in two voyages aboard the American military transport USS "Hermitage," over 1,400 Poles who recently left Russia arrived in San Diego. Shortly thereafter they were taken in special trains to the city of Leon, located in central Mexico. Near it lay the abandoned hacienda of Santa Rosa, which the Mexican government allowed the refugees to use during the time of war. Gradually, thanks to the efforts of the arrivals and help from the outside, the hacienda buildings were remodeled and adapted to the needs of the Poles.

The conditions of life in the settlement were regulated by the agreements between the Polish authorities and Mexico, Great Britain, and the United States. The administration of the settlement was in the hands of the Polish government represented by the delegate of the Ministry of Labor and Social Welfare. An American government agency, the Foreign Relief and Rehabilitation Operations (FRRO), covered, in the form of credit to the Polish government, the cost of maintaining the settlement. An American charitable organization, the National Catholic Welfare Conference (NCWC), financed the cultural activities, sports and recreation. Among the various organizations that came to the assistance of the refugees there was no lack of Polish ones. Right after the arrival of the USS "Hermitage" the Polish-American Council (Rada Polonii Amerykańskiej — RPA) appropriated $25,000 for the purchase of clothes and medicines for their fellow countrymen who came from Russia. Somewhat later the RPA undertook the financing of education and health services in the Santa Rosa settlement and sent its own delegate there. From Chicago and other centers of Polish life delegates of Polish organizations came to Mexico and brought the refugees not only words of encouragement but also material assistance. The Polish Felician Sisters of Chicago who ran the orphanage and the school system also deserve a mention.

Thanks to the efforts of the above-mentioned governments and organizations, the Polish refugees in Santa Rosa were provided with suitable living conditions, conditions about which their compatriots in occupied Poland and the camps located in other nations of the world could only dream. Many of the residents of the hacienda considered their years of stay in Mexico as the most beautiful period of their youth. Undoubtedly, this positive assessment also applies to the work of the excellent educators and caretakers who not only taught the youth but also during their free time inspired them to participate in worthwhile cultural, sporting, and recreational activities.

The settlement of Santa Rosa was to be a place of residence for the refugees only until the liberation of their fatherland from German occupation. Unfortunately, the decision undertaken at Yalta made the return to Poland impossible for most of them. The borderlands from which they hailed were now within the borders of the USSR and the communists seized power in Poland. Given this situation, despite the end of the war in Europe, the process of the liquidation of the settlement lasted until the end of 1946. During that dramatic period their fellow countrymen in the USA again hurried with help. Already in March 1946 the president of the Polish National Alliance, Karol Rozmarek, brought to the United States a group of boys who were placed in the Alliance College in Cambridge Springs. Shortly after the liquidation of the settlement another group of boys was brought to the Polish college and 25 girls were sent to Coraopolis, where they were to be enrolled in a school operated by the Felician Sisters.

The Polish-American Council and their president, F. X. Świetlik, also took part in the relocation of the refugees from Santa Rosa. Over 100 children came to the orphanage of St. Hedwig in Niles, and other groups were placed in Elmsworth (Holy Family), Milwaukee (St. Joseph), Detroit (Guardian Angel), and Buffalo (Immaculate Heart of the Blessed Virgin Mary). Thanks to personal initiatives and the efforts of relatives, about 250 people were brought to the USA.

A certain number of people remained in Mexico. This became possible thanks to President M. A. Camacho who, during his visit to Santa Rosa in the fall of 1945 stated that "to those who would like to remain in Mexico we offer ... open arms to receive them among us on a permanent basis." Several dozen persons found work there; a number of women got married. These people launched the beginning of a small but dynamic Polish community in Mexico.

Other groups of the hacienda residents went to Canada or joined their families in Great Britain; a small number returned to Poland.[1]

Santa Rosa

Account of Tadeusz Pieczko

We arrived in Mexico in November 1943 to join another group already there. In all, there were about 250 orphans in our group. We were housed in two large dormitories: girls in one, the boys in the other. About five or six adults were put in charge of us....

At the beginning, the orphanage was in a state of total chaos. There was no discipline, and if any rules existed they were completely ignored. It was almost impossible to get a true head count of the children because they wandered all over the settlement. Our favorite trick was to take off with a group of friends and go swimming near a dam in the hills without any adult supervision. Not having any swimming trunks, we would try to find a cloth bag with a drawstring. (Some of us still had the bags given to us in Russia in which to carry our belongings.) We would cut off the corners of the bag and end up with a pair of trunks. If we were not swimming at the dam, we would be in the nearby Mexican village. We would steal soap or other goods from the supply room and trade with the Mexicans for candy, beer, soda and puppies. It seemed as though every kid had a puppy under his bed. What a noise and mess they created! After a while the cleaning ladies refused to sweep our dormitory. Given this state of affairs, someone decided to send for the Felician Sisters from Chicago to look after us. At first, we did not like this. It meant going to school regularly, attending church services, and staying within the orphanage area.

One Sunday we were ordered to go to the church to greet the nuns. They arrived in our settlement the previous day so they knew what a wild bunch we were. As they entered the church the crowd parted to let them through and some of the kids quietly hissed and booed. That was meant to give them a taste as to what to expect. These nuns were small in stature but tough, and they shaped us up in no time. Whenever we had to go somewhere in a large group, we were ordered to march in twos. We now had cleaner and better clothes and went to school each day. We even got better schoolbooks. Before the nuns came, reading materials were very scarce. Now there was a library stocked with Polish books. I read, or tried to read, anything I could get my hands on....

Soon a new orphanage was built. To us, it seemed absolutely beautiful. About thirty children were assigned to a room with steel cots and there was a separate recreation room. The nuns hired a carpenter to build some rabbit cages out of the old wooden cots. In no time the rabbit population exploded. My brother and I decided to offer one of our rabbits to the sisters for supper. We killed it and carried it to the kitchen. The cook and one of the nuns screamed when we walked in with the dead rabbit. After the nun realized our good intentions and saw the look on the faces of the kids that accompanied us, she told us that she would cook it, but that we had to skin it first. So we did. No one ever offered the sisters a rabbit for their dinner again.

Our entire settlement had a high wall around it to keep trespassers out. There were bits of broken glass on top of the wall to make it difficult to scale. To exit the settlement one had to use the main gate or go through the holes that we made in the wall....

We kept busy after school by working either in the mechanics or the hobby shops. In the mechanics shop most of the boys made hunting knives, tools and other things. In the hobby shop we learned how to make picture frames, wooden toys and plaster ashtrays. One of the boys decided to make himself a gun. However, it couldn't fire bullets. One day, a group of us decided to go with him to the dam to test it out. When we got there, he packed the barrel with gunpowder, glass, tar and pebbles and plugged it with paper. He then ignited the powder through a small hole on the side of the handgun. When it was fired, a beautiful ball of flame sailed through the air and fell in the water. He then repacked the pistol and we started back to the orphanage. On the way back we spotted some Mexican boys tending cows in the pasture. As we got closer they started chasing us and waving large machetes. After running a few yards the boy with the gun decided to make a stand. We all stopped to watch him. Standing near a large cactus, he aimed his gun at our pursuers. His aim was bad, and the shot ripped the hell out of the cactus. Well, when the Mexican boys saw that they turned around and ran like hell, and we walked very leisurely back to the orphanage. Once, on the outskirts of our compound, we saw a skunk that took off down the road and into a field. So we went after him. When he disappeared down a hole, someone got a pail of water to flush him out. Well, he came out all right, but we weren't prepared for the consequences.

We were able to obtain fireworks from the Mexican villagers fairly easy. One time (this was when the nuns still did not have complete control over us) we got some fireworks and set them off on the orphanage grounds. Actually, we threw them near the girls to scare them. Unfortunately, a low-flying rocket began pursuing one of them. As she ran in panic the rocket went right through her skirt. No one got punished but we had to attend a lecture on the danger of fireworks and how the girl's clothing could have caught on fire and how seriously she could have been burned. Fireworks were forbidden from then on.

Our gym teacher was a handsome, husky Mexican. Once, he took a few days off to take part in a wrestling match in the city. When he came back some of us cried. He was bruised, cut up, black and blue all over, and he limped. We all liked him very much and called him "Lobo."...Looking back, I think that the most memorable and enjoyable time of my life was the time I spent in Mexico. To this day, I love Mexican music. I cannot say the same for their hot food....

While in Mexico, we contacted the International Red Cross in an attempt to locate our parents. Just before we left Mexico we received notice from the Red Cross that our mother was located and that we could expect a letter from her soon.

We received word in early in 1946 that the settlement would be closed. And so the children were split up into small groups (about 50 to 100 each) and sent to different Catholic orphanages in the U.S.[2]

Account of Anita Paschwa (née Kozicka)

The [USS] Hermitage became our home for six weeks. We were to cross the Indian Ocean and then the Pacific en route to California. We were involved in our "normal" daily activities including school work. But the Japanese mines in the Indian Ocean diverted our journey to Melbourne, where we spent a few days waiting for an all clear. From there we sailed past Bora Bora and arrived in Los Angeles, California, on October 24, 1943. Our experience in California was limited to army barracks in Santa Anita where we spent two weeks. From there we went by train to Juarez, a Mexican border town. While in Juarez I passed a man selling oranges. I gave him a half-dollar coin which I received in Santa Anita, and since I couldn't speak Spanish, pointed to the oranges.

He followed me into the train compartment, dumped a whole bushel of fruit on my seat, and left. Everyone laughed at my thinking I was buying one orange, but they all enjoyed my mistake.

The train from Juarez took us to Leon, Guanajuato. We arrived in Colonia Santa Rosa on November 2, 1943. Ours was the second of two transports. There were 1,432 Polish refugees, of which 265 were orphans.

Colonia Santa Rosa was a happy place. We were far from the war still going on Europe, but sadly, I was far away from my sister Maria and could no longer keep track of her. I knew only that she was serving in the army as a nurse. I became very involved in school work. There was much to do. We studied three foreign languages — Latin, English and Spanish — plus Polish and a full curriculum of high school subjects. In addition, there were scouting activities, piano, crocheting club and reading club. Actual study time was so scarce that I often completed reading assignments with a candle under my sheet propped up with a ruler. It's a wonder that none of my 25 dormitory roommates ever turned me in.

There were many field trips also. We often went swimming to the hot springs at Camanjillo and we traveled to Mexico City, Guadalajara, Chapala, Morelia and the volcano Paricutin.

In April 1946, near the end of my third year of high school, we were notified that 104 of the oldest boys and girls were being sent to St. Hedwig's orphanage in Niles, Illinois. There we would finish high school.[3]

Account of Jane [Janina] Żebrowski-Bulmahn

A group of 727 Polish people, including 265 orphans, were accepted for the trip to Mexico. On September 8, 1943, we left the city of Karachi in army trucks which took us to a small ship anchored in the port of Karachi. We were on our way to Bombay, India. It was a very slow ship and although the distance was not great, it took us five days to get there.

When we got to Bombay, army trucks showed up to take us to the American ship called the USS Hermitage. This had been an Italian ship captured by Allies in 1942 and was used to transport American soldiers returning from the South Pacific. We received quite a welcome from the American soldiers, many of whom could speak Polish. We left Bombay on September 16, 1943, for a dangerous trip across the Pacific, heading for Los Angeles....

From the USS Hermitage we were taken by army trucks to camp Santa Anita, close to Los Angeles, previously used as a detention camp for Japanese. We were then assigned to army barracks for a short stay.

Representatives from five organizations came to assist us in whatever way we needed help. These were: The Friends of Poland, United Polish Societies, Polish Relief Fund, The Council of Jewish Women, and the American Friends Service Committee.

The distribution of the fruit and clothing gathered by these organizations started almost immediately. Most of the clothing received did not fit many people, but extra fabric and sewing supplies were given to women to make alterations if necessary. After a prolonged period of going barefoot, shoes did not fit us either. But we took whatever we thought we could use.

The children were given toys, which brought a lot of joy to us. We had forgotten what toys were. Being given toys brought many tears of happiness to our eyes. Yes, these new friends cared for us.

At sunrise each morning the faithful gathered for Catholic Mass under the trees. The priest celebrated the Mass dressed in his own daily attire. However, by the end of the week our new American friends provided him with proper religious vestments.

In a few days, local radio personalities came and brought a band to play American music for us in the camp athletic field. After that the children were encouraged to play ball. This was all new to us but very enjoyable....

After a six-day stay at Santa Anita, we were driven in busses to a waiting train in Los Angeles for the trip to Mexico. We crossed the border on foot after our documents were checked. We then boarded a Mexican train. Our new destination was Colonia Santa Rosa, close to the city of Leon, in the state of Guanajuato.

We reached Santa Rosa in November 1943. This was an old ranch belonging to someone who was killed in one of the revolutions. Since it had been empty for some time, Mexico offered to house Polish war refugees there.

We were not only welcomed by Polish people who got to Santa Rosa four months before us, but also were escorted to our living quarters by uniformed Polish Scouts who explained to us about life in the camp. We were given one room per family, clothing, food, and a small allowance for each family.

The 265 orphans who traveled with us had their own living quarters and activities, but attended school with the rest of the children.

Grade school classes were held in an old mill which had been rebuilt. There was also a small church, more like a chapel. The church was very beautiful with many icons and decorations. However, one outside wall of the church was full of bullet holes from executions during the many revolutions in Mexico. It was frightening to look at that side of the church building.

High school classes were held in the living quarters of one of the previous ranch owners. The building was constructed in a Spanish style, adobe type, with a central courtyard and all the rooms facing the beautiful courtyard. There were enough rooms for all four grades as well as living quarters for the teachers.

Our food, clothing, medicine and school supplies were donated by the Polish War Relief Organization and a loan from the U.S. government to the Polish government-in-exile. The National Catholic Welfare Conference (NCWC) provided activities and educational trips for school children. Two representatives of the organization lived in the nearby city of Leon and worked at Santa Rosa.

There was much construction going on in the camp when we arrived. A new orphanage building was being built, more housing for families, bath houses, extra toilets and laundry facilities, as well as a theater, a bakery, a library, a medical clinic and administrative offices.

We were free to come and go except that it was not safe for children to be roaming the countryside unsupervised because of the possibility of getting lost and/or coming across a wild animal or a poisonous snake. Our transportation to the city of Leon consisted of a horse-drawn trolley. Our camp was located only a few miles from the city.

The organization of the camp was already well established and we fit right in. This was going to be our home for the duration of the war.

We established friendships quickly and shared many hopes and dreams as well as fears and anxieties with other girls approaching their teens. We formed small groups of friends, as young people do, which gave us a feeling of belonging. My group was composed of girls from my grade who traveled with me to Mexico. Our teachers encouraged us to share our feelings with them and doubled as counselors. I was 12 years old and this was my first "normal" way of life since that fateful night in 1941.

I continued in fourth grade when we arrived in Mexico. Our school day always began with morning prayer, gym exercises, then home for breakfast, and back to school.

We had school six days a week which went on all year, with only a few free days in between, to make up for the time lost in Russia. Our lessons were conducted in Polish, but we were also learning Spanish and English. We picked up Spanish very quickly since we mingled with the local people. English presented a problem for us, especially the pronunciation. Since Spanish was of immediate use to us, more stress was put on learning that language. Periodically, we were taken to a school in Leon to participate in Spanish language instructions.

How proud I was to wear a Polish Scout uniform and the scarf of my troop, rather than the hated red scarf I was forced to wear under communism....

Our benefactor, NCWC, provided us with a bus to tour Mexico. All high school students were allowed to go on these tours. They lasted a week and were well supervised. Besides Polish teachers, we had a Mexican tour guide traveling with us and explaining the cultural and historical significance of the places we visited. We enjoyed every minute of it and learned much about Mexico.

Our first stop was at the health spa with sulfur hot springs, called Camanjillo. After visiting the spa, we continued on to Mexico City. Some of the things I remember were: a tour of Mexico City, visiting the National Palace where we saw several of Diego Rivera's murals, and being able to see the Mexican folk dances performed by the National Ballet Company. We also made a stop at the beautiful and historic Chapultepec Park where the residence of Emperor Maxímilian is located.

From there we traveled to Guadalupe, located not far from Mexico City, to visit the shrine of the Virgin of Guadalupe who had appeared to an Indian peasant, Juan Diego, several times. As a proof to the church authorities, the image of the Virgin appeared on the Indian's cloak. Her image is displayed at a church built in her honor.

Also close to Mexico City was an active volcano, Paricutin, which erupted in February 1943. It was an overwhelming experience to see an active volcano with hot lava flowing close to where we were standing. We were also able to see the crater of a dormant volcano Popocatepetl. Our class visited the area in the summer of 1945.

From there we went to Guadalajara, a beautiful city with many very impressive old buildings, churches, and monuments. We also toured one of the silver mines located close to the city of Guadalajara.

Our last stop was Lake Chapala where we spent a whole day swimming and just walking around. After spending a night in a small hotel, we headed back to Santa Rosa.

The tour was a great lesson in the history, geography and culture of Mexico. We learned more than we could have from a book in any classroom....

After we had been in Mexico for about two years, my sister Juzia came down with malaria. We had a Polish doctor in our camp who was allowed to dispense medicine under the direction of a Mexican doctor. The Mexican doctor lived in town and only serious cases were referred to him. Malaria was so common that it was not considered very serious. My sister was given medicine and my parents were told to take her home and make sure she stayed in bed until the fever broke.

Within an hour she became unconscious and her fingers and toenails started turning purple. Father ran with her to the medical clinic pleading for help. The Mexican doctor was called and rushed from Leon. He gave her a shot, an antidote of some sort, and assured my parents that she would be all right.

Several hours later my sister's fingers and toes returned to a normal color, but she did not regain consciousness until the next day. She was very weak and stayed in bed for a long time. The doctor told my parents that the Polish doctor had made a mistake and had given her an adult dosage of quinine. After several weeks she recovered completely.

When the war ended, we were notified by Mexican authorities that our camp in Santa Rosa would be dissolved since they only gave us temporary shelter for the duration of the war. Instead of dissolving it at the end of 1945, they had extended it till the end of 1946 to give us time to make other arrangements. Poland was not free as promised, and we had no country to return to. Of the 1,432 residents of Santa Rosa, only 45 returned to Poland to join their families there, 180 established permanent residence in Mexico, and a small number were able to emigrate to the U.S. right away. The orphans in the camp left for an orphanage in Chicago. The rest of the families were assigned to different areas of Mexico to live and work, hoping to emigrate to the U.S....

While I was in my second year of high school in 1946, there were rumors that some students might have a chance to go to the United States. Soon representatives from the Polish National Alliance, a fraternal organization headquartered in Chicago, came and informed us that their organization would sponsor up to 100 students to go to the United States to study. The students were chosen on the basis of teachers' recommendations, grades, personality and health. The total number accepted was 73 girls and boys. I was one of the lucky ones.[4]

Account of Krystyna Machałowska

This was shortly after the first transport of Poles arrived in Mexico. In that transport were mainly women with children (from three to sixteen years old) and a few men unfit for military service. When we arrived at our settlement, called Santa Rosa, not all the buildings were sufficiently prepared for our use, including the school (an old windmill was being renovated for that purpose). The children were anxious to return to the classroom after their almost three-year hiatus. (In Russia conditions were not conducive to education and later the travels interfered; for example, I finished fifth grade in Tehran.) After a short time lessons resumed but they were not held in a normal setting. Carrying bricks, which served as our seats, we would gather somewhere in a field in the settlement or in the hallways of our living quarters. There were no textbooks and so everything had to be written down; our knees served as our desks. One day our teacher decided to conduct class on the flat roof of a one-storied residential building near the chapel whose steeple would shield us from the hot Mexican sun. The lesson began but the students, who were evidently not all that interested in the subject matter, began to collect small stones and throw them down below. No harm was done but nevertheless someone complained to the school authorities that the children were misbehaving. For punishment, all the students in my class had to write 50 times: "A good student behaves himself (or herself) and does not throw stones." I don't know whether this taught us anything, but it did embed itself permanently on my memory, all the more so because it took so much time to write and used up half of my notebook. Then the conditions improved. The primary and secondary schools received a lot of help from the Polish-American Council and other charitable organizations. We also had a few textbooks and a well-stocked library.

Outings were planned for us, thanks to which we were able to visit many interesting places in this exotic land. I was most impressed by the active volcano Paricutin (it erupted for the first time in the spring of 1943), which we visited at night and therefore were able to see the pillar of fire emanating from the crater and the living fire flowing slowly down the mountainside. Prior to each eruption one could feel a slight tremor, which produced a strange sensation. When the lava reached the bottom of the mountain everyone garnered it closer to himself or herself with a stick, and when it cooled, took some of it for a keepsake. I have very pleasant memories of Mexico in spite of the fact that this was a time of a cruel war and that news would often reach the settlement that someone near and dear to us had died at the front. This is a beautiful land with a rich folklore tradition. To this day I still listen to Mexican music and recall the exciting dances. The local people showed us a lot of sympathy and, when the occasion presented itself, visited us gladly. Our *Śmigus-dyngus* custom appealed to them the most, and they would participate in it with pleasure, sloshing girls they met with water from head to toe. But because there were problems with the water in Mexico, in the years following the water was shut off on this day and the joys of sloshing came to an end.

I recall with pleasure my engagement in scouting and meeting Mexican Scouts. We also participated in parades commemorating Mexican national holidays. I regard this over three-year stay in the settlement of Santa Rosa as being very beneficial to the young people that were studying there because we were raised in a patriotic spirit and were imbued with good principles.[5]

Documents

A: Excerpts from NKVD Instructions Relating to "Anti-Soviet Elements"; Order No. 0054

Source: Third Interim Report *of the U.S. House of Representatives' Select Committee on Communist Aggression, 83rd Cong., 2nd sess. (Washington, D.C.: Government Printing Office, 1954), 471. This order, dated November 28, 1940, was issued by Guzevicius, the People's Commissar for Internal Affairs of the Lithuanian SSR. No doubt this list of "anti-Soviet elements" applied to all Soviet-occupied territories, including Eastern Poland.*

5. Index accounting must embrace all persons who, by reason of their social and political background, national-chauvinistic and religious convictions, and moral and political instability, are opposed to the socialist order and thus might be used for anti-Soviet purposes by the intelligence services of foreign countries and by counter-revolutionary centers.

These elements include:

a) All former members of anti-Soviet political parties, organizations and groups: Trotskyists, Rightists, Socialist Revolutionaries, Mensheviks, Social Democrats, Anarchists, and such like;

b) All former members of national-chauvinistic anti-Soviet parties, organizations and groups: Nationalists, Young Lithuanians, Voldemarists, Populists, Christian Democrats, members of Nationalist terrorist organizations ("The Iron Wolf"), active members of student fraternities, active members of the Riflemen's Association (the National Guard), and the Catholic terrorist organization "The White Steed";

c) Former military police, policemen, former employees of the political and criminal police and of the prisons;

d) Former officers of the Tsarist, Petlyura, and other armies;

e) Former officers and members of the military courts of the armies of Lithuania and Poland;

f) Former political bandits and volunteers of the White and other armies;

g) Persons expelled from the Communist Party and Comm-Youth for anti-Party offenses;

h) All deserters, political emigrés, re-emigrants, repatriates, and contra-bandists;

i) All citizens of foreign countries, representatives of foreign firms, employees of offices of foreign countries, former citizens of foreign countries, former employees of legations, concerns, concessions and stock companies of foreign countries;

j) Persons maintaining personal contacts and correspondence abroad, with foreign legations and consulates, Esperantists and Philatelists;

k) Former employees of the departments of ministries (from Referents upwards);

l) Former workers of the Red Cross and Polish refugees;

m) Religionists (priests, pastors), sectarians and the active worshipers of religious congregations;

n) Former noblemen, estate owners, merchants, bankers, businessmen (who availed themselves of hired labor), shop owners, proprietors of hotels and restaurants.

6. In preparing index accounts of the anti-Soviet element, all sources must be utilized, including: agency (informers') reports, special investigative materials, data of the Party and Soviet organizations, statements of citizens, depositions of arrested persons, and other data. As a rule, statements and other official materials must be verified by means of agents.

B: Basic Instructions on Deportations; Order No. 001223; Dated October 11, 1939

Source: Third Interim Report *of the U.S. House of Representatives' Select Committee on Communist Aggression, 83rd Cong., 2nd sess. (Washington, D.C.: Government Printing Office, 1954), 464–68. This deportation order was also implemented in Soviet-occupied Eastern Poland.*

Instructions Regarding the Procedure for carrying out the Deportation of Anti-Soviet Elements from Lithuania, Latvia, and Estonia.

Strictly Secret

1. General Situation

The deportation of anti-Soviet elements from the Baltic Republics is a task of great political importance. Its successful execution depends upon the extent to which the district operative "troikas" and operative headquarters are capable of carefully working out a plan for executing the operations and for anticipating everything indispensable.

Moreover, care must be taken that the operations are carried out without disturbances and panic, so as not to permit any demonstrations and other troubles not only on the part of those to be deported, but also on the part of a certain section of the surrounding population hostile to the Soviet administration.

Instructions as to the procedure for conducting the operations are given below. They should be adhered to, but in individual cases the collaborators engaged in carrying out the operations shall take into account the special character of the concrete conditions of such operations and, in order correctly to appraise the situation, may and must adopt other decisions directed to the same end, viz., to fulfill the task entrusted to them without noise and panic.

2. Procedure of Instructing

The instructing of operative groups by the district "troika" shall be done as speedily as possible on the day before the beginning of the operations, taking into consideration the time necessary for travelling to the scene of operations.

The district "troika" shall previously prepare the necessary transport for conveyance of the operative groups in the village to the scene of operations.

On the question of allocating the necessary number of motor-cars and wagons for transport, the district "troika" shall consult the leaders of the Soviet party organized on the spot.

Premises for the issue of instructions must be carefully prepared in advance, and their capacity, exits and entrances and the possibility of intrusion by strangers must be considered.

Whilst instructions are being issued the building must be carefully guarded by operative workers.

Should anybody from amongst those participating in the operation fail to appear for instructions, the district "troika" shall at once take steps to replace the absentee from a reserve which shall be provided in advance.

Through police officers the "troika" shall notify to those assembled a division of the government for the deportation of a prescribed number contingent of anti-Soviet elements from the territory of the said republic or region. Moreover, they shall briefly explain what the deportees represent.

The special attention of the (local) Soviet party workers gathered for instructions shall be drawn to the fact that the deportees are enemies of the Soviet people and that the possibility of an armed attack on the part of the deportees cannot be excluded.

3. Procedure for Acquisition of Documents

After the general instructions of the operative groups, documents regarding the deportees should be issued to such groups. The deportees' personal files must be previously collected and distributed among the operative groups, by communes and villages, so that when they are being given out there shall be no delays.

After receipt of personal files, the senior member of the operative groups shall acquaint himself with the personal affairs of the families which he will have to deport. He shall, moreover, ascertain the composition of the family, the supply of essential forms for completion regarding the deportee, the supply of transport for conveyance of the deportee, and he shall receive exhaustive answers to questions not clear to him.

Simultaneously with the issuing of documents, the district "troika" shall explain to each senior member of the operative group where the families to be exported are situated and shall describe the route to be followed to the place of deportation. The roads to be taken by the operative personnel with the deported families to the railway station for entrainment shall be indicated. It is also essential to indicate where reserve military groups are stationed, should it be necessary to call them out during trouble of any kind.

The possession and state of arms and ammunition of the entire operative personnel shall be checked. Weapons must be in complete battle readiness and magazine loaded, but the cartridge shall not be slipped into the rifle breech. Weapons shall be used only as a last resort, when the operative group is attacked or threatened with attack or when resistance is offered.

4. Procedure for Carrying out Deportations

If the deportation of several families is being carried out in a settled locality, one of the operative workers shall be appointed senior as regards deportation in that village, and under his direction the operative personnel shall proceed to the villages in question. On arrival in the villages, the operative group shall get in touch (observing the necessary secrecy) with the local authorities: the chairman, secretary or members of the village soviets, and shall ascertain from them the exact dwelling-place of the families to be deported.

After this operative groups, together with the representatives of the local authorities, who shall be appointed to make an inventory of property, shall proceed to the dwellings of the families to be deported. Operations shall be begun at daybreak. Upon entering the home of the person to be deported, the senior member of the operative group shall assemble the entire family of the deportee into one room, taking all necessary precautionary measures against any possible trouble.

After the members of the family have been checked in conformity with the list, the location of those absent and the number of sick persons shall be ascertained, after which they shall be called upon to give up their weapons. Irrespective of whether or not any weapons are delivered, the deportee shall be personally searched and then the entire premises shall be searched in order to discover hidden weapons.

During the search of the premises one of the members of the operative group shall be appointed to keep watch over the deportees.

Should the search disclose hidden weapons in small quantities, these shall be collected by the operative groups and distributed among them. If many weapons are discovered, they shall be piled into the wagon or motor-car which has brought the operative group, after any ammunition in them has been removed. Ammunition shall be packed together with rifles.

If necessary, a convoy for transporting the weapons shall be mobilised with an adequate guard.

In the discovery of weapons, counter-revolutionary pamphlets, literature, foreign currency, large quantities of valuables etc., a brief report of the search shall be drawn up on the spot, wherein the hidden weapons or counter-revolutionary literature shall be indicated. If there is any armed resistance, the question of the necessity of arresting the parties, showing such armed resistance, and of sending them to the district branch of the People's Commissariat of Public Security shall be decided by the district "troika."

A report shall be drawn up regarding the deportees in hiding or sick ones, and this report shall be signed by the representative of the Soviet party organization.

After completion of the search of the deportees they shall be notified that by a Government decision they will be deported to other regions of the Union.

The deportees shall be permitted to take with them household necessities not exceeding 100 kilograms in weight.

1. Suit. 2. Shoes. 3. Underwear. 4. Bedding. 5. Dishes. 6. Glassware. 7. Kitchen utensils. 8. Food, an estimated month's supply for a family. 9. Money in their possession. 10. Trunk or box in which to pack articles. It is not recommended that large articles be taken.

If the contingent is deported from rural districts, they shall be allowed to take with them small agricultural stocks — axes, saws, and other articles, so that when boarding the deportation train they may be loaded into special goods wagons.

In order not to mix them with articles belonging to others, the Christian name, patronymic and surname of the deportee and name of the village shall be written on the packed property.

When loading these articles into the carts, measure shall be taken so that the deportee cannot make use of them for purposes of resistance while the column is moving along the highway.

Simultaneously with the task of loading by the operative groups, the representatives of the Soviet party organisations present at the time prepare an inventory of the property and of the manner of its protection in conformity with the instructions received by them.

If the deportee possesses his own means of transport, carts shall be mobilised in the village by the local authorities, as instructed by the senior member of the operative group.

All persons entering the home of the deportee during the execution of the operations or found there at the moment of these operations must be detained until the conclusion of the operations, and their relationship to the deportee shall be ascertained. This is done in order to disclose persons hiding from the police, gendarmes and other persons. After verification of the identity of the detained persons and establishment of the fact that they are persons in whom the contingent is not interested they shall be liberated.

If the inhabitants of the village begin to gather round the deportees' home while operations are in progress, they shall be called upon to disperse to their own homes, and crowds shall not be permitted to form. If the deportee refuses to open the door of his home, notwithstanding that he is aware that the members of the People's Commissariat for Public Security have arrived, the door must be broken down. In individual cases neighbouring operative groups carrying out operations in that locality shall be called upon to help.

The delivery of the deportees from the village to the meeting place at the railway station must be effected during daylight; care, moreover, should be taken that the assembling of every family shall not last more than two hours.

In all cases throughout the operations firm and decisive action shall be taken, without the slightest excitement, noise and panic.

It is categorically forbidden to take any articles away from the deportees except weapons, counter-revolutionary literature and foreign currency, as also to make use of the food of the deportees.

All participants in the operations must be warned that they will be held legally accountable for attempts to appropriate individual articles belonging to the deportees.

5. Procedure for Separating a Deportee's Family from the Head of the Family.

In view of the fact that a large number of deportees must be arrested and distributed in special camps and that their families must proceed to special settlements in distant regions, it is essential that the operations of removal of both the members of the deportee's family and its head shall be carried out simultaneously, without notifying them of the separation confronting them. After the domiciliary search has been carried out and the appropriate identification documents have been drawn up in the deportee's home, the operative worker shall complete the documents of the head of the family and deposit them in the latter's personal file, but the documents drawn up for members of his family shall be deposited in the personal file of the deportee's family. The convoy of the entire family to the station shall, however, be effected in one vehicle and only at the station of departure shall the head of the family be placed from his family in a car specially intended for heads of families.

During the assembling (of the family) in the home of the deportee the head of the family shall be warned that personal male effects must be packed in a separate suitcase, as a sanitary inspection of the deported men will be made separately from the women and children.

At the station of entrainment heads of families subject to arrest shall be loaded into cars specially allotted to them, which shall be indicated by operative workers appointed for that purpose.

6. Procedure for Conveying the Deportees

The assistants convoying the column of deportees in horse-carts are strictly forbidden to sit in the said carts. The assistants must follow alongside and behind the column of deportees. The senior assistant of the convoy shall from time to time go the rounds of the entire column to check the correctness of the movement.

When the column of the deportees is passing through inhabited places or when encountering passers-by, the convoy must be controlled with particular care; those in charge must see that no attempts are made to escape, and no conversation of any kind shall be permitted between the deportees and passers-by.

7. Procedure for Entrainment

At each point of entrainment a member of the operative "troika" and a person specially appointed for that purpose shall be responsible for entrainment.

On the day of entrainment the chief of the entrainment point, together with the chief of the deportation train and of the convoying military forces of the People's Commissariat of Internal Affairs, shall examine the railway cars provided in order to see that they are supplied with everything necessary, and the chief of the entrainment point shall agree with the chief of the deportation train on the procedure to be observed by the latter in accepting delivery of the deportees.

Red Army men of the convoying forces of the People's Commissariat of Internal Affairs shall surround the entrainment station.

The senior members of the operative group shall deliver to the chief of the deportation train one copy of the nominal roll of the deportees in each railway-car. The chief of the deportation train shall, in conformity with this list, call out the name of each deportee, shall carefully check every name and assign the deportee's place in the railway-car.

The deportee's effects shall be loaded into the car, together with the deportee, with the exception of small agricultural inventory, which shall be loaded in a separate car.

The deportees shall be loaded into railway-cars by families; it is not permitted to break up a family (with the exception of heads of families subject to arrest). An estimate of twenty-five persons to a car should be observed.

After the railway-car has been filled with the necessary number of families, it shall be locked.

After the people have been taken over and placed in the deportation train, the chief of the train shall bear responsibility for all persons handed over to him and for their delivery to their destination. After handing over the deportees the senior member of the operative group shall draw up a report on the operation carried out by him and briefly indicate the name of the deportee, whether any weapon and counter-revolutionary literature have been discovered, and also how the operation was carried out.

After having placed the deportees on the deportation train and having submitted reports of the results of the operations to be thus discharged, the members of the operative group shall be considered free and shall act in accordance with the instructions of the chief of the district branch of the People's Commissariat of Public Security.

Deputy People's Commissar of Public Security of the USSR, Commissar of Public Security of the Third Rank (signed):

SEROV.

Authentic: (Signature)

C: Katyn Document from Beria to Stalin Signed by Stalin and Politburo Members Kliment Voroshilov, Vyacheslav Molotov and Anastas Mikoyan

Source: Louisa Vinton, "The Katyn Documents: Politics and History," RFE/RL Research Report, *2, no. 4 (January 22, 1993): 22.*

TOP SECRET

5 March 1940

USSR People's Commissariat for Internal Affairs
March 1940
Moscow

To Comrade Stalin:

A large number of former officers of the Polish Army, former employees of the Polish police and intelligence agencies, members of Polish nationalist, counterrevolutionary parties, members of exposed counterrevolutionary resistance organizations, escapees, and others, all of them sworn enemies of Soviet authority [and] full of hatred for the Soviet system, are currently being held in prisoner-of-war camps of the USSR NKVD and in prisons in the western oblasts of Ukraine and Belarus.

The military and police officers in the camps are attempting to continue their counterrevolutionary activities and are carrying out anti-Soviet agitation. Each of them is waiting only for his release in order to enter actively into the struggle against Soviet authority.

The organs of the NKVD in the western oblasts of Ukraine and Belarus have uncovered a number of counterrevolutionary rebel organizations. Former officers of the Polish Army and police as well as gendarmes have played an active, leading role in all of these organizations.

Among the detained escapees and violators of the state border a considerable number of people have been identified as belonging to counterrevolutionary espionage and resistance organizations.

14,736 former officers, government officials, landowners, policemen, gendarmes, prison guards, settlers in the border region, and intelligence officers (more than 97% of them are Poles) are being kept in prisoner-of-war camps. This number excludes soldiers and junior officers.

They include:

Generals, colonels and lieutenant colonels — 295
Majors and captains — 2,080
Lieutenants, second lieutenants, and ensigns — 6,049
Officers and junior officers of the police, border troops, and gendarmerie —1,030
Rank-and-file police officers, gendarmes, prison guards, and intelligence officers — 5,138
Government officials, landowners, priests, and settlers in border regions —144

18,632 detained people are being kept in prisons in western regions of Ukraine and Belarus (10,685 of them are Poles).

They include:

Former officers —1,207
Former intelligence officers of the police and gendarmerie — 5,141
Spies and saboteurs — 347
Former landowners, factory owners, and government officials — 465
Members of various counterrevolutionary and resistance organizations and various counterrevolutionary elements — 5,345
Escapees — 6,127

In view of the fact that all are hardened and uncompromising enemies of Soviet authority, the USSR NKVD considers it necessary:

1. To instruct the USSR NKVD that it should try before special tribunals
    1) the cases of the 14,700 former Polish officers, government officials, landowners, police officers, intelligence officers, gendarmes, settlers in border regions, and prison guards being kept in prison-of-war camps
    2) and also the cases of 11,000 members of various counterrevolutionary organizations of spies and saboteurs, former landowners, factory owners, former Polish officers, government officials, and escapees who have been arrested and are being held in prisons in the western oblasts of Ukraine and Belarus and apply to them the supreme penalty: shooting.
2. Examination of the cases is to be carried out without summoning those detained

and without bringing charges; the statements concerning the conclusion of the investigation and the final verdict [should be issued] as follows:

a) for persons being held in prison-of-war camps, in the form of certificates issued by the Administration for the Affairs of Prisoners of War of the USSR NKVD;

b) for arrested persons, in the form of certificates issued by the NKVD of the Ukrainian SSR and the NKVD of the Belarusian SSR.

3. The cases should be examined and the verdicts pronounced by a three-person tribunal [*troika*] consisting of Comrades Merkulov, Kabulov, and Bashtakov [head of the first special department of the USSR NKVD].

People's Commissar for Internal Affairs of the USSR

L. Beria

D: Soviet Deportation of the Inhabitants of Eastern Poland in 1939–1941 (Confidential Report, London, December 1943)

Source: "Soviet Deportation of the Inhabitants of Eastern Poland in 1939–1941," Confidential P-66020 Report (London), December 1943, U.S. Department of State, National Archives and Research Administration, Washington, DC (NND 1500, NARS date, July 31, 1973).

The aim of the present report is not to contribute to any further dispute in the camps of the United Nations. We are fully aware that it is in the interests both of Poland and the Soviet Union to re-establish friendly relations based on solid foundations.

Nevertheless, it seems advisable that a few persons, especially selected for this purpose, be confidentially informed of the fate of Polish citizens under Soviet rule, and this to avoid any misunderstanding which may arise and to refute certain false statements emanating from specific sources. It might also prevent a repetition of the regrettable events which took place in Eastern Poland in 1939–1941.

At 3 A.M. on September 17, 1939, M. POTEMKIN, the Deputy People's Commissar for Foreign Affairs, invited M. GRZYBOWSKI, the Polish Ambassador in Moscow and handed him the text of the Soviet Government's note. The Soviet Government declared in their note that in view of the disintegration of authority on Polish territory they found themselves forced to extend their protection to the kindred Ukrainian and White-Ruthenian nations and thus to assure them peace and safety. By their unilateral act the Soviet Government violated the peace treaty they concluded with Poland in 1921 in Riga, and the Polish-Soviet non-aggression pact of 1932, extended five years before the outbreak of the present war until 1945.

It is interesting to juxtapose the text of the Soviet note of September 17, 1939, with the texts of the notes of Catherine the Great, sent between 1766 and 1795 to a number of European powers with a view to justifying the three consecutive partitions of Poland. The argumentation used is incredibly similar. Both Catherine and M. POTEMKIN refer to the alleged state of anarchy in Poland and both of them extend their protection to the Ukrainians and White-Ruthenians, with the sole distinction that the Empress speaks of followers of the Orthodox Church while the Soviet diplomat refers to nationalities.

The analogy in the two argumentations is by no means accidental. M. Vladimir POTEMKIN was the editor of a history of diplomacy in which Catherine's the Great notes were quoted. Therefore they must have been fresh in his memory. /At this time, Catherine failed to realise her aims as the "Ukrainian territories" were never joined in Tsarist Russia and it was only Soviet Russian which endeavored to annex them/.

As a matter of fact, the Soviet "History of Diplomacy" contains a passage which characterises Catherine's diplomatic activities most eloquently:

> Of the old methods of diplomatic action one especially widely in use in Catherine's time was demagogic agitation among the Orthodox population in foreign states. In fact everywhere where Christians were concerned "the Tsars could adopt the pose of liberators" /Marx and Engles/ so as to further their own aims /page 293/.

The theses of M. POTEMKIN received large scale military support, for at 4 A.M. on the day the note was delivered, Soviet troops crossed the Polish frontier. What, at the time, was the position of Poland? Having refused to surrender to German demands and having rejected suggestions of common action against Russia, Poland had to face the first onslaught of the German military machine. The situation was difficult, but not hopeless. Warsaw, Hel, Modlin and the armies fighting near Lublin could have defended themselves much longer, while the last big-scale battle took place on October 4th. Meanwhile in Eastern Poland vast stocks of armaments were amassed and reserves of the Polish Army were concentrating in preparation for a counter-offensive. It was here that 700.000 soldiers of the Red Army fully equipped in tanks and planes, struck their blow. The Polish Army unable naturally enough, to resist blows directed simultaneously from the East and the West, was therefore forced to succumb.

M. MOLOTOV, the People's Commissar for Foreign Affairs, speaking on October 31, 1939, at a meeting of the Supreme Council of the USSR announced the number of prisoners and booty taken by the Red Army and described the course of events in the following words:

> There have been important changes in the international situation during the past two months. This applies above all to Europe but also to countries far beyond the confines of Europe. In this connection we have to bear in mind three principal circumstances which are of decisive importance. Firstly, mention should be made of changes that have taken place in the relations between the Soviet Union and Germany. Since the conclusion of the Soviet-German Non-Aggression Pact on August 23, an end has been put to the abnormal relations that have existed between the Soviet Union and Germany for a number of years. Instead of the enmity which was fostered in every way by certain European powers, we now have a RAPROCHEMENT [sic] and the establishment of friendly relations between the U.S.S.R. and Germany.
>
> The further improvement of these new and good relations, found its reflection in the German-Soviet Treaty on amity and frontier fixation signed in Moscow on Sep-

tember 28. This radical change in the relations between the Soviet Union and Germany two of the biggest States in Europe, was bound to have its effect on the entire international situation. Furthermore events have entirely confirmed the estimation of the political significance of the Soviet-German Rapprochement given at the last Session of the Supreme Soviet.

Secondly, mention must be made of such a fact as the military defeat of Poland and the collapse of the Polish State. The ruling circles of Poland boasted quite a lot about the "stability" of their State and the "might" of their army. However one swift blow to Poland, first by the German Army and then by the Red Army, and nothing was left of this ugly offspring of the Versailles Treaty which had existed by oppressing non-Polish nationalities. The "traditional policy" of unprincipled manoeuvring between Germany and the U.S.S.R., and the playing off of one against the other has proved unsound and has suffered complete bankruptcy.

Thirdly, it must be admitted that the big war that has flared up in Europe has caused radical changes in the entire international situation. This war began as a war between Germany and Poland and turned into a war between Germany on the one hand, and Britain and France on the other. The war between Germany and Poland ended quickly owing to the utter bankruptcy of the Polish leaders. As we know neither British nor French guarantees were of help to Poland. To this day in fact nobody knows what these "guarantees" were. /General laughter/....

The efforts of the British and French Governments to justify this new position of theirs on the ground of their undertakings to Poland, are, obviously unsound. Everybody realizes that there can be no question of restoring old Poland. It is therefore, absurd to continue the present war under the flag of restoration of the former Polish State.

Although the Governments of Britain and France understand this they do not want war stopped and peace restored, but are seeking new excuses for continuing the war with Germany. The ruling circles of Britain and France have been lately attempting to depict themselves at champions of the democratic rights of nations against Hitlerism and the British Government has announced that its aim in the war with Germany is nothing more nor less than the "destruction of Hitlerism". It amounts to this that the British and with them the French supporters of the war have declared something in the nature of an "ideological" war on Germany, reminiscent of the religious wars of olden times. In fact religious wars against heretics and religious dissenters were once the fashion....

In any case under the "ideological" flag there has now been started a war of even greater dimensions and fraught with even greater danger for the peoples of Europe and of the whole world. But there is absolutely no justification for a war of this kind. One may accept or reject the ideology of Hitlerism as well as any other ideological system, that is a matter of political views. But everybody should understand that an ideology cannot be destroyed by force, that it cannot be eliminated by war. It is therefore, not only senseless but criminal to wage such a war as a war for the "destruction of Hitlerism" camouflaged as a fight for "democracy"....

Subsequent events fully confirmed that the new Soviet-German relations were based on a firm foundation of mutual interest. After the Red Army units entered the territory of the former Polish State serious questions arose relating to the delimination [sic] of the State interests of the U.S.S.R. and Germany. Those questions were promptly settled by mutual agreement. The German-Soviet Treaty of amity and delimitation of the frontiers between the two countries which was concluded at the end of September has consolidated our relations with the German State....

/The above quotation is taken from M. Molotov's speeches which were published in London in 1941 by D. N. Pritt, K. C., M. P., but the publication was subsequently withdrawn from circulation. The original text is to be found in "The Fifth Extraordinary Session of the Supreme Council of the USSR," Stenographic Report, published by the Supreme Council of the USSR in 1939/.

Briefly, it can be said that the action against Poland carried out by the German and Soviet armies was based on the Soviet-German pact of August 23, 1939, concluded after the long and fruitless negotiations with the British and French delegations in Moscow. The plans had thus been laid down long in advance of Hitler's attack on Poland and removed the threat of a second front once Poland has been beaten. Having overpowered the Polish Army with their combined forces the German and Soviet Governments accomplished in the Ribbentrop-Molotov pact of September 28, 1939, a fourth partition of Poland. The new Russo-German frontier left 72.800 square miles of Polish territory inhabited by 22.000.000 Polish citizens under German rule and 77.720 square miles inhabited by 13.000.000 Polish citizens under Soviet rule.

The 13.000.000 Polish citizens who found themselves under Soviet occupation comprised /according to the census made in 1931/:

Poles	5.278.400	i.e. 40%
Ukrainians and Ruthenians	4.486.600	i.e. 34%
White-Ruthenians	1.055.680	i.e. 8%
Jews	1.055.680	i.e. 8%
Without declared nationality	923.720	i.e. 7%
Russians	131.060	i.e. 1%
Other nationalities	263.920	i.e. 2%

Thus ten nationalities of five religious creeds inhabit these territories. None of them has an absolute majority, as is evident from the above table, but the Poles constitute the strongest group, both numerically and culturally.

Both Governments undertook in their treaty to safeguard peace on the territories they had conquered and assumed all responsibility for their organisation. Soviet activity in the occupied territories did not at first indicate any intention to refer to the will of the people; on the contrary, the Soviet authorities considered these territories to have been joined to the Soviet Union once and for all by means of the Ribbentrop-Molotov frontier agreement. It so happened, however, that despite the adverse course of the war Poland succeeded in saving the legal continuity of her Government. General Sikorski's constitutional cabinet, appointed by the Polish President in France, received the recognition of all Allied Governments as the legal Polish Government. It was probably therefore in connection with this event that the Soviet Government arrived at the conclusion that it was necessary to create an appearance of legality and decided to refer themselves to the will of the people. Evidently, however, they felt too weak to carry out a plebiscite so they chose a form which neither international law, nor the Soviet constitution envisaged: Commander-in-Chief of the Soviet Army of occupation issued a proclamation fixing October 22nd as the date for an election to two institutions created ad hoc under the name of the National Assembly of Western Ukraine and the National Assembly of Western White-Ruthenia. The proclamation gave no indication of the fact that the Assemblies were to vote either for joining to the Soviet Union or remaining under Polish rule. It was in fact withdrawn two days later and no further pronouncement whether made by the administrative or military Soviet authorities threw any light whatever on the role to be played by the body in question.

The elections to both the national assemblies were carried out according to principles which no democratic state had ever applied. The whole occupied area was divided into constituencies with only one candidate in each. The electorate were left to vote either for or against the candidate. Should the candidate obtain less than half the votes of his constituencies, new elections would have to take place. In fact, however, this procedure was quite useless for candidates were purely and simply appointed by the Soviet authorities which in certain sporadic cases convened open meetings which were alleged to have approved the candidates. Moreover voting "against" implied a quite definite danger, as the voters voted in premises guarded by NKVD officials and the Red Army: if voting "against" they had to cross the card they received, if voting "for," they just threw the card into the urn. In practice voting was compulsory, as the army and political police went round private houses and forced people to go to the voting centres. No wonder therefore that with such a system of franchise the Government candidates obtained more than 90% of the votes.

A full list of the names of the members of both Assemblies has never been published, though it is known from official sources that among the candidates proposed were M. MOLOTOV and Marshal VOROSHILOV, a number of generals of the army of occupation and political personages who had come from Russia and that in the Presidium of the Assemblies among the 43 members whose names were made public in the Soviet press, 11 were personnel of the Red Army. In the Assemblies thus selected the Soviet Government easily found unanimous support for a resolution for the incorporation of Eastern Poland in the Soviet Union. The sole member who opposed the resolution, Mr. VINNICKENKO, a Ukrainian lawyer from Lvov, was subsequently arrested and sentenced to 8 years in prison camp. The agenda of both Assemblies were dealt with with lighting [sic] rapidity: the National Assembly of Western White-Ruthenia sat for a day and a half and the Assembly of Western Ukraine for two days and a half, after which they never met again.

In spite of such proofs of the "will of the people" the Soviet Government never felt secure in the occupied territories. They were well aware that despite the unanimous resolutions /which were neither a plebiscite nor a parliamentary election/ the great majority of the population was ill suited for a communist régime and a considerable proportion was in favour of remaining within the Polish State. Therein lay the reason for the mass deportations of the population to the interior of Russia in the hope that the deportees would disappear in the vast spaces of the Soviet Union and that their place in Poland would be taken by disciplined Soviet citizens. Thus the Soviet authorities adopted the traditional Tsarist policy which in the 18th and 19th centuary [sic] let [sic] to the mass deportation of Poles, Latvians, Lithuanians, Estonians and Ukrainians from their homes to the vast expanses of Russia.

The elimination of active politicians from the area was carried out immediately on the entry of the Red Army into Poland. The political commissars must have been in possession of lists of all the more prominent men in politics, trade unions and cultural associations, for they arrested them literally within the first few days. The first on the lists of those to be arrested were the leaders of Polish, Jewish, Ukrainian and White-

Ruthenian socialist organisations and of the Socialist trade unions. A similar fate met all representatives of every single political party of the four nationalities inhabiting these areas. Most of them, following lengthy investigations were sentenced to anything between five and fifteen years forced labour in concentration camps while many of them were executed. A speech in their memory was delivered by Camille Huysmans, President of the Socialist International, on March 23, 1943, in Caxton Hall, London, when he said inter alia:

> After September 17, 1939, many Socialists met with systematic destruction. They all belonged either to the Polish Socialist Party /PPS/ or to the "Bund". They all played a prominent part in the workers' movement and in the struggle of democracy against fascism and Hitlerism.

Camille Huysmans then quoted the names of 22 Polish, Jewish and Ukrainian leaders of the workers' movement and added:

> Moreover more than 200 members of local Jewish Bund committees and Jewish trade unions were arrested in the towns of Eastern Poland immediately following the entry of the Red Army. The fate of these comrades is still unknown. In all probability they are no longer among the living.

The arrests of members of political, social and professional societies were carried out during the first days of the occupation, and those affected by them were tried and sentenced by special courts of the NKVD. The deportations on the other hand, did not follow upon any specific charges, not even upon sentences of the NKVD special courts, but simply upon orders of the NKVD territorial administrative authorities which transported hundreds of thousands of people to the interior of Russia. Persons subjected to this type of deportation did not know for what period of time they were to be deported. It is therefore to be presumed that it was a case of deportation for life.

The deportations were preceded by a secret registration by the NKVD of all persons who were considered "socially dangerous". What was the criterion employed by the political authorities for including certain individuals among those to be deported? An idea of the criteria used can be had from the examination of an order issued by GUZEVITIUS, People's Commissar for the Interior of Soviet Lithuania, on November 28, 1940, under No.0054. The order instructed the local authorities to compile registers of individuals considered anti-Soviet and socially undesirable. These were classified thus:-

1/ Members of Russian pre-revolutionary political parties; S-R Mensheviks, D-D, Trotskites, anarchists;

2/ Members of contemporary Lithuanian political parties: nationalists, Valdemarasites /pro-German/, Peasants, Christian-Democrats, university students belonging to students' organizations, Shaulisists;

3/ Members of the State Police, gendarmerie and prison staffs;

4/ Officers of the former Tsarist Army and other anti-Bolshevik armies of 1918–1921;

5/ Officers and military judges of the modern Polish and Lithuanian armies;

6/ Volunteers of all non-Bolshevik armies;

7/ Persons removed from the Communist Party;

8/ Refugees, political emigrés and re-emigrés and contraband runners;

9/ Citizens of foreign states, representatives of foreign firms etc.

10/ Persons who have travelled abroad; who are in contact with representatives of foreign states; who are Esperantists or Philatelists;

11/ Officials of Lithuanian ministries;

12/ The staff of the Red Cross and refugees from Poland;

13/ Persons active in local religious parishes: clergymen and secretaries and "active members of religious communities";

14/ Aristocrats, landowners, wealthy merchants, bankers, industrialists, hotel and restaurant proprietors.

This order may be taken as representative of all occupied territories. On carefully examining the categories of deportees it will be seen that they include the majority of persons active in political, social and even economic life. The lists for Lithuania occupied by the Soviets in 1940 included about 700.000 out of a total population of three million. The extent of this action in South-Eastern Poland, Polesie and the Grodno district exceeded the limits laid down in the order we have just quoted. The following were added to the list of socially dangerous elements: university professors, teachers, doctors, engineers, the forestry service, well-to-do peasants and even poor peasants and certain categories of workmen, the families of soldiers of all ranks who went abroad, refugees from other parts of Poland and "speculators," which was a term applied to small traders and merchants. Thus the registers included three to four million people out of a total population of thirteen million.

The registration and the deportations which followed extended also over the families of the persons ennumerated [sic] above, a fact which is characteristic of the communist point of view of guilt and punishment. It is a point of view based on the assumption that an individual is the product of his environment, and therefore if a certain environment produces criminals it must be destroyed. Thus the registers of persons to be deported included even relatively distant connections, sometimes even friends and collaborators, etc. Hence the mass scale of the deportations and the large number of women and children they affected. It is not excluded that the economic factor also played a large part in this connection and that the authorities were simply looking for a labour force with which to fill empty camps, villages, collective farms and "sov-khozs" in Central Russia.

After the registration was completed the Deputy Commissar for the Interior, M. SEROV, signed a decree describing the way in which deportations are to be carried out. The decree says: "The deportation of anti-Soviet elements is a problem of great political importance. The plans for carrying it out must be worked out in minute detail and realised by the "Executive troikas" of each district. This task must be carried out as quietly as possible so as to avoid demonstrations or panic among the local population". The decree covers over ten pages of instructions describing even the minutest detail of the deportations. "In principle the whole operation shall be carried out by the above-mentioned "Executive troikas" at night-time". The deportees may be allowed 20 to 60 minutes time for packing their things. The weight of the baggage of one family cannot exceed 100 kilos /200 lbs/ and can only contain clothes, footwear, underwear, bed-linen, kitchen utensils, food for one month and fishing tackle. Farmers can also take certain simple farming implements with them, though these must be packed in a separate truck so that they cannot be used as arms. Trains must be ready for departure before dawn. Before embarking on the trains, heads of families must be separated and placed in special carriages /hence the great number of families separated even before deportation/. After entrainment the doors and windows of the carriages must be blocked up leaving only an opening for the introduction of food and for eliminating excreta. The decree ends by saying that close collaboration with local communist elements should help in making the final choice of who is to be deported and in ensuring peace among the population remaining behind in the country.

The mass deportation of the population of occupied territories were carried out, apart from the individual arrests of prominent individuals, which were a constantly recurring phenomenon, in four great waves: In February 1940, in April 1940, in June 1940 and in June 1941. The first to go — in February 1940 — were the officials of various branches of the State administration in towns, and settlers, forestry workers and whole villages of farmers and the rural proletariat in the country. This deportation took place during the worst period, in the winter; it found its victims unprepared both materially and psychologically. It affected for the greater part families burdened with small children. One who took part in this drama, a village teacher, thus describes the deportation:

> Beginning with February 10, 1940, the Soviet authorities proceeded systematically to deport, village by village, Polish citizens living in the Eastern provinces. In their action the Soviet authorities did not spare either the sick whom frequently they had to drag out of their beds, nor the poor, the peasants or the farm labourers burdened with enormous families of small children. Epidemics of typhus, measles and whooping-cough soon decimated these children.
>
> It must be taken into consideration that tho fathers of so many small children neither had very great savings nor sufficient strength to work heavily in the severe Russian winter conditions, to which in Poland they were wholly unaccustomed. Under such conditions it is difficult to earn a living for one, let alone for a whole family.

The author of the letter goes on to enumerate the names of over a dozen villages of which the entire populations were deported. He provides the names of the deportees, the number of their dependants, their financial status, etc., all of which indicates that the victims in the country were recruited from the poorest class of workers, tradesmen and peasants.

In April of the same year the second deportation took place. The victims of this were the families of anyone who had been previously arrested or who was suspected of having gone abroad, been a policeman, officer or high official of the State. Among these there were very few able-bodied men and very many women, children and old people. As in the February deportations there were also glaring examples of accidental deportation or deportation of Poles just because they were Poles. Thus for example Maria Smolek and Bronislava Gembarovicz of Lvov, both paralysed old ladies of over 70, were deported just because they were staying with acquaintances in Delatyn; Stanislav Szymanski a deaf-mute tailor was deported from Lvov together with his wife and three small children.

The deportation of June 1940 affected almost exclusively refugees from Western Poland. These were people tired out by the war and their exile and almost every one of them had left another victim of the war on the other side of the Ribbentrop-Molotov line. The compilation of a list of these people was an extremely easy matter as the authorities had announced a few months earlier that every refugee wishing to return to his home under the German occupation must register in a special office where he will receive a special pass for crossing the frontier. This registration included tens of thousands of unfortunates who were later told that their applications for a pass were the reason for their deportation to the interior of the U.S.S.R. To this group were added members of the free professions who were earmarked as counter-revolutionary and small merchants, mostly Jews, defined as "speculators."

The fourth and last wave of deportations took place on the eve of the outbreak of the Russo-German war. In the face of the threat of war the authorities decided to get rid of all the witnesses of and collaborators in their activities in the occupied territories. Thus were deported the members of the so-called local committees consisting of communists and semi-communists, members of the workers' militia and even members of air raid precaution squods [sic]; in a word all those who collaborated with the Soviet authorities. Apart from those the fourth deportation included members of the Polish and Jewish intelligentsia who had so far succeeded in remaining, those who had had anything to do with the army, owners of shops, unemployed who have registered for work and persons inscribed in the files of Committees for Refugees, organised for charitable purposes.

To sum up them, the following categories of citizens were affected by the four mass deportations in the following order:

I. February 1940. In towns: civil servants and local government officials, judges, members of the police forces; in the country: forest workers, settlers, Polish, Ukrainian and White-Ruthenian small farmers /several entire villages/.

II. April 1940. Families of those previously arrested, families of persons escaped abroad, tradesmen /mostly Jews/, farm-labourers from liquidated estates and another group of small farmers of the three nationalities.

III. June 1940. Practically all refugees from Central and Western Poland, small merchants, doctors, engineers, lawyers, journalists, university professors, teachers.

IV June 1941. All belonging to categories enumerated above who had so far evaded deportation, children from summer camps and orphanages.

Independently of the four mass deportations small batches of a dozen or even several score persons were continually being banished to the interior of the USSR.

The deportation plan was not carried out in full on account of the outbreak of the Russo-German war. The four mass deportations included only a part of those figuring in the registers, and this part amounted to about 1.000.000 men, women and children.

It is of course, impossible to compile statistics according to the sex, occupation and nationality of the deportees. According to letters, reports and accounts it has, however, been found possible to establish the following round estimate:

About half the deportees were women and children, for we must remember that the families of persons who had escaped abroad or were simply missing, were also deported. The number of children was increased also as a result of the deportation just before the outbreak of the Russo-German war, and during the first days of the war in June 1941, of the inmates of summer camps and orphanages. These children were placed in Soviet orphanages in Russia and even after the resumption of Polish-Soviet relations only a small number were returned to their parents or were transferred to Polish relief institutions, as the Soviet authorities held that they were children of Soviet citizens. It need not be added that on the way to Russia and in exile the greatest death-rate was among the children.

It is very difficult to classify the deportees according to occupation. A certain idea can, however, be got from the data concerning 120,000 persons registered individually or by their families with the Polish Red Cross in Teheran. Of these 50.2% are workers, tradesmen, farmers and members of the forestry service. Thus half of the deportees belong to the poorest class which the Soviet régime was to liberate from capitalist oppression and bestow with freedom and property. The other groups are soldiers /3%/, judges /8%/, clergymen of all creeds, professors, members of the university teaching staffs /total 11%/, lawyers and engineers /7%/, secondary and elementary school-teachers /4%/, and 12% other small groups.

The deportations affected all the four nationalities inhabiting the occupied areas: Poles, Jews, Ukrainians and White-Ruthenians. As far as politically active elements were concerned those were all affected to an equal degree, whether Poles, Jews, Ukrainians or White-Ruthenians, though in practice left-wing groups were the principal victims. The proportion of those included in mass deportations on the other hand differ for each nationality. About 52% of all the deportees were Poles, 30% Jews, while Ukrainians and White-Ruthenians constituted about 18% to 20%. We cannot however, tell what these figures would have been if the deportation plans had been fully carried out.

The conditions accompanying the deportations were incompatible with the most elementary humane standards. The deportees travelled to their exile in unheated goods trucks, 30 to 50 people per truck with very often no other sustenance that a bucket of hot water once or twice in a day. A train journey like this lasted a fortnight and was followed by another journey by sleigh or cart. No wonder, therefore that the death-rate — especially among old people and children — was appalling.

On reaching their destination the deportees began their new way of life. There were roughly three types of exile:

The first, and undoubtedly the hardest to bear, were the forced labour concentration camps. Persons sentenced to anything from 5 to 15 years by the NKVD courts were sent to those. This did not mean however, that the prisoner, once having served his sentence, would leave the camp, for this, in the Soviet interpretation of a penal system, had as its objective the re-education of a citizen; if the beneficial influence of the camp, had not left its imprint on the prisoner, then his sentence could be extended. In practice "political offenders" rarely come out of a camp even if their health should withstand the severe camp régime, the lack of food and the heavy work.

The forced labour of the concentration camps is employed on canal, railway and factory buildings and in the normal exploitation of Russia's natural riches, i.e. timber felling in almost inaccessible forests, gold mining, work in the sub-arctic mines and work in industries which impair the health. Thus three aims are achieved: large scale pioneer work is done such as no free worker would undertake; elements which in the opinion of the Soviet Government are dangerous to society are separated from the rest of the people; and lastly an enormously profitable undertaking is made possible which constitutes the principle source for financing the administration and army of the NKVD. It is a system which, according to its authors, is more humane than the capital punishment or even prison sentence. It curtails the lives of the prisoners by fact and not by sentence.

A network of such camps covers the whole of Russia and especially its northern areas. The camps are surrounded by characteristic barbed-wire fences with guards' turrets every 60–120 yards. As a rule the camps are located in groups and divided into units and columns of several or even several tens of thousands of men. Dispersed over great scarcely populated regions, equipped with primitive, generally wooden barracks, they are well guarded by the NKVD. Inside these camps political prisoners live together with ordinary criminals who occupy a privileged position and are even engaged on junior administrative jobs. The working day is 12 hours, not including the time spent on parade and on the march to and from work which is often several miles from the camps. The amount of food received depends on the amount of work done, for a piece-work system which is applied. Prisoners who have completed more than 50% but less than 100% of the standard are fed by kitchen No. 1. They receive 1 lb. to 1 and a half lb. of bread once a day and watery soup three times a day. Those who have performed 100% of the standard of work demanded from them get food from the 2nd kitchen: 1½ lbs to 2 lbs. of bread daily and the same watery soup three times a day and some millet gruel after dinner. The third category are the "Stakhanovites" /record workers/ who have accomplished more than 100% of the standard. These get 2 lbs to 2¾ lbs of bread, the rest from the second kitchen plus a slice of dried fish for supper. The fourth kitchen is for the staff and is the best of all, while the fifth is the "penal kitchen" for those who have done less than 50% of the standard and who get ¾ lb to 1 lb. of bread and soup only once a day. Modest money allowances are given only to the "Stakhanovites."

Under conditions such as these the span of human life is indeed very effectively curtailed, especially if we still take into account the severe climate, the very high standard of work demanded of the prisoners /e.g. intellectuals rarely succeed in obtaining 50%/, the absence of adequate clothing and the iron discipline which is in the hands of common criminals. Man falls here to the very depth of moral and physical degradation, he breaks down nervously and exhausts himself physically and soon becomes the victim of one of the many camp epidemics: typhoid, tuberculosis and "tsinga" /a type of scurvy/. One who experienced this gehenna relates that during the winter of 1940–1941 at least 25% of the prisoners in the northern camps met with their death.

The second penal system was applied chiefly to whole families of deportees. These were settled in empty villages far from railway lines or towns. Each village has its own "commander," usually an N.C.O. of the NKVD. The deportees have to work in forests, felling trees and collecting resin, and on roads etc. If they work for other concerns /e.g. saw-mills etc./ the NKVD takes 10% off their wages. The deportees receive no food but are paid for piece-work according to the same system as in the camps. For their money they can buy primitive products in the village shops kept by the authorities while those who do less than 50% of the demanded standard of work are subject to sanctions. The source of livelihood of the Polish deportees were not their wages, but what they obtained from selling the few objects they had brought with them from Poland and parcels sent to them by their families, friends and relations in Poland. The death-rate among this group was smaller than in the camps but those who spent 1939, 1940 and 1941 in the villages of Central Russia did not remain unaffected as regards bodily and mental condition.

The third and last system was applied to persons either single or in families, deported to Kazakhstan and Yakutsk Country etc. Here they were settled in collective farms in the capacity of hired farm labourers for carrying out the most primitive duties such as guarding flocks of sheep in the steppes, digging, carzing [sic, carting] manure and turning manure into fuel, etc. The local population — the Kazakhs, Kirghiz, Yakuts, etc., semi-savages, hardly transformed from the nomadic pastoral stage to the stage of settled farmers, lead a primitive mode of life dwelling in clay huts and "yurts" (tents). To the arrivals from Europe they could only offer the same primitive living conditions, farm-work, sleeping quarters in stables and cow-sheds, and a limited amount of food consisting of a kind of porrage [sic], milk and vegetables. This group of deportees was not in principle subjected to any sort of control, and could move about freely in certain specified areas. Any attempt of escape was of course futile in view of the great desert epanses [sic], the absence of roads and the impossibility of procuring foodstuffs. In conditions like these the deportees were to spend the remainder of their lives, in order to populate remote regions of the Soviet Empire and to supply labour for their semi-savage population.

An end — at least a formal one — to this tragedy of the Polish deportees was to have been put by the Polish-Soviet agreement. The agreement of July 30, 1941, signed in London, stipulated that everyone sentenced for whatever reason, to forced labour in concentration camps, "villages" and places of exile, shall be set free and shall have the right to choose a new place to live in.

In was then that the treck [sic] began of a mass of Polish citizens from camps, villages and places of exile to the seat of the Polish Embassy, to regions where the Polish Army was being organised and to Central Asia where better living conditions were expected to prevail. The Polish Government, aided very effectively by their Allies and by hundreds of social organisations in Britain and the United States, organised immediate relief for all Polish citizens in the form of food, clothing and medical supplies comprising in all some 5.000 tons of valuable commodities. By their regional organisation the Polish authorities accorded their citizens relief in various forms, totaling 110.000.000 roubles. In the course of 1942 and the first half of 1943 about 800 different Polish relief institutions were set up, including orphanages, homes for the disabled, shools [sic], and hospitals. During the second half of 1942 about 115.000 Polish soldiers and civilians left Russia. The men are now serving in the Polish Forces, while the women, children and old people are under the care of Allied governments in Persia, East Africa, India and Mexico.

When the great south-bound treck [sic] ended and the deportees settled down, it became possible to ascertain how many were saved. It was found that barely half of those deported, i.e. about 500.000 could be located. The remainder, i.e. also about half a million had either been retained in the forced labour camps or else remained in the Far North /e.g. in the regions surrounding the Kolyma river/ and could neither leave nor get in touch with the Polish authorities. It can be estimated on the basis of incomplete relations and reports that about 200.000 Polish citizen children and adults died during the period of deportation.

At present, after the severance by Russia of her relations with Poland, those Polish citizens who remained in the Soviet Union are considered by the Soviet authorities as Soviet citizens, while the relief institutions and stores of relief goods, set up by the Polish Government, have been taken over by the Soviet Government. Of the Polish citizens now in Russia who have been located and retained their freedom there are 272.000 including 76.000 children, 96.000 women, 30.000 old persons unfit for work, and about 30.000 members of the families of Polish soldiers serving in the Middle East and the United Kingdom, of Polish airmen, sailors and merchant seamen.

From the day the Soviet Union severed diplomatic relations with Poland, i.e. from April 25, 1943, it has been impossible to accord them any form of organised help whatever.

London, December 1943.

Chapter Notes

Introduction

1. Schulenburg Dispatch, September 10, as cited in William Shirer, *The Rise and Fall of the Third Reich* (Greenwich, CT: Fawcett, 1960), 832.

2. Cited in Shirer, 835.

3. Zbigniew S. Siemaszko, "The Mass Deportations of the Polish Population to the USSR, 1940–1941," in Keith Sword (ed.), *The Soviet Takeover of the Polish Eastern Provinces, 1939–1941* (New York: St. Martin's Press, 1991), 234, n. 9.

As a result of the February 10, 1940, German-Soviet pact, the Soviet Union agreed to provide Germany, in twelve months' time, with 800 million reichsmarks' worth of raw materials and food, specifically, 1 million tons of grain, 900,000 tons of oil derivatives, 100,000 tons of cotton, 500,000 tons of phosphates, 100,000 tons of chromium ore, 500,000 tons of iron ore, 300,000 tons of pig iron, 2,400 kilograms of platinum, and many other raw materials. Aleksander Bregman, *Najlepszy sojusznik Hitlera: Studium o współpracy niemiecko-sowieckiej 1939–1941,* 3d ed. (London: Orbis, 1967), 104. See his chapter 9, "Współpraca wojskowa i gospodarcza."

German military records indicate that until June 1941 the Soviet Union actually did provide the Wehrmacht with English zinc and rubber, one million tons of grain, 500,000 tons of wheat, 900,000 tons of oil derivatives, 100,000 tons of flax, 80 million reichsmarks' worth of lumber, and an unspecified amount of manganese and platinum. See Documentary Survey by Vice-Admiral Ossman, *Trials of War Criminals Before the Nuremberg Military Tribunals*, vol. 34 (Washington, D.C.: U.S. Government Printing Office, 1951–52), 674.

See also Edward E. Ericson, *Feeding the German Eagle: Soviet Economic Aid to Nazi Germany, 1933–1941* (Westport, CT: Praeger, 1999).

4. Some of these measures have been documented, albeit in a summary fashion, in Tadeusz Piotrowski, *Poland's Holocaust: Ethnic Strife, Collaboration with Occupying Forces and Genocide in the Second Republic, 1918–1947* (Jefferson, NC: McFarland, 1998), chapters 1 and 2.

5. George Kennan, *Siberia and the Exile System* (London: James R. Osgood, McIlvaine & Co., 1891; New York: Praeger Publishers, 1970), vol. 1, 82.

6. Kennan, vol. 2, 280, n. 1, basing himself on Sergei Maxímof (who had access to the official records), *Siberia and Penal Servitude* (St. Petersburg, 1871), vol. 3, 80–81.

7. Stanisław Ciesielski, Wojciech Materski, Andrzej Paczkowski, *Represje sowieckie wobec Polaków i obywateli polskich* (Warszawa: Ośrodek Karta, 2002), 4–6.

8. Józef Lewandowski, "Rosjanie o Europie Wschodniej i Polsce," *Zeszyty Historyczne*, no. 126 (1998): 180–82. See also Mikołaj Iwanow, *Pierwszy naród ukarany: Polacy w Związku Radzieckim 1921–1939* (Warszawa: Państwowe Wydawnictwo Naukowe, 1991), 324–78; Stanisław Morozow, "Deportacje polskiej ludności cywilnej z

radzieckich terenów zachodnich w głąb ZSRR w latach 1935–1936," *Pamięc i sprawiedliwość: Biuletyn Głównej Komisji Badania Zbrodni przeciwko Narodowi Polskiemu—Instytutu Pamięci Narodowej* 40 (1997–98): 267–81; and Andrzej Paczkowski, "Poland, the 'Enemy Nation,'" in Stéphene Courtois, et al., *The Black Book of Communism: Crimes, Terror, Repression,* trans. by Jonathan Murphy and Mark Kramer (Cambridge, MA: Harvard University Press, 1999), 366–67.

9. Ciesielski et al., 33.

10. Keith Sword, *Deportation and Exile: Poles in the Soviet Union, 1939–48* (London: St. Martin's Press, 1994), viii-ix, 17–18.

11. *Dokumenty uzyskane przez Wojskową Komisję Archiwalną w okresie wrzesień 1992-czerwiec 1993* (Warszawa, 1993). (Xerox copies.)

12. See the URL Internet posting: http:// www.indeks.karta.org.pl. For a summary of the findings see Ciesielski et al.

13. Daniel Boćkowski, *Czas nadziei: Obywatele Rzeczypospolitej Polskiej w ZSRR i opieka nad nimi placówek polskich w latach 1940–1943* (Warszawa: Neriton and Instytut Historii PAN, 1999), 59–66.

14. Wojciech Materski, "Martyrologia obywateli polskich na wschodzie po 17 września 1939 r.," in Andrzej Skrzypek et al., eds. *Zbrodnicza ewakuacja więzień i arresztów NKWD na Kresach Wschodnich II Rzeczypospolitej w czerwcu-lipcu 1941 roku: Materiały z sesji naukowej w 55. rocznicę ewakuacji więźniów NKWD w głąb ZSRR (Łódź, 10 czerwca 1996 r.)* (Warszawa: Główna Komisja Badania Zbrodni przeciwko Narodowi Polskiemu, Instytut Pamięci Narodowej, 1997), 8–9.

15. Ciesielski et al., 15–21. The table on p. 33 (see below) presents different figures for the second and third deportations: 61,000 and 79,000, respectively. The text in that work differs somewhat from the total presented in the table: table total deported—320,000; text (p. 18) total deported—309,000–327,000. The various categories in the table are as follows (most totals are rounded off to the nearest thousand):

Soviet Repressions Against the Poles

I. 1939–41	
A. Total POWs and internees	45,387
1. POWs shot [Katyn, Kharkov, Kalinin (now Tver)]	14,587
2. POWs and internees in captivity to Aug. 1941	26,200
3. Deceased and missing POWs	2,300
4. Discharged, arrested in camps and handed over to Germans (1940–41	2,300
B. Total arrested in Eastern Poland (*Kresy Wschodnie*)	110,000
1. In so-called Western Ukraine	65,000
2. In so-called Western Belorussia	43,000
3. In Lithuania [*Wileńszczyzna* area of Poland]	2,000
C. Total deported	320,000
1. On February 10, 1940	140,000
2. On April 13, 1940	61,000
3. In June 1940	79,000
4. In June 1941	40,000
II. 1941–44	
A. Arrested	3,000
III. After 1944	
A. Interned 1944–45	42,000
B. Arrested and deported	50,000
Grand Total	570,387

16. Lewandowski, 182–83.

17. Boćkowski, 92, 377.

18. See Elżbieta Wróbel and Janusz Wróbel, *Rozproszeni po świecie: Obozy i osiedla uchodźców polskich ze Związku Sowieckiego 1942–1950* (Chicago: n.p., 1992), 12–13.

19. See Sławomir Kalbarczyk, "Żydzi wśród ofiar zbrodni sowieckich w latach 1939–1941," *Pamięc i sprawiedliwość: Biuletyn Głównej Komisji Badania Zbrodni przeciwko Narodowi Polskiemu—Instytutu Pamięci Narodowej* 40 (1997–1998): table on p. 194.

20. See Skrzypek et al., especially pp. 10–11 of the article by Materski. See also Sławomir Kalbarczyk, "Zbrodnie sowieckie na obywatelach polskich w okresie wrzesień 1939—sier-

pień 1941: Próba oceny skali zjawiska oraz szacunku strat ludzkich," *Pamięc i sprawiedliwość: Biuletyn Głównej Komisji Badania Zbrodni przeciwko Narodowi Polskiemu—Instytutu Pamięci Narodowej* 39 (1996): 28, 34, 268.

21. See, for example: Bogdan Musiał, "Stosunki polsko-żydowskie na Kresach Wschodnich RP pod okupacją sowiecką (1939–1941)," *Biuletyn Kwartalny Radomskiego Towarzystwa Naukowego,* 34, no. 1 (1999): 103–25; Jerzy Robert Nowak, *Przemilczane zbrodnie: Żydzi i Polacy na Kresach w latach 1939–1941* (Warszawa: von Borowiecky, 1999); and Mark Paul, "Jewish-Polish Relations in Soviet-Occupied Eastern Poland, 1939–1941" in the collective work, *The Story of Two Shtetls: Brańsk and Ejszyszki,* Part Two (Toronto: The Polish Educational Foundation in North America, 1998), 173–230.

22. In Irena Grudzińska-Gross and Jan Tomasz Gross, eds., *W czterdziestym nas matko na Sybir zesłali... Polska a Rosja 1939–1942* (London: Aneks, 1983), 307. This is a much larger volume with many more accounts than the English edition (see following note).

23. In Irena Grudzińska-Gross and Jan Tomasz Gross, eds., *War Through Children's Eyes: The Soviet Occupation of Poland and the Deportations, 1939–1941* (Stanford, CA: Hoover Institution Press, 1985), 118–19.

24. "The Life of Archpriest Avvakum by Himself," cited in Serge A. Zenkovsky (ed.), *Medieval Russia's Epics, Chronicles, and Tales* (New York: E. P. Dutton, 1963), 331, 338–39. Avvakum became a priest at the age of 20 and joined, in early 1640s, the revival movement of the Zelots of Piety, or Seekers After God (Bogoliubtsy). For this, he and his followers were persecuted by Patriarch Nikon and the government.

25. Cited in Wróbel and Wróbel (1992), 21.

26. Cited in Zenkovsky (ed.), 339.

27. In Kalbarczyk, 1996, 14, n. 4.

28. Cited in Wróbel and Wróbel (1992), 31–32.

29. Ibid., 28, n. 38.

30. See the May 25, 1942, report of a deputy delegate in Samarkand, cited in Wróbel and Wróbel (1992), 52.

31. Ciesielski et al., 20–21.

32. Wróbel and Wróbel (1992), 63.

33. In Grudzińska-Gross and Gross, eds., *War Through Children's Eyes,* xxv.

34. See the penultimate paragraph in the British Document D (above): "Soviet Deportation of the Inhabitants of Eastern Poland in 1939–1941."

35. Klaus Hergt, *Exiled to Siberia: A Polish Child's World War II Journey* (Cheboygan, MI: Crescent Lake Publishers, 2000), 182.

36. Ibid., 183.

1. Deportation

1. Milewski family memoir in my possession, compiled and translated by Stanisław Antoni Milewski, consisting of the diary of his mother (Sabina) and sister (Teresa) as well as his own recollections.

2. Nina and Janusz Smenda (eds.), *Unforgettable Memories: Memoirs of Polish Exiles in the Soviet Union, 1940–1942* (Perth, Western Australia: Polish Siberian Group [WA], 1996), 10–13.

3. Alicia A. Zarzycki and Stefania Buczak -Zarzycka, *Kwaheri Africa: A Polish Experience 1939–1950, from Deportation to Freedom* (Perth, Western Australia: n.p., [1985]), 1–3.

4. Tadeusz Pieczko's memoir, in my possession.

5. Smenda, 69.

6. Ibid., 147.

7. Ibid., 256.

8. Marysia Pienta, "Only a Chapter in the Road to Freedom," in *Poles of Santa Rosa: Our 50th Anniversary, 1946–1996,* a commemoration booklet without pagination published in Chicago in 1996.

9. Smenda, 107–10.

10. Ibid., 169–70.

11. Ibid., 64.

12. Anita Paschwa-Kozicka, *My Flight to Freedom: An Autobiography* (Chicago: Panorama Publishing Co., 1996), 24, 27–28.

13. Eva [Ursula Sowińska, *née* Rossowska], "Trial by Torture: Out of the Depths," *Pier Illini* (University Archives, University of Illinois at Chicago) (Literary Supplement, May 24, 1954): 1.

14. Anna Mineyko, "Through the Mists of Time," http://www.interlog.com/~mineykok/anna.html#war

15. Smenda, 266–68.

16. Ibid., 121–24.
17. Ibid., 51–52.
18. Maria Gabiniewicz, *W stronę domu ojczystego przez Syberię, Kazachstan, Uzbekistan, Turkmenię, Persję, Indie, Afrykę* (Warszawa: Oficyna Wydawniczo-Poligraficzna "Adam," 2000), 9, 11–12.
19. Jane [Janina] Żebrowski-Bulmahn, *Long Journey Home* (New York: iUniverse.com, 2000), 1–3, 17–18.

2. Soviet Union

1. Milewski family memoir.
2. Smenda, 14–15.
3. Zarzycki and Buczak-Zarzycka, 4–6.
4. Pieczko memoir.
5. Smenda, 71–72.
6. Ibid., 147–49.
7. Ibid., 257–58.
8. Pienta.
9. Smenda, 110–11.
10. Ibid., 172–73.
11. Ibid., 85–86.
12. Ibid., 236–38.
13. Paschwa-Kozicka, *My Flight to Freedom*, 28–32.
14. Eva, 1–2.
15. Mineyko.
16. Smenda, 268–69.
17. Ibid., 54–55.
18. Gabiniewicz, 12–13.
19. Żebrowski-Bulmahn, 23–25.

3. Amnesty

1. Milewski family memoir.
2. Smenda, 20–25.
3. Zarzycki and Buczak-Zarzycka, 7–16.
4. Pieczko memoir.
5. Smenda, 3–76.
6. Ibid., 149–50.
7. Ibid., 259–60.
8. Ibid., 91–92.
9. Anita Paschwa-Kozicka, "My Road to Freedom," in *Poles of Santa Rosa: Our 50th Anniversary, 1946–1996*, a commemoration booklet without pagination published in Chicago in 1996.
10. Smenda, 56–60.
11. Gabiniewicz, 13–15.
12. Żebrowski-Bulmahn, 27–44.

4. Near and Middle East

1. *Tułacze dzieci, Exiled Children* (Warszawa: Fundacja Archiwum Fotograficzne Tułaczy, 1995), 22–27.
2. Milewski family memoir.
3. Smenda, 26–28.
4. Zarzycki and Buczak-Zarzycka, 17–19.
5. Pieczko memoir.
6. Smenda, 76.
7. Paschwa-Kozicka, "My Road to Freedom."
8. Smenda, 60.
9. Żebrowski-Bulmahn, 47–48.
10. *Tułacze dzieci*, 18–20.
11. Milewski family memoir.
12. Smenda, 29.
13. Zarzycki and Buczak-Zarzycka, 19–22.
14. Pieczko memoir.
15. From Marysia Pienta's letter (2.14.03) to me.
16. Paschwa-Kozicka, "My Road to Freedom."
17. Gabiniewicz, 16–17.
18. Żebrowski-Bulmahn, 48–53.
19. *Tułacze dzieci*, 29–31.
20. Smenda, 81.
21. Ibid., 245–46.
22. Paschwa-Kozicka, "My Road to Freedom."
23. *Tułacze dzieci*, 38–40.
24. Smenda, 30–31.
25. Zarzycki and Buczak-Zarzycka, 22–23.
26. *Tułacze dzieci*, 48.
27. Ibid., 60.
28. Ibid., 68–69.
29. Ibid., 72.
30. Milewski family memoir.
31. Ibid.

5. India

1. *Tułacze dzieci*, 80–83.
2. Ibid., 84–86.
3. Ibid., 92–93.
4. Ibid., 100–01.
5. Smenda, 32.
6. Zarzycki and Buczak-Zarzycka, 23.
7. Pieczko memoir.
8. Żebrowski-Bulmahn, 54–57.
9. Pieczko memoir.
10. Paschwa-Kozicka, "My Road to Freedom."

6. *Africa*

1. *Tułacze dzieci*, 128–32.
2. Smenda, 33–34.
3. *Tułacze dzieci*, 133.
4. Smenda, 36–37.
5. Ibid., 272–74.
6. *Tułacze dzieci*, 138–39.
7. Henryka Utnik-Łappo, "Afrykańczycy — Wspominając tamte dni," *Związkowiec,* no. 19 (December 10, 1998): section B, 22.
8. Smenda, 34–36.
9. *Tułacze dzieci*, 145–47.
10. Zarzycki and Buczak-Zarzycka, 24–72.
11. Smenda, 246–47.
12. Ibid., 61–62.
13. *Tułacze dzieci*, 156–58.
14. Ibid., 159–62.
15. Ibid., 172–73.
16. Ibid., 178.
17. Ibid., 186–87.
18. Ibid., 191–92.
19. Ibid., 196–97, 202–05.
20. Smenda , 232–33.
21. *Tułacze dzieci*, 209–11.
22. Ibid., 221–23.
23. Ibid., 227.
24. Ibid., 231–32.
25. Ibid., 237–38.
26. Ibid., 245–47.

7. *New Zealand*

1. *Tułacze dzieci*, 256–57.
2. Ibid., 262–65.
3. Krystyna Skwarko, *The Invited: The Story of 733 Polish Children who Grew up in New Zealand* (Ngaio, Wellington 4, New Zealand: Millwood Press, 1974), 51–80.
4. Maria van der Linden, *An Unforgettable Journey* (Palmerston North, NZ: Dunmore Press, 1994). Electronic version by Roman Antoszewski. Retrieved from http://polish.ssni.ca/BIBL-CONS/LINDEN/HTM/L13.HTM

8. *Mexico*

1. Elżbieta Wróbel and Janusz Wróbel. "Spotkanie w Santa Rosa." *Dziennik Związkowy* (July 23–25, 1993).
2. Pieczko memoir.
3. Paschwa-Kozicka, "My Road to Freedom."
4. Żebrowski-Bulmahn, 58–77.
5. *Tułacze dzieci*, 274–75.

Bibliography

Achmatowicz, Teresa, et al., eds. *Zbiegli się żurawie z daleka: Światowy zjazd koła Polaków z Indii z lat 1942–1948. Warszawa, 25–26 lipca, 1992.* N.p.: n.p., 1993.

Ain Karem — Ośrodek polskich dziewcząt. Palestyna 1942–1947. London: Związek Ain Karem, 1988.

Allbrook, Maryon, and Helen Cattalini. *The General Langfitt Story: Polish Refugees Recount Their Experiences of Exile, Dispersal, and Resettlement.* Canberra: Australian Govt. Pub. Service, 1995.

Baczkowski, Włodzimierz. "Polacy w Czerwonej Rosji." *Myśl Polska* 11/33 (1937).

Bak, Eugene. *Life's Journey: Autobiography.* Boulder, CO: East European Monographs, 2002.

Barański, Kamil. *W trzy strony świata: Szkolnictwo polskie poza granicami kraju w czasie drugiej wojny światowej.* Hove: Caldra House, 1991.

Bardach, Janusz, and Kathleen Gleeson. *Man is Wolf to Man: Surviving the Gulag.* Berkeley: University of California Press, 1998.

Bardel, Marcin. *Z Krasnobrodu przez obozy i obczyznę do rodzinnych stron.* Lublin: Oddział Lubelski Stowarzyszenia "Wspólnota Polska," 1994.

Beaupré-Stankiewicz, Irena, Danuta Waszczuk-Kamieniecka, and Jadwiga Lewicka-Howells, eds. *Isfahan: City of Polish Children.* 3d ed. Hove, Sussex, UK: Association of Former Pupils of Polish Schools, Isfahan and Lebanon, 1989. Polish ed. *Isfahan: Miasto polskich dzieci.* London: Koło Wychowanków Szkół Polskich Isfahan i Liban, 1987.

Bełdowski, Leszek, et al., eds. *Polacy w Indiach 1942–1948 w świetle dokumentów i wspomnień. Praca zbiorowa.* London: Koło Polaków z Indii 1942–1948, 2000.

Boćkowski, Daniel. *Czas nadziei: Obywatele Rzeczypospolitej Polskiej w ZSRR i opieka nad nimi placówek polskich w latach 1940–1943.* Warszawa: Neriton and Instytut Historii PAN, 1999.

______. *Jak pisklęta z gniazd: Dzieci polskie w ZSRR w okresie II wojny światowej.* Wrocław: Polskie Towarzystwo Ludoznawcze; Warszawa: Urząd d/s Kombatantów i Osób Represjonowanych, 1995.

Bodnar, Tadeusz. *Znad Niemna przez Sybir do II Korpusu.* Wrocław: Nortom, 1997.

Bogusz, Janina. *Koszmarne Wspomnienia: Wspomnienia deportacji do sowieckiego imperium w latach 1940–1943.* Montreal: n.p., 2002.

Buczek, Roman. "Działalność opiekuńcza Ambasady R.P. w ZSRR w latach 1941–1943." *Zeszyty Historyczne* 29 (1974): 42–115.

Budziarek, Marek, et al., eds. *My Sybiracy.* Łódź: Związek Sybiraków. Oddział Wojewódzki, 1990.

Bugaj, Nikołaj F. "'Specjalna teczka Stalina' Deportacje i reemigracja Polaków." *Zeszyty Historyczne* 107 (1994): 76–140.

Bugaj, Tadeusz. *Dzieci polskie w krajach pozaeuropejskich 1939–1949.* Jelenia Góra, 1984.

Bukowiński, Władysław. *Wspomnienia z Kazachstanu.* Lublin: "Spotkania," 1980.

Byrska, Maria. *Ucieczka z zesłania.* Gdańsk: "Suplement 2," 1987.

Caban, Ireneusz. *Polacy internowani w ZSRR w latach 1944–1947: Transporty i obozy.* Lublin: Wydawnictwo Lubelskie, 1990.

Ciesielski, Stanisław. *Polacy w Kazachstanie 1940–1946: Zesłańcy lat wojny.* Worcław: W Kolorach Tęczy, 1997.

_____, Grzegorz Hryciuk, and Aleksander Srebrakowski. *Masowe deportacje radzieckie w okresie II wojny światowej.* 2d ed. Wrocław: Instytut Historyczny Uniwersytetu Wrocławskiego i Wrocławskie Towarzystwo Miłośników Historii, 1994.

_____, Wojciech Materski, and Andrzej Paczkowski. *Represje sowieckie wobec Polaków i obywateli polskich.* Warszawa: Ośrodek Karta, 2002.

Cisek, Andrzej. *Nieludzka ziemia w oczach dziecka.* Kaków: Jagiellonian University Press, 2000.

Conquest, Robert. *Kolyma: The Arctic Death Camps.* New York: Oxford University Press, 1979.

_____. *The Soviet Deportation of Nationalities.* New York: St. Martin's Press, 1960.

Courtois, Stéphene, et al. *The Black Book of Communism: Crimes, Terror, Repression.* Trans. by Jonathan Murphy and Mark Kramer. Cambridge, MA: Harvard University Press, 1999.

Czapski, Józef. *The Inhuman Land.* Trans. by Gerald Hopkins. London: Polish Cultural Foundation, 1987.

Czerniakiewicz, Jan. *Przemieszczenia Polaków i Żydów na kresach wschodnich II Rzeczpospolitej i w ZSRR 1939–1959.* Warszawa: Centrum Badania Wschodnich UW, 1991.

_____. *Repatriacja ludności z ZSRR 1944–1948.* Warszawa: Państwowe Wydawnictwo Naukowe, 1987.

D'Arc, Mary. "Colonia Santa Rosa in Mexico." *Polish American Studies* 19, no. 1 (1962): 45–56.

"Deportacje." *Biuletyn Historycznej Agencji Informacyjnej* 3 (January 31, 1995): 5–6.

Deutsch, Leo. *Sixteen Years in Siberia: Some Experiences of a Russian Revolutionist.* Trans. by Helen Chisholm. Westport, CT: Hyperion Press, 1977; London: John Murray, 1905.

Doktor, Grażyna, et al., comps. *Deportacje i przemieszczenia ludności polskiej w głąb ZSRR 1939–1945: Przegląd piśmiennictwa.* Warszawa: Państwowe Wydawnictwo Naukowe, 1989.

Dokumenty uzyskane przez Wojskową Komisję Archiwalną w okresie wrzesień 1992-czerwiec 1993. Warszawa, 1993. (Xerox copies.)

Dowling, Alick. *Janek: A Story of Survival.* Letchworth, Herts, England: Ringpress, 1989.

Draus, Jan. *Junacka szkoła kadetów w Palestynie 1942–1946.* Kraków: Rocznik Komisji Nauk Pedagogicznych, 1988.

_____. *Oświata i nauka polska na Bliskim i Środkowym Wschodzie 1939–1950.* Lublin: Towarzystwo Naukowe Katolickiego Uniwersytetu Lubleskiego, 1993.

_____. *Polskie szkoły w Tel-Awiwie 1940–1947.* Kraków: Rocznik Komisji Nauk Pedagogicznych, 1987.

Dubanowicz, Edward and Magdalena. *Na placówce w Ajaguz, 1941–2r.: Wspomnienia z zesłania do Kazakstanu 1940–1942, spisane w 1942–1945 r.* London: Polish Cultural Foundation, 1976.

Dubanowicz, Magdalena. *Na mongolskich bezdrożach: Wspomnienia z zesłania 1940–1942 spisane w 1943–45.* London: Polska Fundacja Kulturalna, 1974.

Dzierżek, Edward W. *Free the White Eagle.* Horning's Mills, ON: Self-published, 1981.

Egan, Eileen. *For Whom There Is No Room: Scenes from the Refugee World.* New York: Paulist Press, 1995.

Ekart, Antoni. *Vanished Without Trace: The Story of Seven Years in Soviet Russia.* London: Max Parrish, 1954.

Eva [Ursula Sowińska, *née* Rossowska]. "Trial by Torture: Out of the Depths." *Pier Illini* (University Archives, University of Illinois at Chicago) (Literary Supplement, May 24, 1954): 1–2.

Fedorowicz, Tadeusz. *Drogi opatrzności.* Lublin: Norbertinum, 1991.

Gabel, Dina. *Behind the Ice Curtain.* Lakewood, NJ: C.I.S. Publishers, 1992.

Gabiniewicz, Maria. *W stronę domu ojczystego przez Syberię, Kazachstan, Uzbekistan, Turkmenię, Persję, Indie, Afrykę.* Warszawa: Oficyna Wydawniczo-Poligraficzna "Adam," 2000.

Garbacz, Dionizy, and Andrzej Zagórski. *W kleszczach Czerwonych.* Rzeszów-Brzozów: Muzeum

Regionalne im. A. Fastnachta w Brzozowie i Zarząd Regionu NSZZ "Solidarność" w Rzeszowie, 1991.

Gladun, Christopher. "Poland's Holocaust: A Family Chronicle of Soviet and Nazi Terror." http://www.geocities.com/CapitolHill/Parliament/6764/intro.html

Gliksman, Jerzy. *Tell the West: An Account of His Experiences as a Slave Laborer in the Union of Soviet Socialist Republics.* New York: The Gresham Press, 1948.

Głowacki, Albin. *Ocalić i repatriować: Opieka nad ludnością polską w głębi terytorium ZSRR 1943–1946.* Łódź: Wydawnictwo Uniwersytetu Łódzkiego, 1994.

_____. *Sowieci wobec Polaków na ziemiach wschodnich II Rzeczypospolitej, 1939–1941.* Łódź: Wydawnictwo Uniwersytetu Łódzkiego, 1997.

Goldberger, Janka. *Stalin's Little Guest.* London: Janus Publishing Company, 1995.

Górski, Jerzy W. *Głodne stepy.* London: Polska Fundacja Kulturalna, 1989.

Gross, Jan Tomasz. *Revolution from Abroad: The Soviet Conquest of Poland's Western Ukraine and Western Belorussia.* Princeton: Princeton University Press, 1988.

Grudzińska-Gross, Irena, and Jan Tomasz Gross, eds. *W czterdziestym nas matko na Sybir zesłali... Polska a Rosja 1939–1942.* London: Aneks, 1983. Engl. ed. *War Through Children's Eyes: The Soviet Occupation of Poland and the Deportations, 1939–1941.* Stanford, CA: Hoover Institution Press, 1985.

Gurjanow, Aleksandr. "Cztery deportacje 1940–1941." *Karta* 12 (1994): 114–36.

Hautzig, Esther Rudomin. *The Endless Steppe: Growing Up in Siberia.* New York: Thoman Y. Crowell Co., 1968.

Haw, Irena. *Na szlaku Praojców: Sowieckie wspomnienia z lat 1940–1941.* Wrocław: Polskie Towarzystwo Ludoznawcze, 1995.

Hergt, Klaus. *Exiled to Siberia: A Polish Child's World War II Journey.* Cheboygan, MI: Crescent Lake Publishers, 2000.

Herling, Gustaw. *A World Apart.* Trans. by Joseph Marek. Westport, CT: Greenwood Press, 1974.

Hobler, Janina. *Polonistka w mundurze: Ze Lwowa przez Sowiety, Iran, Irak, Palestyne do Wielkiej Brytanii.* London: Oficyna Poetów i Malarzy, 1982.

Hort, Weronika (Hanka Ordonówna, pseud.). *Tułacze dzieci.* Warszawa: Państwowy Instytut Wydawniczy, 1990.

Iwanow, Mikołaj. *Pierwszy naród ukarany: Polacy w Związku Radzieckim 1921–1939.* Warszawa: Państwowe Wydawnictwo Naukowe, 1991.

_____. *Polacy w Związku Radzieckim w latach 1921–1939.* Wrocław: Wydawnictwo Uniwersytety Wroławskiego, 1990.

Jacewicz, Alfons. *Santa Rosa: Osiedle polskie w Meksyku.* London: n.p., 1965.

Januszkiewicz, Maria. *Kazachstan.* Paris: Instytut Literacki, 1981.

Jarzębowski, J. "Polskie szkoły w Meksyku," *Wychowanie Ojczyste* 1, no. 32 (January–February 1961).

Jolluck, Katherine. *Exile and Identity: Polish Women in the Soviet Union During World War II.* Pittsburgh: University of Pittsburgh Press, 2002.

Kalbarczyk, Sławomir. *Wykaz łagrów sowieckich miejsc przymusowej pracy obywateli polskich w latach 1939–1943.* Part One. Warszawa: Główna Komisja Badania Zbrodni przeciwko Narodowi Polskiemu — Instytut Pamięci Narodowej, 1993.

_____. "Zbrodnie sowieckie na obywatelach polskich w okresie wrzesień 1939 — sierpień 1941: Próba oceny skali zjawiska oraz szacunku strat ludzkich." *Pamięc i sprawiedliwość: Biuletyn Głównej Komisji Badania Zbrodni przeciwko Narodowi Polskiemu— Instytutu Pamięci Narodowej* 39 (1996): 13–35.

_____. "Żydzi wśród ofiar zbrodni sowieckich w latach 1939–1941." *Pamięc i sprawiedliwość: Biuletyn Głównej Komisji Badania Zbrodni przeciwko Narodowi Polskiemu— Instytutu Pamięci Narodowej* 40 (1997–98): 173–94.

Kant, Anna, and Norbert Kant. *Extermination: Killing Poles in Stalin's Empire.* Trans. by Barbara O'Driscoll. London: Roma Kant-Ravid Foundation, Unicorn Publishing Studio, 1991. Polish ed. *Zesłani na zagładę.* London: Unicorn, 1990.

Karol, K. S. *Between Two Worlds: The Life of a Young Pole in Russia, 1939–46*. Trans. by Eamonn McArdle. New York: Holt, 1987.

_____. Solik: *Life in the Soviet Union, 1939–1946*. Trans. by Eamonn McArdle. Wolfeboro, NH: Pluto Press, 1986.

Kawecka, Zdzisława Krystyna. *Do Anglii przez Syberię*. Wrocław: Polskie Towarzystwo Ludoznawcze, 1994. Engl. ed. *Journey Without a Ticket: To England Through Siberia*. Nottingham, England: Z. K. Kawecka, 1994.

Kaz-Ostaszewicz, Kazimierz. *Długie drogi Syberii*. London: Oficyna Poetów i Malarzy, 1984. Gdańsk: "Prymat," 1997.

Kennan, George. *Siberia and the Exile System*. 2 vols. London: James R. Osgood, McIlvaine & Co., 1891; New York: Praeger Publishers, 1970.

Kesting, Robert W. "American Support of Polish Refugees and Their Santa Rosa Camp." *Polish American Studies* 48, no. 1 (1991): 79–90.

Klukowski, Bogdan, comp. *My deportowani: Wspomnienie Polaków z więzień, łagrów i zsyłek w ZSRR [Czapski, Grubiński, Herling-Grudziński, Krakowiecki, Obertyńska, Umiastowski]*. Warszawa: Alfa, 1989.

Kochanowicz, Tadeusz. *W Komi i gdzie indziej: Wspomnienia z pobytu z ZSRR, 1939–1942*. Warszawa: Pelikan, 1989.

Kojder, Apolonja Maria, and Barbara Głogowska. *Marynia Don't Cry: Memoir of Two Polish-Canadian Families*. Toronto: Multicultural History Society of Ontario, 1995.

Kopisto, Wacław. *Droga cichociemnego do łagrów Kołymy*. Warszawa: Oficyna Wydawnicza Volumen, 1990.

Kowal, Jan S. *My First Survival or My Life in Poland and in the USSR*. Ann Arbor, MI: n.p., 1992.

Kowalska, Ewa. *Przeżyć, aby wrócić! Polscy zesłańcy lat 1940–1941 w ZSRR i ich losy do roku 1946*. Warszawa: Neriton and Instytut Historii PAN, 1998.

Krakowiecki, Anatol. *Książka o Kołymie*. London: Veritas, 1987.

Kramek, John S. *Refugee's Trails*. St. Clair Shores, MI: Refugee's Trails Fund, Inc., 1990.

Kranc, Remigiusz. *W drodze z Ostroga na Kołymę*. Kraków: Ośrodek "Wołanie z Wołynia," 1998.

Królikowski, Lucjan. *Skradzione dzieciństwo*. London: Veritas, 1960. Engl. ed. *Stolen Childhood: A Saga of Polish War Children*. Trans. by Kazimierz J. Rozniatowski. Buffalo, NY: Father Justin Rosary Hour, 1983.

Krupa, Michael. *Shallow Graves in Siberia*. Ed. by Thomas Lane. London: Minerva Press, 1995.

Krupa, Stanisław. "Wspomnienia z czasów deportacji na Sybir w roku 1940." *Posłaniec Matki Boskiej Saletyńskiej*, no. 9 (June 1992) to no. 9 (September 1993).

Krzysztoporska, Maria. *Ze wspomnień tułaczych*. London: Veritas, 1981.

Kubiak, Hieronim, and Andrzej Pilch, eds. *Stan i potrzeby badań nad zbiorowościami polonijnymi [międzynarodowa konferencja naukowa: Kraków, 30 sierpnia-5 września, 1975]*. Wrocław, Kraków: Zakład Narodowy im. Ossolińskich, 1976.

Kucharski, Józef. *Jogła: Obóz NKWD (1944–1946)*. Lublin: Norbertinum, 1995.

Kunert, Andrzej Krzysztof, comp. *Polacy w Iranie 1942–1945*. Warszawa: Oficyna Wydawnicza "Adiutor," 2001.

Kusiński, Witold. *Deportacje ludności polskiej w ZSRR*. Warsawa: Uniwersytet Warszawski Centrum Badań Radzieckich, 1991.

Lachocki, Eugene. *No Return*. New Smyrna Beach, FL: Luthers, 1996.

Levin, Dov. *The Lesser of Two Evils: Eastern European Jewry Under Soviet Rule, 1939–1941*. Philadelphia: The Jewish Publication Society, 1995.

Lewandowski, Józef. "Rosjanie o Europie Wschodniej i Polsce." *Zeszyty Historyczne* 126 (1998): 175–90.

Linden, Maria van der. *An Unforgettable Journey*. Palmerston North, NZ: Dunmore Press, 1994.

Łojek, Jerzy (Leopold Jerzewski, pseud.). *Agresja 17 września 1939: Studium aspektów politycznych*. Warszawa: Instytut Wydawniczy Pax, 1990.

Lukas, Richard C. "Polish Refugees in Mexico: An Historical Footnote." *The Polish Review* 22, no. 2 (1977): 73–75.

Łysakowski, Richard. *Syberyjskie wizje: Pieśń rogu obfitości.* Chicago: Feniks Publ., 1987. Engl. ed. *Siberian Odyssey.* New York: Vantage Press, 1990.

Majewski, Witold. *Polish Children Suffer.* London: F.P. agency, 1944.

Malcher, George C. *Blank Pages: Soviet Genocide Against the Polish People.* Woking: Pyrford Press, 1993.

Martin, Terry. "The Origins of Soviet Ethnic Cleansing." *The Journal of Modern History* 70 (December 1998): 813–61.

Maxímof, Sergei. *Siberia and Penal Servitude.* Vol. 3. St. Petersburg, 1871.

Mazur, Grzegorz. "Polityka sowiecka na 'Zachodniej Ukrainie' 1939–1941 (zarys problematyki)." *Zeszyty Historyczne* 130 (1999): 68–95.

Milewski Family Memoir. Compiled and translated by Stanisław Antoni Milewski, consisting of the diary of his mother (Sabina) and sister (Teresa) as well as his own recollections. Copy in the possession of Tadeusz Piotrowski.

Milewski, Henryk. "Sytuacja poprzedzająca zesłanie i warunki bytowe zesłańców polskich w ZSRR w latach 1940–1946." *Studia Łomżyńskie* 5 (1995): 109–17.

Mineyko, Anna. "Through the Mists of Time." http://www.interlog.com/~mineykok/anna.html#war

Mikosz-Hintzke, Teresa. *Six Years Till Spring: A Polish Family's Odyssey.* New York: iUniverse.com, 2001.

Mora, Sylwester [Kazimierz Zamorski], and Piotr Zwierniak [Stanisław Starzewski]. *Sprawiedliwość sowiecka.* Italy: n.p., 1945; Warsaw: Alfa-Wero, 1994.

Morozow, Stanisław. "Deportacje polskiej ludności cywilnej z radzieckich terenów zachodnich w głąb ZSRR w latach 1935–1936." *Pamięc i sprawiedliwość: Biuletyn Głównej Komisji Badania Zbrodni przeciwko Narodowi Polskiemu—Instytutu Pamięci Narodowej* 40 (1997–98): 267–81.

Musiał, Bogdan. "Stosunki polsko-żydowskie na Kresach Wschodnich RP pod okupacją sowiecką, 1939–1941." *Biuletyn Kwartalny Radomskiego Towarzystwa Naukowego* 34, no. 1 (1999): 103–26.

Niebuda, Zofia. *My Guardian Angel.* Toronto: Easy Printing, 1996.

Nowak, Jerzy Robert. *Przemilczane zbrodnie: Żydzi i Polacy na Kresach w latach 1939–1941.* Warszawa: von Borowiecky, 1999.

Oanica, Sandra. *Remember: Helen's Story.* Calgary: Detselig Enterprises, 1997.

Obertyńska, Beata (Marta Rudzka). *W domu niewoli.* 2d ed. Chicago: Grono Przyjaciół, 1968.

Ochocki, Adam. *Raz, dwa, wziali! Wspomnienia z ZSRR 1939–1946.* Łódź: Wydawnictwo Towarzystwa Krzewienia Kultury Świeckiej, 1988.

Orłowski, Hubert, and Andrzej Sakson, eds. *Utracona ojczyzna: Przymusowe wysiedlenia, deportacje i przesiedlenia, jako wspólne doświadczenie.* Poznań: Instytut Zachodni, 1996.

Ożarowski, Bohdan. *Droga do Ojczyzny: ZSRR, Środkowy Wschód, Italia, Anglia: Wiersze.* London: Oficyna Poetów in Marlrzy, 1990.

Paschwa-Kozicka, Anita. *My Flight to Freedom: An Autobiography.* Chicago: Panorama Publishing Co., 1996.

Pieczko, Tadeusz. Memoir. Copy in the possession of Tadeusz Piotrowski.

Piekarski, Henryk. *Z nad Niemna przez Syberię do Kanady.* Rome: Tipografia pont. Universita Gregoriana, 1967.

Piesakowski, Tomasz. *The Fate of Poles in the USSR 1939–1989.* London: Gryf, 1990.

Pinchuk, Ben-Cion. *Shtetl Jews under Soviet Rule: Eastern Poland on the Eve of the Holocaust.* Cambridge, MA: Basil Blackwell, 1991.

Piotrowska-Dubik, Barbara. *Kwiaty na stepie: Pamiętnik z zesłania.* Warszawa: "Soli Deo," 1997.

Piotrowski, Henryk. *My Siberian Experience.* Toronto: H. Piotrowski, 1996, 2000.

Piotrowski, Tadeusz. *Poland's Holocaust: Ethnic Strife, Collaboration with Occupying Forces and Genocide in the Second Republic, 1918–1947.* Jefferson, NC: McFarland, 1998.

_____. *Vengeance of the Swallows: Memoir of a Polish Family's Ordeal Under Soviet Aggression,*

Ukrainian Ethnic Cleansing and Nazi Enslavement, and Their Emigration to America. Jefferson, NC: McFarland, 1995.

Pohl, J. Otto. *The Stalinist Penal System: A Statistical History of Soviet Repression and Terror, 1930–1953.* Jefferson, NC: McFarland, 1997.

Poles of Santa Rosa: Our 50th Anniversary, 1946–1996, a commemoration booklet without pagination published in Chicago in 1996.

Pomykalski, Wanda E. *The Horror Trains: A Polish Woman Veteran's Memoir of World War II.* Pasadena, MD: The Minerva Center, 1999.

Porajska, Barbara. *From the Steppes to the Savannah.* Port Erin, Isle of Man, UK: Ham, 1988.

Ptasnik, Zofia Ludwika Malachowska. "A Polish Woman's Daily Struggle to Survive: Her Diary of Deportation, Forced Labor, and Death in Kazakhstan: April 13, 1940–May 26, 1941." (In subsequent issues: "Death by a Thousand Cuts: A Polish Woman's Diary of Deportation, Forced Labor, and Death in Kazakhstan: April 13, 1940—May 26, 1941). *Sarmatian Review*, series beginning with Vol. 22, No. 2 (2002).

Rachlin, Rachel. *Sixteen Years in Siberia: Memoirs of Rachel and Israel Rachlin.* Trans. by Brigitte M. de Weille. Tuscaloosa: University of Alabama Press, 1988.

Rawicz, Slavomir. *The Long Walk.* New York: Harper, 1956; North Salem, NY: Adventure Library, 1999.

Rdułkowski, Konstanty. *Notatki z wygnania.* Warszawa: Polskie Towarzystwo Ludoznawcze, 1996.

Romanko, Maria Alina. *The Story of Maria Alina and Aleksander Romanko. http://www.romanko.net/book/book.htm*

Rudnicki, Klemens. *Na polskim szlaku: wspomnienia z lat 1939–1947.* Worcław: Zakład Narodowy im. Ossolińskich, 1990.

Ryzner, Janina. *Droga do Polski: Od syberyjskiej tajgi przez afrykański busz.* Przemyśl: PTK, 1993.

Saski, Witold. *Crossing Many Bridges: Memoirs of a Pharmacist in Poland, the Soviet Union, the Middle East, Italy, the United Kingdom, and Nebraska.* Manhattan, KS: Sunflower University Press, 1988. Polish ed. *Przez wiele mostów: Przeżycia absolwenta farmacji Uniwersytetu Stefana Batorego w Wilnie—od pracy w kraju, przez sowieckie lagry, Armię Andersa, pobyt w Anglii i w Włoszech do profesury w USA.* Warszawa: Vademecum, 1992.

Sawicka-Brockie, T. "The 'Polish' Experience and Identity of the 'Pahiatua Children' in New Zealand." Ph.D. dissertation. University of Auckland, 1987.

Sendek-Biliczka, Eugenia. *W sowieckim raju.* Perth, Australia: Kurier Press, 1990.

Siedlecki, Julian. *Losy Polaków w ZSRR w latach 1939–1986.* London: Gryf, 1987.

Siemaszko, Zbigniew S. *W sowieckim osaczeniu* 1939–1943. London: Polish Cultural Foundation, 1991.

Skrzypek, Andrzej, et al., eds. *Zbrodnicza ewakuacja więzień i arresztów NKWD na Kresach Wschodnich II Rzeczypospolitej w czerwcu-lipcu 1941 roku: Materiały z sesji naukowej w 55. rocznicę ewakuacji więźniów NKWD w głąb ZSRR (Łódź, 10 czerwca 1996 r.)* Warszawa: Główna Komisja Badania Zbrodni przeciwko Narodowi Polskiemu, Instytut Pamięci Narodowej, 1997.

Skrzypek, Stanisław. *Rosja jaką widziałem: Wspomnienia z lat 1939–1942.* Newtown, MT: Montgomeryshire Printing Co., [1949]; Warszawa: "Wola," 1987.

Skwarko, Krystyna. *Osiedlenie młodzierzy polskiej w Nowej Zelandii w r. 1944.* London: Poets' and Painters' Press, 1972. Engl. Ed. *The Invited: The Story of 733 Polish Children who Grew up in New Zealand.* Ngaio, Wellington 4, New Zealand: Millwood Press, 1974.

Smenda, Nina and Janusz, eds. *Unforgettable Memories: Memoirs of Polish Exiles in the Soviet Union, 1940–1942.* Perth, Western Australia: Polish Siberian Group (WA), 1996.

"Soviet Deportation of the Inhabitants of Eastern Poland in 1939–1941," Confidential P-66020 Report (London), December 1943, the U.S. Department of State, National Archives and Research Administration, Washington, D.C. (NND 1500, NARS date, July 31, 1973). Copy in the possession of Tadeusz Piotrowski.

Spis. Delegatura Ministerstwa Pracy i Opieki Społecznej w Meksyku. Delegat: Bohdan Szmejko.

Leon, Guanajuato. November 15, 1944. A complete listing of the names, dates of birth, places of birth, parents' names, and addresses in Poland before the war of 1,453 deportees residing in Colonia Santa Rosa, Mexico. This document also contains the names, dates of birth, places of birth, and parental names of children born in Santa Rosa between September 6 and November 1, 1944 (ten of them — not included in the above list of 1,453 refugees), as well as a list of marriages (36) contracted in the settlement. Copy in the possession of Tadeusz Piotrowski.

"Sprawozdanie z dyskusji dotyczącej liczby obywateli polskich wywiezionych do Związku Sowieckiego w latach 1939–1941." *Studia z Dziejów Rosji i Europy Środkowo-Wschodniej,* vol. 31 (1996): 117–48.

Strzembosz, Tomasz, ed. *Okupacja sowiecka (1939–1941) w świetle tajnych dokumentów: Obywatele polscy na Kresach Północno-Wschodnich II Rzeczypospolitej pod okupacją sowiecką w latach 1939–1941.* Warszawa: Instytut Studiów Politycznych PAN, 1996.

Stypulkowski, Zbigniew. *Invitation to Moscow.* London: Thames and Hudson, 1951.

Sukiennicki, Wiktor. *Biała Księga.* Paris: Instytut Literacki, 1964.

Sword, Keith. *Deportation and Exile: Poles in the Soviet Union, 1939–48.* London: St. Martin's Press, 1994.

_____, ed. *The Soviet Takeover of the Polish Eastern Provinces, 1939–1941.* New York: St. Martin's Press, 1991.

Synowiec-Tobis, Stella H. *The Fulfillment of Visionary Return: A Historical Narrative Based on Two Memoirs Written by the Author at Ages 13 & 15.* Northbrook, IL: Artpol, 1998.

Szymczyk, Wanda. *Z pożogi w busz.* Warszawa: "Iskry," 1982.

Tańska, Irena, ed. *Wspomnienia Sybiraków.* Warszawa: Comandor, 2001.

Teczarowska, Danuta. *Deportation into the Unknown.* Braunton, Devon: Merlin Books, 1985. Polish ed. *Deportacja w nieznane: Wspomnienia 1939–1942.* London: Veritas, 1981.

Thompson, Ewa M. *Imperial Knowledge: Russian Literature and Colonialism.* Westport, CT: Greenwood Press, 2000.

Toczek, Edward. *Wspomnienia syberyjskiego zesłańca.* Warszawa: Novum, 1989.

Topolski, Aleksander. *Without Vodka: Adventures in Wartime Russia.* South Royalton, VT: Steerforth Press, 2001.

Truchanowicz, Tadeusz. *Związek harcerstwa polskiego na wschodzie: Z dziejów harcerstwa na obczyznie 1940–1946.* Kraków: Harcerska Oficyna Wydawnicza, 1987.

Tułacze dzieci. Exiled Children. Warszawa: Fundacja Archiwum Fotograficzne Tułaczy, 1995.

Tuszyński, Marek. "Soviet War Crimes Against Poland During the Second World War and Its Aftermath: A Review of the Factual Record and Outstanding Questions." *The Polish Review* 44, no. 2 (1999): 183–216.

Umiastowski, Jan Kazimierz. *Przez kraj niewoli: Wspomnienia z Litwy i Rosji z lat 1939–1942.* Warszawa: "Kret," 1985.

Utnik-Łappo, Henryka. "Afrykańczycy — Wspominając tamte dni," *Związkowiec,* no. 19 (December 10, 1998): section B, 22.

Wasilewska, Eugenia. *The Silver Madonna.* New York: The John Day Company, 1971.

Wasilewska, Irena. *Suffer Little Children.* London: Maxlove, 1946.

Wat, Aleksander. *My Century: The Odyssey of a Polish Intellectual.* Berkeley: University of California Press, 1988. Polish ed. *Mój wiek: Pamiętnik mówiony.* London: Polonia Book Fund, 1977.

Whiteman, Dorit Bader. *Escape via Siberia: A Jewish Child's Odyssey of Survival.* New York and London: Holmes & Meier, 1999.

Wielhorski, Władysław. *Wspomnienia z przeżyć w niewoli sowieckiej.* London: Orbis, 1965; Łódź: Towarzystwo Oświaty Niezależnej, 1985.

Wójcik, Zbigniew K., and Andrzej Zagórski. *Na katorżniczym szlaku.* Warszawa: Polonia, 1994.

Wołczuk, Janina. *Listy sybiraków: 1939–1955.* Wrocław: Wydawnictwo Uniwersytetu Wrocławskiego, 1994.

Wróbel, Elżbieta, and Janusz Wróbel. *Rozproszeni po świecie: Obozy i osiedla uchodźców polskich ze Związku Sowieckiego 1942–1950.* Chicago: Panorama, 1992.

_____. "Spotkanie w Santa Rosa." *Dziennik Związkowy* (July 23–25, 1993).

Wróbel, Janusz, and Elżbieta Wróbel. "Dzieci z Santa Rosa. Cz. 1: Z syberyjskiej tajgi na kontynent amerykański." *Dziennik Związkowy* (July 6–7, 1991).

Z Kresów Wschodnich RP na wygnanie: Opowieści zesłańców 1940–1946. London: Ognisko Rodzin Osadników Kresowych, 1996. Engl. ed. *Stalin's Ethnic Cleansing in Eastern Poland.* London: Association of the Families of the Borderland Settlers, 2000.

[Zajdlerowa, Zoe]. *The Dark Side of the Moon.* Preface by T. S. Eliot. London: Faber and Faber, 1946; London: Harvester Wheatsheaf, 1989.

Zalewski, Jan. *Stala się omyłka...: Wspomnienia z niewoli sowieckiej wrzesień 1939-sierpień 1941.* Warszawa: Kolejowa Oficyna Wydawnicza, 1994.

Żarnecki, Anna. *Polonia, Viento y Tinieblas.* Mexico, D.F.: EDAMEX, 1982.

Zarod, Kazimierz. *Inside Stalin's Gulag: A True Story of Survival.* Sussex, England: The Book Guild Ltd., 1990.

Żaroń, Piotr. *Agresja Związku Radzieckiego na Polskę 17 września 1939: Los jeńców polskich.* Toruń: Adam Marszałek, 1998.

_____. *Deportacja na kresach [1939–1941].* Warszawa: Ministerstwo Obrony Narodowej, 1990.

Zarzycki, Alicia A., and Stefania Buczak-Zarzycka. *Kwaheri Africa: A Polish Experience 1939–1950, from Deportation to Freedom.* Perth, Western Australia: n.p., [1985].

Żebrowski-Bulmahn, Jane [Janina]. *Long Journey Home.* New York: iUniverse.com, 2000.

Zenkovsky, Serge A., ed. *Medieval Russia's Epics, Chronicles and Tales.* New York: E.P. Dutton, 1963.

Index